MONTAGUE TERRACE

WARREN & GARY PLEECE

Jonathan Cape
London

Published by Jonathan Cape 2013

2 4 6 8 10 9 7 5 3 1

First published in Great Britain in 2013 by
Jonathan Cape
Random House UK Ltd
20 Vauxhall Bridge Road,
London SW1V 2SA

www.vintage-books.co.uk

Addresses for companies within The Random House Group Limited can be found at:
www.randomhouse.co.uk/offices.htm

The Random House Group Limited Reg. No. 954009

A CIP catalogue record for this book is available from the British Library

ISBN 9780224090629

Printed and bound in Great Britain by MPG Books Group Ltd

Thanks to Dean Haspiel
and Simon Fraser at
activatecomix.com,
Dan Franklin and Mr
Scott Engel, for original
inspiration.

Also available from
Pleece Brothers,
The Great Unwashed
escape-books.com

montagueterrace.co.uk
pleecebrothers.com
warrenpleece.com

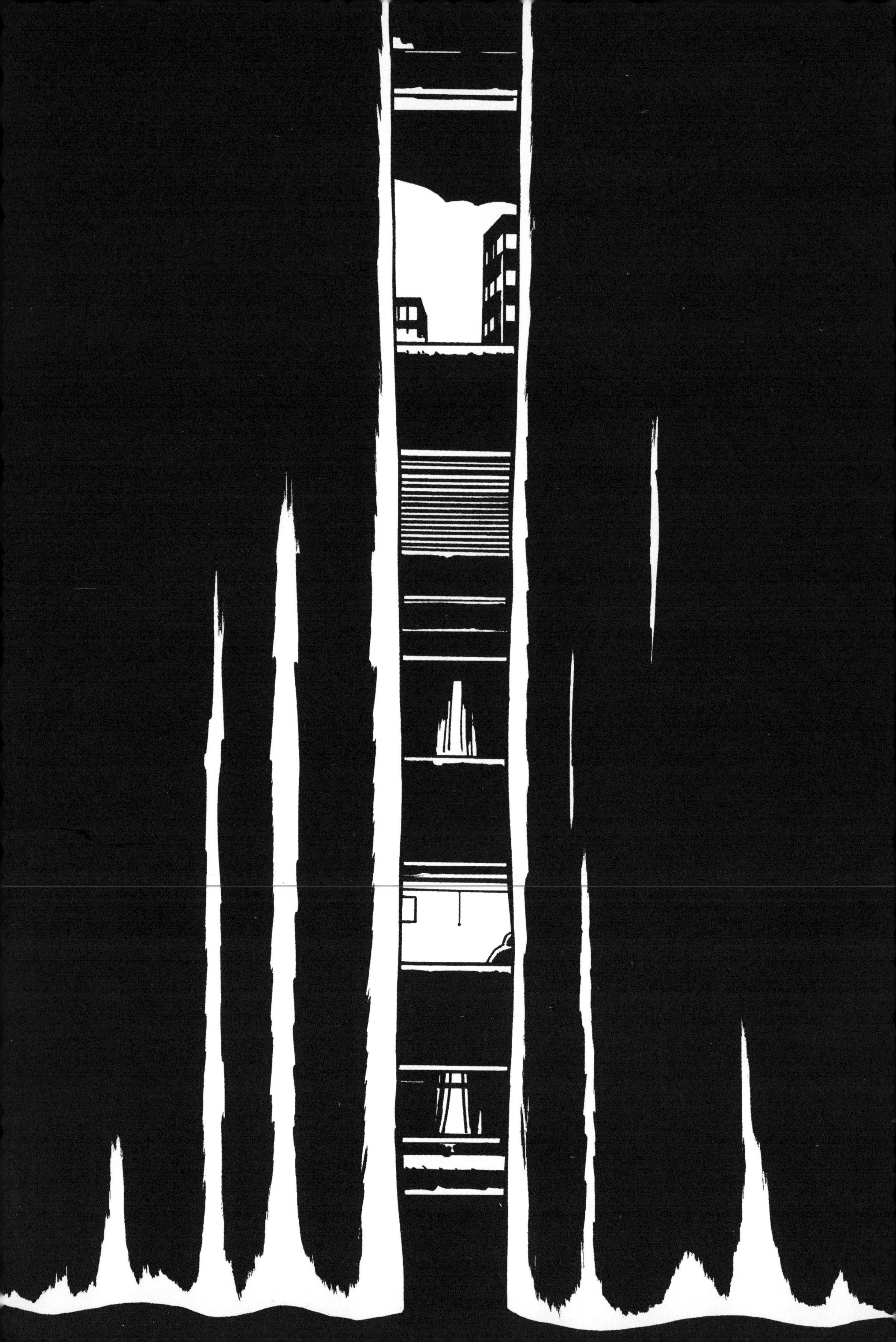

MONTAGUE TERRACE

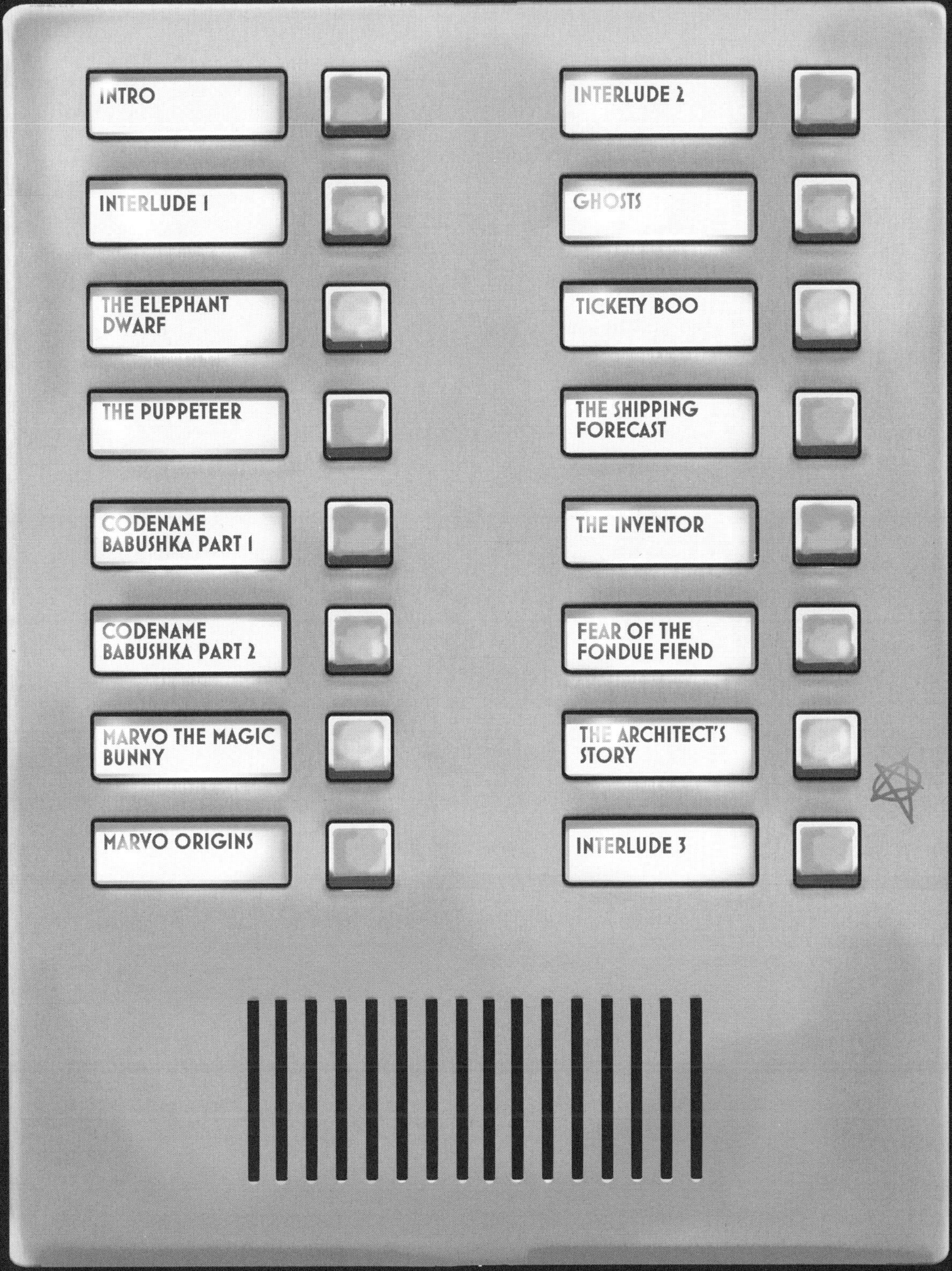
INTRO
INTERLUDE 1
THE ELEPHANT DWARF
THE PUPPETEER
CODENAME BABUSHKA PART 1
CODENAME BABUSHKA PART 2
MARVO THE MAGIC BUNNY
MARVO ORIGINS
INTERLUDE 2
GHOSTS
TICKETY BOO
THE SHIPPING FORECAST
THE INVENTOR
FEAR OF THE FONDUE FIEND
THE ARCHITECT'S STORY
INTERLUDE 3

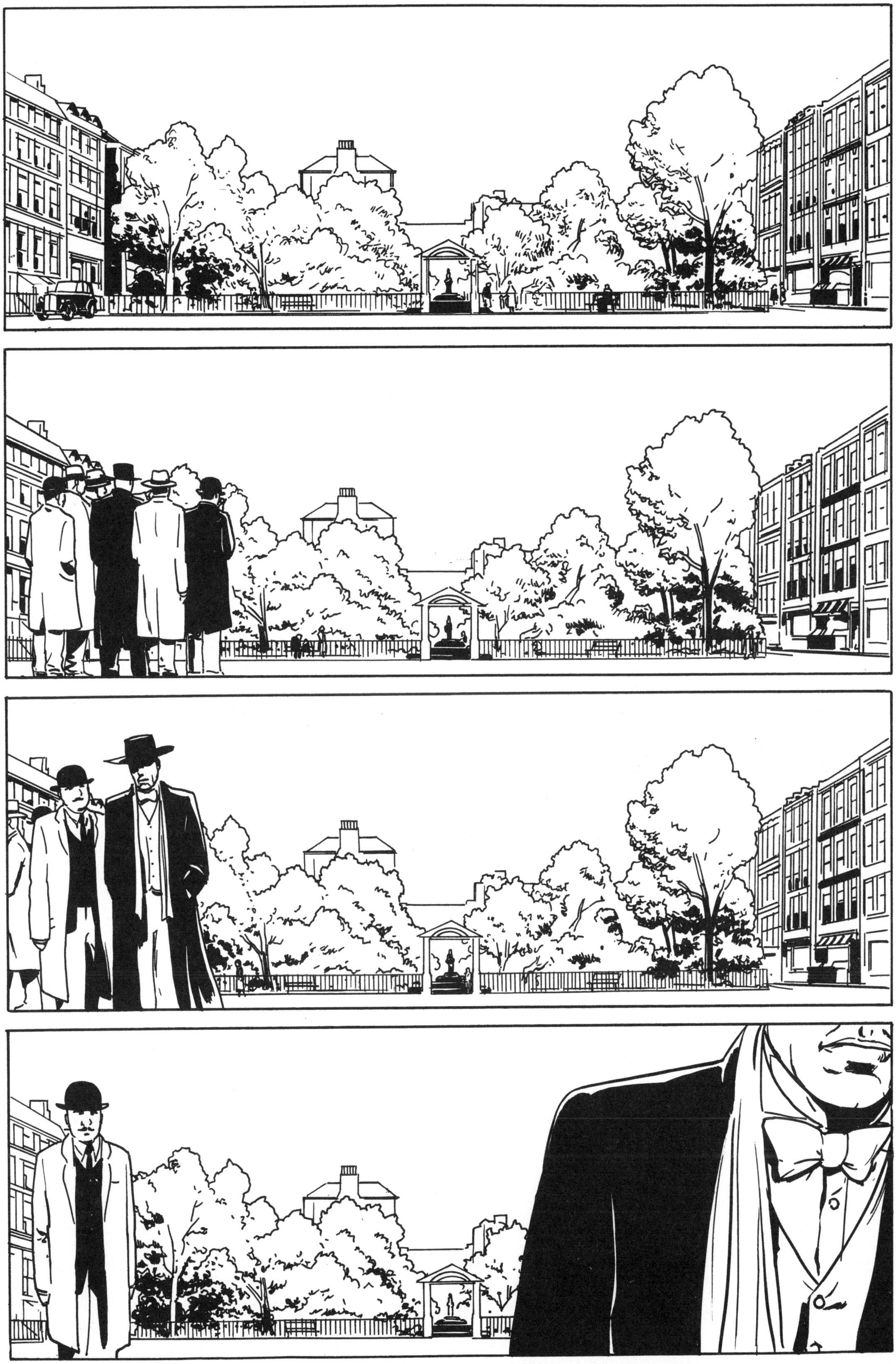

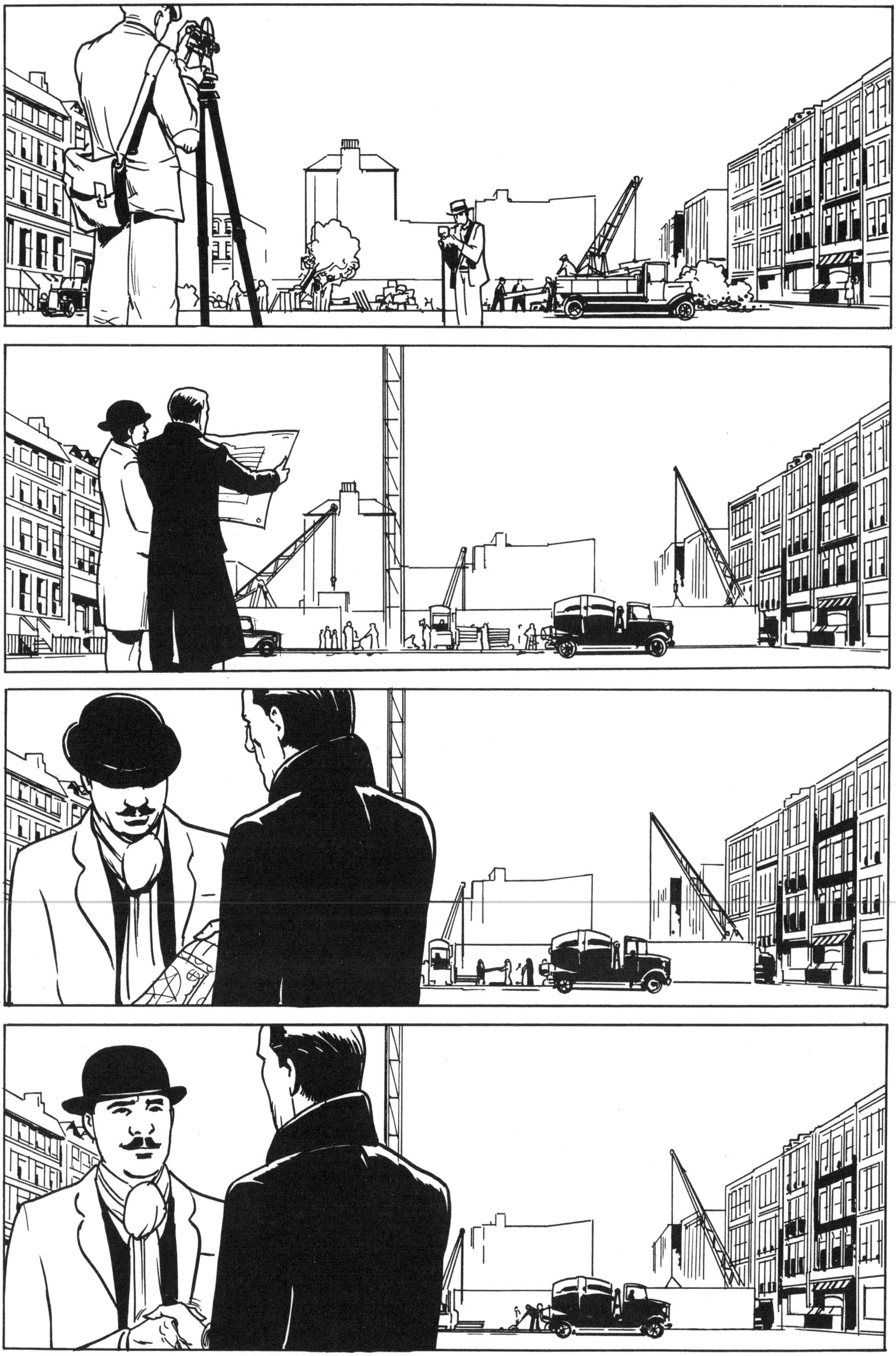

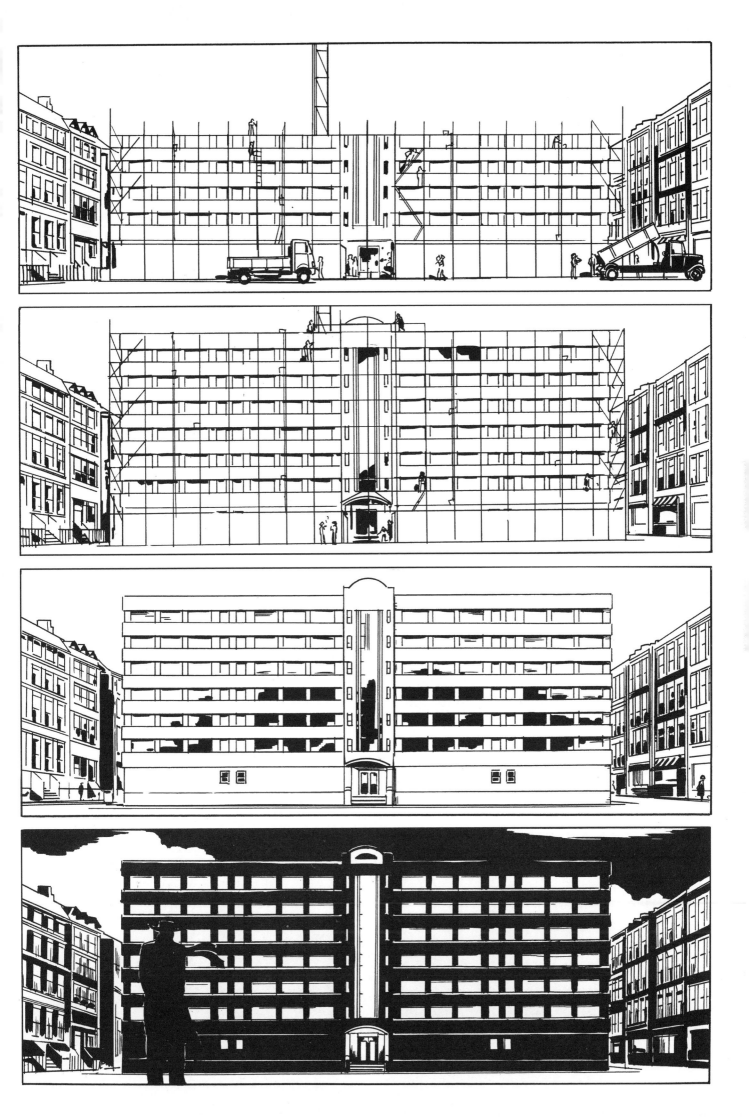

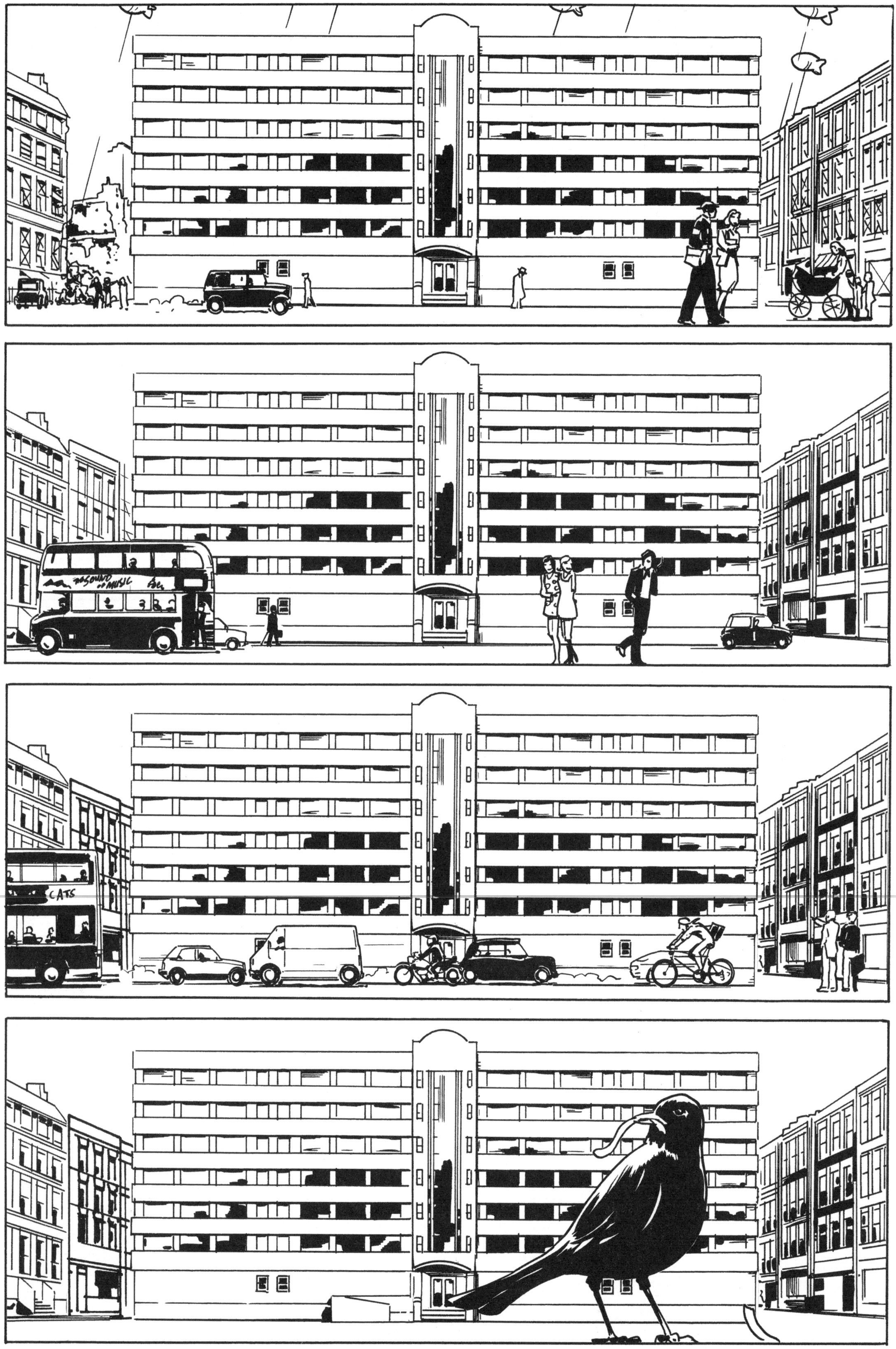
SOUND
MUSIC
CATS

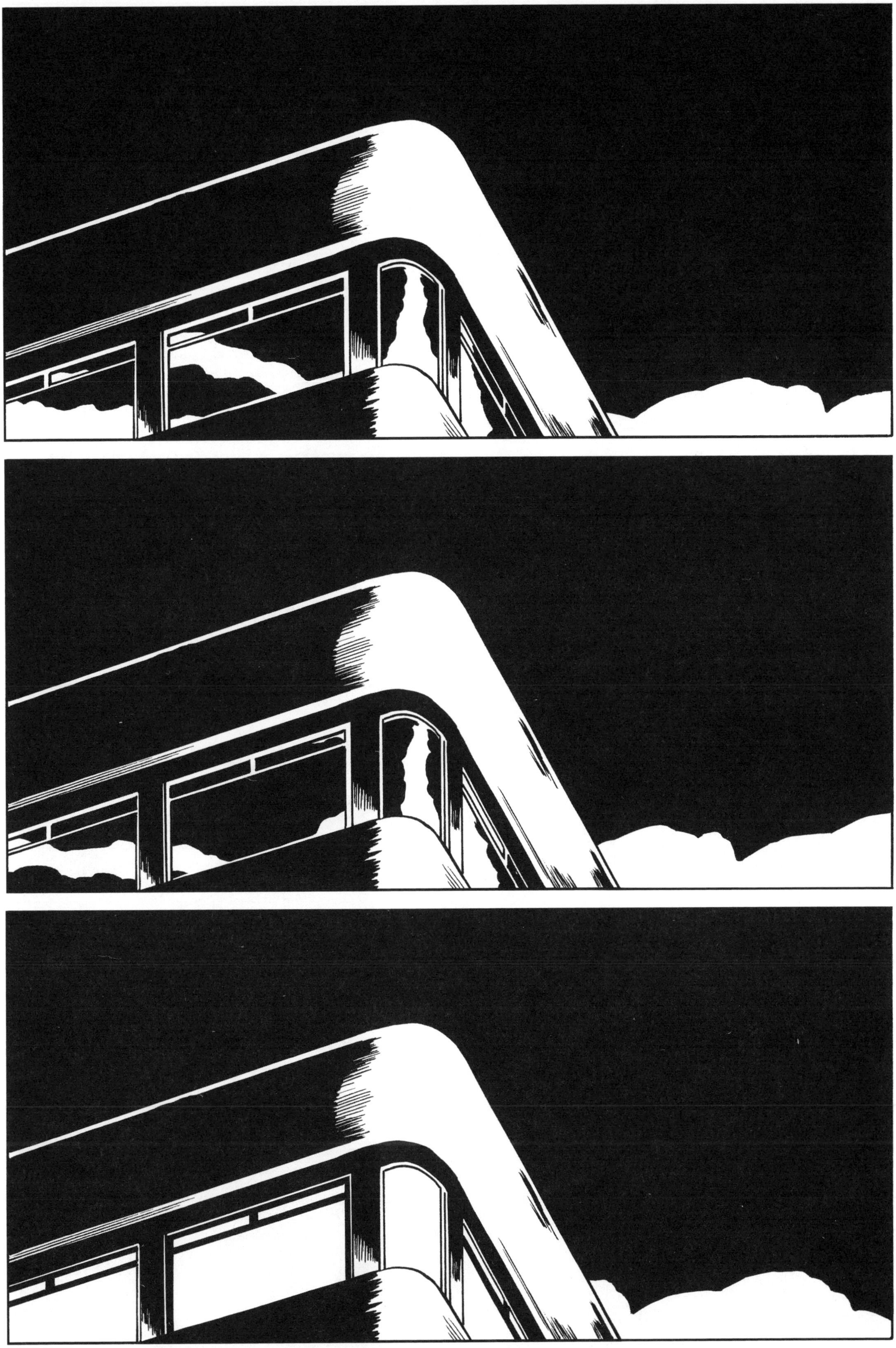

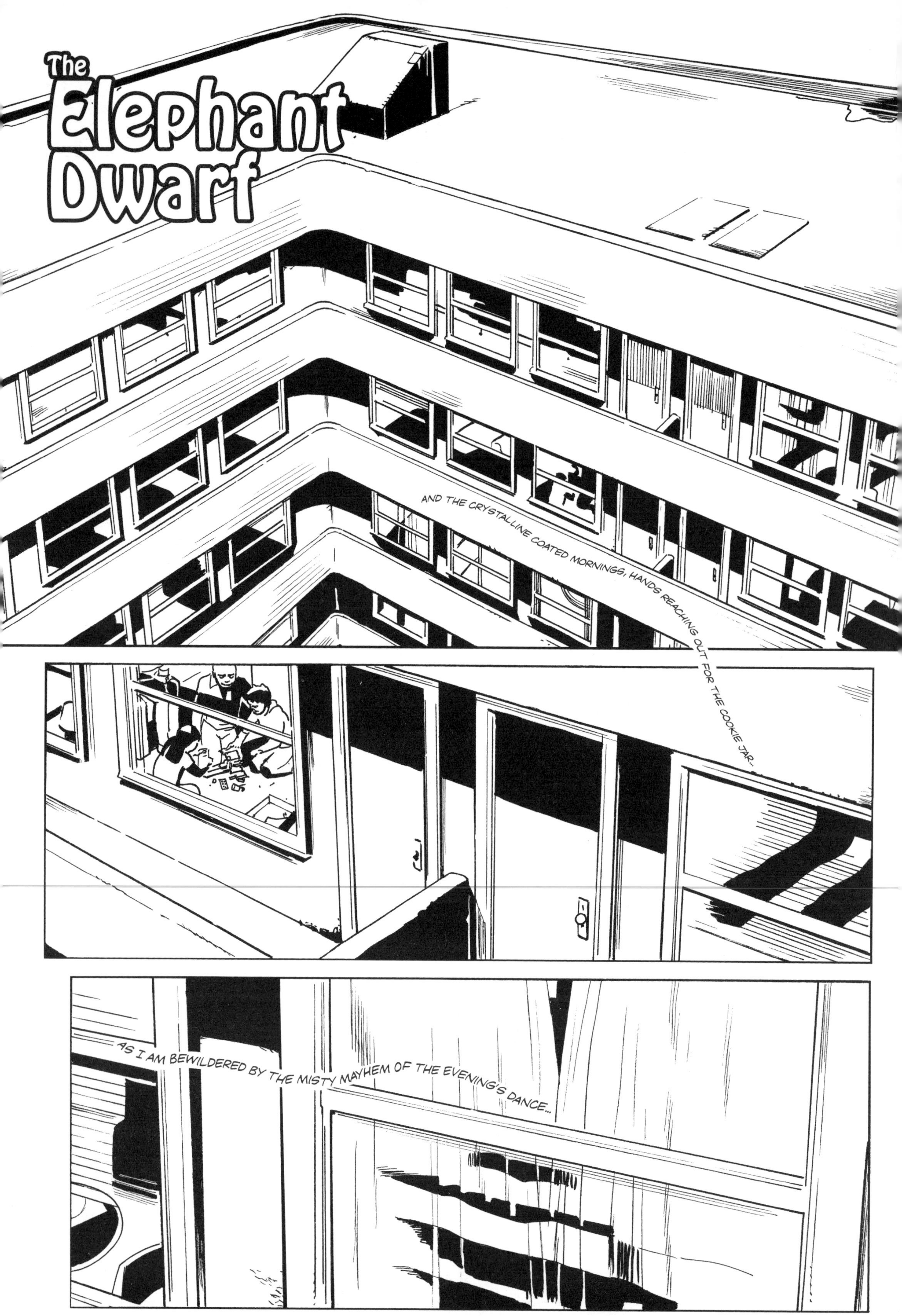
The Elephant Dwarf
AND THE CRYSTALLINE COATED MORNINGS, HANDS REACHING OUT FOR THE COOKIE JAR...
AS I AM BEWILDERED BY THE MISTY MAYHEM OF THE EVENING'S DANCE...

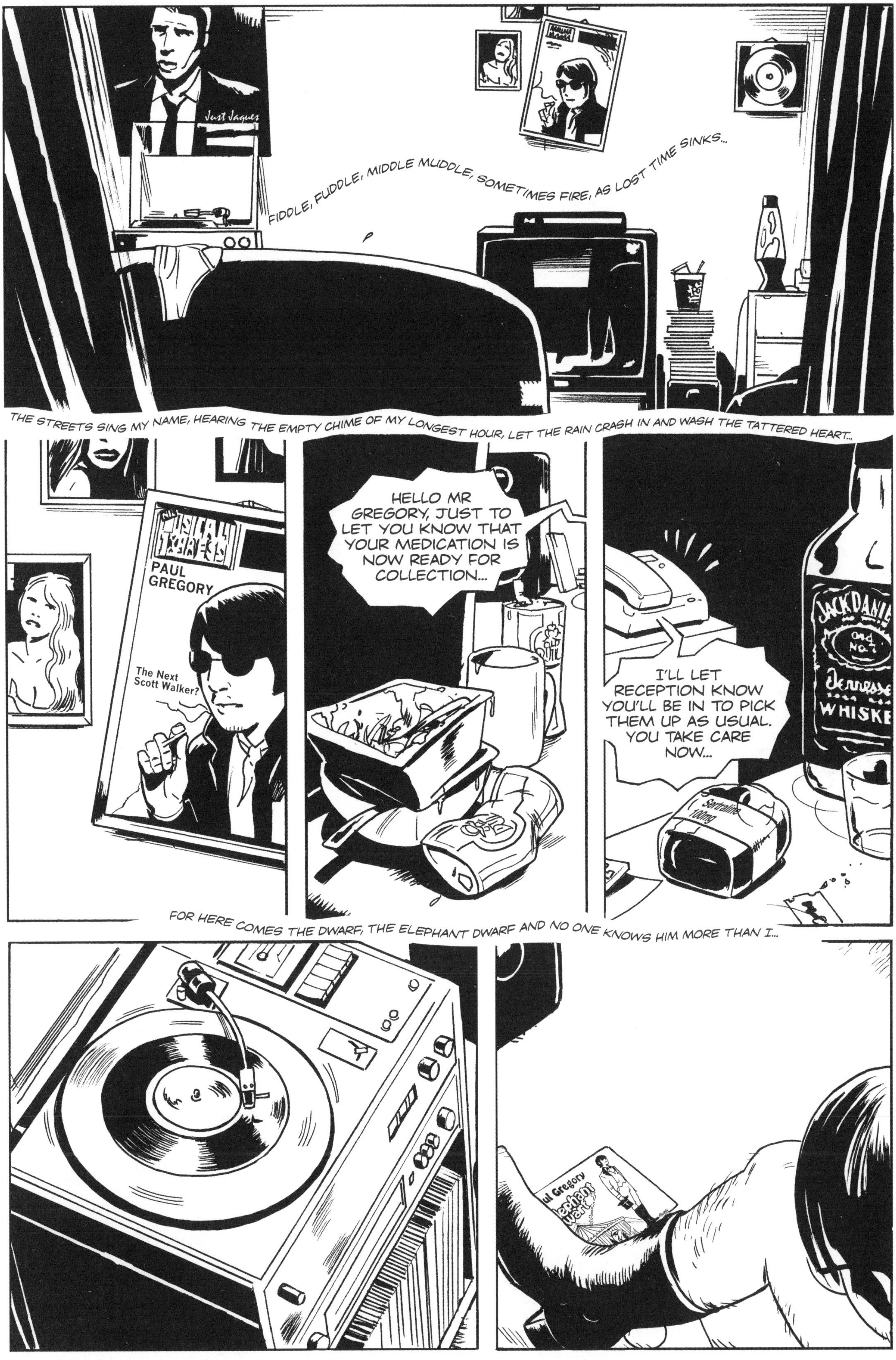
Just Jaques
FIDDLE, FUDDLE, MIDDLE MUDDLE, SOMETIMES FIRE, AS LOST TIME SINKS...
THE STREETS SING MY NAME, HEARING THE EMPTY CHIME OF MY LONGEST HOUR, LET THE RAIN CRASH IN AND WASH THE TATTERED HEART...
PAUL GREGORY
The Next Scott Walker?
HELLO MR GREGORY, JUST TO LET YOU KNOW THAT YOUR MEDICATION IS NOW READY FOR COLLECTION...
I'LL LET RECEPTION KNOW YOU'LL BE IN TO PICK THEM UP AS USUAL. YOU TAKE CARE NOW...
Sertraline 100mg
WHISKE
FOR HERE COMES THE DWARF, THE ELEPHANT DWARF AND NO ONE KNOWS HIM MORE THAN I...
ul Gregory

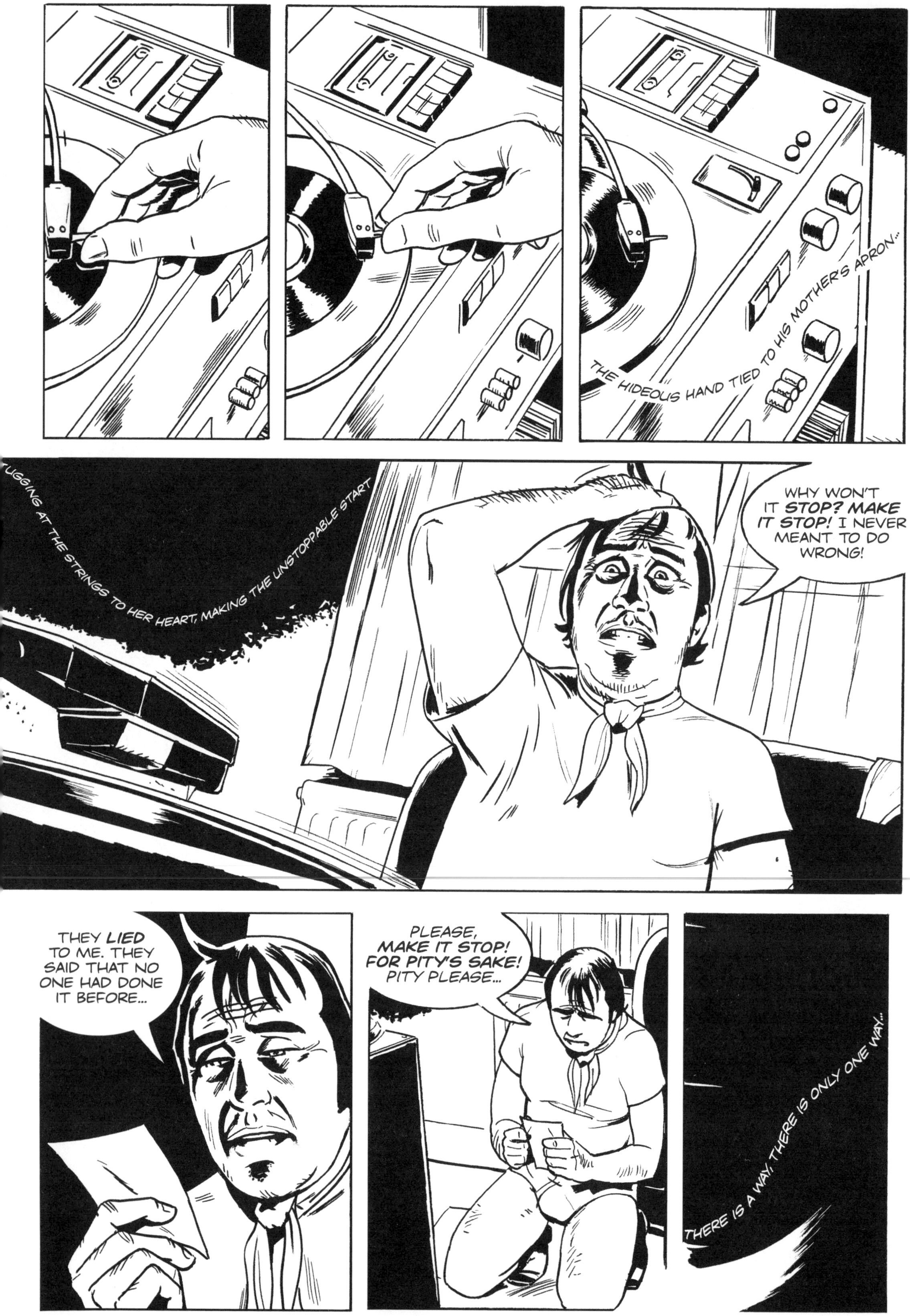
THE HIDEOUS HAND TIED TO HIS MOTHER'S APRON...
TUGGING AT THE STRINGS TO HER HEART, MAKING THE UNSTOPPABLE START
WHY WON'T IT STOP? MAKE IT STOP! I NEVER MEANT TO DO WRONG!
THEY LIED TO ME. THEY SAID THAT NO ONE HAD DONE IT BEFORE...
PLEASE, MAKE IT STOP! FOR PITY'S SAKE! PITY PLEASE...
THERE IS A WAY. THERE IS ONLY ONE WAY...

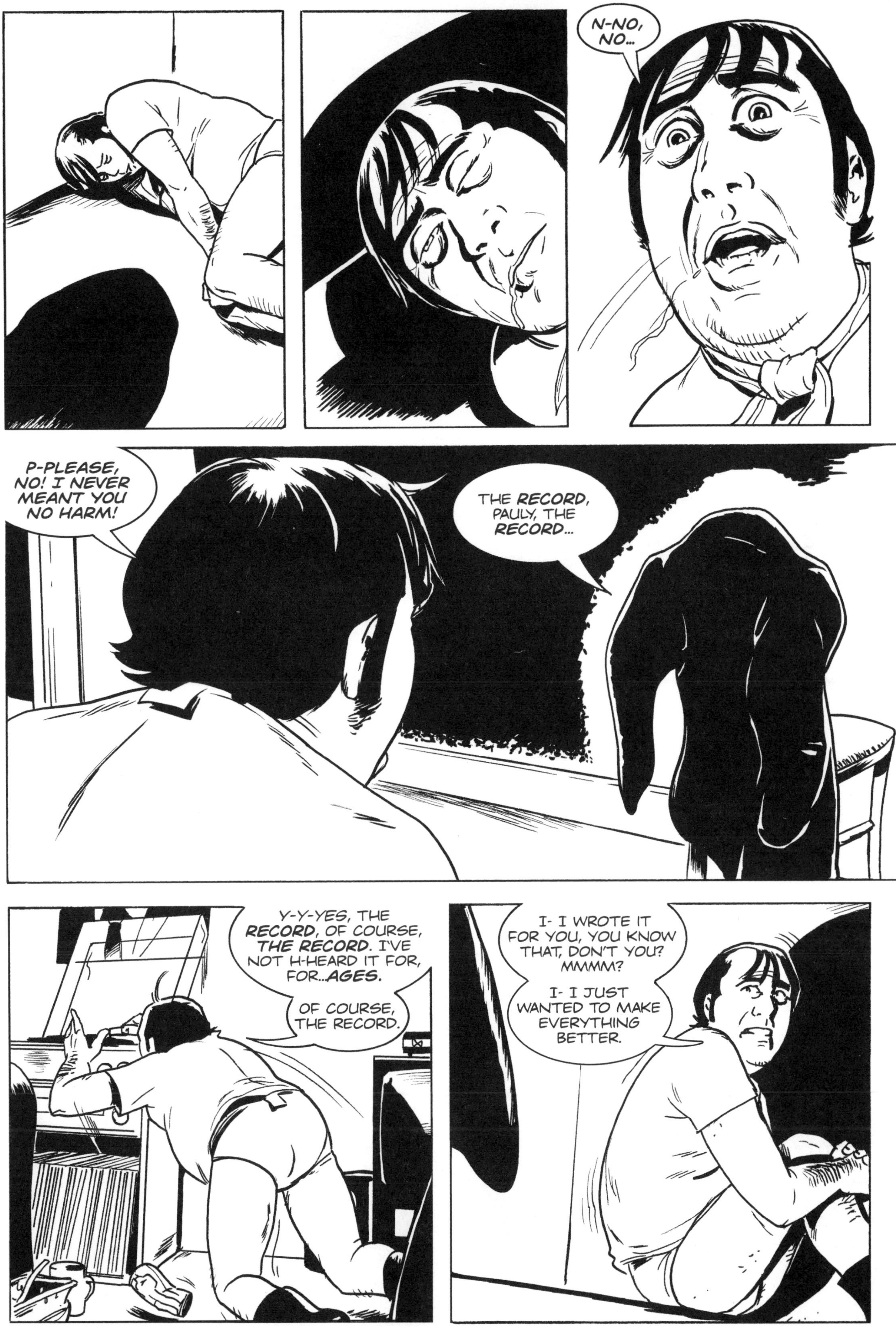
N-NO, NO...
P-PLEASE, NO! I NEVER MEANT YOU NO HARM!
THE RECORD, PAULY, THE RECORD...
Y-Y-YES, THE RECORD, OF COURSE, THE RECORD. I'VE NOT H-HEARD IT FOR, FOR...AGES.
OF COURSE, THE RECORD.
I- I WROTE IT FOR YOU, YOU KNOW THAT, DON'T YOU? MMMM?
I- I JUST WANTED TO MAKE EVERYTHING BETTER.

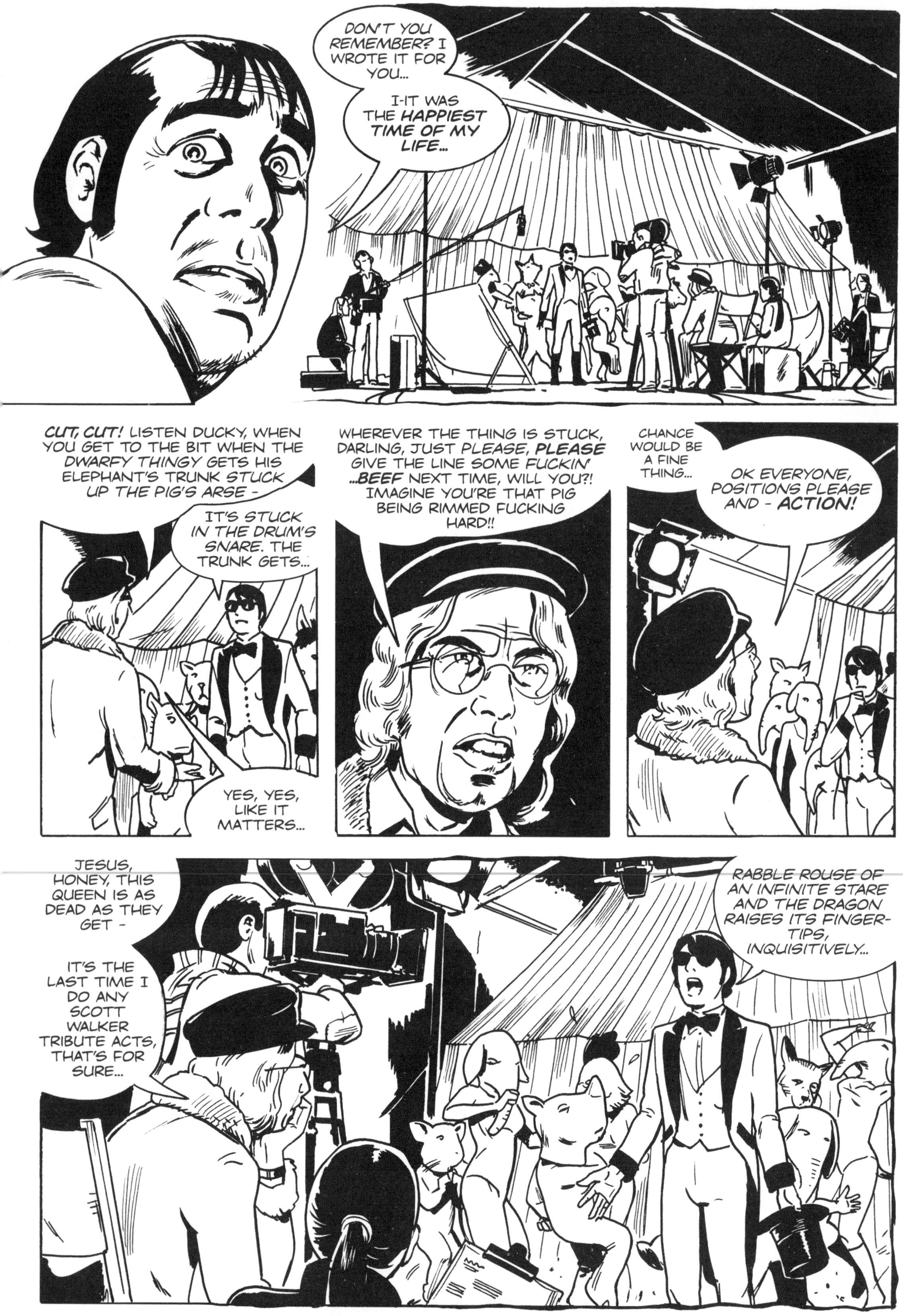
DON'T YOU REMEMBER? I WROTE IT FOR YOU...
I-IT WAS THE HAPPIEST TIME OF MY LIFE...
CUT, CUT! LISTEN DUCKY, WHEN YOU GET TO THE BIT WHEN THE DWARFY THINGY GETS HIS ELEPHANT'S TRUNK STUCK UP THE PIG'S ARSE -
IT'S STUCK IN THE DRUM'S SNARE. THE TRUNK GETS...
YES, YES, LIKE IT MATTERS...
WHEREVER THE THING IS STUCK, DARLING, JUST PLEASE, PLEASE GIVE THE LINE SOME FUCKIN' ...BEEF NEXT TIME, WILL YOU?! IMAGINE YOU'RE THAT PIG BEING RIMMED FUCKING HARD!!
CHANCE WOULD BE A FINE THING...
OK EVERYONE, POSITIONS PLEASE AND - ACTION!
JESUS, HONEY, THIS QUEEN IS AS DEAD AS THEY GET -
IT'S THE LAST TIME I DO ANY SCOTT WALKER TRIBUTE ACTS, THAT'S FOR SURE...
RABBLE ROUSE OF AN INFINITE STARE AND THE DRAGON RAISES ITS FINGER-TIPS, INQUISITIVELY...

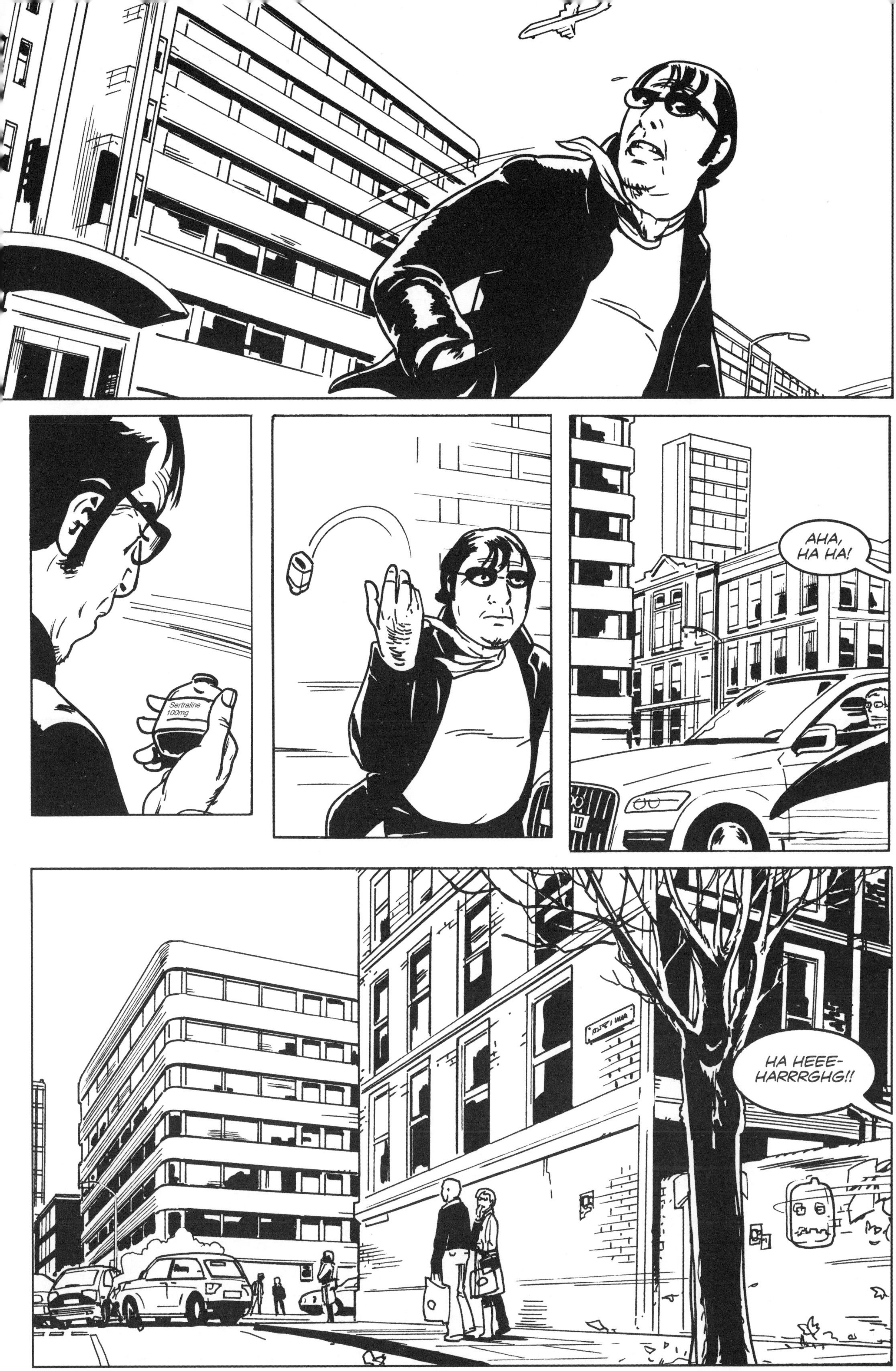
Sertraline
100mg
AHA, HA HA!
HA HEEE-HARRRGHG!!

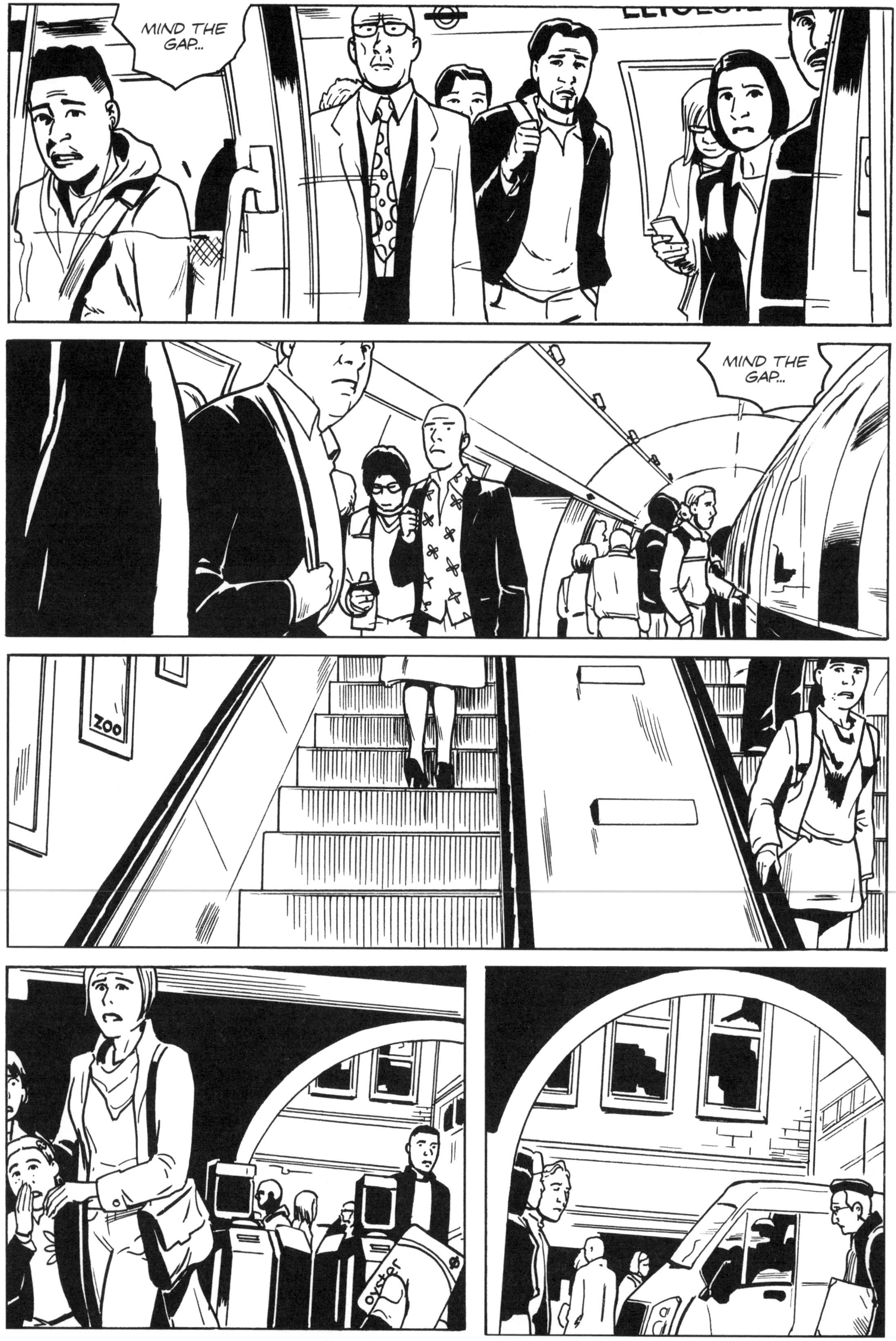
MIND THE GAP...
MIND THE GAP...
ZOO
oyster

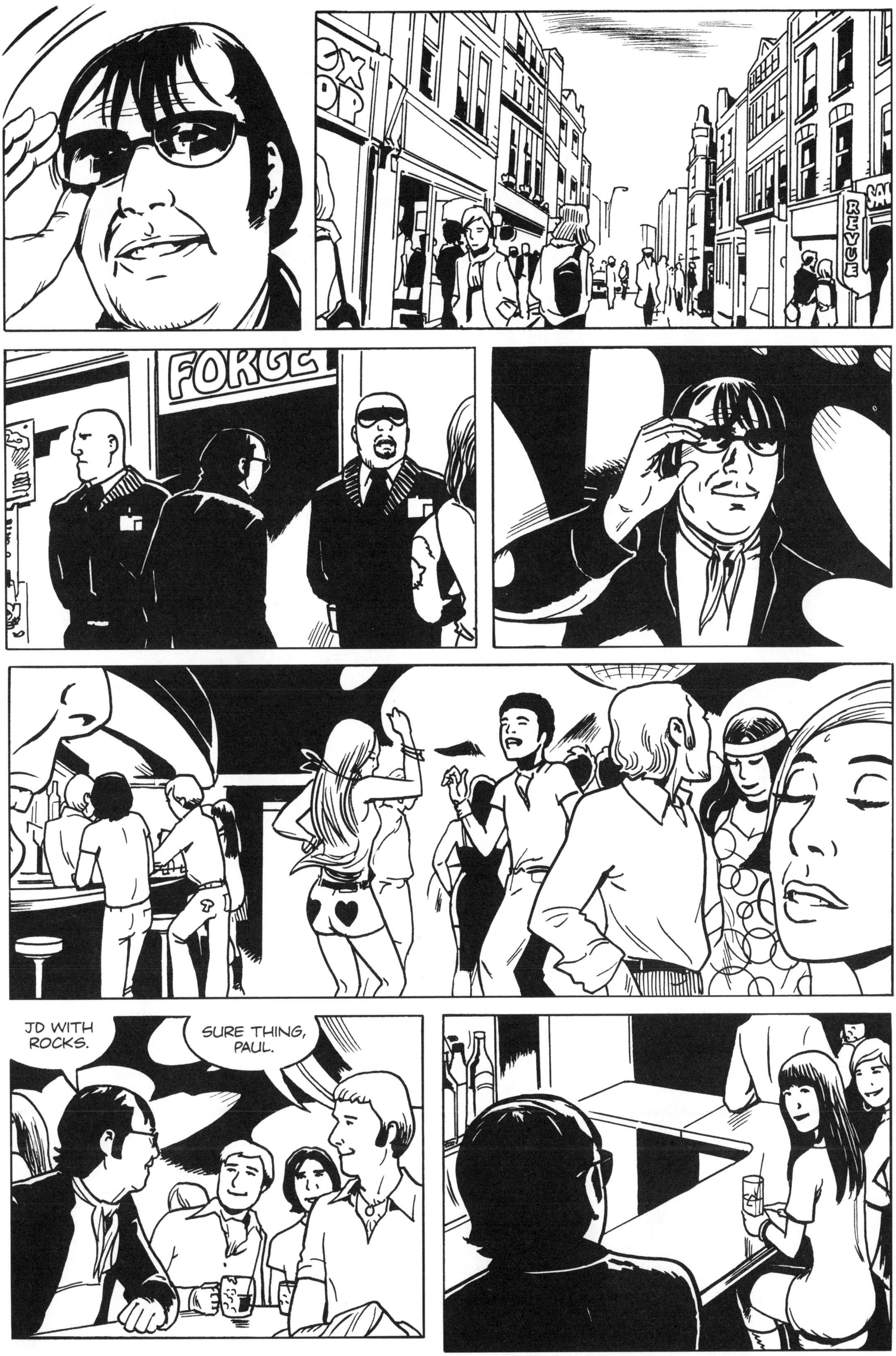
REVUE
FORGE
JD WITH ROCKS.
SURE THING, PAUL.

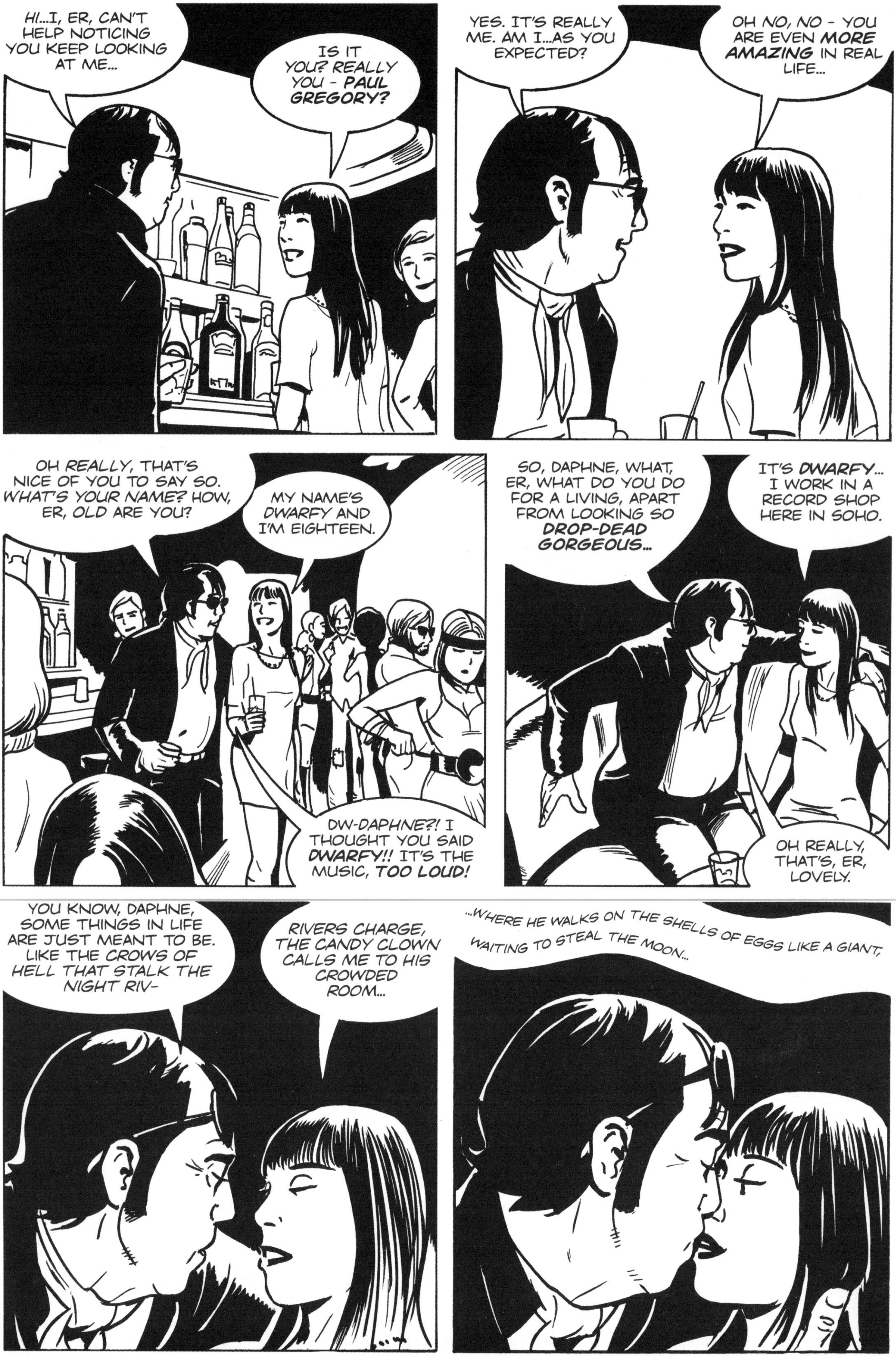
HI...I, ER, CAN'T HELP NOTICING YOU KEEP LOOKING AT ME...
IS IT YOU? REALLY YOU - PAUL GREGORY?
YES. IT'S REALLY ME. AM I...AS YOU EXPECTED?
OH NO, NO - YOU ARE EVEN MORE AMAZING IN REAL LIFE...
OH REALLY, THAT'S NICE OF YOU TO SAY SO. WHAT'S YOUR NAME? HOW, ER, OLD ARE YOU?
MY NAME'S DWARFY AND I'M EIGHTEEN.
DW-DAPHNE?! I THOUGHT YOU SAID DWARFY!! IT'S THE MUSIC, TOO LOUD!
SO, DAPHNE, WHAT, ER, WHAT DO YOU DO FOR A LIVING, APART FROM LOOKING SO DROP-DEAD GORGEOUS...
IT'S DWARFY... I WORK IN A RECORD SHOP HERE IN SOHO.
OH REALLY, THAT'S, ER, LOVELY.
YOU KNOW, DAPHNE, SOME THINGS IN LIFE ARE JUST MEANT TO BE. LIKE THE CROWS OF HELL THAT STALK THE NIGHT RIV-
RIVERS CHARGE, THE CANDY CLOWN CALLS ME TO HIS CROWDED ROOM...
...WHERE HE WALKS ON THE SHELLS OF EGGS LIKE A GIANT, WAITING TO STEAL THE MOON...

WHEN I FIRST SAW YOUR FACE, I COULD NOT IGNORE THE DISGRACE...

DAPHNE, OH DAPHN —

IT'S DWARFY, I TELL YOU...

I DON'T BELONG TO ME, I AM NOT YOUR GATE KEEPER, NOT YOUR PEEPHOLE PEEPER...

DWARFY.

I CAN HIDE FROM THE TORTURED IRE, BUT YOU WILL ALWAYS FEEL THE FURNACE OF A THOUSAND STARES...

YYYYYYYYYYAAAAAAAARRRRRHHHHHHHHHGGGGGGGGGHHHHHHHHH!!!!!!!!

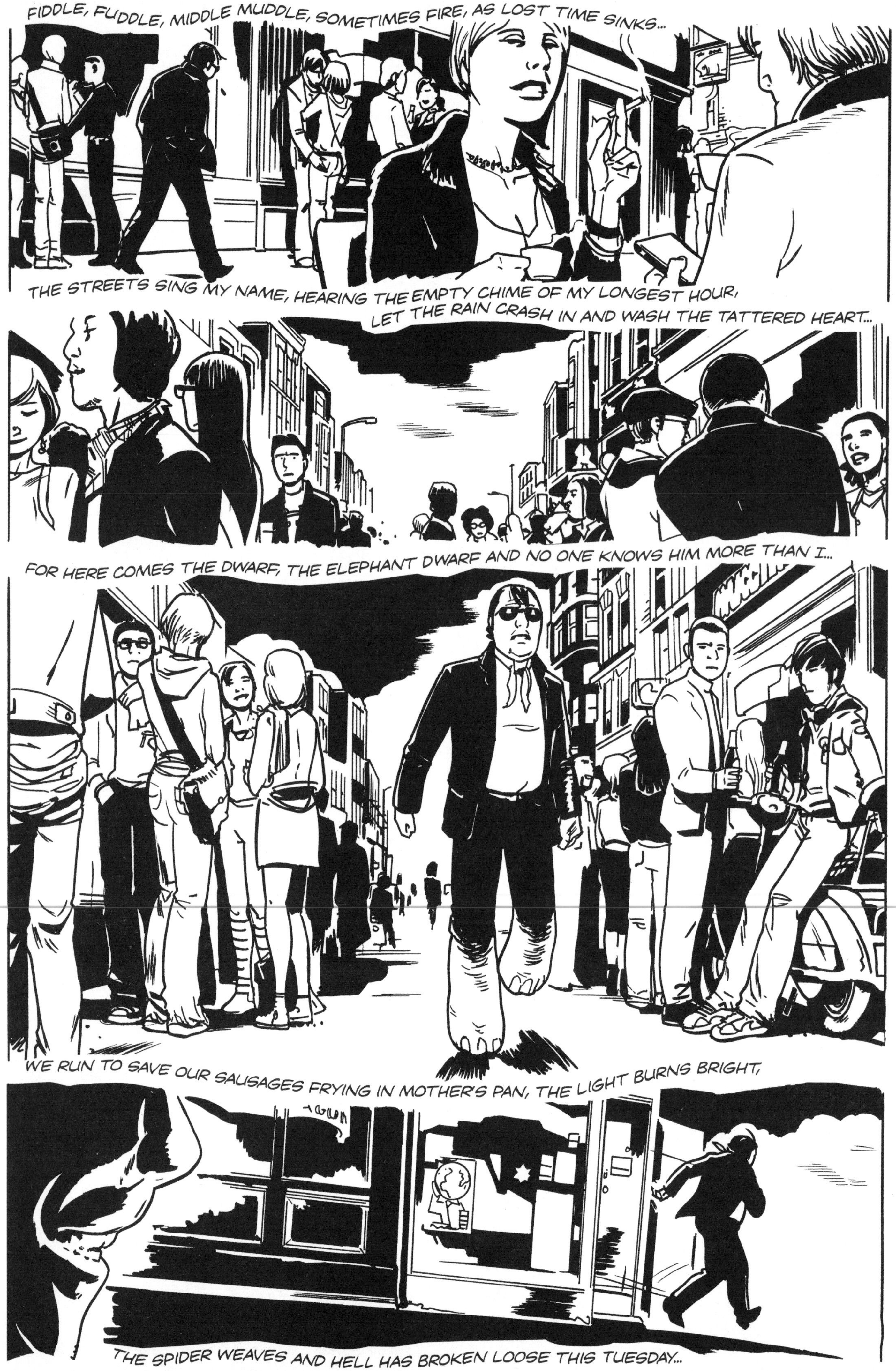
FIDDLE, FUDDLE, MIDDLE MUDDLE, SOMETIMES FIRE, AS LOST TIME SINKS...
THE STREETS SING MY NAME, HEARING THE EMPTY CHIME OF MY LONGEST HOUR,
LET THE RAIN CRASH IN AND WASH THE TATTERED HEART...
FOR HERE COMES THE DWARF, THE ELEPHANT DWARF AND NO ONE KNOWS HIM MORE THAN I...
WE RUN TO SAVE OUR SAUSAGES FRYING IN MOTHER'S PAN, THE LIGHT BURNS BRIGHT,
THE SPIDER WEAVES AND HELL HAS BROKEN LOOSE THIS TUESDAY...

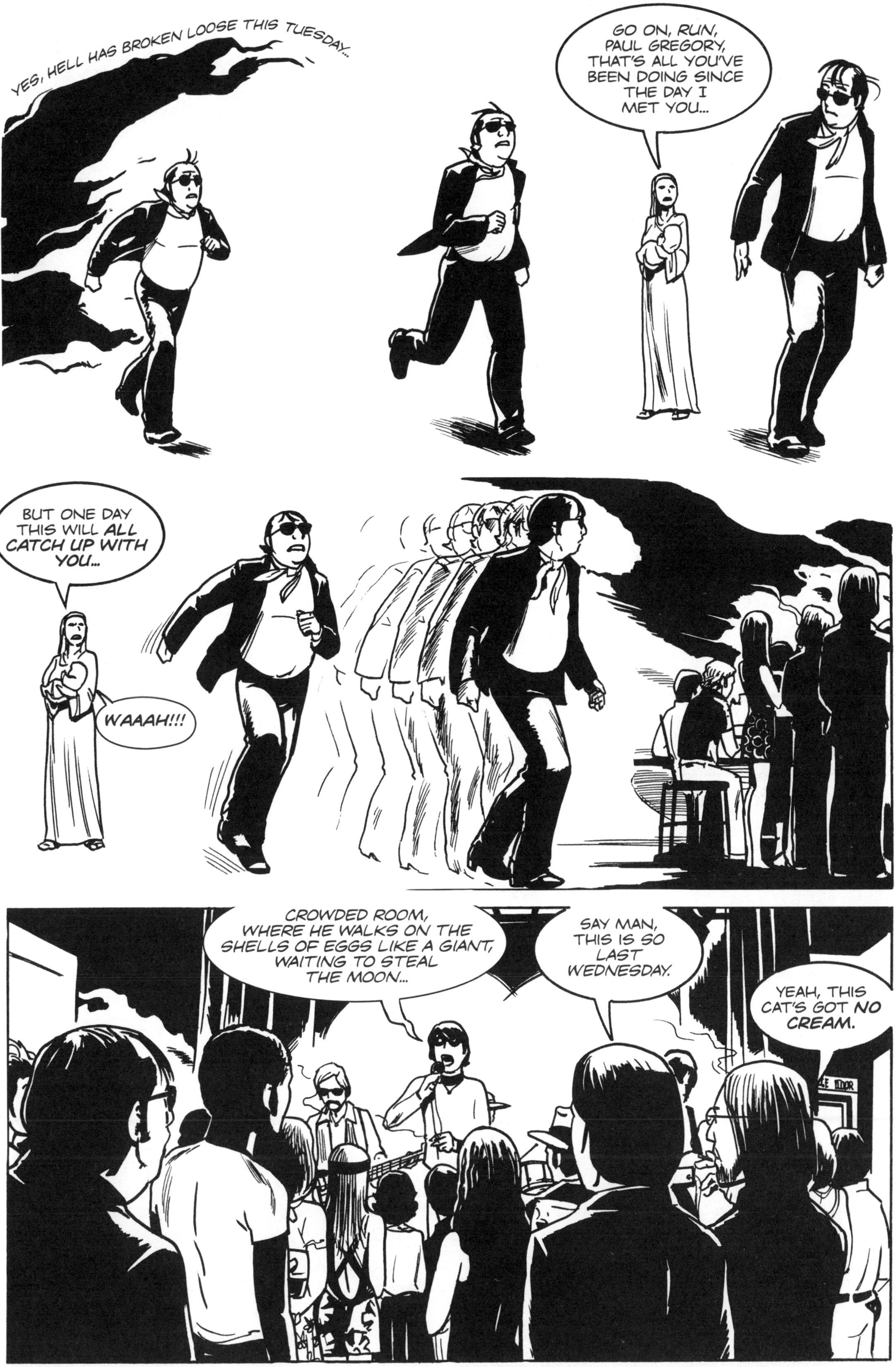
YES, HELL HAS BROKEN LOOSE THIS TUESDAY...
GO ON, RUN, PAUL GREGORY, THAT'S ALL YOU'VE BEEN DOING SINCE THE DAY I MET YOU...
BUT ONE DAY THIS WILL ALL CATCH UP WITH YOU...
WAAAH!!!
CROWDED ROOM, WHERE HE WALKS ON THE SHELLS OF EGGS LIKE A GIANT, WAITING TO STEAL THE MOON...
SAY MAN, THIS IS SO LAST WEDNESDAY.
YEAH, THIS CAT'S GOT NO CREAM.

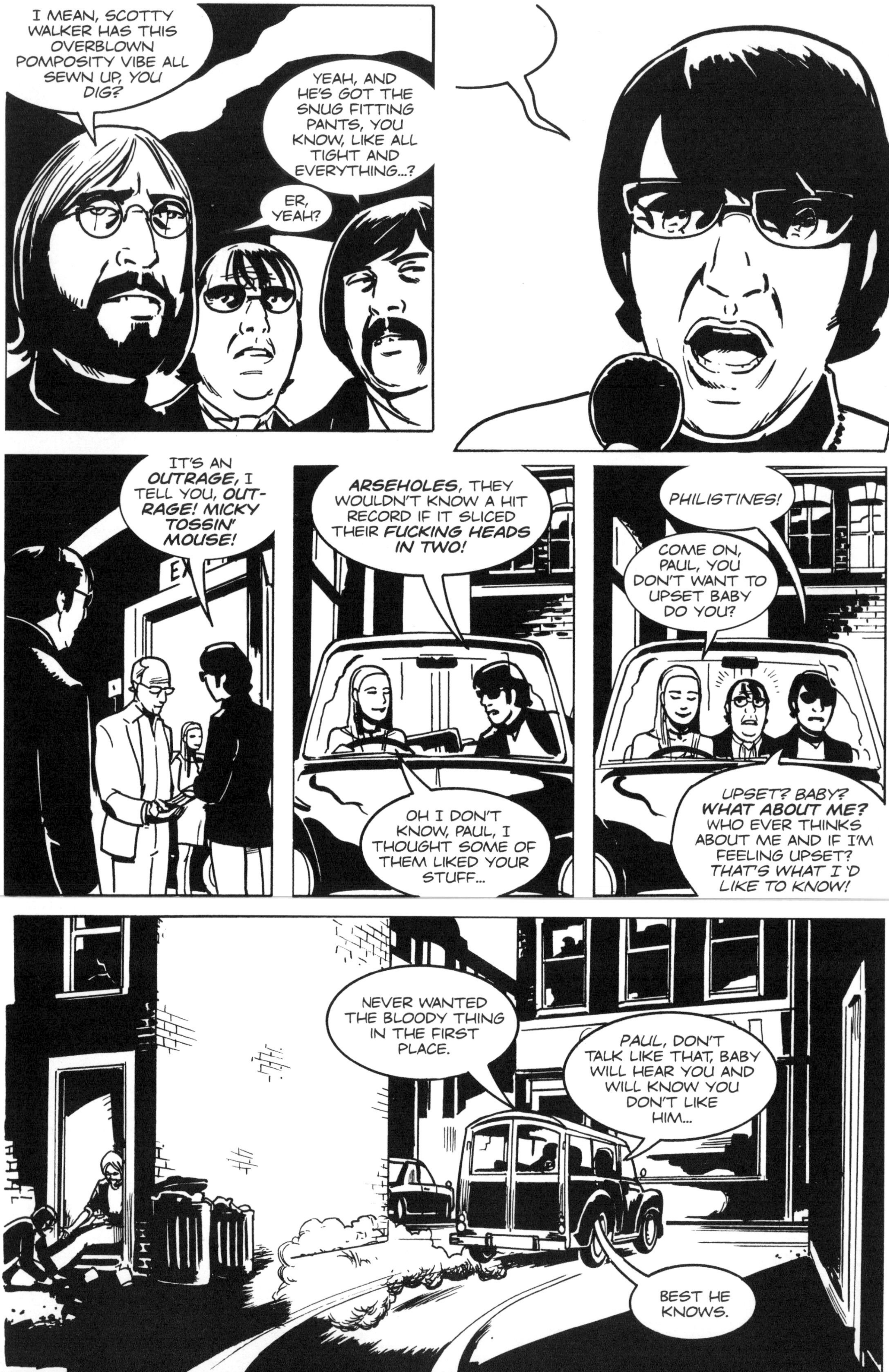

I MEAN, SCOTTY WALKER HAS THIS OVERBLOWN POMPOSITY VIBE ALL SEWN UP, YOU DIG?
YEAH, AND HE'S GOT THE SNUG FITTING PANTS, YOU KNOW, LIKE ALL TIGHT AND EVERYTHING...?
ER, YEAH?
IT'S AN OUTRAGE, I TELL YOU, OUT-RAGE! MICKY TOSSIN' MOUSE!
ARSEHOLES, THEY WOULDN'T KNOW A HIT RECORD IF IT SLICED THEIR FUCKING HEADS IN TWO!
OH I DON'T KNOW, PAUL, I THOUGHT SOME OF THEM LIKED YOUR STUFF...
PHILISTINES!
COME ON, PAUL, YOU DON'T WANT TO UPSET BABY DO YOU?
UPSET? BABY? WHAT ABOUT ME? WHO EVER THINKS ABOUT ME AND IF I'M FEELING UPSET? THAT'S WHAT I 'D LIKE TO KNOW!
NEVER WANTED THE BLOODY THING IN THE FIRST PLACE.
PAUL, DON'T TALK LIKE THAT, BABY WILL HEAR YOU AND WILL KNOW YOU DON'T LIKE HIM...
BEST HE KNOWS.

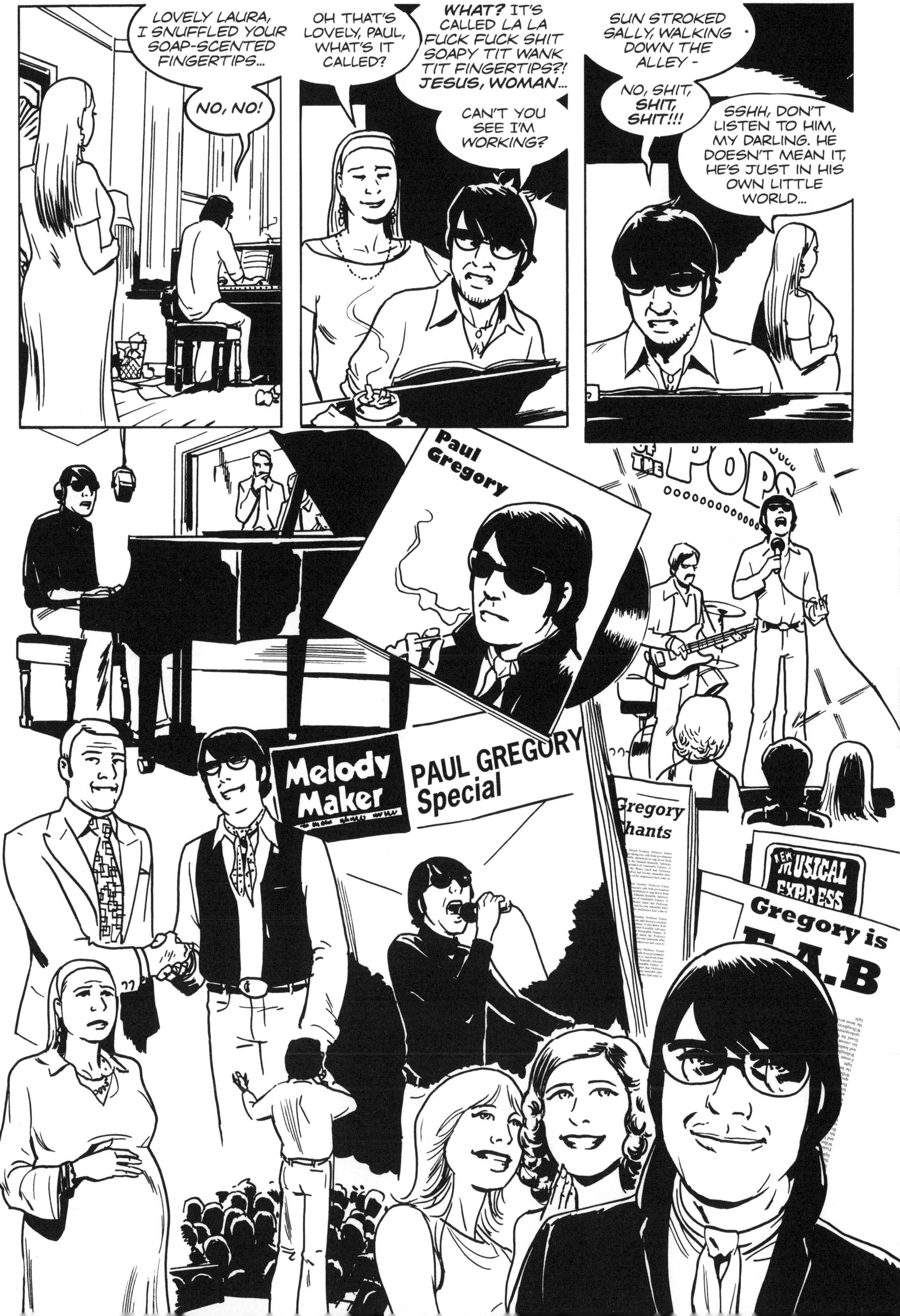
LOVELY LAURA, I SNUFFLED YOUR SOAP-SCENTED FINGERTIPS...
NO, NO!
OH THAT'S LOVELY, PAUL, WHAT'S IT CALLED?
WHAT? IT'S CALLED LA LA FUCK FUCK SHIT SOAPY TIT WANK TIT FINGERTIPS?! JESUS, WOMAN...
CAN'T YOU SEE I'M WORKING?
SUN STROKED SALLY, WALKING DOWN THE ALLEY -
NO, SHIT, SHIT, SHIT!!!
SSHH, DON'T LISTEN TO HIM, MY DARLING. HE DOESN'T MEAN IT, HE'S JUST IN HIS OWN LITTLE WORLD...
Paul Gregory
Melody Maker
PAUL GREGORY Special
Gregory
NEW MUSICAL EXPRESS
Gregory is F.A.B

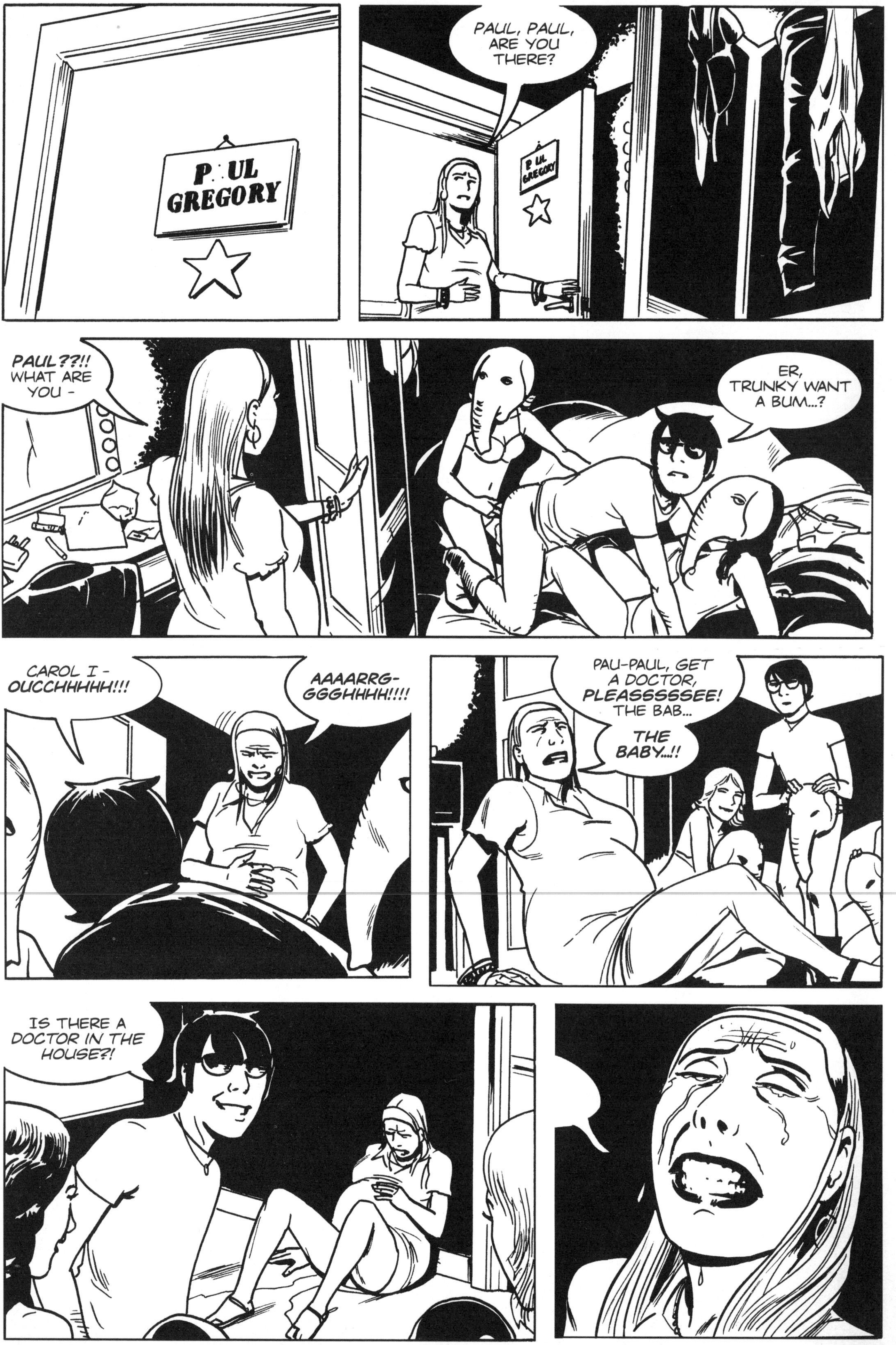
P UL
GREGORY
PAUL, PAUL, ARE YOU THERE?
P UL
GREGORY
PAUL??!! WHAT ARE YOU -
ER, TRUNKY WANT A BUM...?
CAROL I - OUCCHHHHH!!!
AAAARRG-GGGHHHH!!!!
PAU-PAUL, GET A DOCTOR, PLEASSSSSEE! THE BAB...
THE BABY...!!
IS THERE A DOCTOR IN THE HOUSE?!

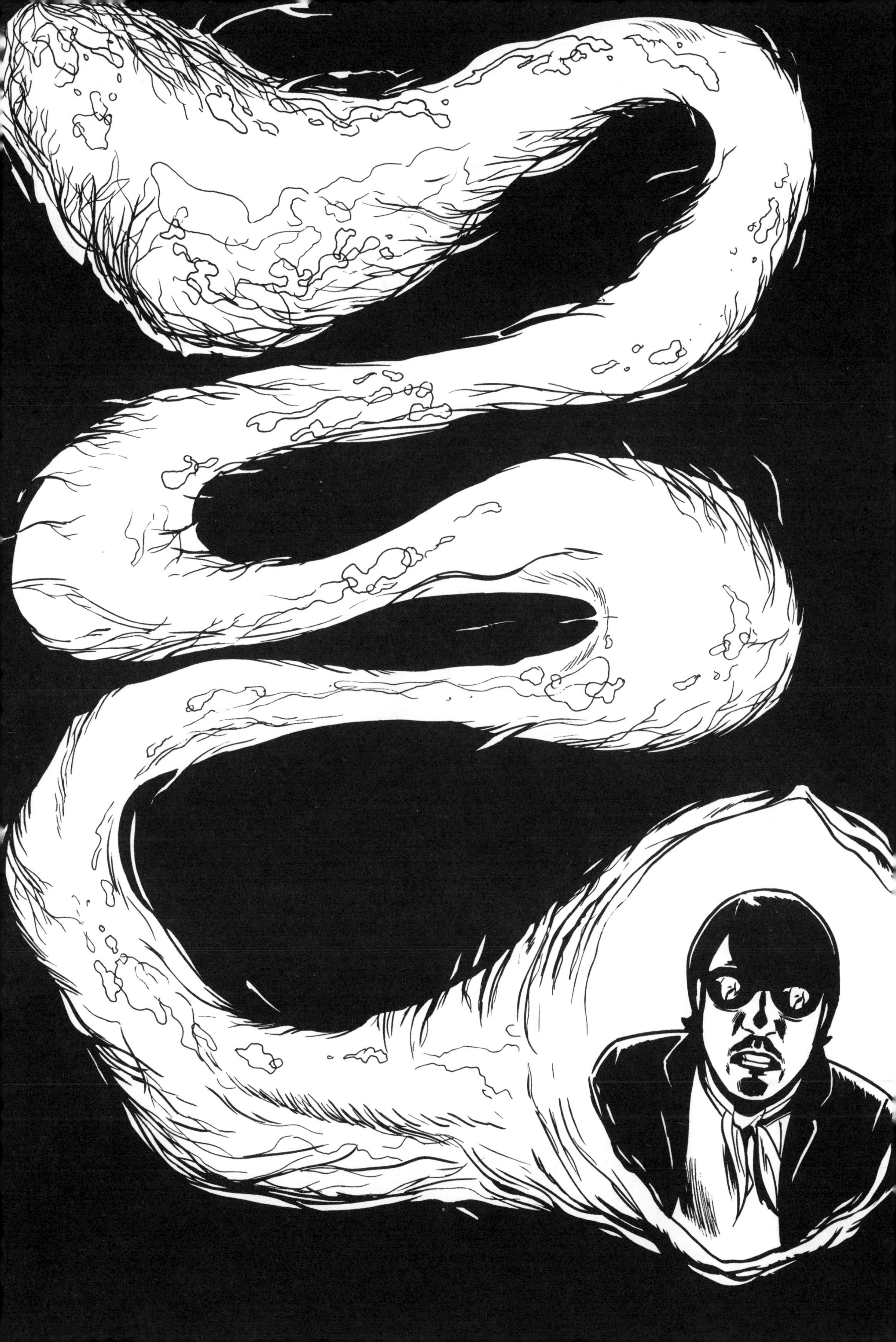

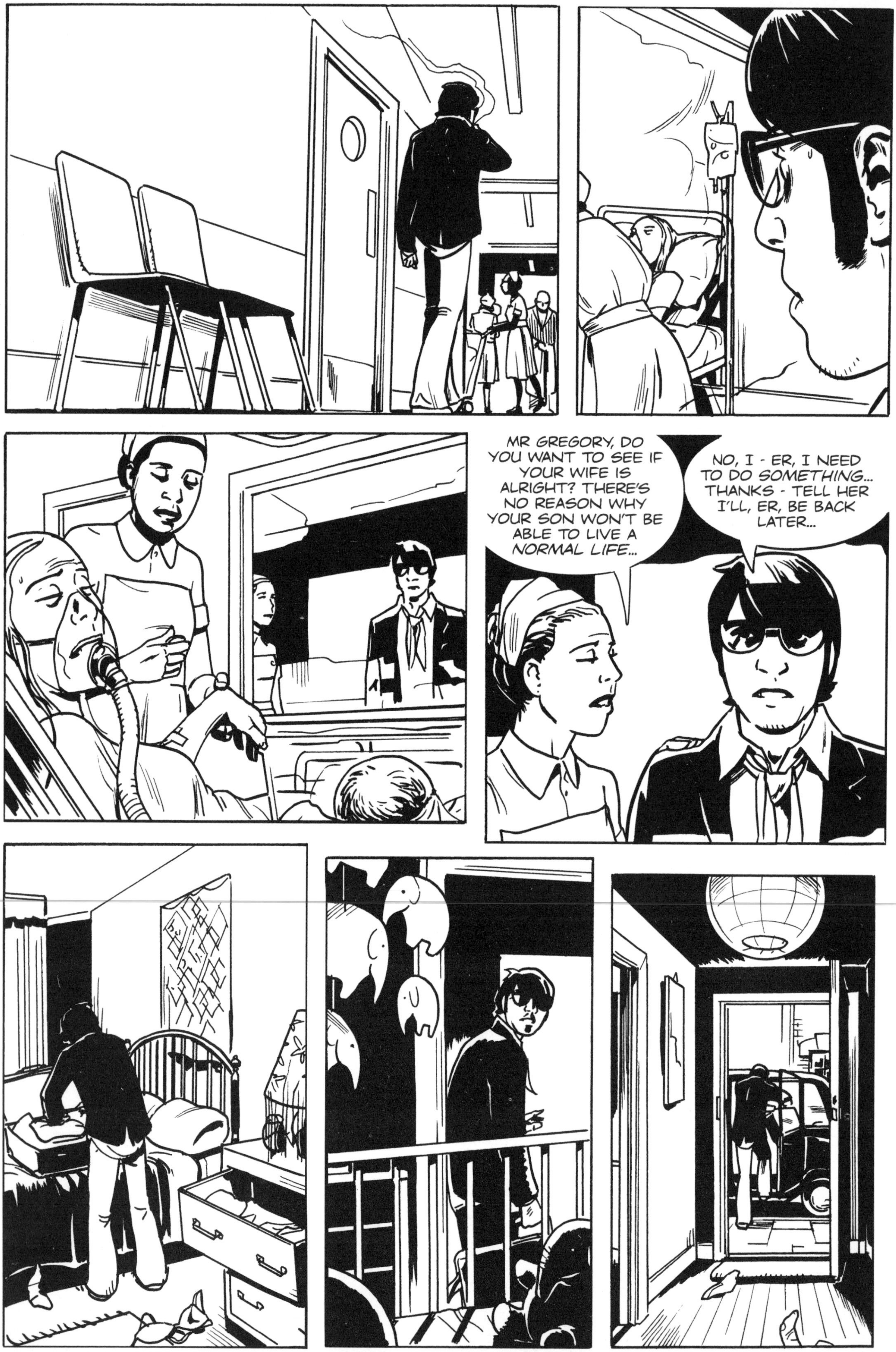
MR GREGORY, DO YOU WANT TO SEE IF YOUR WIFE IS ALRIGHT? THERE'S NO REASON WHY YOUR SON WON'T BE ABLE TO LIVE A NORMAL LIFE...
NO, I - ER, I NEED TO DO SOMETHING... THANKS - TELL HER I'LL, ER, BE BACK LATER...

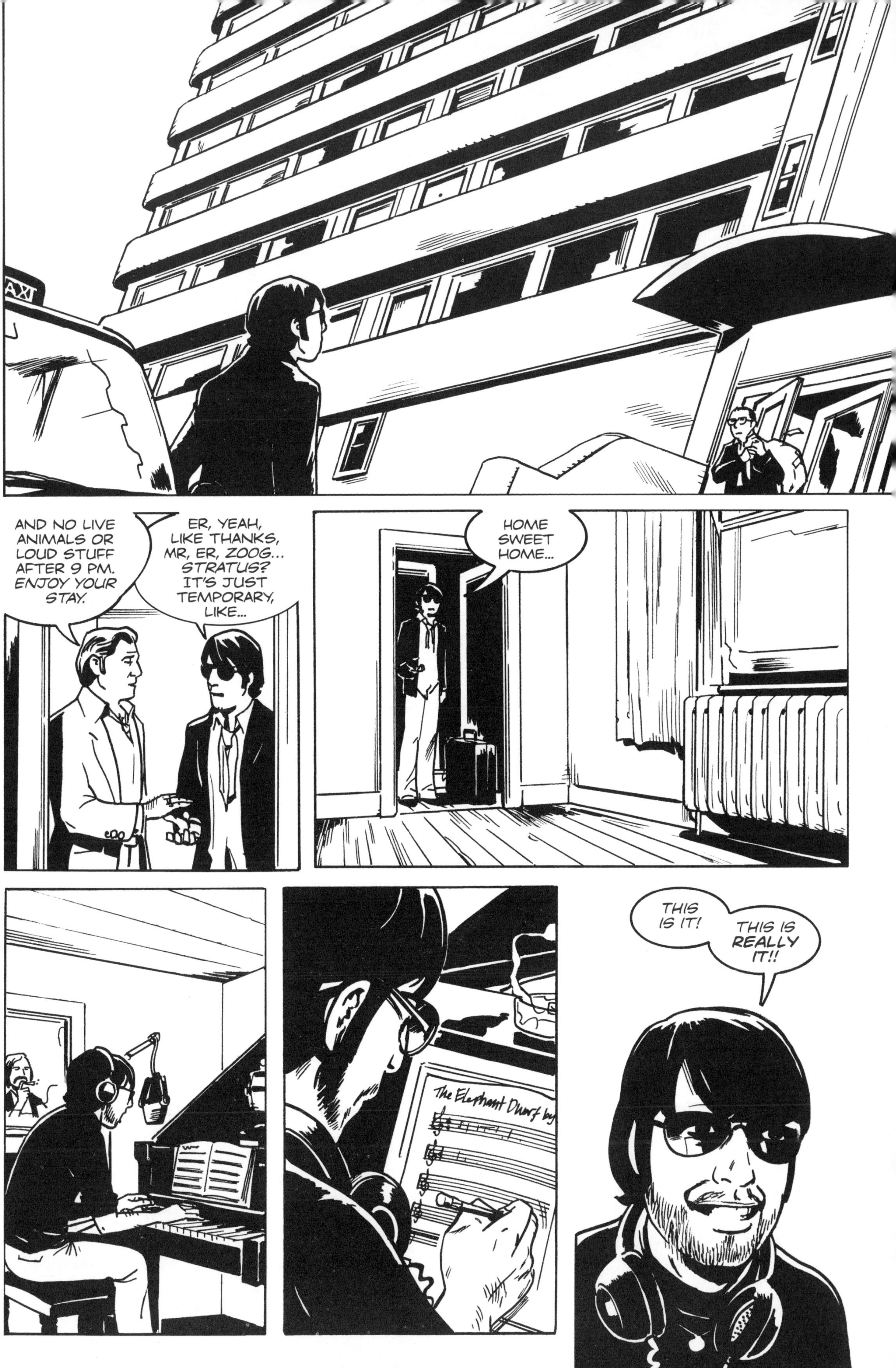
AXI
AND NO LIVE ANIMALS OR LOUD STUFF AFTER 9 PM. ENJOY YOUR STAY.
ER, YEAH, LIKE THANKS, MR, ER, ZOOG... STRATUS? IT'S JUST TEMPORARY, LIKE...
HOME SWEET HOME...
The Elephant Dwarf by
THIS IS IT!
THIS IS REALLY IT!!

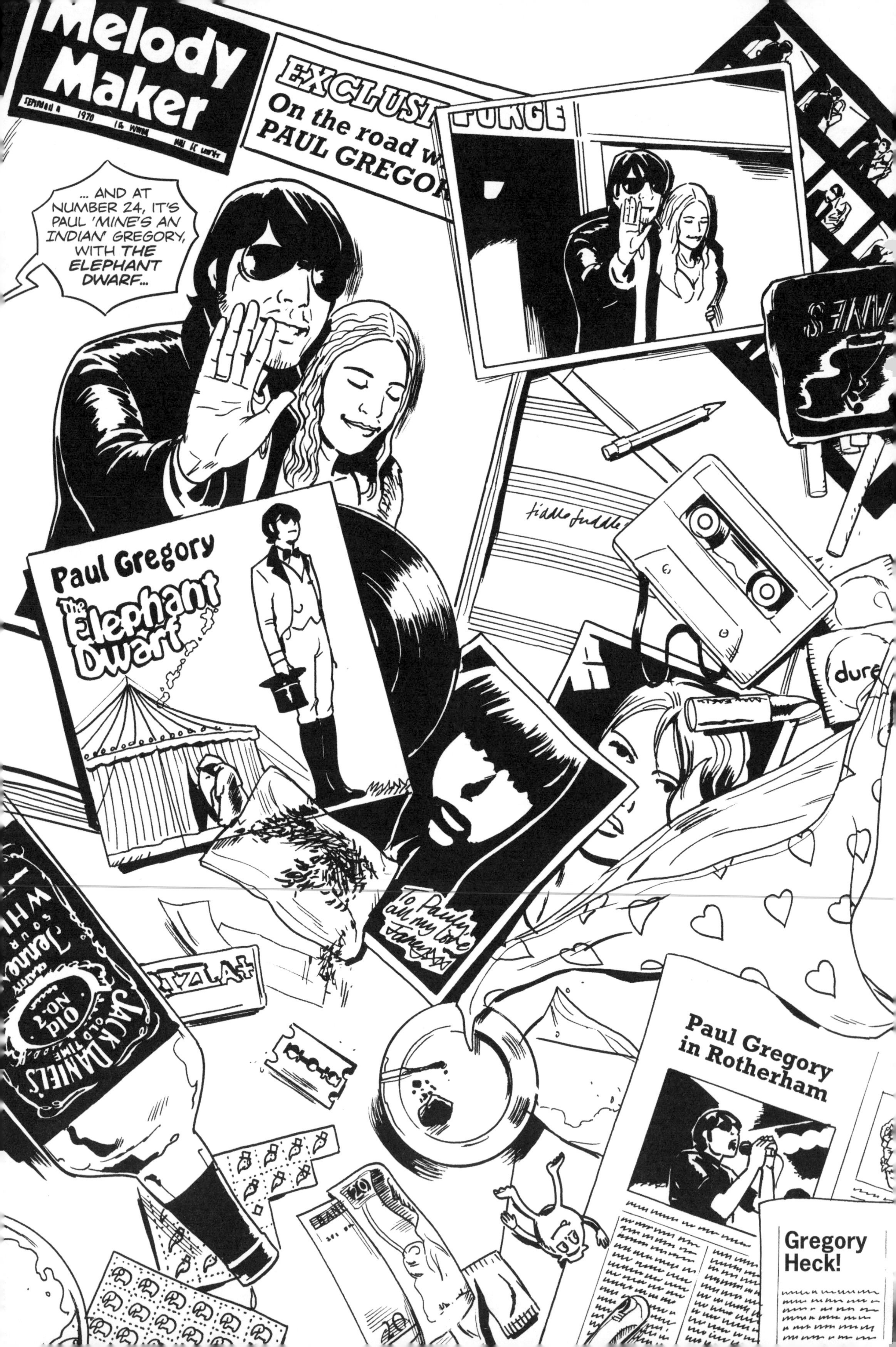
Melody Maker
EXCLUSI
On the road w
PAUL GREGOR
... AND AT NUMBER 24, IT'S PAUL 'MINE'S AN INDIAN' GREGORY, WITH THE ELEPHANT DWARF...
Paul Gregory
The Elephant Dwarf
To Pauly all my love
Paul Gregory in Rotherham
Gregory Heck!
JACK DANIEL'S
Old No. 7

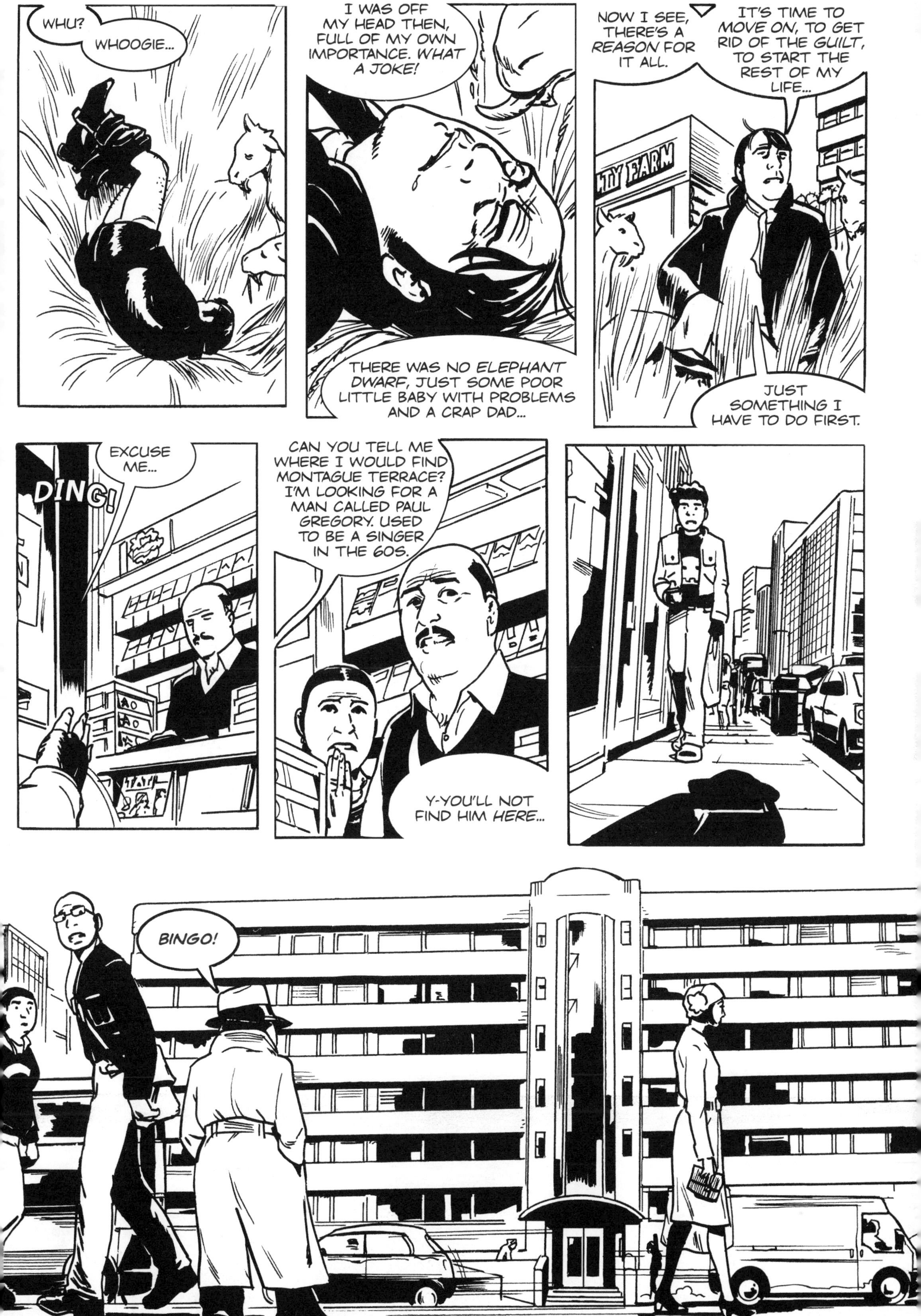
WHU?
WHOOGIE...
I WAS OFF MY HEAD THEN, FULL OF MY OWN IMPORTANCE. *WHAT* A JOKE!
THERE WAS NO *ELEPHANT DWARF*, JUST SOME POOR LITTLE BABY WITH PROBLEMS AND A CRAP DAD...
NOW I SEE, THERE'S A *REASON* FOR IT ALL.
IT'S TIME TO *MOVE ON*, TO GET RID OF THE GUILT, TO START THE REST OF MY LIFE...
JUST SOMETHING I HAVE TO DO FIRST.
EXCUSE ME...
DING!
CAN YOU TELL ME WHERE I WOULD FIND MONTAGUE TERRACE? I'M LOOKING FOR A MAN CALLED PAUL GREGORY. USED TO BE A SINGER IN THE 60S.
Y-YOU'LL NOT FIND HIM *HERE*...
BINGO!

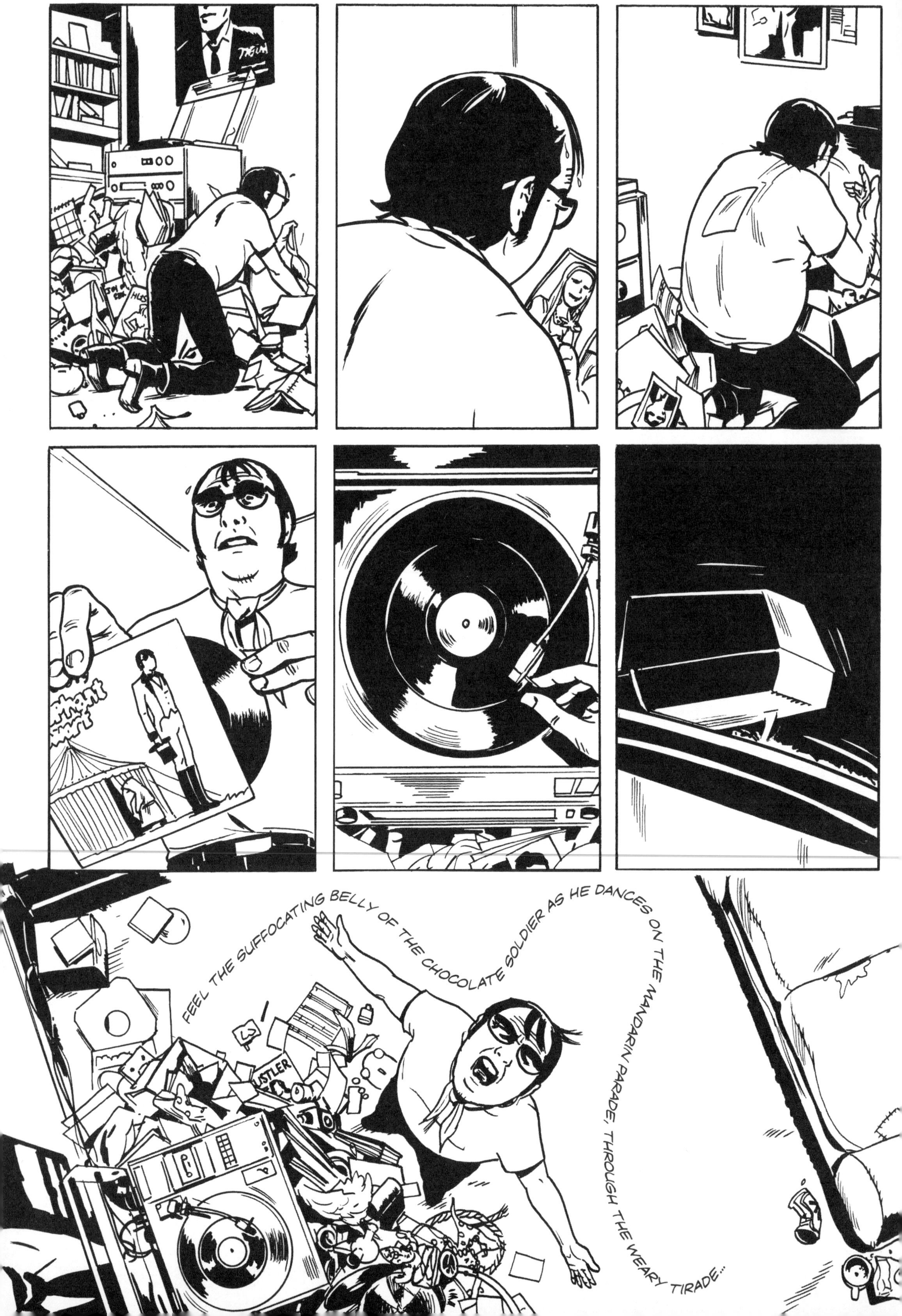
FEEL THE SUFFOCATING BELLY OF THE CHOCOLATE SOLDIER AS HE DANCES ON THE MANDARIN PARADE, THROUGH THE WEARY TIRADE...

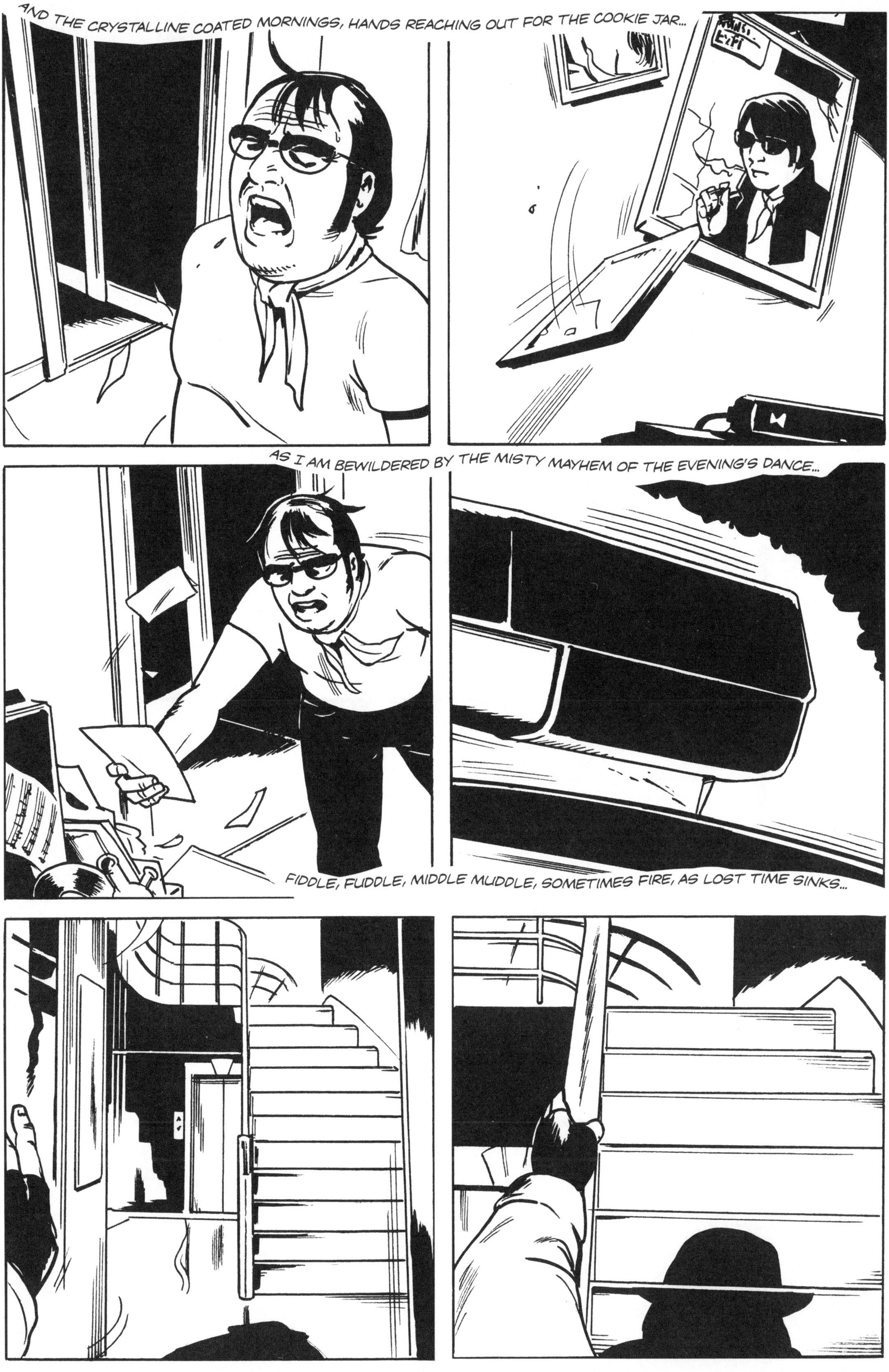
AND THE CRYSTALLINE COATED MORNINGS, HANDS REACHING OUT FOR THE COOKIE JAR...
AS I AM BEWILDERED BY THE MISTY MAYHEM OF THE EVENING'S DANCE...
FIDDLE, FUDDLE, MIDDLE MUDDLE, SOMETIMES FIRE, AS LOST TIME SINKS...

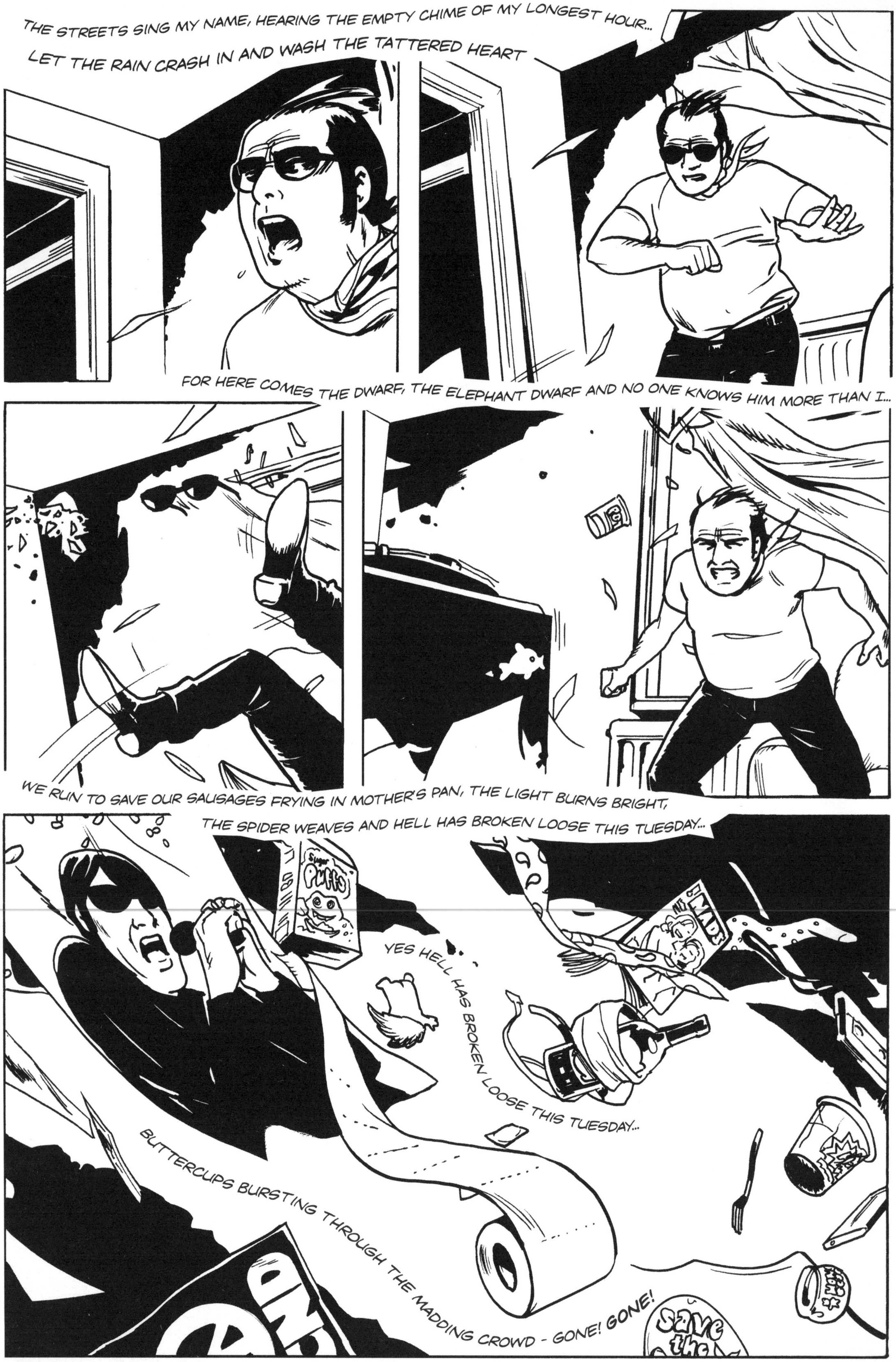
THE STREETS SING MY NAME, HEARING THE EMPTY CHIME OF MY LONGEST HOUR...
LET THE RAIN CRASH IN AND WASH THE TATTERED HEART
FOR HERE COMES THE DWARF, THE ELEPHANT DWARF AND NO ONE KNOWS HIM MORE THAN I...
WE RUN TO SAVE OUR SAUSAGES FRYING IN MOTHER'S PAN, THE LIGHT BURNS BRIGHT,
THE SPIDER WEAVES AND HELL HAS BROKEN LOOSE THIS TUESDAY...
YES HELL HAS BROKEN LOOSE THIS TUESDAY...
BUTTERCUPS BURSTING THROUGH THE MADDING CROWD - GONE! GONE!

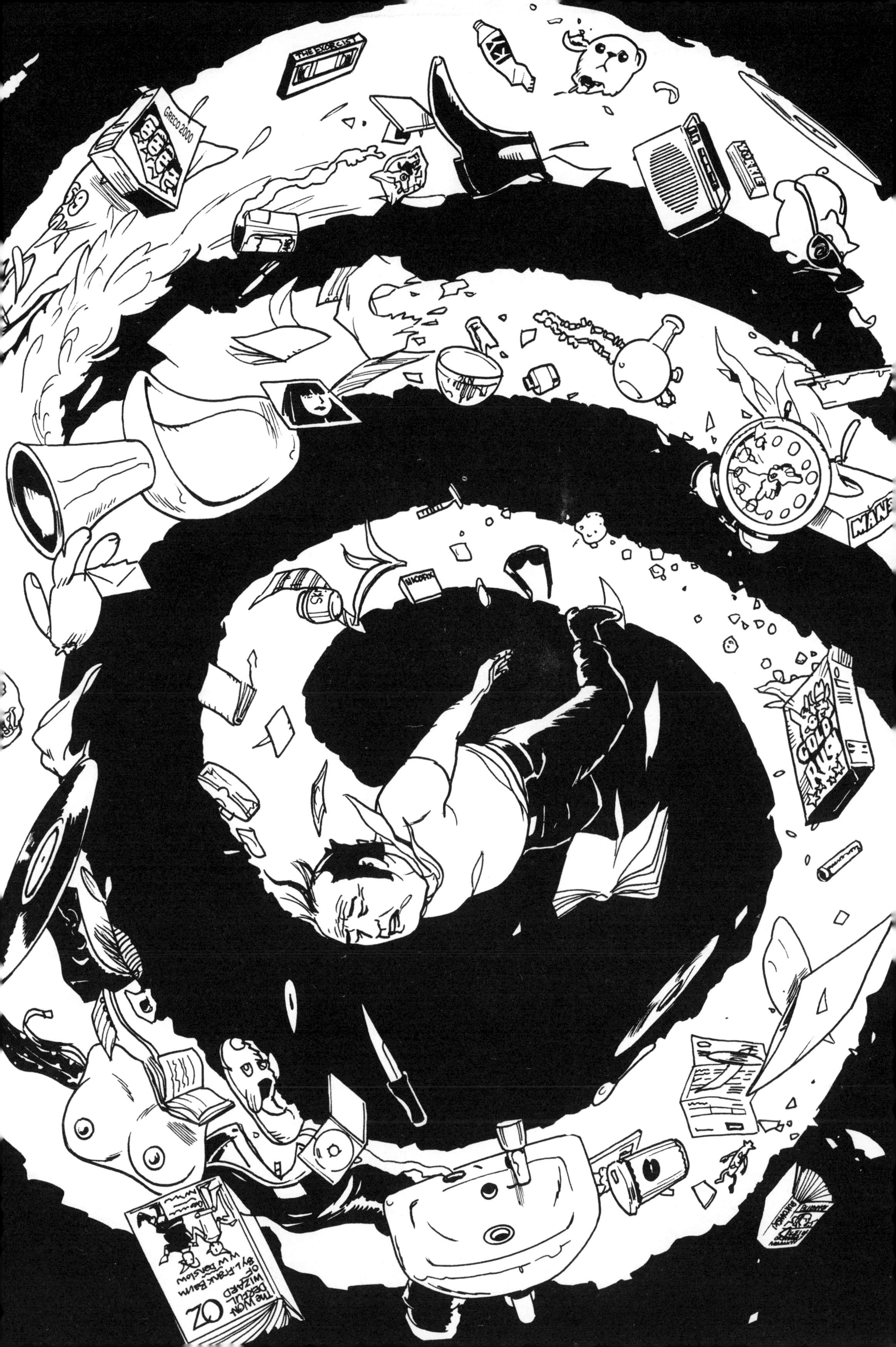
THE EXORCIST
GRECO 2000

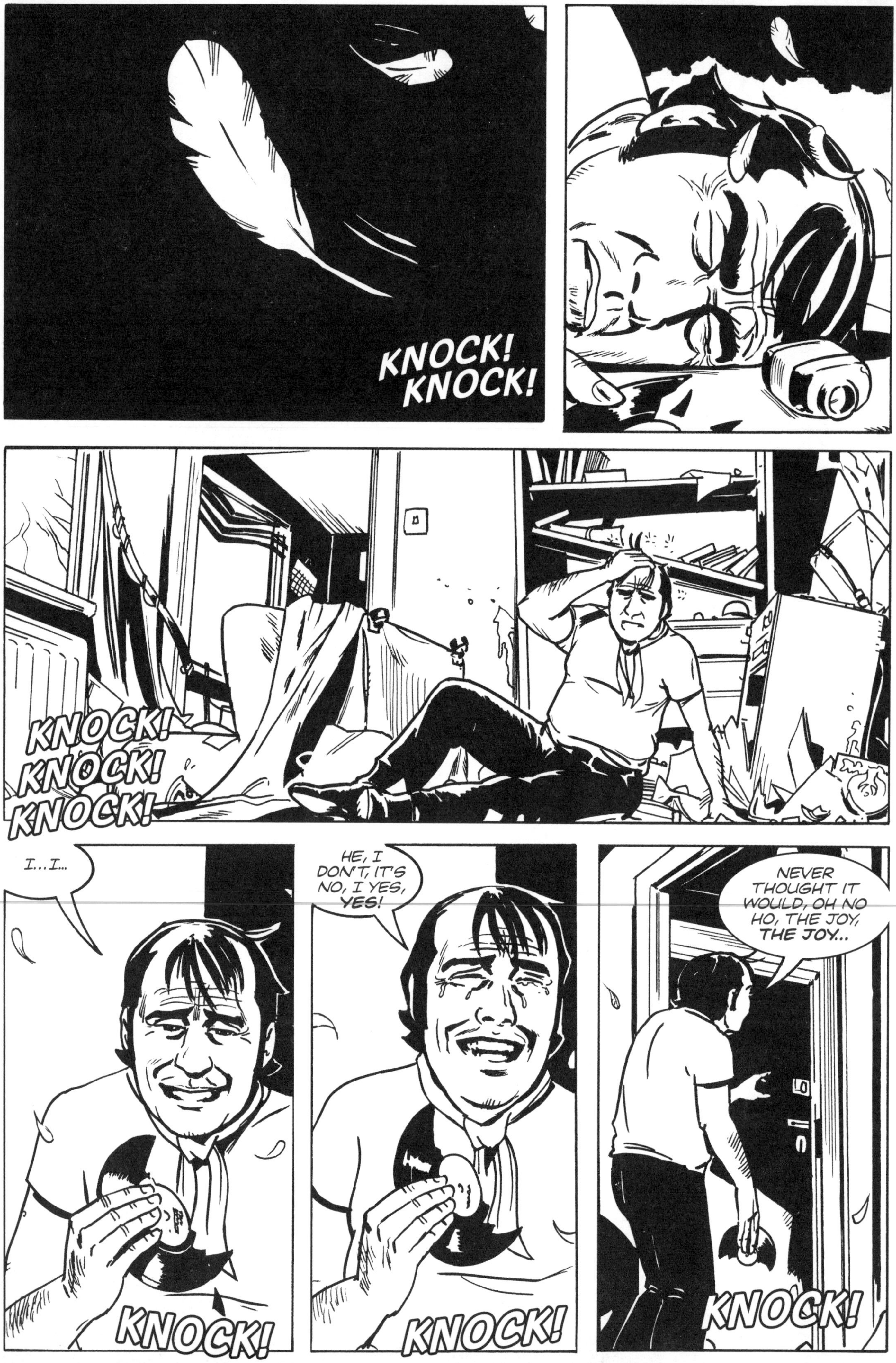
KNOCK! KNOCK!
KNOCK! KNOCK! KNOCK!
I... I...
KNOCK!
HE, I DON'T, IT'S NO, I YES, YES!
KNOCK!
NEVER THOUGHT IT WOULD, OH NO HO, THE JOY, THE JOY...
KNOCK!

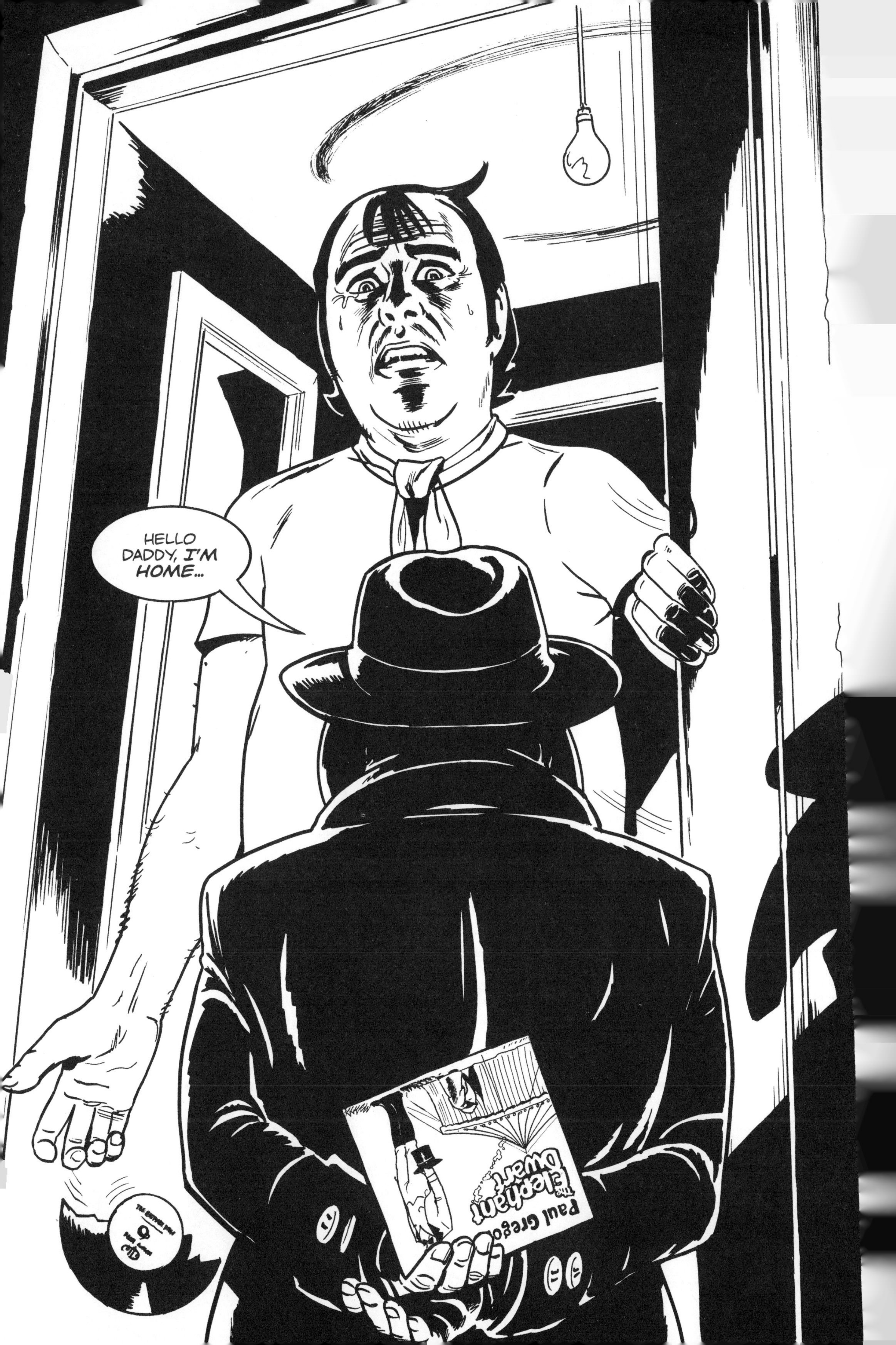
HELLO DADDY, I'M HOME...

the Puppeteer

THOUGH I LIVE AND WORK AMONGST THE FOOLS,

THEY SUSPECT NOTHING OF MY MASTER PLANS,

THE VERY POWER I WIELD BETWIXT MY FINGERTIPS,

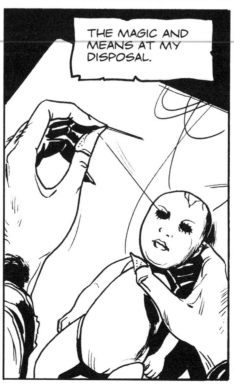

THE MAGIC AND MEANS AT MY DISPOSAL.

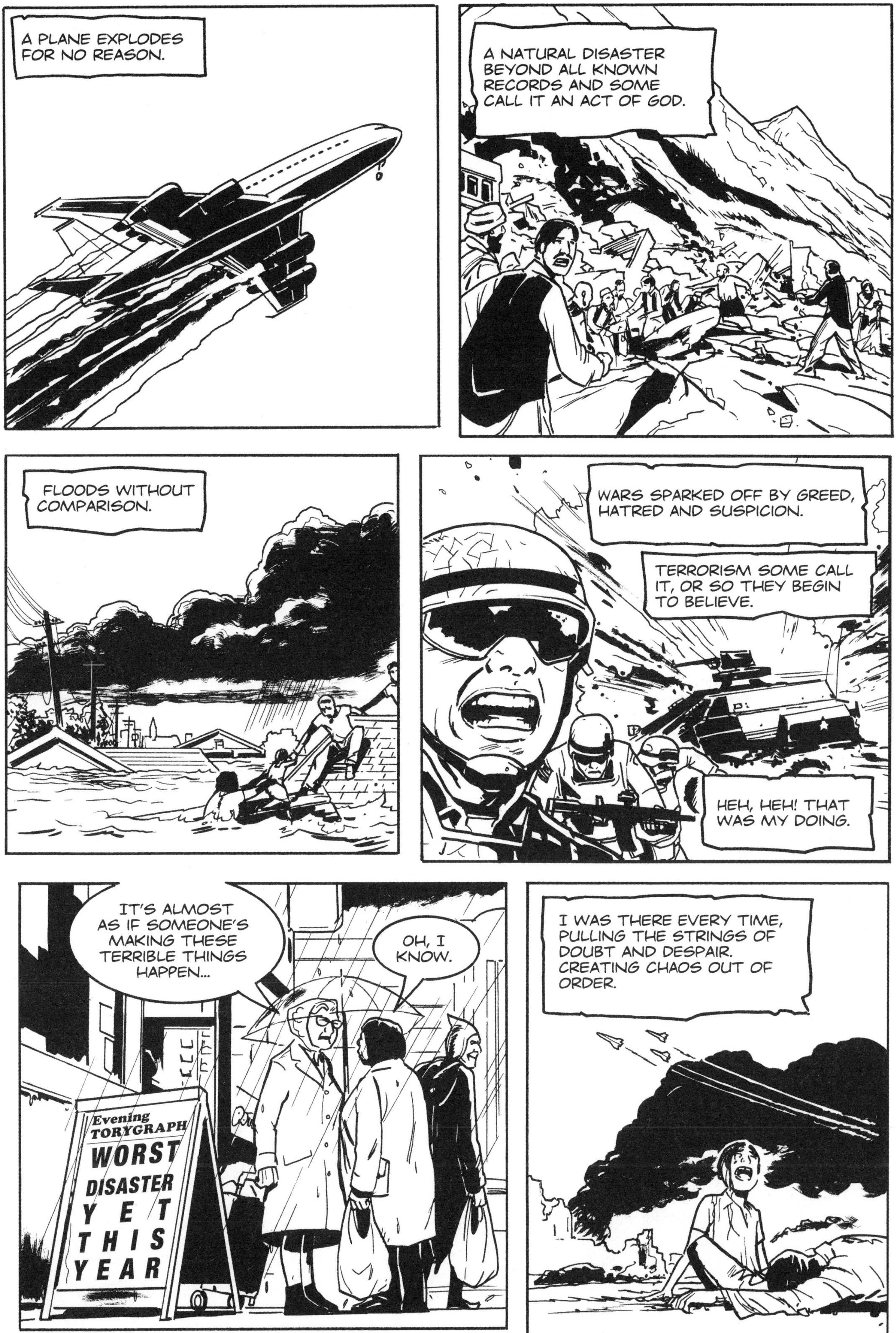
A PLANE EXPLODES FOR NO REASON.
A NATURAL DISASTER BEYOND ALL KNOWN RECORDS AND SOME CALL IT AN ACT OF GOD.
FLOODS WITHOUT COMPARISON.
WARS SPARKED OFF BY GREED, HATRED AND SUSPICION.
TERRORISM SOME CALL IT, OR SO THEY BEGIN TO BELIEVE.
HEH, HEH! THAT WAS MY DOING.
IT'S ALMOST AS IF SOMEONE'S MAKING THESE TERRIBLE THINGS HAPPEN...
OH, I KNOW.
Evening TORYGRAPH
WORST DISASTER YET THIS YEAR
I WAS THERE EVERY TIME, PULLING THE STRINGS OF DOUBT AND DESPAIR. CREATING CHAOS OUT OF ORDER.

BUSH

DOOM AND DESPONDENCY ARE MY PLAYTHINGS, TO DO WITH WHAT I WILL...

...UNTIL THAT FATEFUL DAY WHEN THEY SHALL FINALLY KNOW THAT IT WAS *I, THE PUPPETEER* WHO WAS RESPONSIBLE...

AS I STAND BEFORE THEM, MY LEGIONS OF MANIKINS BY MY SIDE READY TO RISE UP, TO TAKE CONTROL, TO...

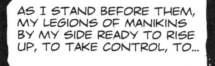

zzzZZZZZZTTCHH-*POP!*

ACH! SCHEISSE!!! NOT AGAIN!

DUMMKOPF FUSE-BOX PIECE OF SH—

HELPING YOU TO DO IT YOURSELF

FUSES FUSES FUSES 2 FOR 1

Afternoon TOERAG

THINGS ARE LOOKING UP!

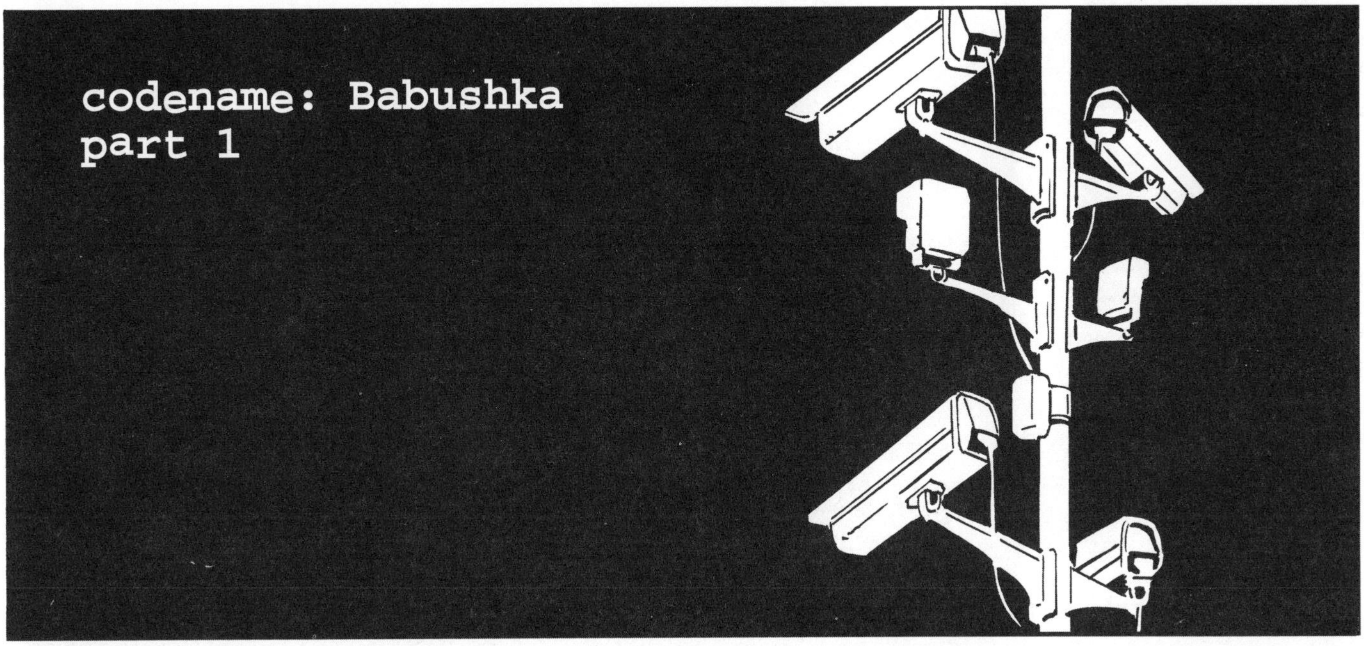
codename: Babushka
part 1

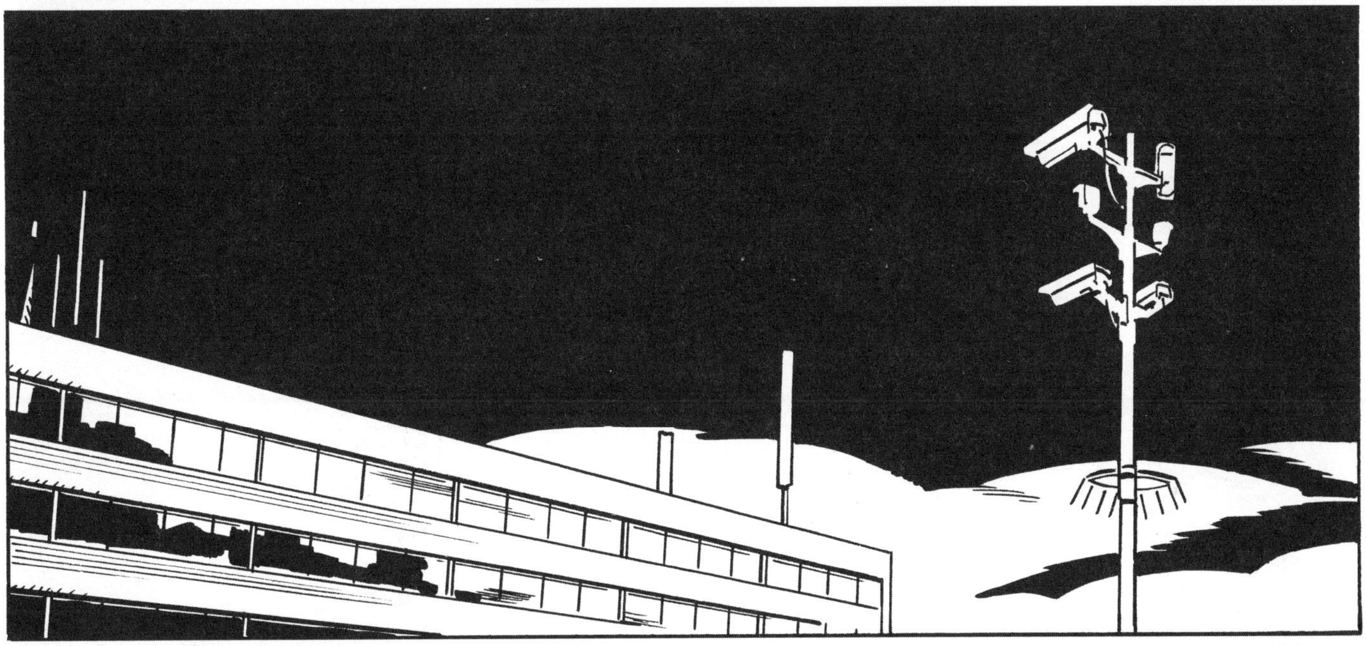

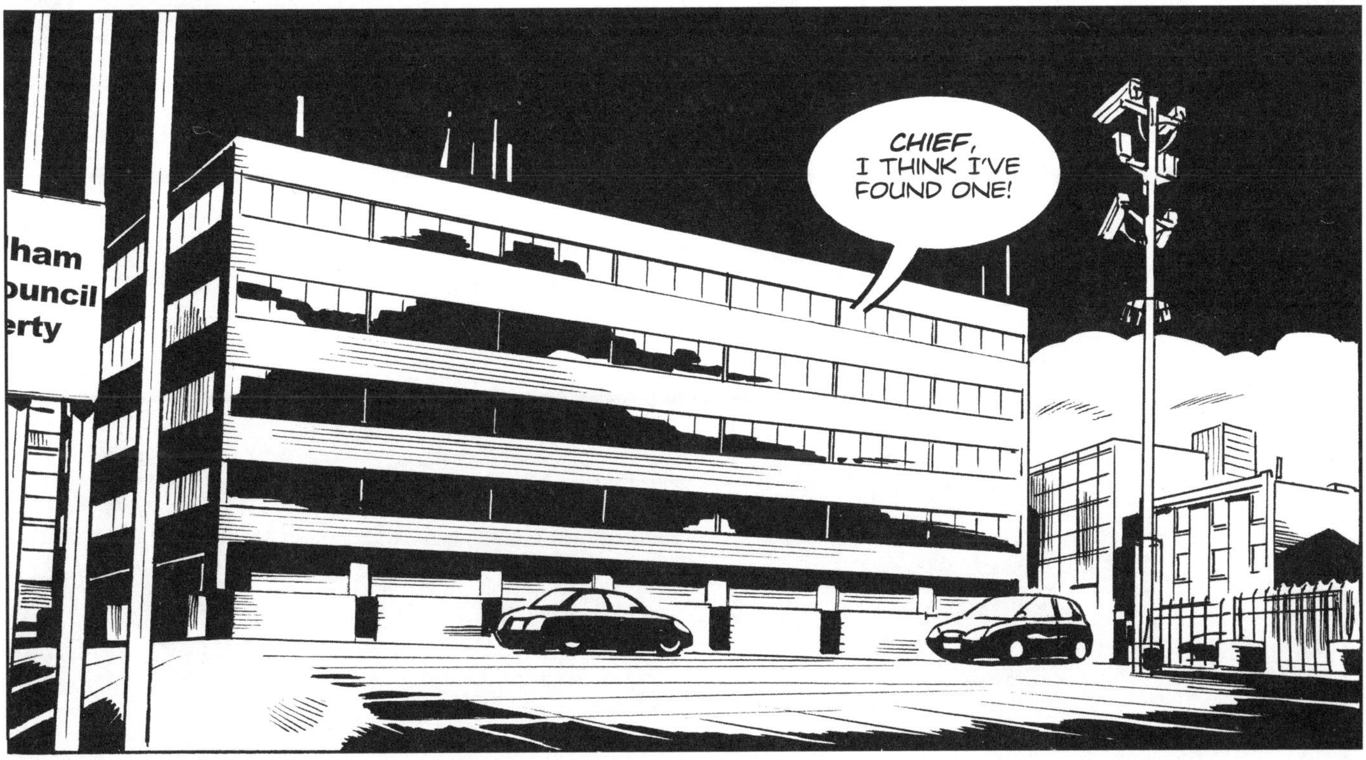
ham
ouncil
erty
CHIEF, I THINK I'VE FOUND ONE!

DON'T KNOW HOW SHE SLIPPED THROUGH THE NET UP TILL NOW, BUT SHE'S IDEAL MATERIAL.

EIGHTY-NINE YEARS OLD, INCAPACITY BENEFITS LEFT RIGHT AND CENTRE, OWNS HER OWN PROPERTY, NO KNOWN NEXT OF KIN.

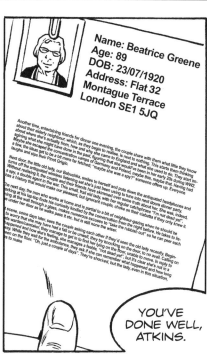

Name: Beatrice Greene
Age: 89
DOB: 23/07/1920
Address: Flat 32 Montague Terrace London SE1 5JQ

LET'S GO TO WORK!

YOU'VE DONE WELL, ATKINS.

NOW JUST LET ME DO THE TALKING. I HAVE A FEELING SHE MAY PROVE A TRICKY CUSTOMER.

YES BOSS.

FK

FK

FK'N

FK!

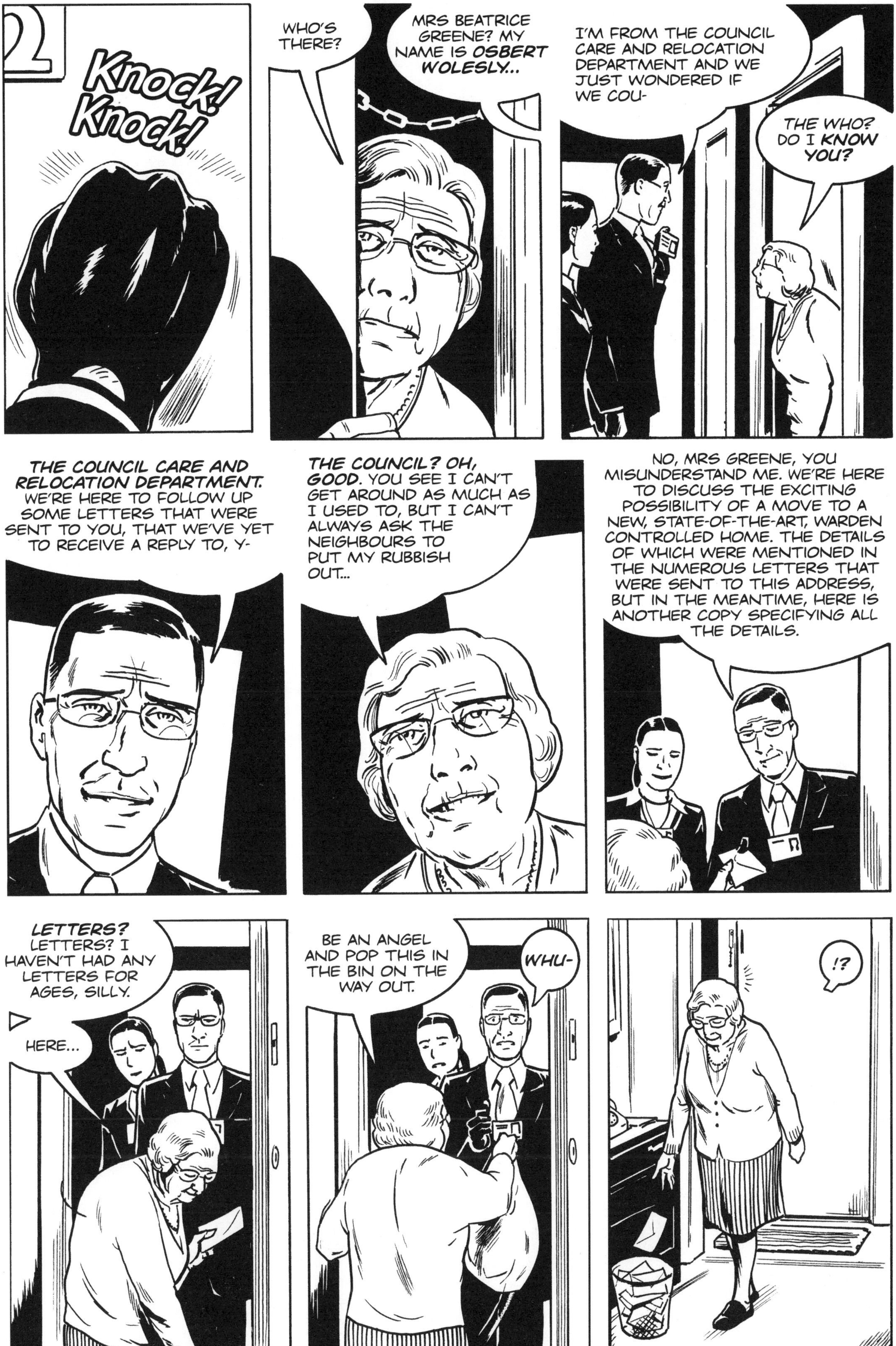
2
Knock! Knock!
WHO'S THERE?
MRS BEATRICE GREENE? MY NAME IS OSBERT WOLESLY...
I'M FROM THE COUNCIL CARE AND RELOCATION DEPARTMENT AND WE JUST WONDERED IF WE COU-
THE WHO? DO I KNOW YOU?
THE COUNCIL CARE AND RELOCATION DEPARTMENT. WE'RE HERE TO FOLLOW UP SOME LETTERS THAT WERE SENT TO YOU, THAT WE'VE YET TO RECEIVE A REPLY TO, Y-
THE COUNCIL? OH, GOOD. YOU SEE I CAN'T GET AROUND AS MUCH AS I USED TO, BUT I CAN'T ALWAYS ASK THE NEIGHBOURS TO PUT MY RUBBISH OUT...
NO, MRS GREENE, YOU MISUNDERSTAND ME. WE'RE HERE TO DISCUSS THE EXCITING POSSIBILITY OF A MOVE TO A NEW, STATE-OF-THE-ART, WARDEN CONTROLLED HOME. THE DETAILS OF WHICH WERE MENTIONED IN THE NUMEROUS LETTERS THAT WERE SENT TO THIS ADDRESS, BUT IN THE MEANTIME, HERE IS ANOTHER COPY SPECIFYING ALL THE DETAILS.
LETTERS? LETTERS? I HAVEN'T HAD ANY LETTERS FOR AGES, SILLY.
HERE...
BE AN ANGEL AND POP THIS IN THE BIN ON THE WAY OUT.
WHU-
!?

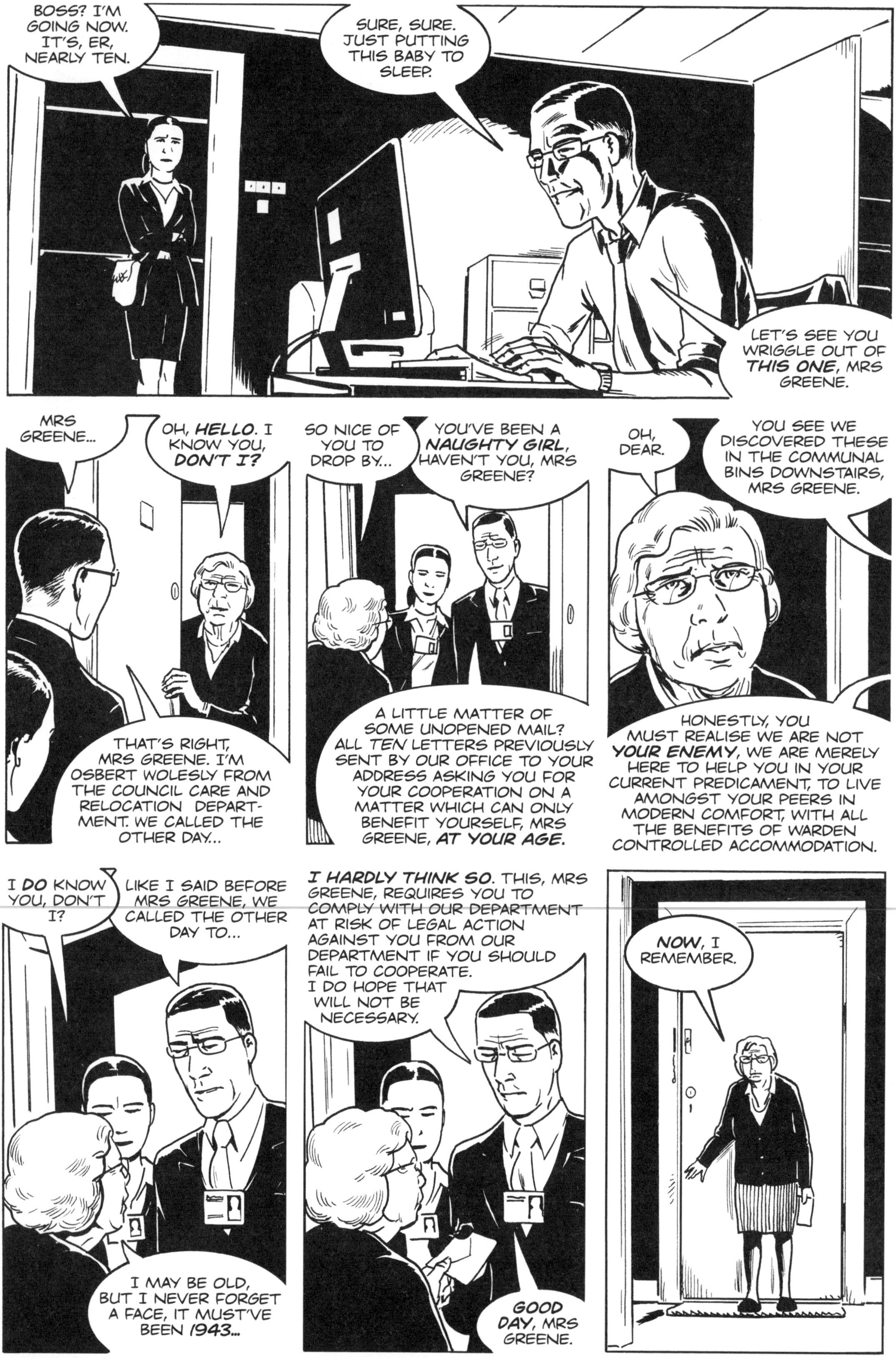
BOSS? I'M GOING NOW. IT'S, ER, NEARLY TEN.
SURE, SURE. JUST PUTTING THIS BABY TO SLEEP.
LET'S SEE YOU WRIGGLE OUT OF ***THIS ONE***, MRS GREENE.
MRS GREENE...
OH, ***HELLO***. I KNOW YOU, ***DON'T I?***
THAT'S RIGHT, MRS GREENE. I'M OSBERT WOLESLY FROM THE COUNCIL CARE AND RELOCATION DEPARTMENT. WE CALLED THE OTHER DAY...
SO NICE OF YOU TO DROP BY...
YOU'VE BEEN A ***NAUGHTY GIRL***, HAVEN'T YOU, MRS GREENE?
A LITTLE MATTER OF SOME UNOPENED MAIL? ALL *TEN* LETTERS PREVIOUSLY SENT BY OUR OFFICE TO YOUR ADDRESS ASKING YOU FOR YOUR COOPERATION ON A MATTER WHICH CAN ONLY BENEFIT YOURSELF, MRS GREENE, ***AT YOUR AGE***.
OH, DEAR.
YOU SEE WE DISCOVERED THESE IN THE COMMUNAL BINS DOWNSTAIRS, MRS GREENE.
HONESTLY, YOU MUST REALISE WE ARE NOT ***YOUR ENEMY***, WE ARE MERELY HERE TO HELP YOU IN YOUR CURRENT PREDICAMENT, TO LIVE AMONGST YOUR PEERS IN MODERN COMFORT, WITH ALL THE BENEFITS OF WARDEN CONTROLLED ACCOMMODATION.
I ***DO*** KNOW YOU, DON'T I?
LIKE I SAID BEFORE MRS GREENE, WE CALLED THE OTHER DAY TO...
I MAY BE OLD, BUT I NEVER FORGET A FACE, IT MUST'VE BEEN ***1943...***
I HARDLY THINK SO. THIS, MRS GREENE, REQUIRES YOU TO COMPLY WITH OUR DEPARTMENT AT RISK OF LEGAL ACTION AGAINST YOU FROM OUR DEPARTMENT IF YOU SHOULD FAIL TO COOPERATE. I DO HOPE THAT WILL NOT BE NECESSARY.
GOOD DAY, MRS GREENE.
NOW, I REMEMBER.

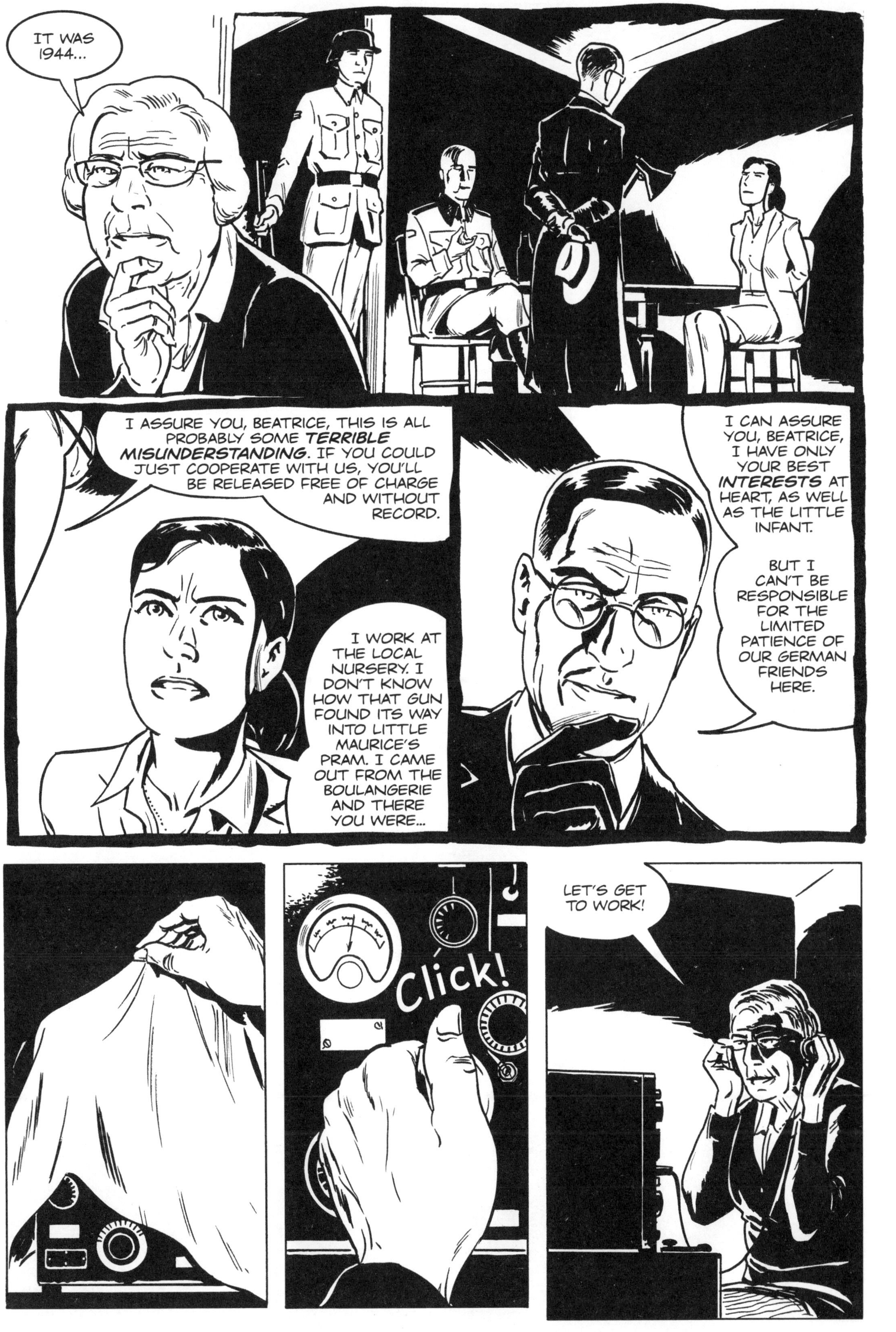
IT WAS 1944...
I ASSURE YOU, BEATRICE, THIS IS ALL PROBABLY SOME TERRIBLE MISUNDERSTANDING. IF YOU COULD JUST COOPERATE WITH US, YOU'LL BE RELEASED FREE OF CHARGE AND WITHOUT RECORD.
I WORK AT THE LOCAL NURSERY. I DON'T KNOW HOW THAT GUN FOUND ITS WAY INTO LITTLE MAURICE'S PRAM. I CAME OUT FROM THE BOULANGERIE AND THERE YOU WERE...
I CAN ASSURE YOU, BEATRICE, I HAVE ONLY YOUR BEST INTERESTS AT HEART, AS WELL AS THE LITTLE INFANT.
BUT I CAN'T BE RESPONSIBLE FOR THE LIMITED PATIENCE OF OUR GERMAN FRIENDS HERE.
Click!
LET'S GET TO WORK!

Dah-di-dah-dit
dah-dah-dah
dah-di-dit

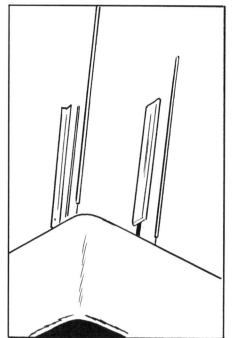

0010001010010
1010001001000
0101000100010
0100001110010
0100100101001
0101001000101
1001000100101
0101010101010
0100100100010
10010010...

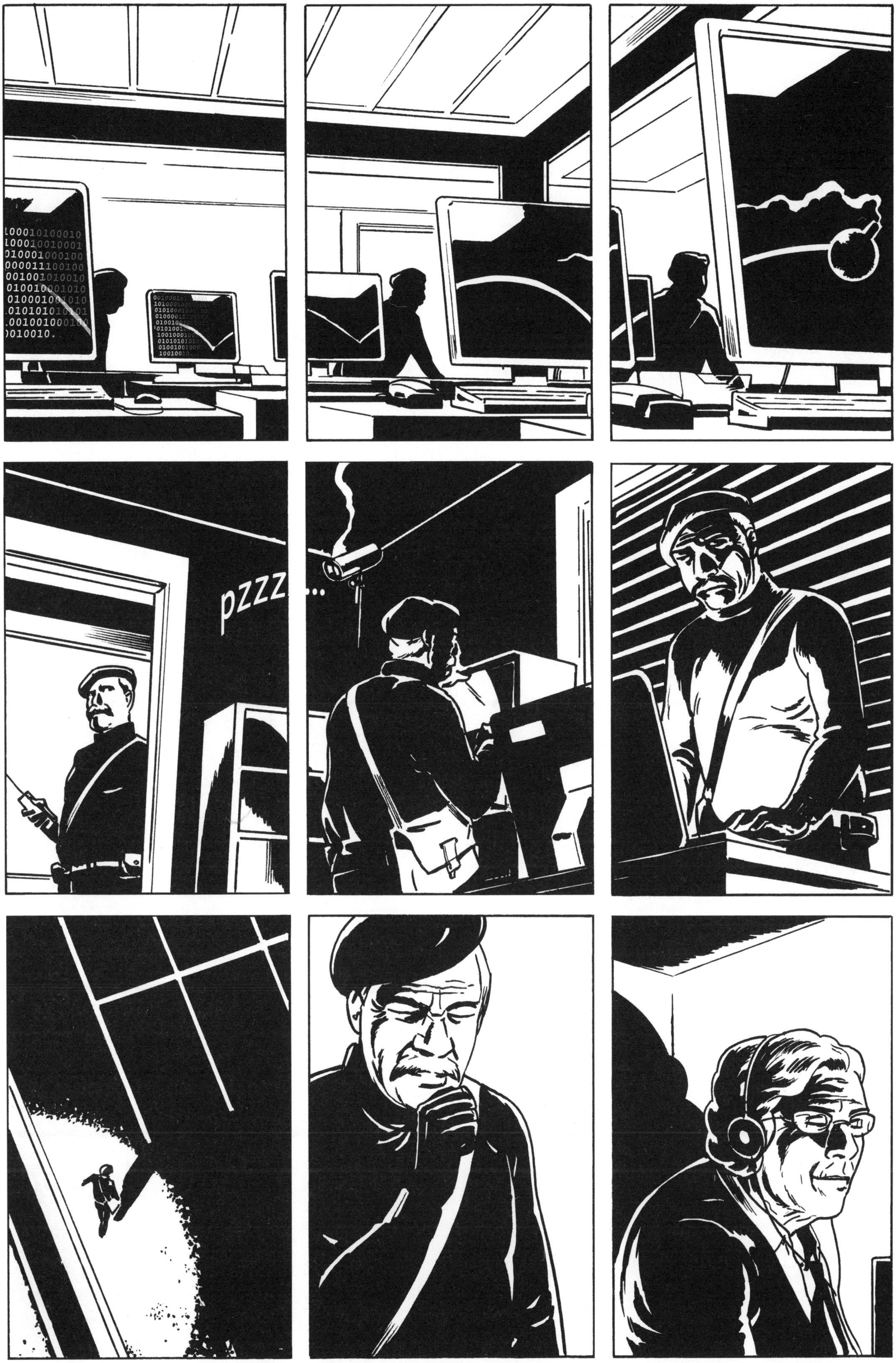
pzzz...

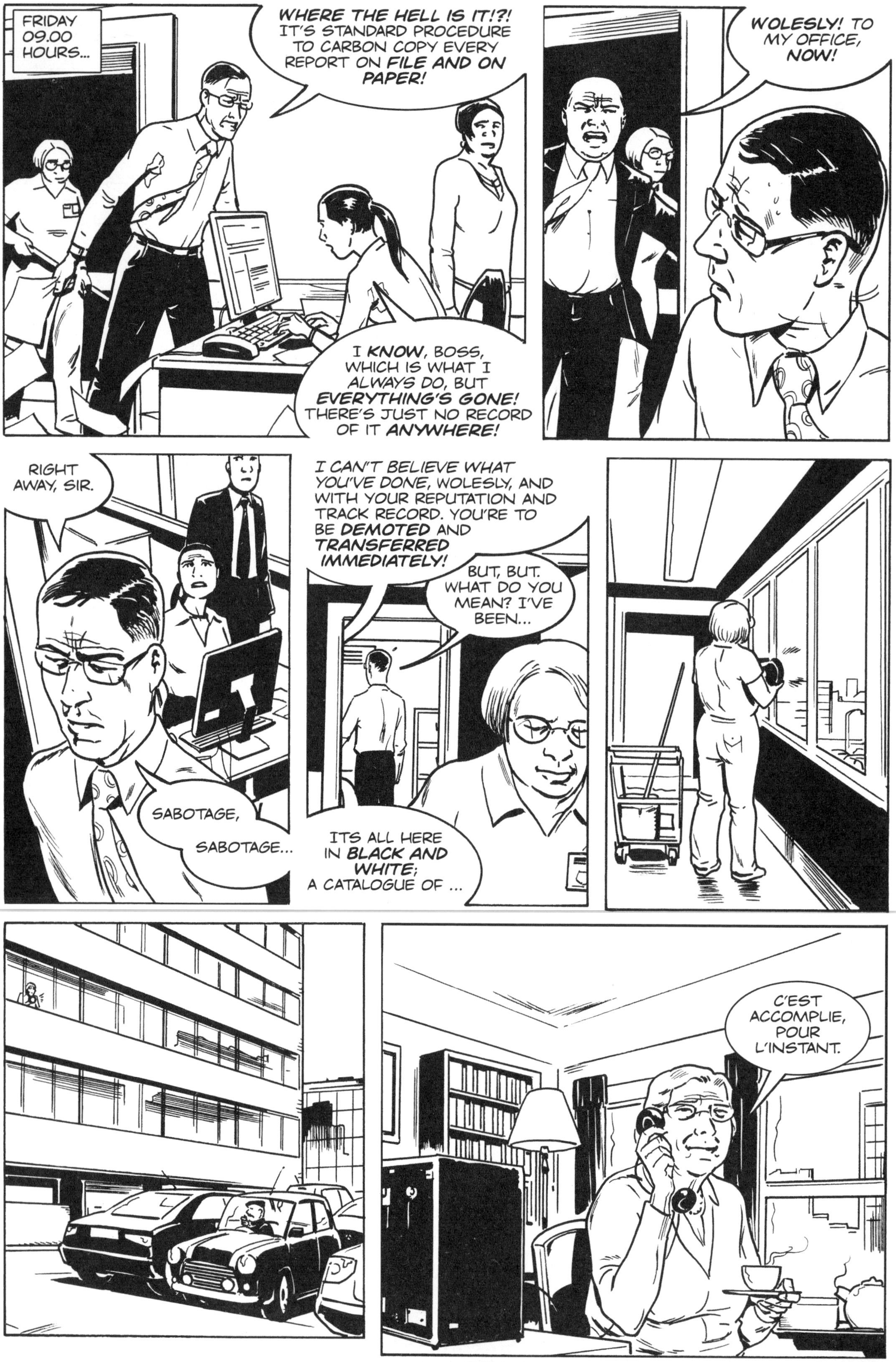
FRIDAY
09.00
HOURS...
WHERE THE HELL IS IT!?! IT'S STANDARD PROCEDURE TO CARBON COPY EVERY REPORT ON FILE AND ON PAPER!
I KNOW, BOSS, WHICH IS WHAT I ALWAYS DO, BUT EVERYTHING'S GONE! THERE'S JUST NO RECORD OF IT ANYWHERE!
WOLESLY! TO MY OFFICE, NOW!
RIGHT AWAY, SIR.
SABOTAGE,
SABOTAGE...
I CAN'T BELIEVE WHAT YOU'VE DONE, WOLESLY, AND WITH YOUR REPUTATION AND TRACK RECORD. YOU'RE TO BE DEMOTED AND TRANSFERRED IMMEDIATELY!
BUT, BUT. WHAT DO YOU MEAN? I'VE BEEN...
ITS ALL HERE IN BLACK AND WHITE; A CATALOGUE OF ...
C'EST ACCOMPLIE, POUR L'INSTANT.

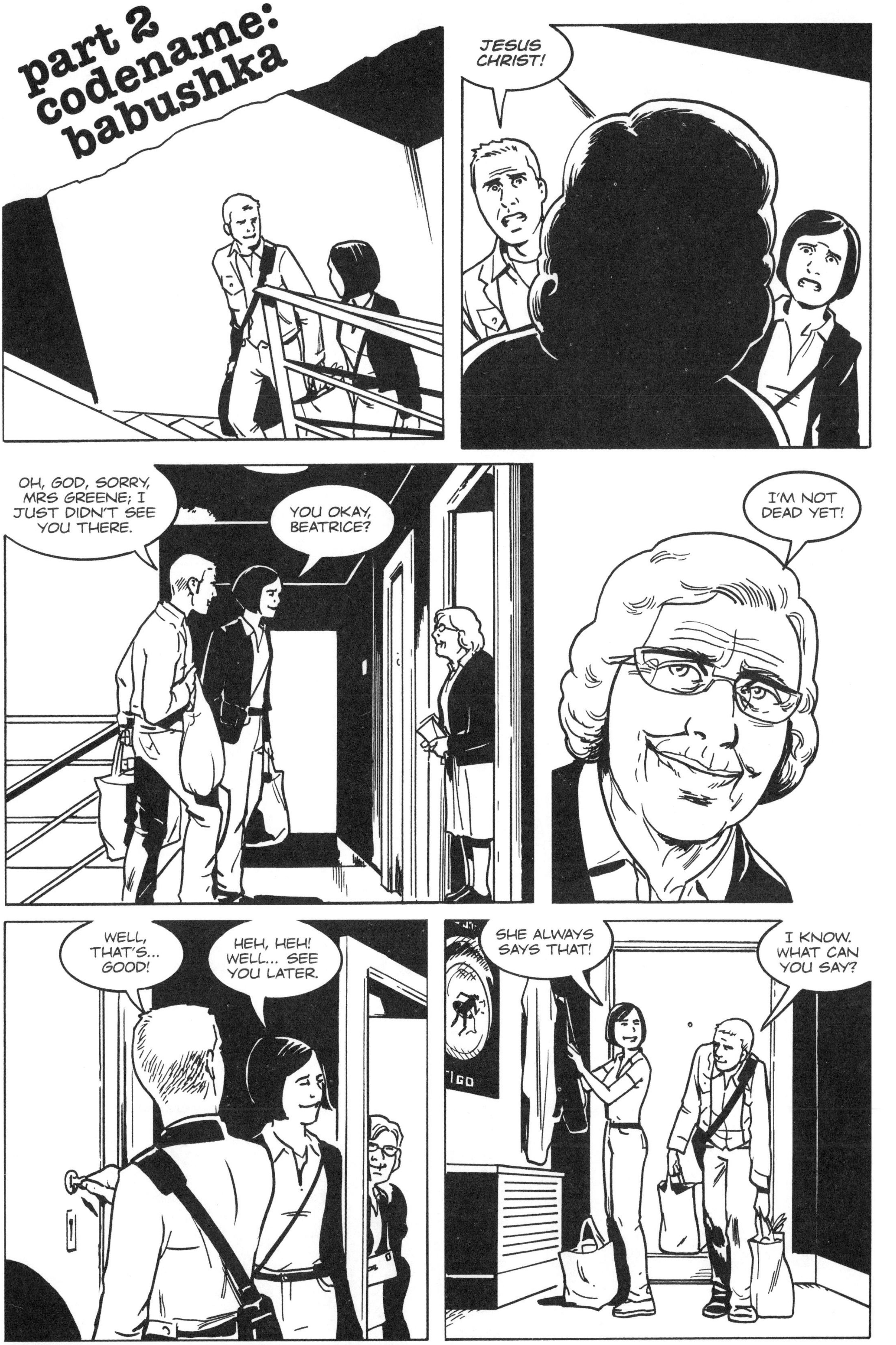
part 2
codename:
babushka
JESUS CHRIST!
OH, GOD, SORRY, MRS GREENE; I JUST DIDN'T SEE YOU THERE.
YOU OKAY, BEATRICE?
I'M NOT DEAD YET!
WELL, THAT'S... GOOD!
HEH, HEH! WELL... SEE YOU LATER.
SHE ALWAYS SAYS THAT!
I KNOW. WHAT CAN YOU SAY?

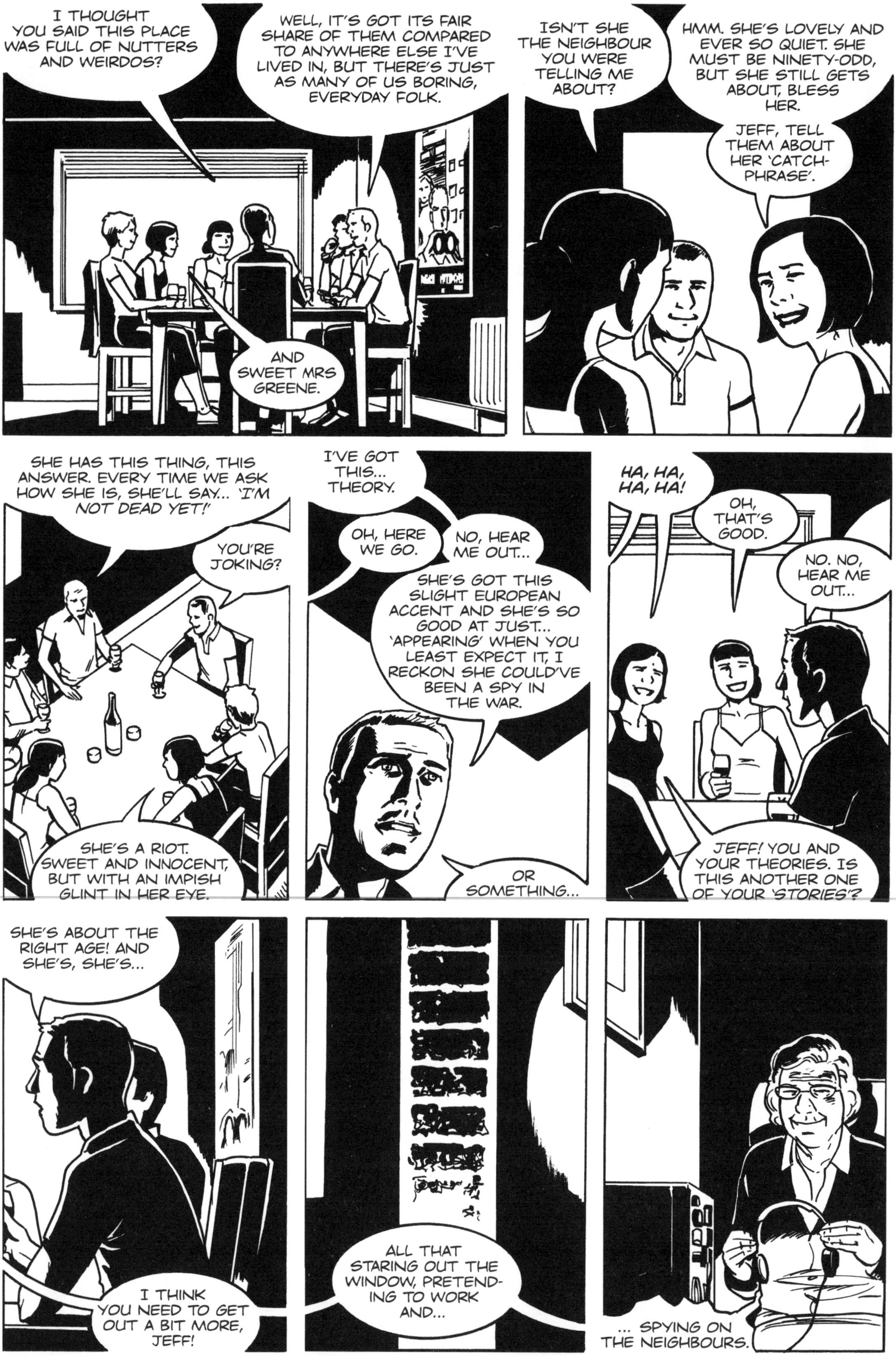
I THOUGHT YOU SAID THIS PLACE WAS FULL OF NUTTERS AND WEIRDOS?
WELL, IT'S GOT ITS FAIR SHARE OF THEM COMPARED TO ANYWHERE ELSE I'VE LIVED IN, BUT THERE'S JUST AS MANY OF US BORING, EVERYDAY FOLK.
AND SWEET MRS GREENE.
ISN'T SHE THE NEIGHBOUR YOU WERE TELLING ME ABOUT?
HMM. SHE'S LOVELY AND EVER SO QUIET. SHE MUST BE NINETY-ODD, BUT SHE STILL GETS ABOUT, BLESS HER.
JEFF, TELL THEM ABOUT HER 'CATCH-PHRASE'.
SHE HAS THIS THING, THIS ANSWER. EVERY TIME WE ASK HOW SHE IS, SHE'LL SAY... *'I'M NOT DEAD YET!'*
YOU'RE JOKING?
SHE'S A RIOT. SWEET AND INNOCENT, BUT WITH AN IMPISH GLINT IN HER EYE.
I'VE GOT THIS... THEORY.
OH, HERE WE GO.
NO, HEAR ME OUT...
SHE'S GOT THIS SLIGHT EUROPEAN ACCENT AND SHE'S SO GOOD AT JUST... 'APPEARING' WHEN YOU LEAST EXPECT IT, I RECKON SHE COULD'VE BEEN A SPY IN THE WAR.
OR SOMETHING...
HA, HA, HA, HA!
OH, THAT'S GOOD.
NO. NO, HEAR ME OUT...
JEFF! YOU AND YOUR THEORIES. IS THIS ANOTHER ONE OF YOUR 'STORIES'?
SHE'S ABOUT THE RIGHT AGE! AND SHE'S, SHE'S...
I THINK YOU NEED TO GET OUT A BIT MORE, JEFF!
ALL THAT STARING OUT THE WINDOW, PRETEND-ING TO WORK AND...
... SPYING ON THE NEIGHBOURS.

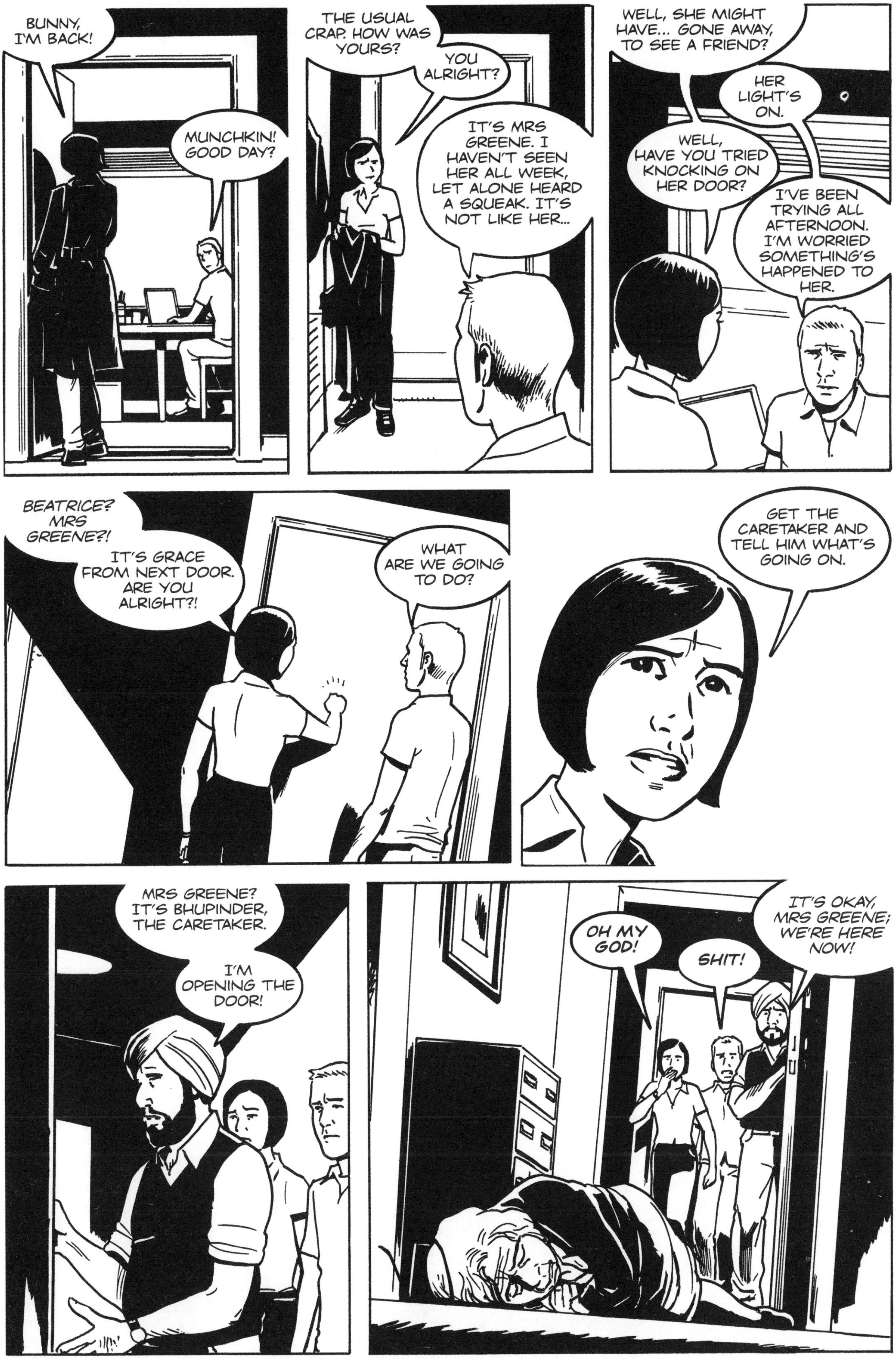
BUNNY, I'M BACK!
MUNCHKIN! GOOD DAY?
THE USUAL CRAP. HOW WAS YOURS?
YOU ALRIGHT?
IT'S MRS GREENE. I HAVEN'T SEEN HER ALL WEEK, LET ALONE HEARD A SQUEAK. IT'S NOT LIKE HER...
WELL, SHE MIGHT HAVE... GONE AWAY, TO SEE A FRIEND?
HER LIGHT'S ON.
WELL, HAVE YOU TRIED KNOCKING ON HER DOOR?
I'VE BEEN TRYING ALL AFTERNOON. I'M WORRIED SOMETHING'S HAPPENED TO HER.
BEATRICE? MRS GREENE?!
IT'S GRACE FROM NEXT DOOR. ARE YOU ALRIGHT?!
WHAT ARE WE GOING TO DO?
GET THE CARETAKER AND TELL HIM WHAT'S GOING ON.
MRS GREENE? IT'S BHUPINDER, THE CARETAKER.
I'M OPENING THE DOOR!
OH MY GOD!
SHIT!
IT'S OKAY, MRS GREENE; WE'RE HERE NOW!

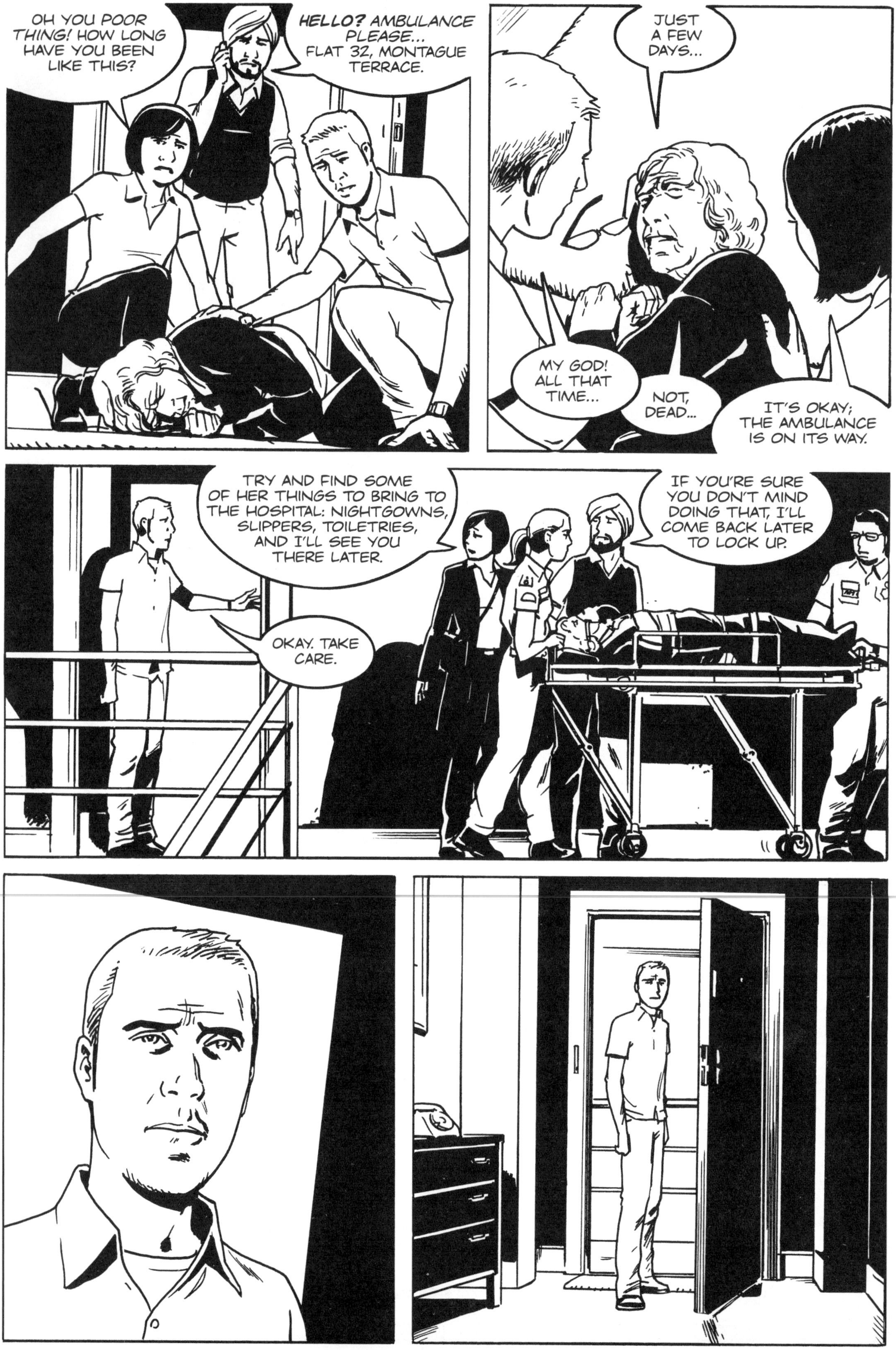
OH YOU POOR THING! HOW LONG HAVE YOU BEEN LIKE THIS?
HELLO? AMBULANCE PLEASE... FLAT 32, MONTAGUE TERRACE.
JUST A FEW DAYS...
MY GOD! ALL THAT TIME...
NOT, DEAD...
IT'S OKAY; THE AMBULANCE IS ON ITS WAY.
TRY AND FIND SOME OF HER THINGS TO BRING TO THE HOSPITAL: NIGHTGOWNS, SLIPPERS, TOILETRIES, AND I'LL SEE YOU THERE LATER.
OKAY. TAKE CARE.
IF YOU'RE SURE YOU DON'T MIND DOING THAT, I'LL COME BACK LATER TO LOCK UP.

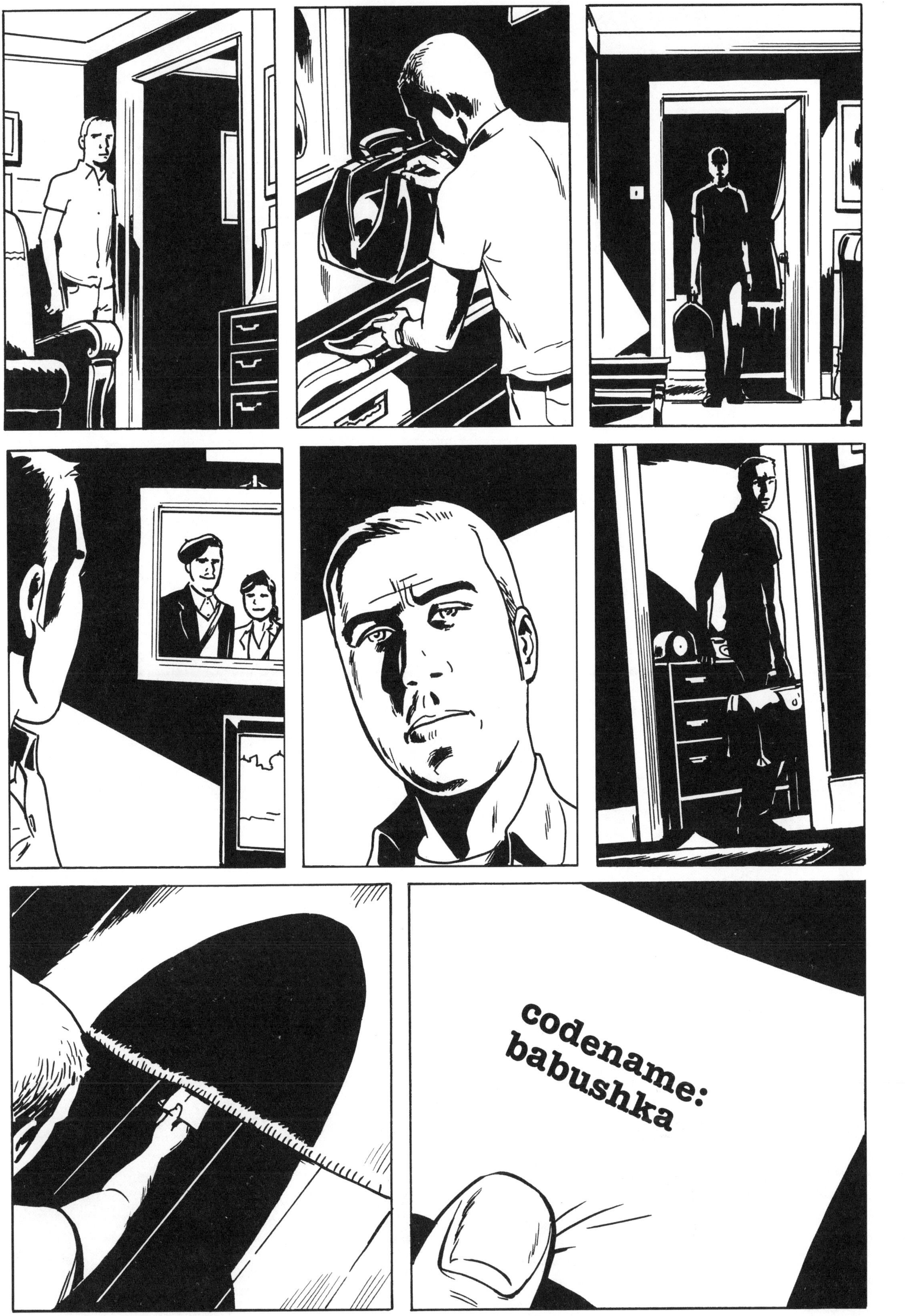
codename:
babushka

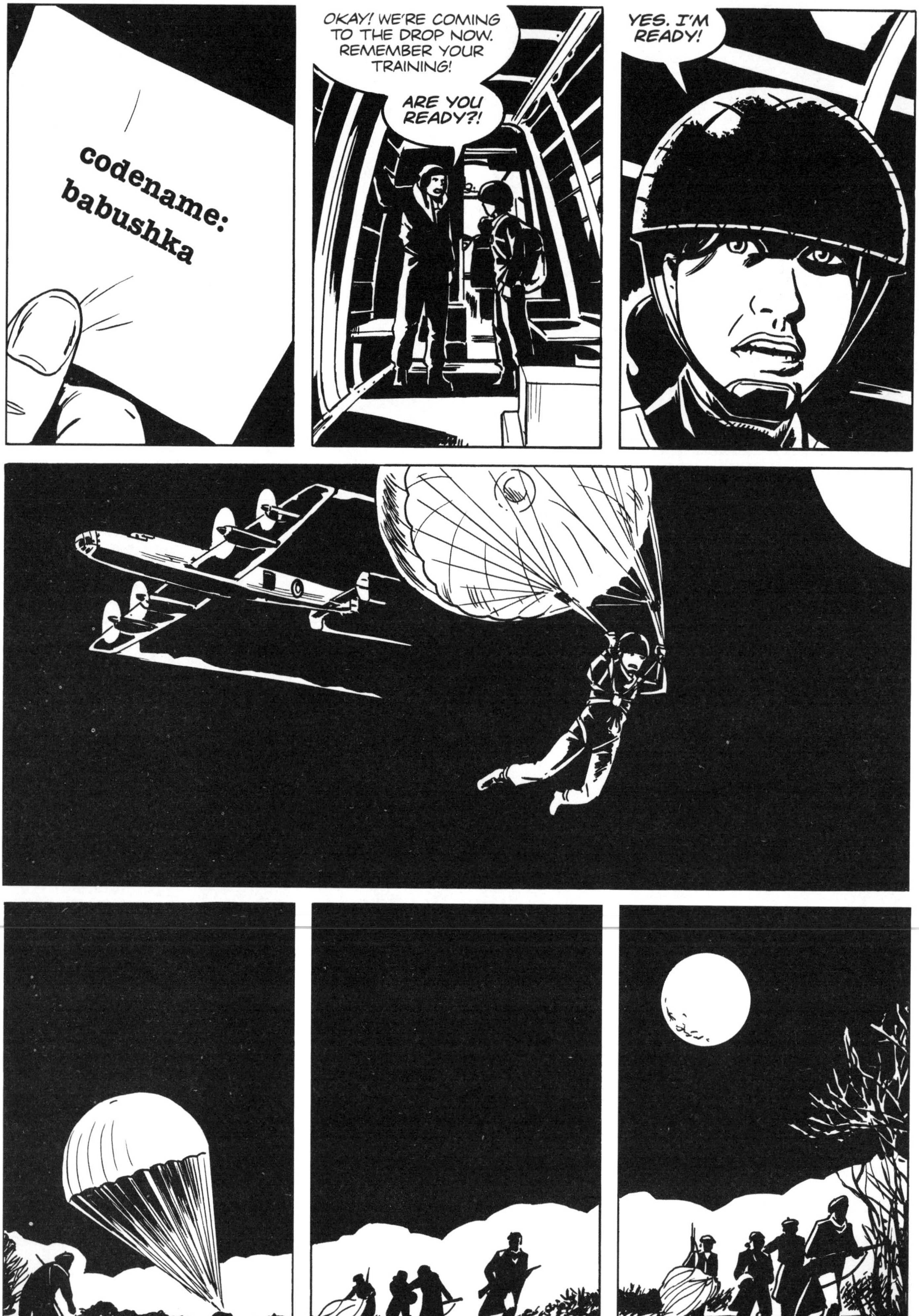
codename: babushka
OKAY! WE'RE COMING TO THE DROP NOW. REMEMBER YOUR TRAINING!
ARE YOU READY?!
YES. I'M READY!

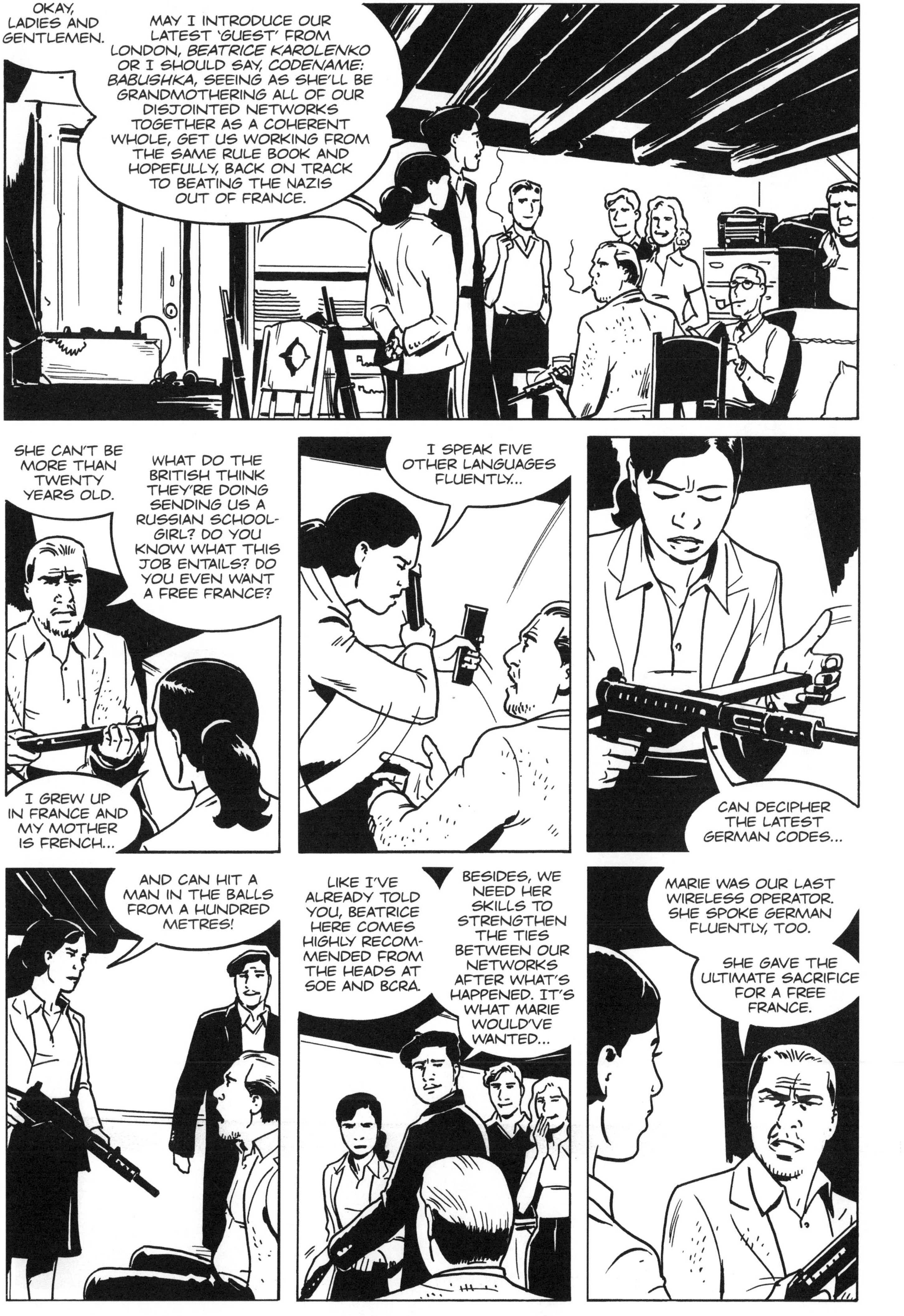
OKAY, LADIES AND GENTLEMEN.
MAY I INTRODUCE OUR LATEST 'GUEST' FROM LONDON, BEATRICE KAROLENKO OR I SHOULD SAY, CODENAME: BABUSHKA, SEEING AS SHE'LL BE GRANDMOTHERING ALL OF OUR DISJOINTED NETWORKS TOGETHER AS A COHERENT WHOLE, GET US WORKING FROM THE SAME RULE BOOK AND HOPEFULLY, BACK ON TRACK TO BEATING THE NAZIS OUT OF FRANCE.
SHE CAN'T BE MORE THAN TWENTY YEARS OLD.
WHAT DO THE BRITISH THINK THEY'RE DOING SENDING US A RUSSIAN SCHOOL-GIRL? DO YOU KNOW WHAT THIS JOB ENTAILS? DO YOU EVEN WANT A FREE FRANCE?
I GREW UP IN FRANCE AND MY MOTHER IS FRENCH...
I SPEAK FIVE OTHER LANGUAGES FLUENTLY...
CAN DECIPHER THE LATEST GERMAN CODES...
AND CAN HIT A MAN IN THE BALLS FROM A HUNDRED METRES!
LIKE I'VE ALREADY TOLD YOU, BEATRICE HERE COMES HIGHLY RECOMMENDED FROM THE HEADS AT SOE AND BCRA.
BESIDES, WE NEED HER SKILLS TO STRENGTHEN THE TIES BETWEEN OUR NETWORKS AFTER WHAT'S HAPPENED. IT'S WHAT MARIE WOULD'VE WANTED...
MARIE WAS OUR LAST WIRELESS OPERATOR. SHE SPOKE GERMAN FLUENTLY, TOO.
SHE GAVE THE ULTIMATE SACRIFICE FOR A FREE FRANCE.

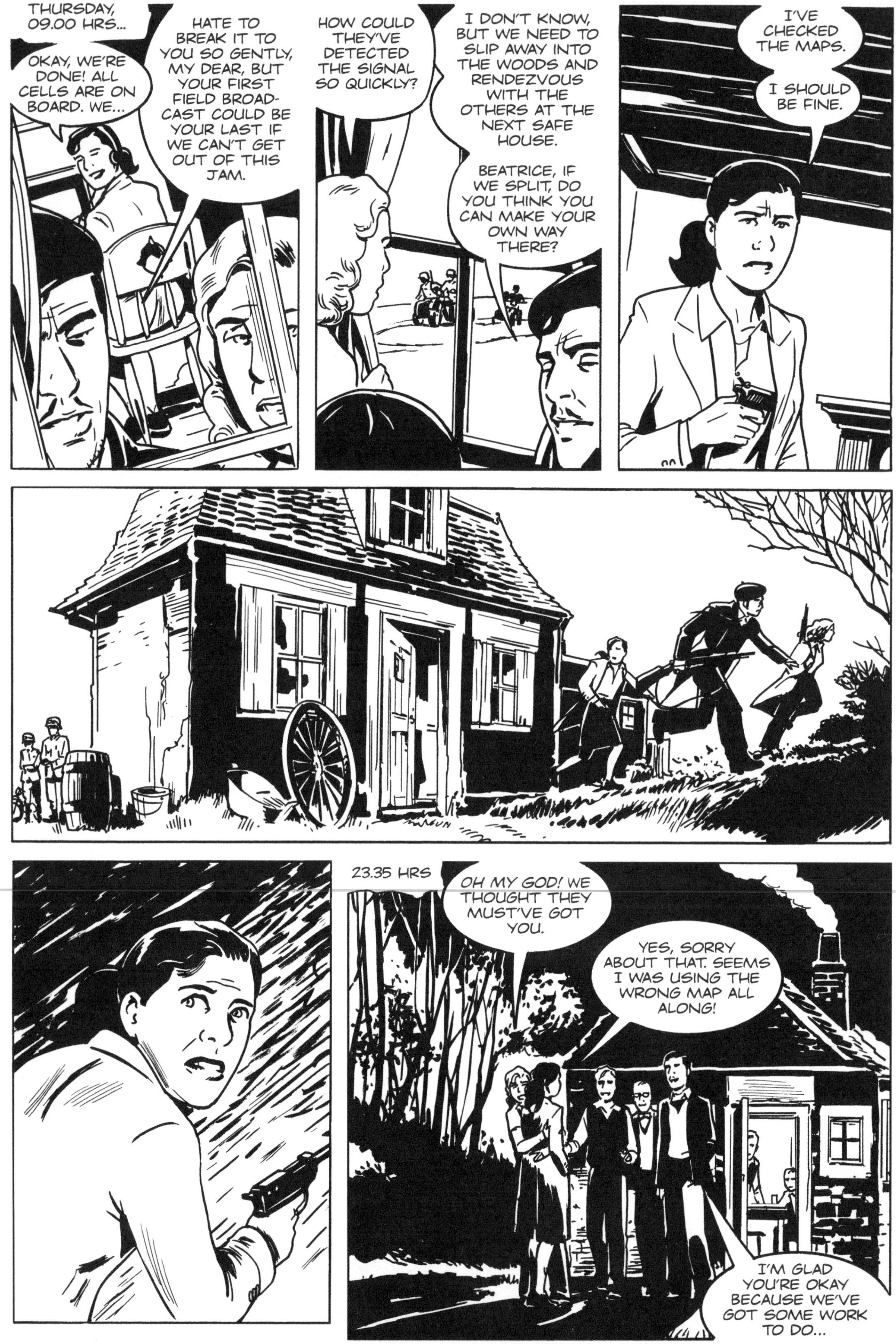
THURSDAY, 09.00 HRS...
OKAY, WE'RE DONE! ALL CELLS ARE ON BOARD. WE...
HATE TO BREAK IT TO YOU SO GENTLY, MY DEAR, BUT YOUR FIRST FIELD BROAD-CAST COULD BE YOUR LAST IF WE CAN'T GET OUT OF THIS JAM.
HOW COULD THEY'VE DETECTED THE SIGNAL SO QUICKLY?
I DON'T KNOW, BUT WE NEED TO SLIP AWAY INTO THE WOODS AND RENDEZVOUS WITH THE OTHERS AT THE NEXT SAFE HOUSE.
BEATRICE, IF WE SPLIT, DO YOU THINK YOU CAN MAKE YOUR OWN WAY THERE?
I'VE CHECKED THE MAPS.
I SHOULD BE FINE.
23.35 HRS
OH MY GOD! WE THOUGHT THEY MUST'VE GOT YOU.
YES, SORRY ABOUT THAT. SEEMS I WAS USING THE WRONG MAP ALL ALONG!
I'M GLAD YOU'RE OKAY BECAUSE WE'VE GOT SOME WORK TO DO...

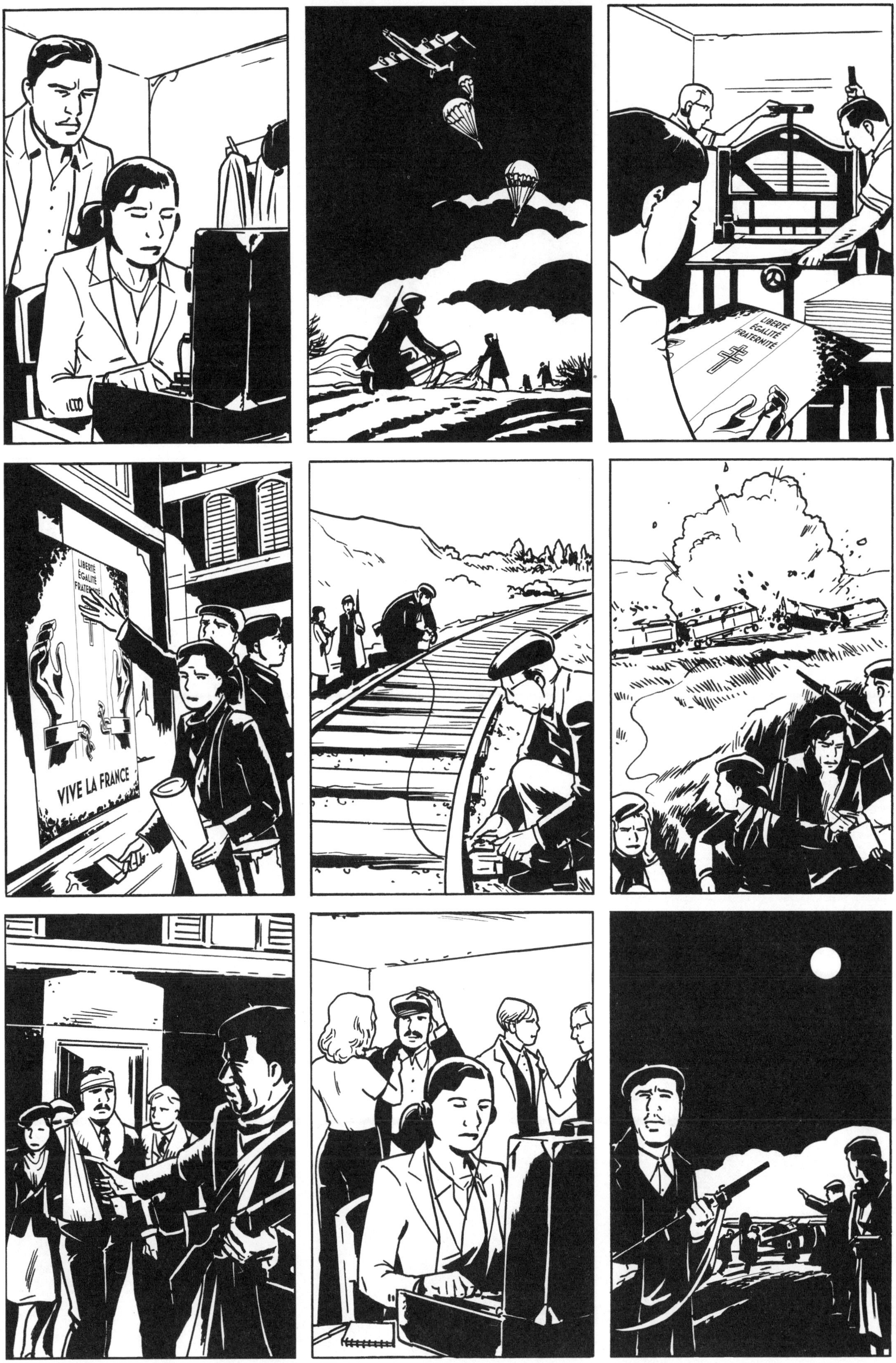
LIBERTÉ
ÉGALITÉ
FRATERNITÉ
LIBERTÉ
ÉGALITÉ
VIVE LA FRANCE

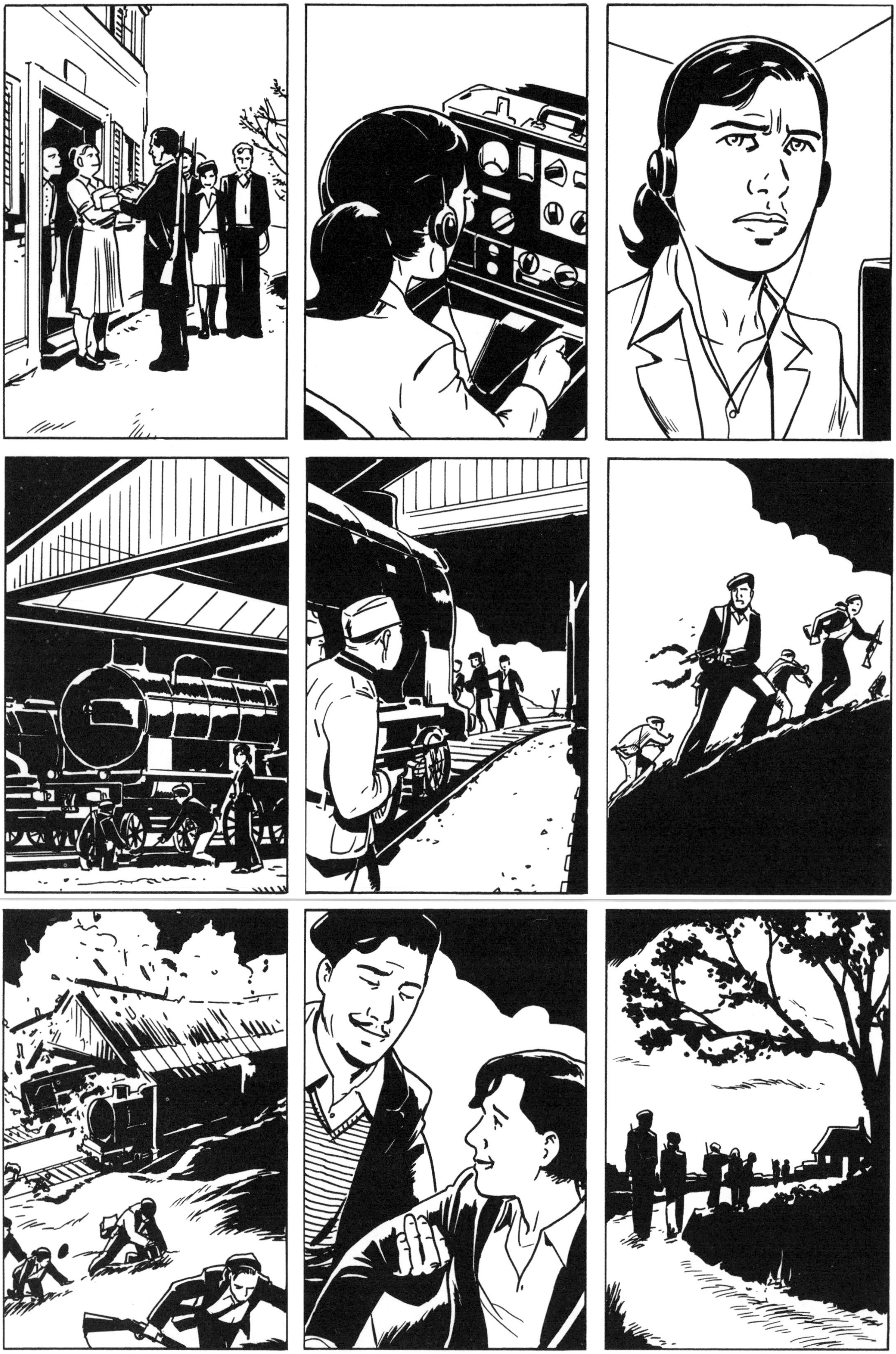

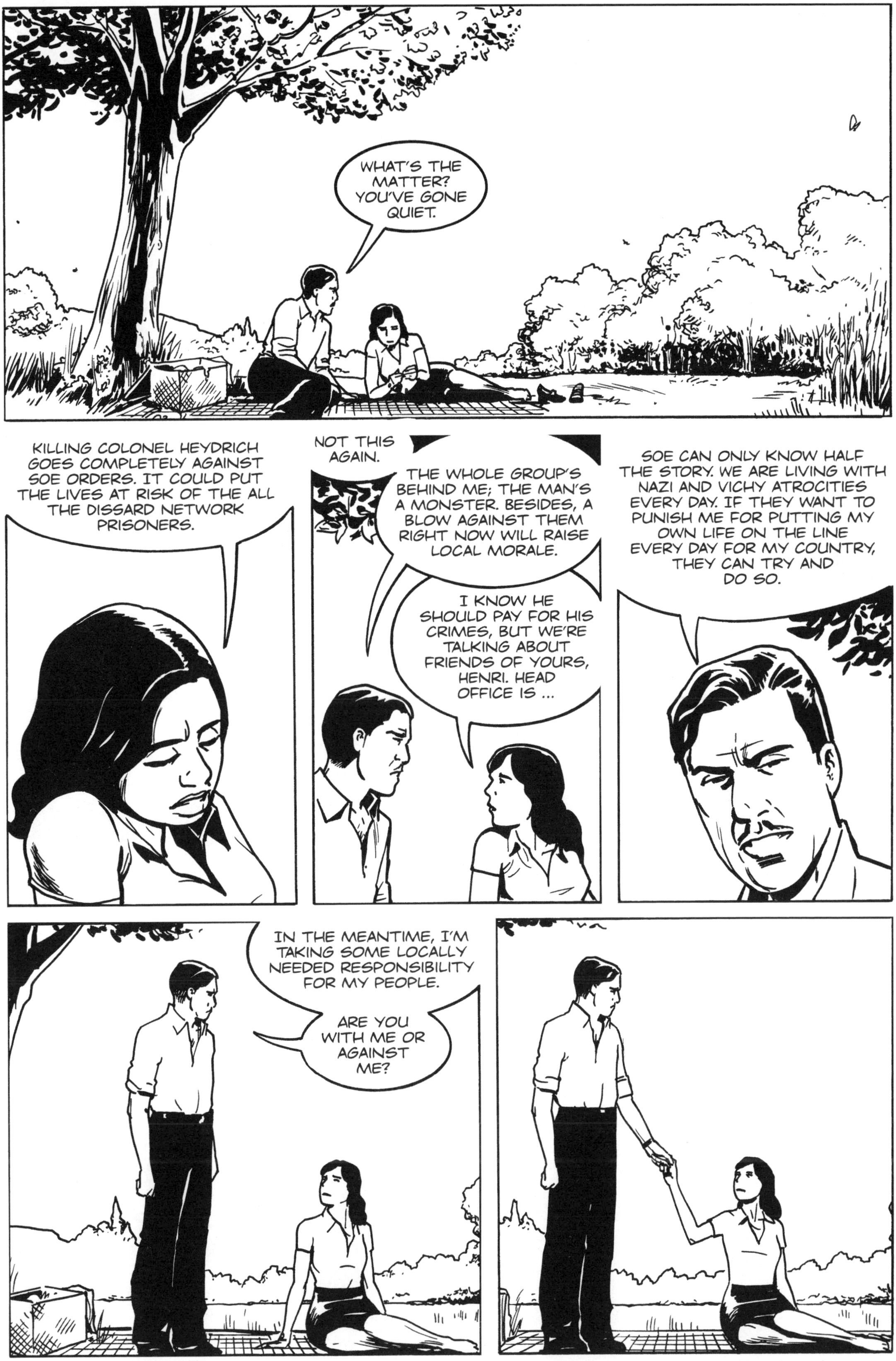
WHAT'S THE MATTER? YOU'VE GONE QUIET.
KILLING COLONEL HEYDRICH GOES COMPLETELY AGAINST SOE ORDERS. IT COULD PUT THE LIVES AT RISK OF THE ALL THE DISSARD NETWORK PRISONERS.
NOT THIS AGAIN.
THE WHOLE GROUP'S BEHIND ME; THE MAN'S A MONSTER. BESIDES, A BLOW AGAINST THEM RIGHT NOW WILL RAISE LOCAL MORALE.
I KNOW HE SHOULD PAY FOR HIS CRIMES, BUT WE'RE TALKING ABOUT FRIENDS OF YOURS, HENRI. HEAD OFFICE IS ...
SOE CAN ONLY KNOW HALF THE STORY. WE ARE LIVING WITH NAZI AND VICHY ATROCITIES EVERY DAY. IF THEY WANT TO PUNISH ME FOR PUTTING MY OWN LIFE ON THE LINE EVERY DAY FOR MY COUNTRY, THEY CAN TRY AND DO SO.
IN THE MEANTIME, I'M TAKING SOME LOCALLY NEEDED RESPONSIBILITY FOR MY PEOPLE.
ARE YOU WITH ME OR AGAINST ME?

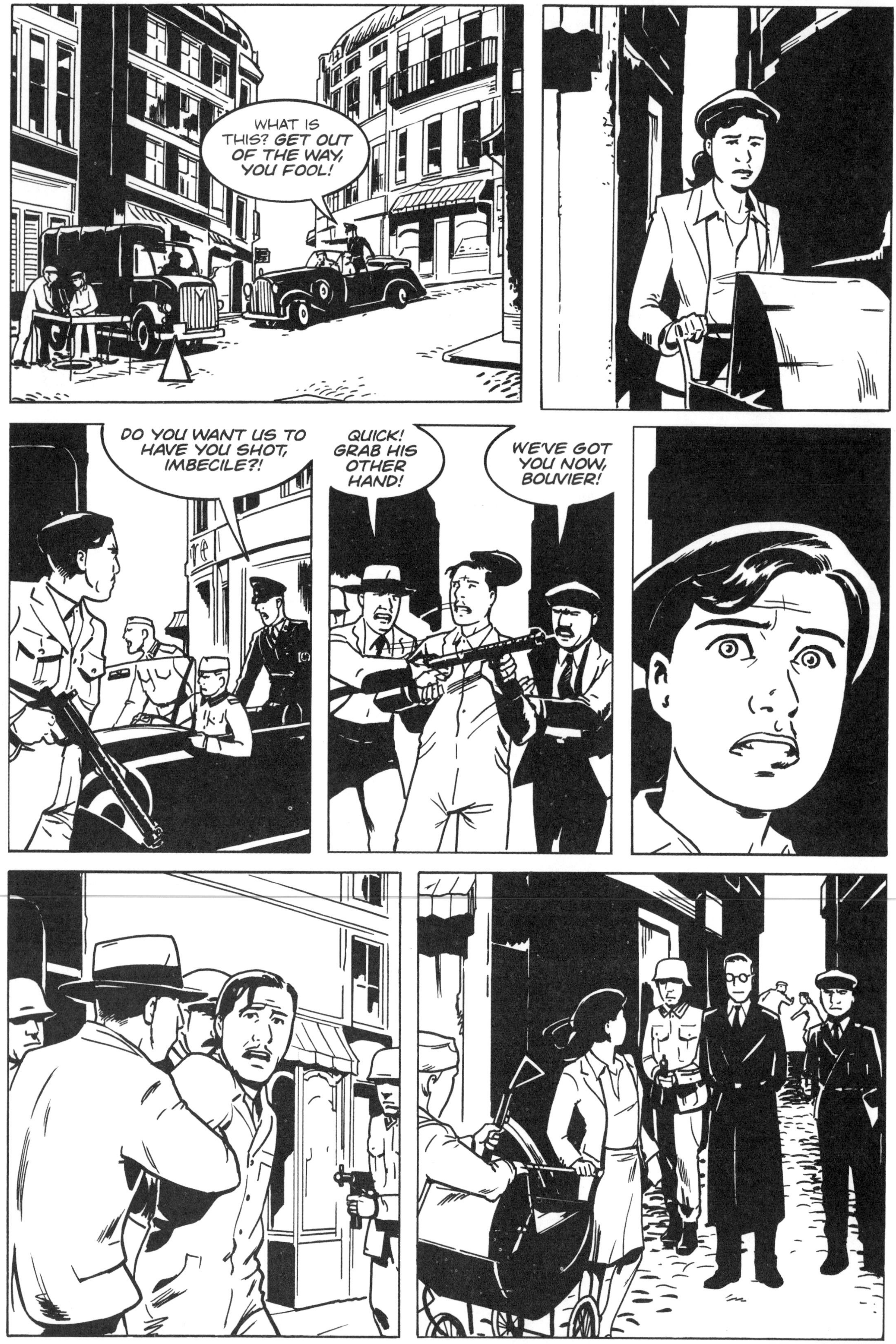
WHAT IS THIS? GET OUT OF THE WAY, YOU FOOL!
DO YOU WANT US TO HAVE YOU SHOT, IMBECILE?!
QUICK! GRAB HIS OTHER HAND!
WE'VE GOT YOU NOW, BOUVIER!

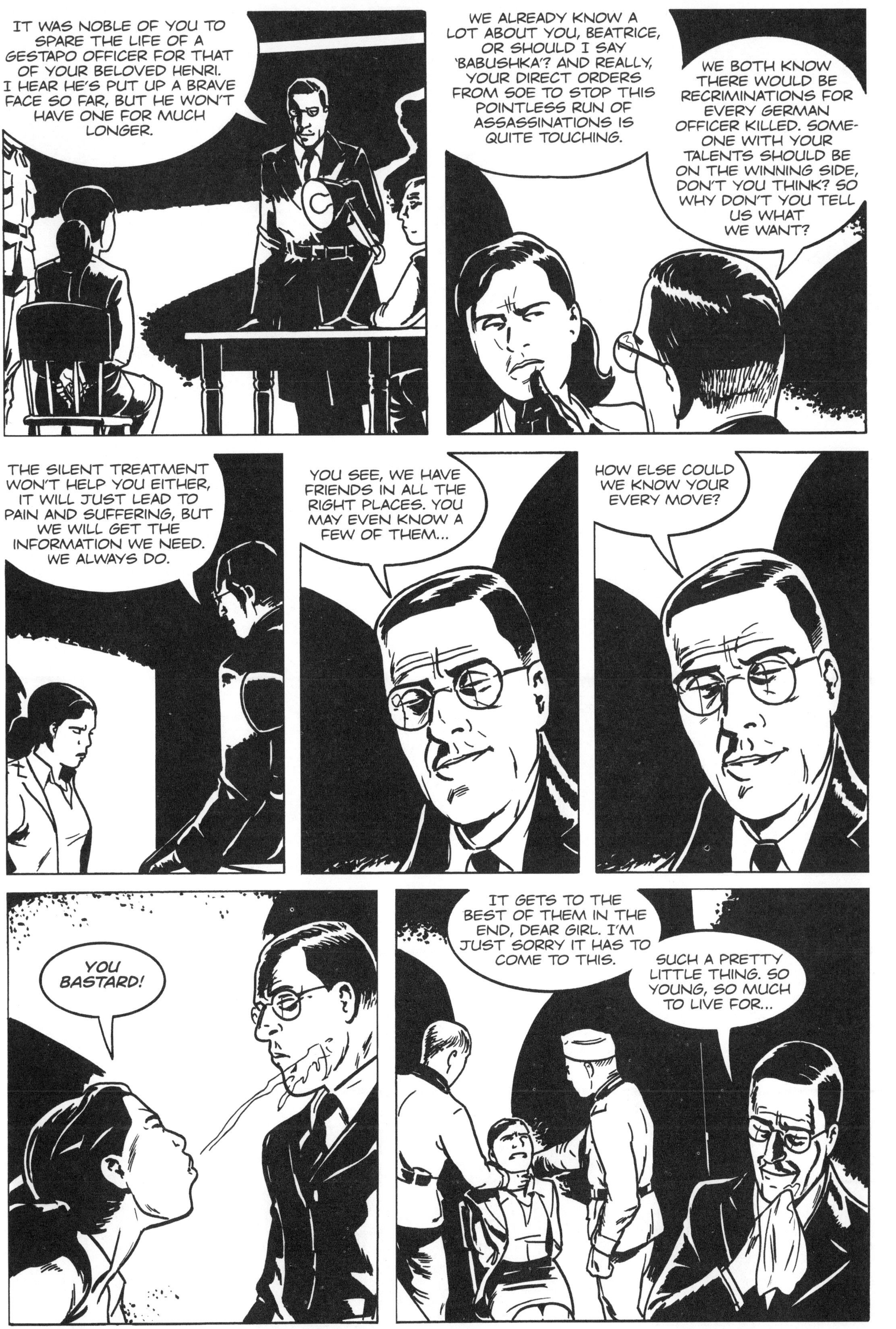
IT WAS NOBLE OF YOU TO SPARE THE LIFE OF A GESTAPO OFFICER FOR THAT OF YOUR BELOVED HENRI. I HEAR HE'S PUT UP A BRAVE FACE SO FAR, BUT HE WON'T HAVE ONE FOR MUCH LONGER.
WE ALREADY KNOW A LOT ABOUT YOU, BEATRICE, OR SHOULD I SAY 'BABUSHKA'? AND REALLY, YOUR DIRECT ORDERS FROM SOE TO STOP THIS POINTLESS RUN OF ASSASSINATIONS IS QUITE TOUCHING.
WE BOTH KNOW THERE WOULD BE RECRIMINATIONS FOR EVERY GERMAN OFFICER KILLED. SOME-ONE WITH YOUR TALENTS SHOULD BE ON THE WINNING SIDE, DON'T YOU THINK? SO WHY DON'T YOU TELL US WHAT WE WANT?
THE SILENT TREATMENT WON'T HELP YOU EITHER, IT WILL JUST LEAD TO PAIN AND SUFFERING, BUT WE WILL GET THE INFORMATION WE NEED. WE ALWAYS DO.
YOU SEE, WE HAVE FRIENDS IN ALL THE RIGHT PLACES. YOU MAY EVEN KNOW A FEW OF THEM...
HOW ELSE COULD WE KNOW YOUR EVERY MOVE?
YOU BASTARD!
IT GETS TO THE BEST OF THEM IN THE END, DEAR GIRL. I'M JUST SORRY IT HAS TO COME TO THIS.
SUCH A PRETTY LITTLE THING. SO YOUNG, SO MUCH TO LIVE FOR...

FIVE DAYS LATER...

STILL REFUSING TO SPEAK, EH?

THE NETWORK IS FINISHED. YOUR BOYFRIEND SQUEALED LIKE A PIG BEFORE HIS PATHETIC HEART GAVE OUT.

WHAT DO YOU HAVE TO SAY FOR YOURSELF NOW?!

I'M...

NOT... DEAD... YET.

YOU BITCH!

IT'S A RAID! QUICK, TO THE SHELTERS!

WWWWOOOOOOOOOOOO

OOOOOOOOOOOO

COME ON YOU FOOL!

OOOOOOOOOOO

I'LL BE BACK! THEY CAN'T SAVE YOU FROM THIS!

OOOOOOOOOOOOOOOOO...

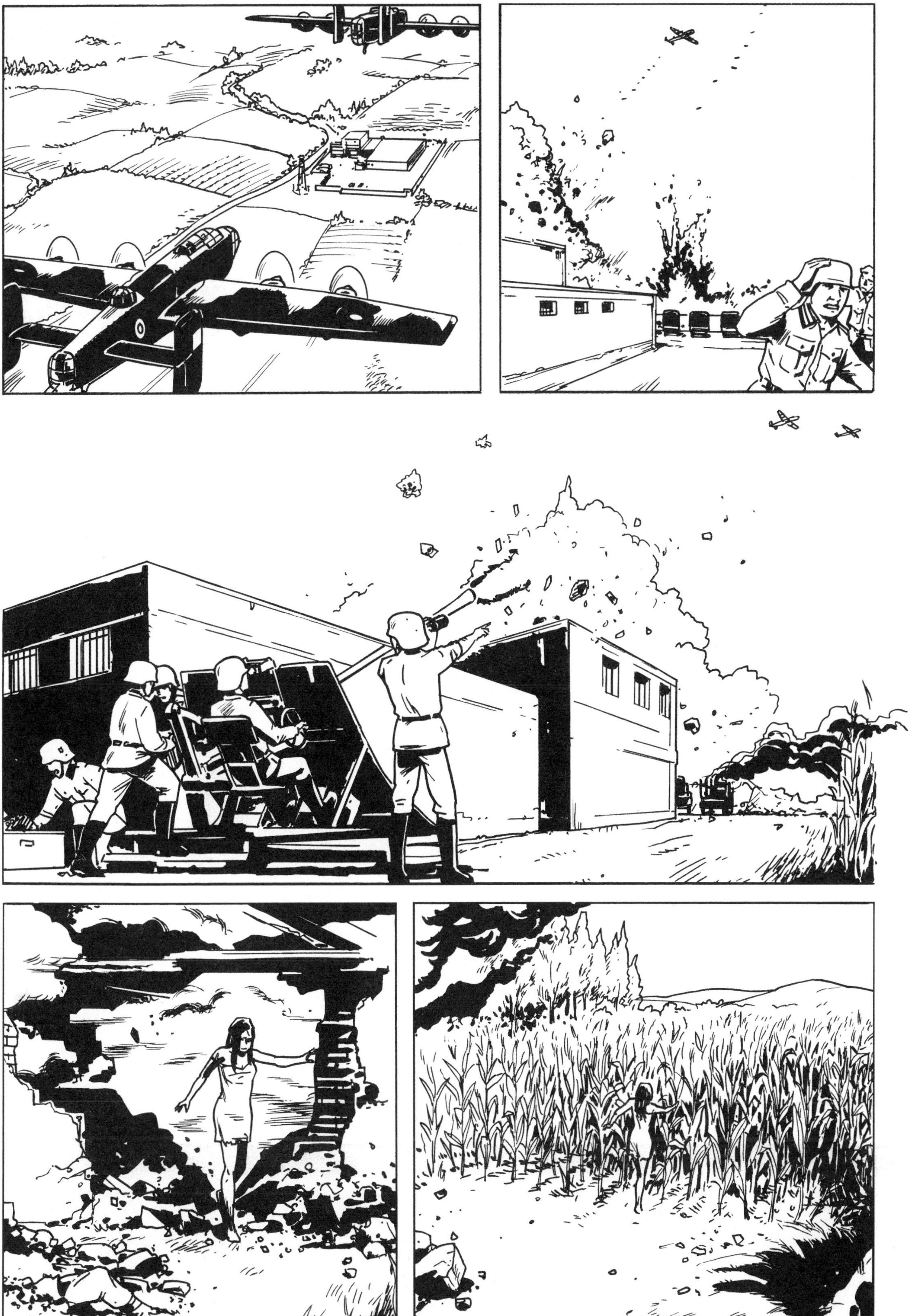

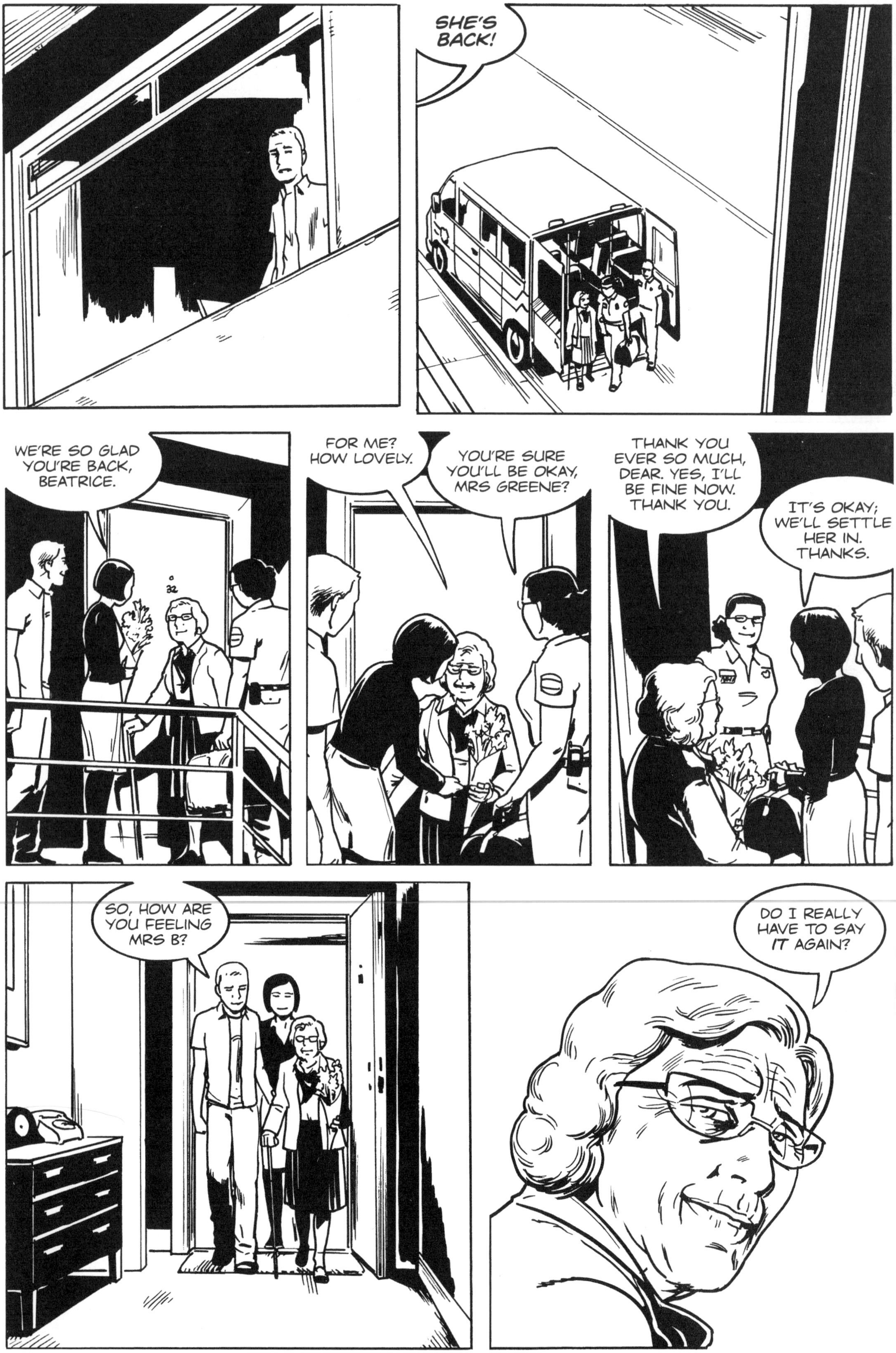
SHE'S BACK!
WE'RE SO GLAD YOU'RE BACK, BEATRICE.
FOR ME? HOW LOVELY.
YOU'RE SURE YOU'LL BE OKAY, MRS GREENE?
THANK YOU EVER SO MUCH, DEAR. YES, I'LL BE FINE NOW. THANK YOU.
IT'S OKAY; WE'LL SETTLE HER IN. THANKS.
SO, HOW ARE YOU FEELING MRS B?
DO I REALLY HAVE TO SAY IT AGAIN?

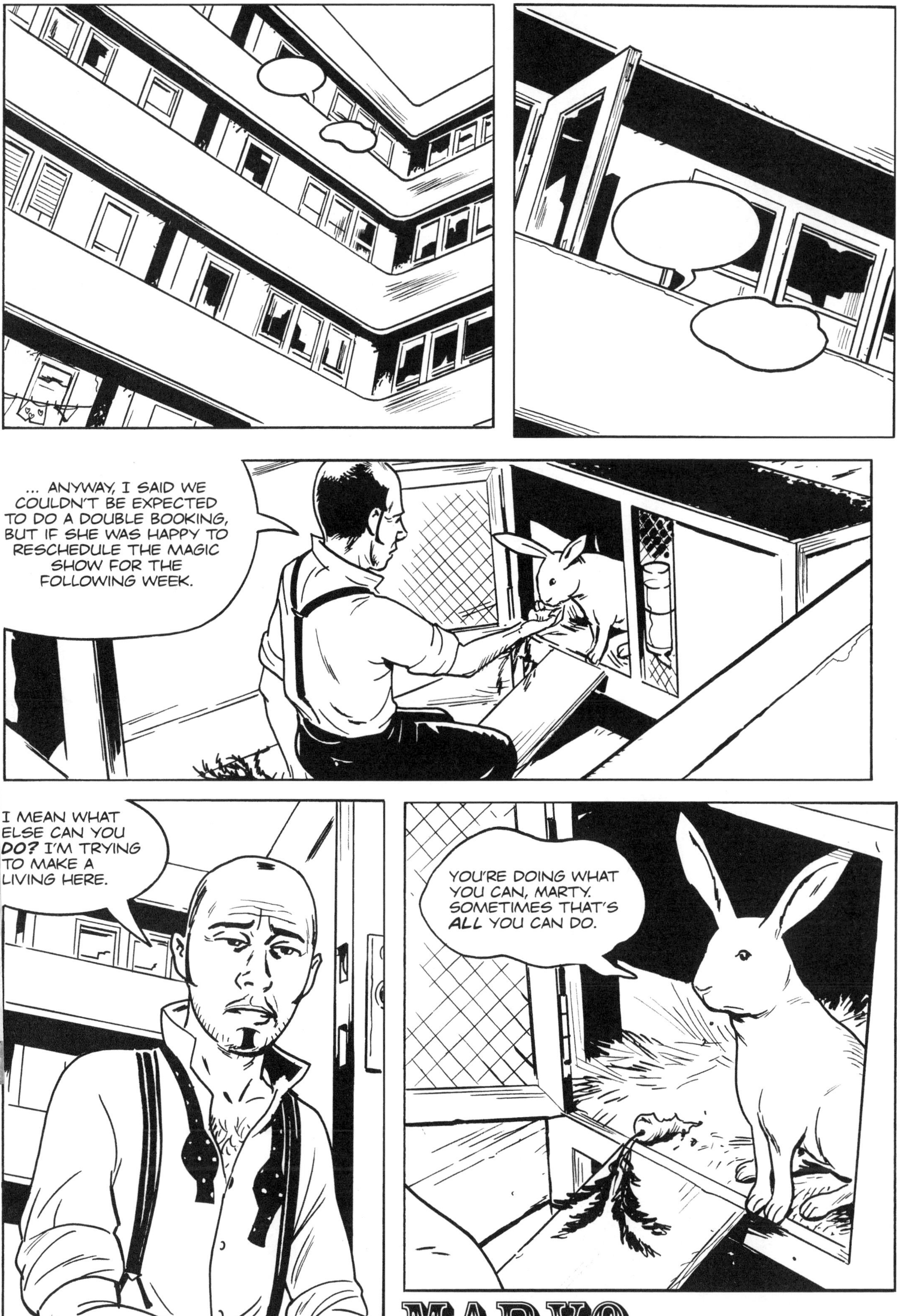
... ANYWAY, I SAID WE COULDN'T BE EXPECTED TO DO A DOUBLE BOOKING, BUT IF SHE WAS HAPPY TO RESCHEDULE THE MAGIC SHOW FOR THE FOLLOWING WEEK.
I MEAN WHAT ELSE CAN YOU DO? I'M TRYING TO MAKE A LIVING HERE.
YOU'RE DOING WHAT YOU CAN, MARTY. SOMETIMES THAT'S ALL YOU CAN DO.

MARVO THE MAGIC BUNNY

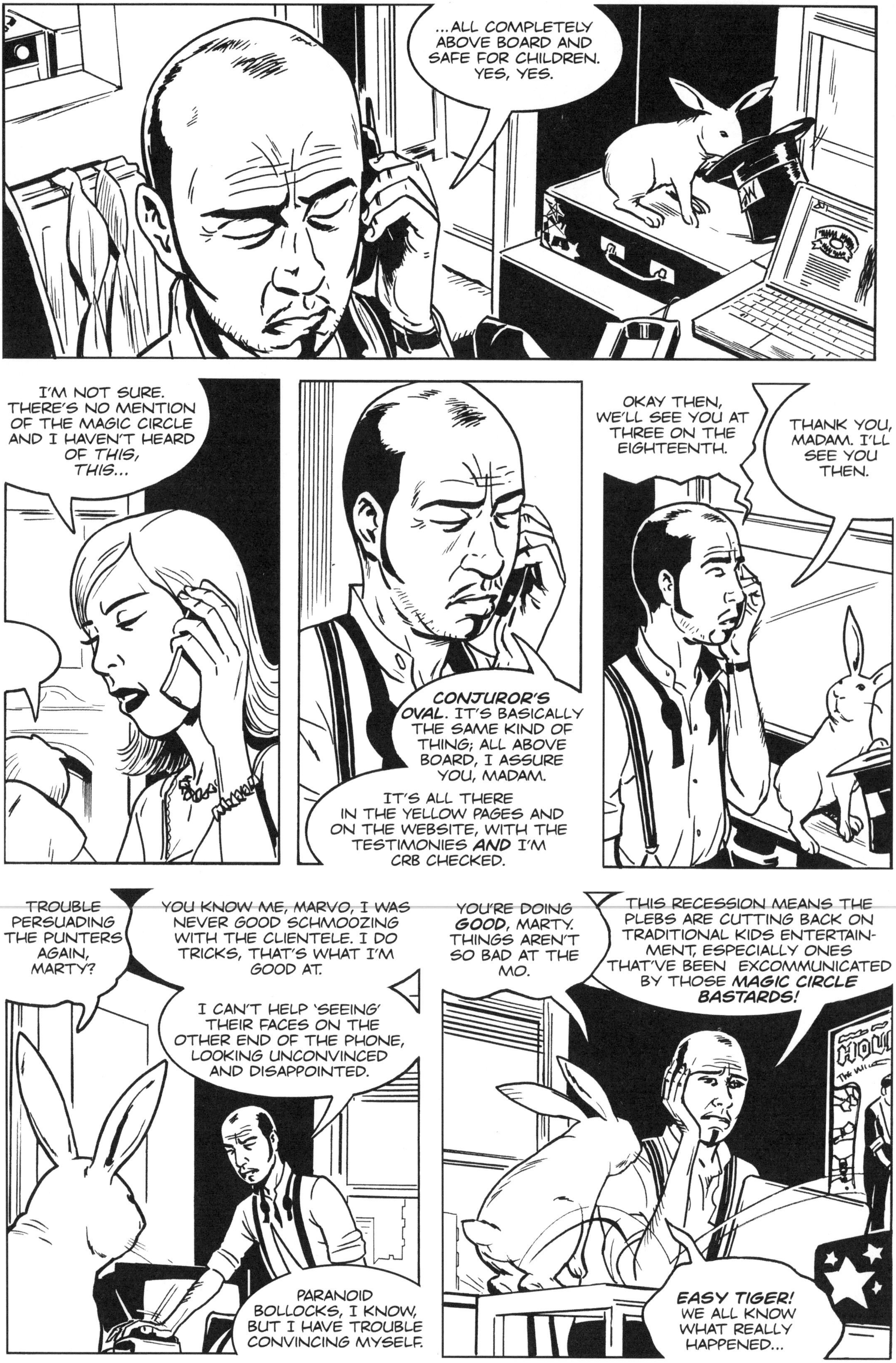
...ALL COMPLETELY ABOVE BOARD AND SAFE FOR CHILDREN. YES, YES.
I'M NOT SURE. THERE'S NO MENTION OF THE MAGIC CIRCLE AND I HAVEN'T HEARD OF *THIS*, THIS...
CONJUROR'S OVAL. IT'S BASICALLY THE SAME KIND OF THING; ALL ABOVE BOARD, I ASSURE YOU, MADAM.
IT'S ALL THERE IN THE YELLOW PAGES AND ON THE WEBSITE, WITH THE TESTIMONIES ***AND*** I'M CRB CHECKED.
OKAY THEN, WE'LL SEE YOU AT THREE ON THE EIGHTEENTH.
THANK YOU, MADAM. I'LL SEE YOU THEN.
TROUBLE PERSUADING THE PUNTERS AGAIN, MARTY?
YOU KNOW ME, MARVO, I WAS NEVER GOOD SCHMOOZING WITH THE CLIENTELE. I DO TRICKS, THAT'S WHAT I'M GOOD AT.
I CAN'T HELP 'SEEING' THEIR FACES ON THE OTHER END OF THE PHONE, LOOKING UNCONVINCED AND DISAPPOINTED.
PARANOID BOLLOCKS, I KNOW, BUT I HAVE TROUBLE CONVINCING MYSELF.
YOU'RE DOING ***GOOD***, MARTY. THINGS AREN'T SO BAD AT THE MO.
THIS RECESSION MEANS THE PLEBS ARE CUTTING BACK ON TRADITIONAL KIDS ENTERTAINMENT, ESPECIALLY ONES THAT'VE BEEN EXCOMMUNICATED BY THOSE ***MAGIC CIRCLE BASTARDS!***
EASY TIGER! WE ALL KNOW WHAT REALLY HAPPENED...

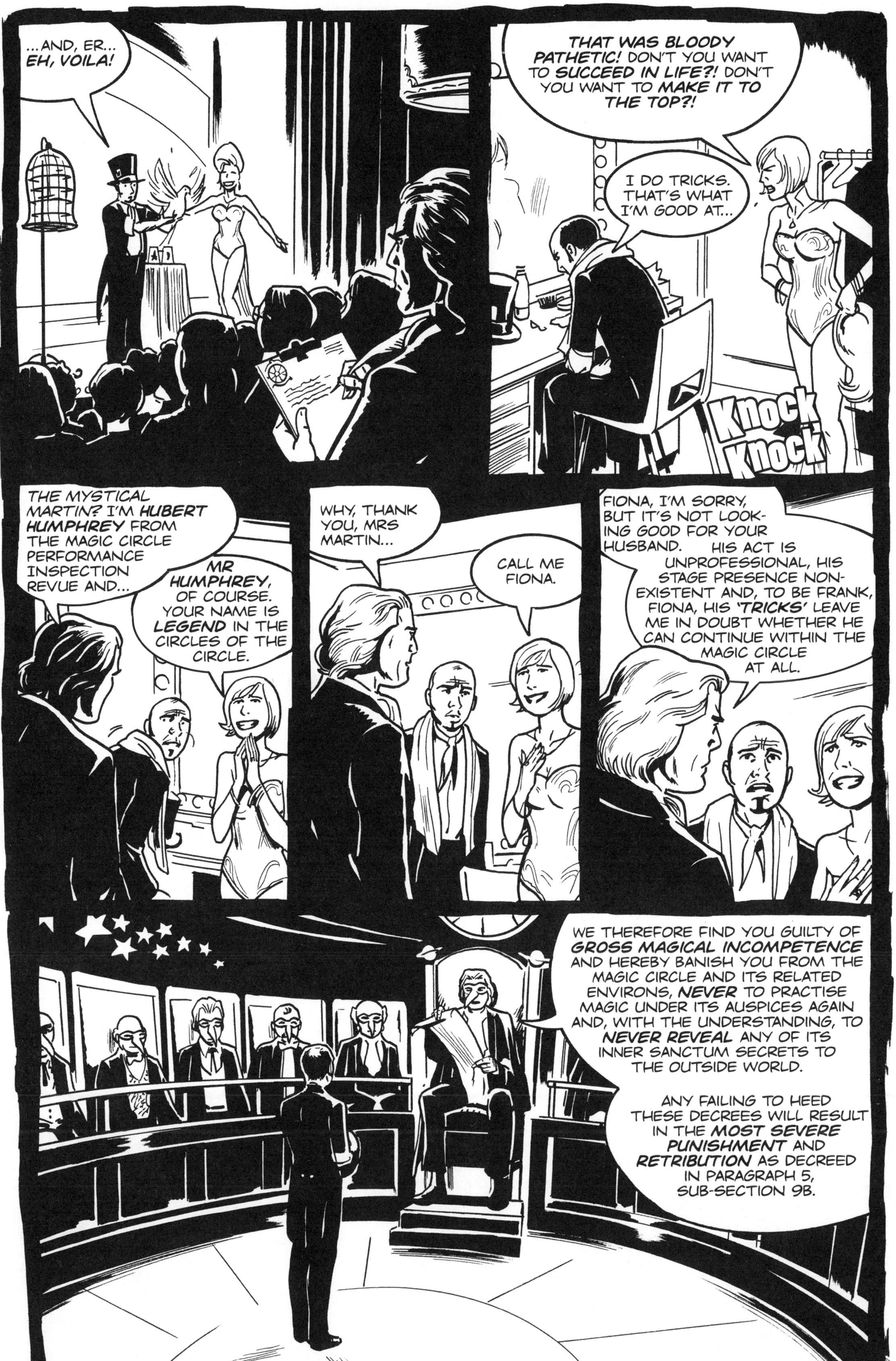
...AND, ER... EH, VOILA!
THAT WAS BLOODY PATHETIC! DON'T YOU WANT TO SUCCEED IN LIFE?! DON'T YOU WANT TO MAKE IT TO THE TOP?!
I DO TRICKS. THAT'S WHAT I'M GOOD AT...
Knock Knock
THE MYSTICAL MARTIN? I'M HUBERT HUMPHREY FROM THE MAGIC CIRCLE PERFORMANCE INSPECTION REVUE AND...
MR HUMPHREY, OF COURSE. YOUR NAME IS LEGEND IN THE CIRCLES OF THE CIRCLE.
WHY, THANK YOU, MRS MARTIN...
CALL ME FIONA.
FIONA, I'M SORRY, BUT IT'S NOT LOOKING GOOD FOR YOUR HUSBAND. HIS ACT IS UNPROFESSIONAL, HIS STAGE PRESENCE NON-EXISTENT AND, TO BE FRANK, FIONA, HIS 'TRICKS' LEAVE ME IN DOUBT WHETHER HE CAN CONTINUE WITHIN THE MAGIC CIRCLE AT ALL.
WE THEREFORE FIND YOU GUILTY OF GROSS MAGICAL INCOMPETENCE AND HEREBY BANISH YOU FROM THE MAGIC CIRCLE AND ITS RELATED ENVIRONS, NEVER TO PRACTISE MAGIC UNDER ITS AUSPICES AGAIN AND, WITH THE UNDERSTANDING, TO NEVER REVEAL ANY OF ITS INNER SANCTUM SECRETS TO THE OUTSIDE WORLD.
ANY FAILING TO HEED THESE DECREES WILL RESULT IN THE MOST SEVERE PUNISHMENT AND RETRIBUTION AS DECREED IN PARAGRAPH 5, SUB-SECTION 9B.

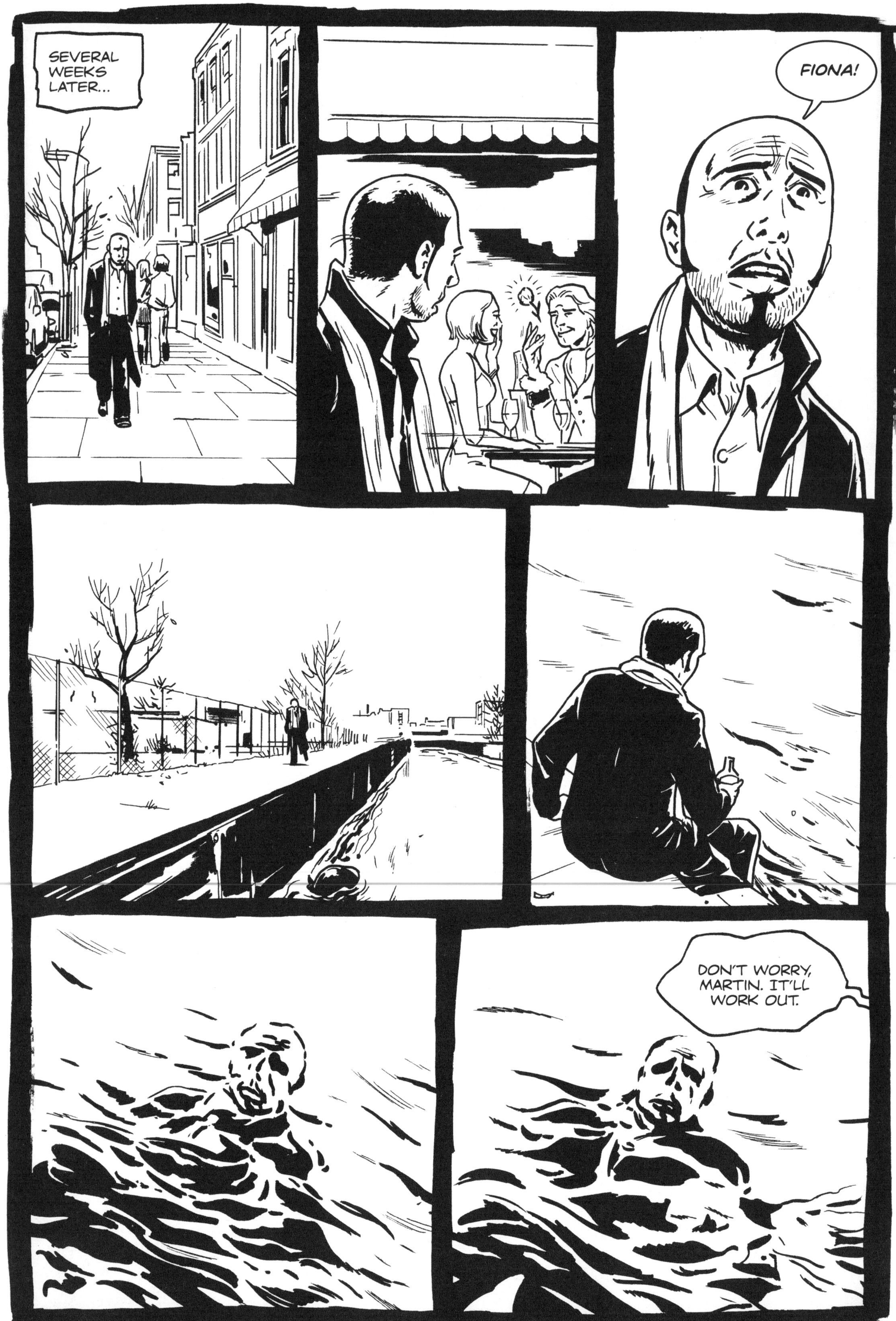
SEVERAL WEEKS LATER...
FIONA!
DON'T WORRY, MARTIN. IT'LL WORK OUT.

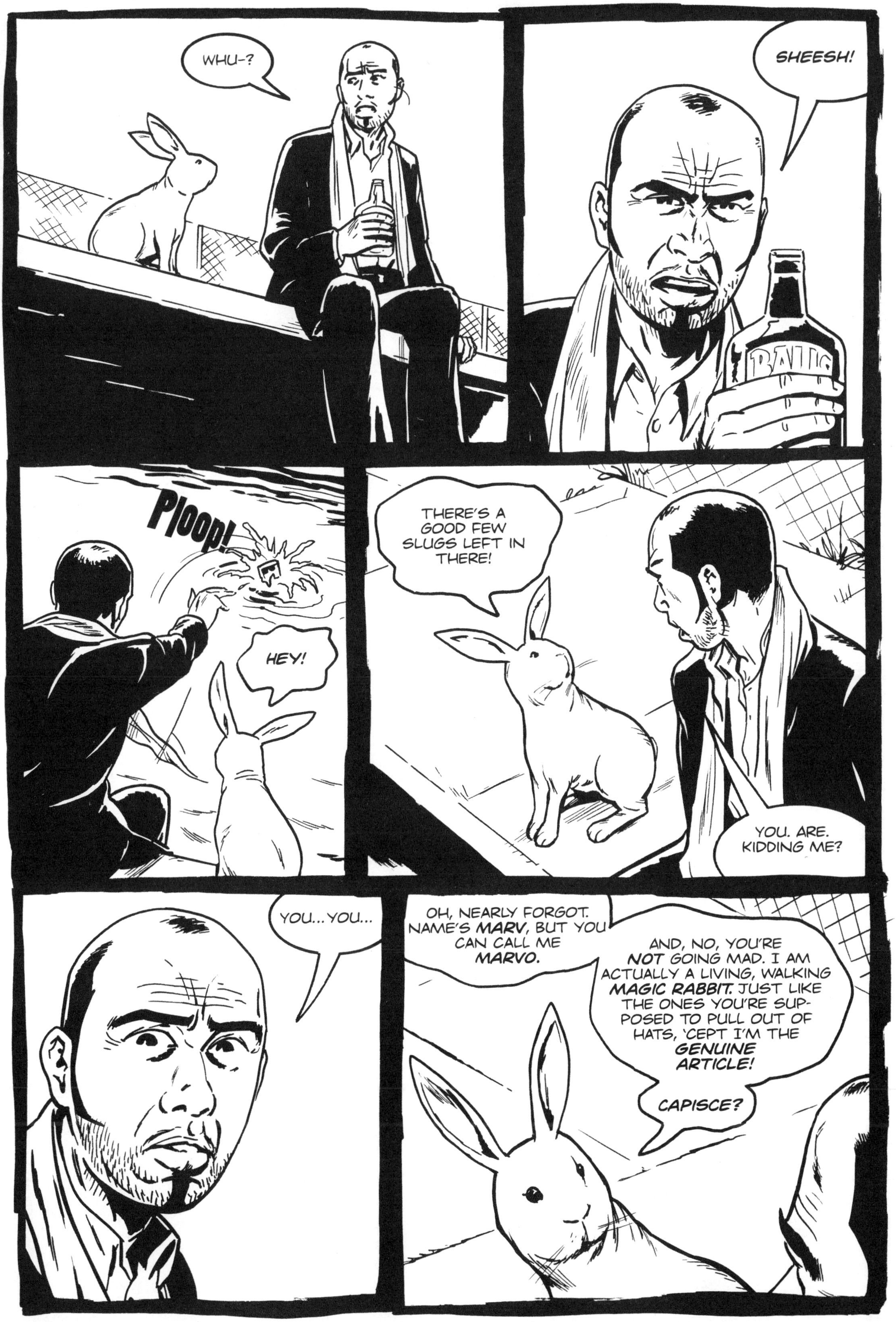
WHU-?
SHEESH!
BALLS
Ploop!
HEY!
THERE'S A GOOD FEW SLUGS LEFT IN THERE!
YOU. ARE. KIDDING ME?
YOU...YOU...
OH, NEARLY FORGOT. NAME'S MARV, BUT YOU CAN CALL ME MARVO.
AND, NO, YOU'RE NOT GOING MAD. I AM ACTUALLY A LIVING, WALKING MAGIC RABBIT. JUST LIKE THE ONES YOU'RE SUP-POSED TO PULL OUT OF HATS, 'CEPT I'M THE GENUINE ARTICLE!
CAPISCE?

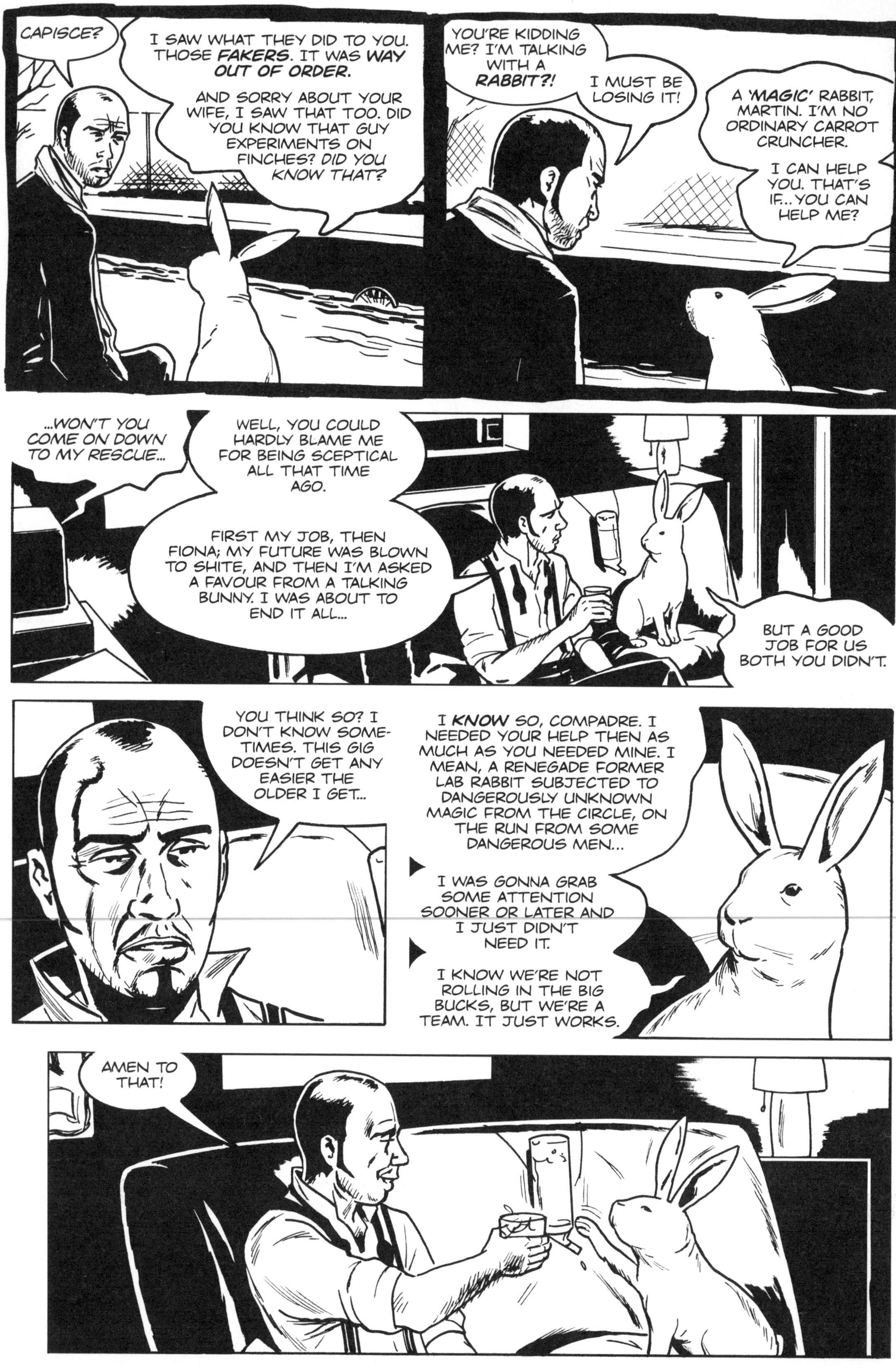
CAPISCE?
I SAW WHAT THEY DID TO YOU. THOSE FAKERS. IT WAS WAY OUT OF ORDER.
AND SORRY ABOUT YOUR WIFE, I SAW THAT TOO. DID YOU KNOW THAT GUY EXPERIMENTS ON FINCHES? DID YOU KNOW THAT?
YOU'RE KIDDING ME? I'M TALKING WITH A RABBIT?!
I MUST BE LOSING IT!
A 'MAGIC' RABBIT, MARTIN. I'M NO ORDINARY CARROT CRUNCHER.
I CAN HELP YOU. THAT'S IF... YOU CAN HELP ME?
...WON'T YOU COME ON DOWN TO MY RESCUE...
WELL, YOU COULD HARDLY BLAME ME FOR BEING SCEPTICAL ALL THAT TIME AGO.
FIRST MY JOB, THEN FIONA; MY FUTURE WAS BLOWN TO SHITE, AND THEN I'M ASKED A FAVOUR FROM A TALKING BUNNY. I WAS ABOUT TO END IT ALL...
BUT A GOOD JOB FOR US BOTH YOU DIDN'T.
YOU THINK SO? I DON'T KNOW SOMETIMES. THIS GIG DOESN'T GET ANY EASIER THE OLDER I GET...
I KNOW SO, COMPADRE. I NEEDED YOUR HELP THEN AS MUCH AS YOU NEEDED MINE. I MEAN, A RENEGADE FORMER LAB RABBIT SUBJECTED TO DANGEROUSLY UNKNOWN MAGIC FROM THE CIRCLE, ON THE RUN FROM SOME DANGEROUS MEN...
I WAS GONNA GRAB SOME ATTENTION SOONER OR LATER AND I JUST DIDN'T NEED IT.
I KNOW WE'RE NOT ROLLING IN THE BIG BUCKS, BUT WE'RE A TEAM. IT JUST WORKS.
AMEN TO THAT!

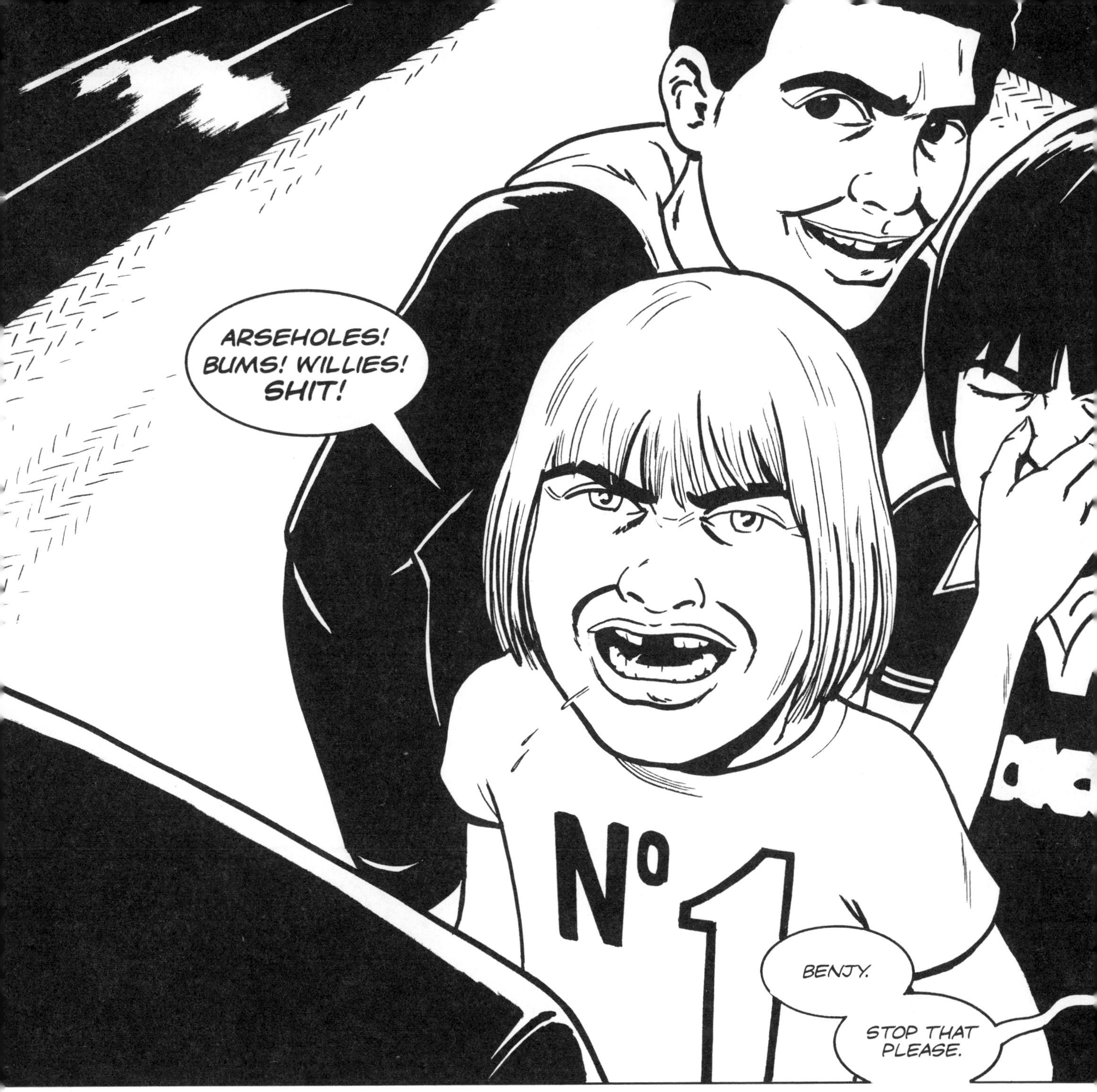
ARSEHOLES! BUMS! WILLIES! SHIT!
BENJY.
STOP THAT PLEASE.

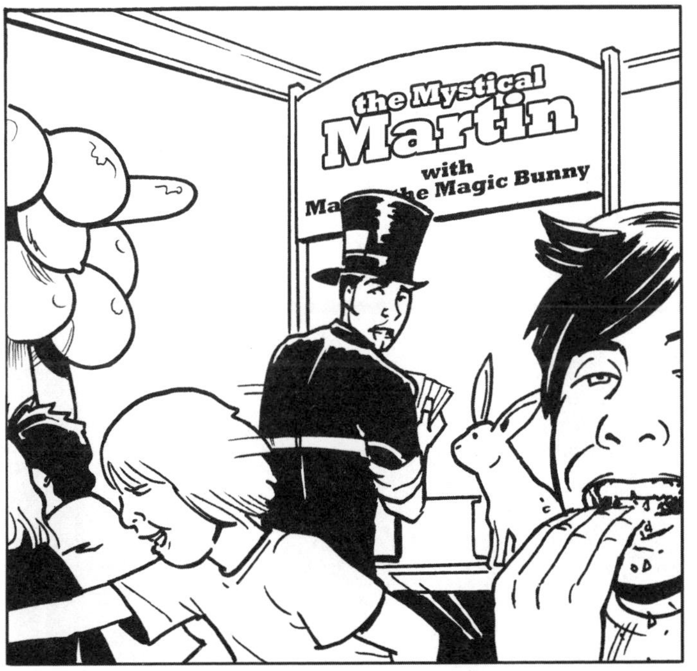
the Mystical
Martin
with

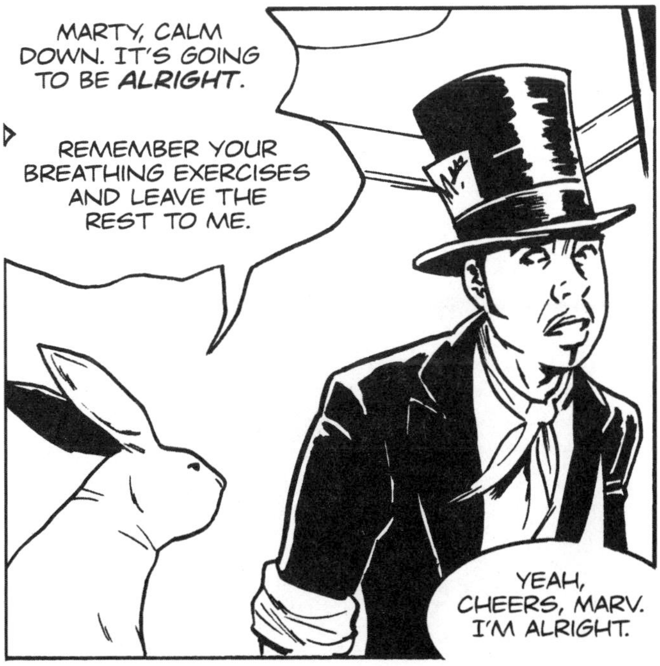
MARTY, CALM DOWN. IT'S GOING TO BE *ALRIGHT*.
REMEMBER YOUR BREATHING EXERCISES AND LEAVE THE REST TO ME.
YEAH, CHEERS, MARV. I'M ALRIGHT.

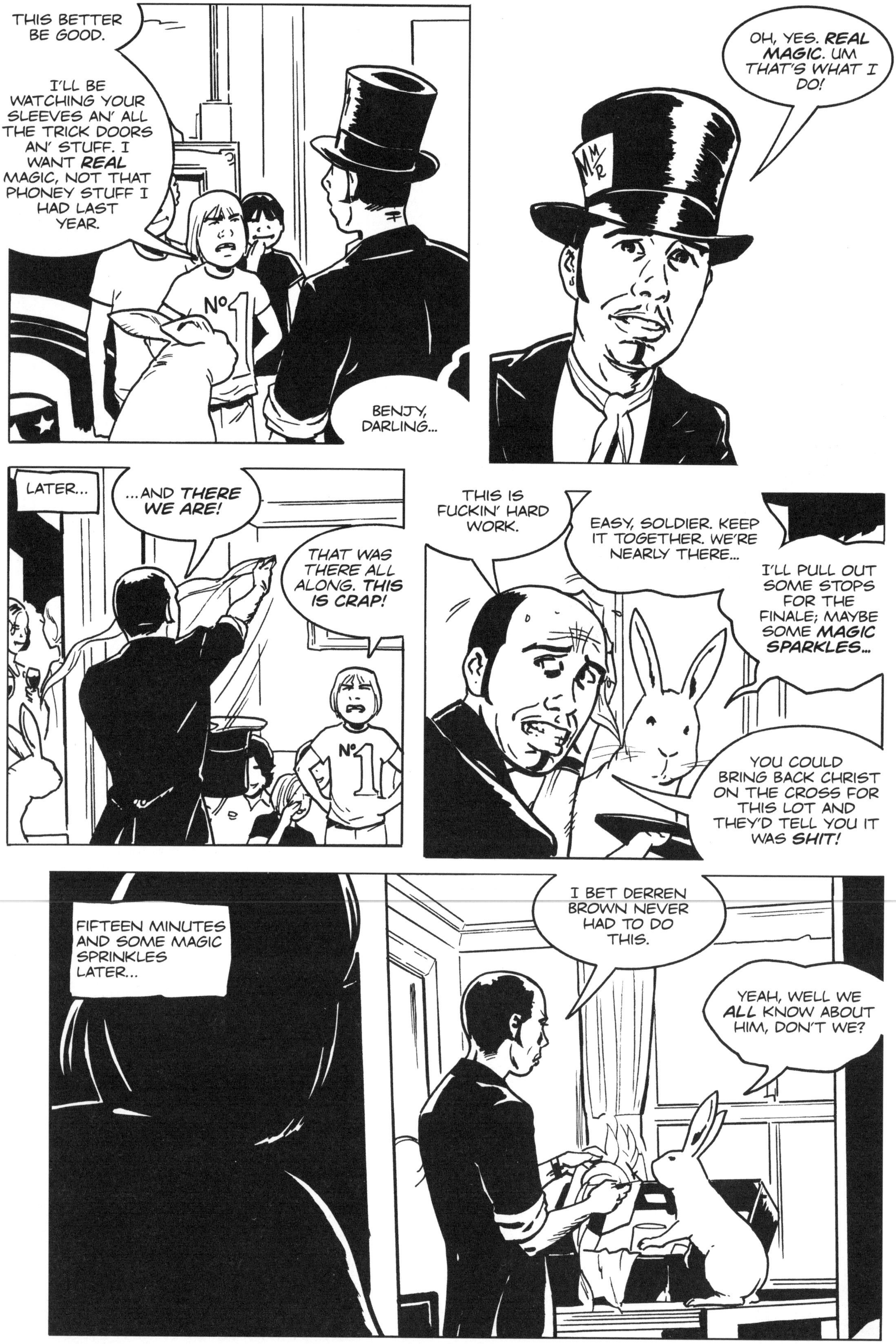
THIS BETTER BE GOOD.
I'LL BE WATCHING YOUR SLEEVES AN' ALL THE TRICK DOORS AN' STUFF. I WANT REAL MAGIC, NOT THAT PHONEY STUFF I HAD LAST YEAR.
BENJY, DARLING...
OH, YES. REAL MAGIC. UM THAT'S WHAT I DO!
LATER...
...AND THERE WE ARE!
THAT WAS THERE ALL ALONG. THIS IS CRAP!
THIS IS FUCKIN' HARD WORK.
EASY, SOLDIER. KEEP IT TOGETHER. WE'RE NEARLY THERE...
I'LL PULL OUT SOME STOPS FOR THE FINALE; MAYBE SOME MAGIC SPARKLES...
YOU COULD BRING BACK CHRIST ON THE CROSS FOR THIS LOT AND THEY'D TELL YOU IT WAS SHIT!
FIFTEEN MINUTES AND SOME MAGIC SPRINKLES LATER...
I BET DERREN BROWN NEVER HAD TO DO THIS.
YEAH, WELL WE ALL KNOW ABOUT HIM, DON'T WE?

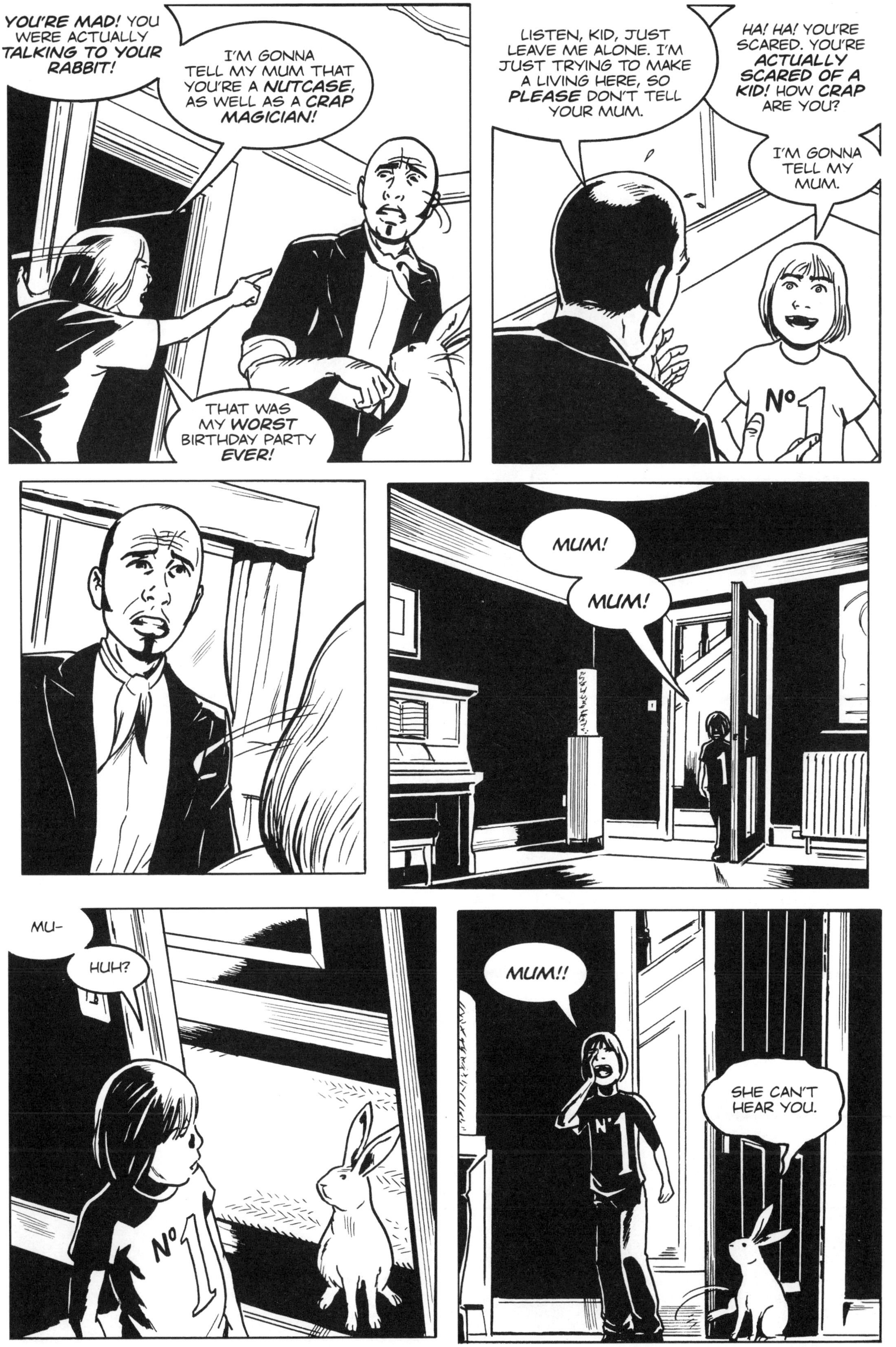
YOU'RE MAD! YOU WERE ACTUALLY TALKING TO YOUR RABBIT!
I'M GONNA TELL MY MUM THAT YOU'RE A NUTCASE, AS WELL AS A CRAP MAGICIAN!
THAT WAS MY WORST BIRTHDAY PARTY EVER!
LISTEN, KID, JUST LEAVE ME ALONE. I'M JUST TRYING TO MAKE A LIVING HERE, SO PLEASE DON'T TELL YOUR MUM.
HA! HA! YOU'RE SCARED. YOU'RE ACTUALLY SCARED OF A KID! HOW CRAP ARE YOU?
I'M GONNA TELL MY MUM.
MUM!
MUM!
MU-
HUH?
MUM!!
SHE CAN'T HEAR YOU.

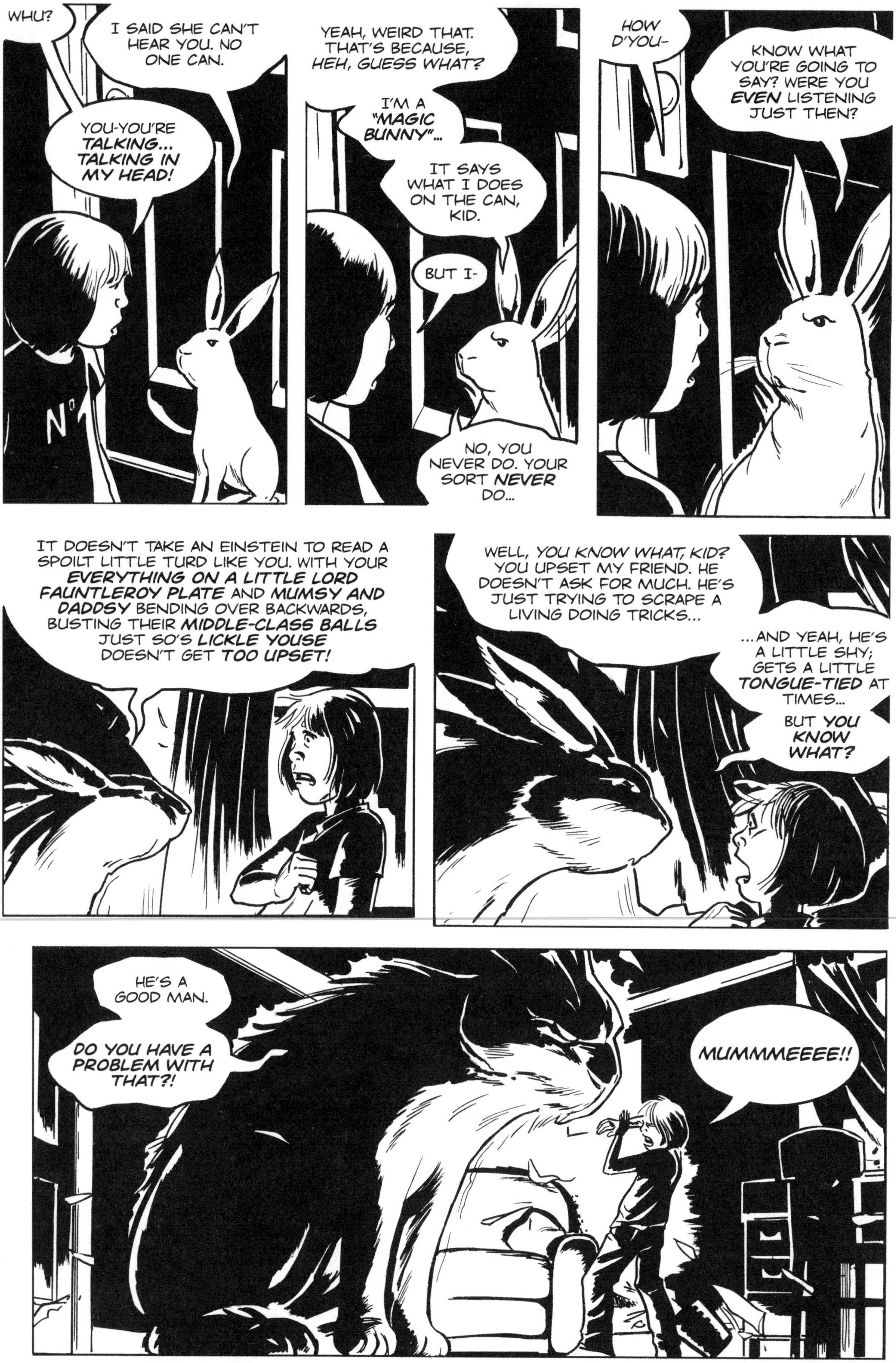
WHU?
I SAID SHE CAN'T HEAR YOU. NO ONE CAN.
YOU-YOU'RE TALKING... TALKING IN MY HEAD!
YEAH, WEIRD THAT. THAT'S BECAUSE, HEH, GUESS WHAT?
I'M A "MAGIC BUNNY"...
IT SAYS WHAT I DOES ON THE CAN, KID.
BUT I-
NO, YOU NEVER DO. YOUR SORT NEVER DO...
HOW D'YOU-
KNOW WHAT YOU'RE GOING TO SAY? WERE YOU EVEN LISTENING JUST THEN?
IT DOESN'T TAKE AN EINSTEIN TO READ A SPOILT LITTLE TURD LIKE YOU. WITH YOUR EVERYTHING ON A LITTLE LORD FAUNTLEROY PLATE AND MUMSY AND DADDSY BENDING OVER BACKWARDS, BUSTING THEIR MIDDLE-CLASS BALLS JUST SO'S LICKLE YOUSE DOESN'T GET TOO UPSET!
WELL, YOU KNOW WHAT, KID? YOU UPSET MY FRIEND. HE DOESN'T ASK FOR MUCH. HE'S JUST TRYING TO SCRAPE A LIVING DOING TRICKS...
...AND YEAH, HE'S A LITTLE SHY; GETS A LITTLE TONGUE-TIED AT TIMES...
BUT YOU KNOW WHAT?
HE'S A GOOD MAN.
DO YOU HAVE A PROBLEM WITH THAT?!
MUMMMEEEE!!

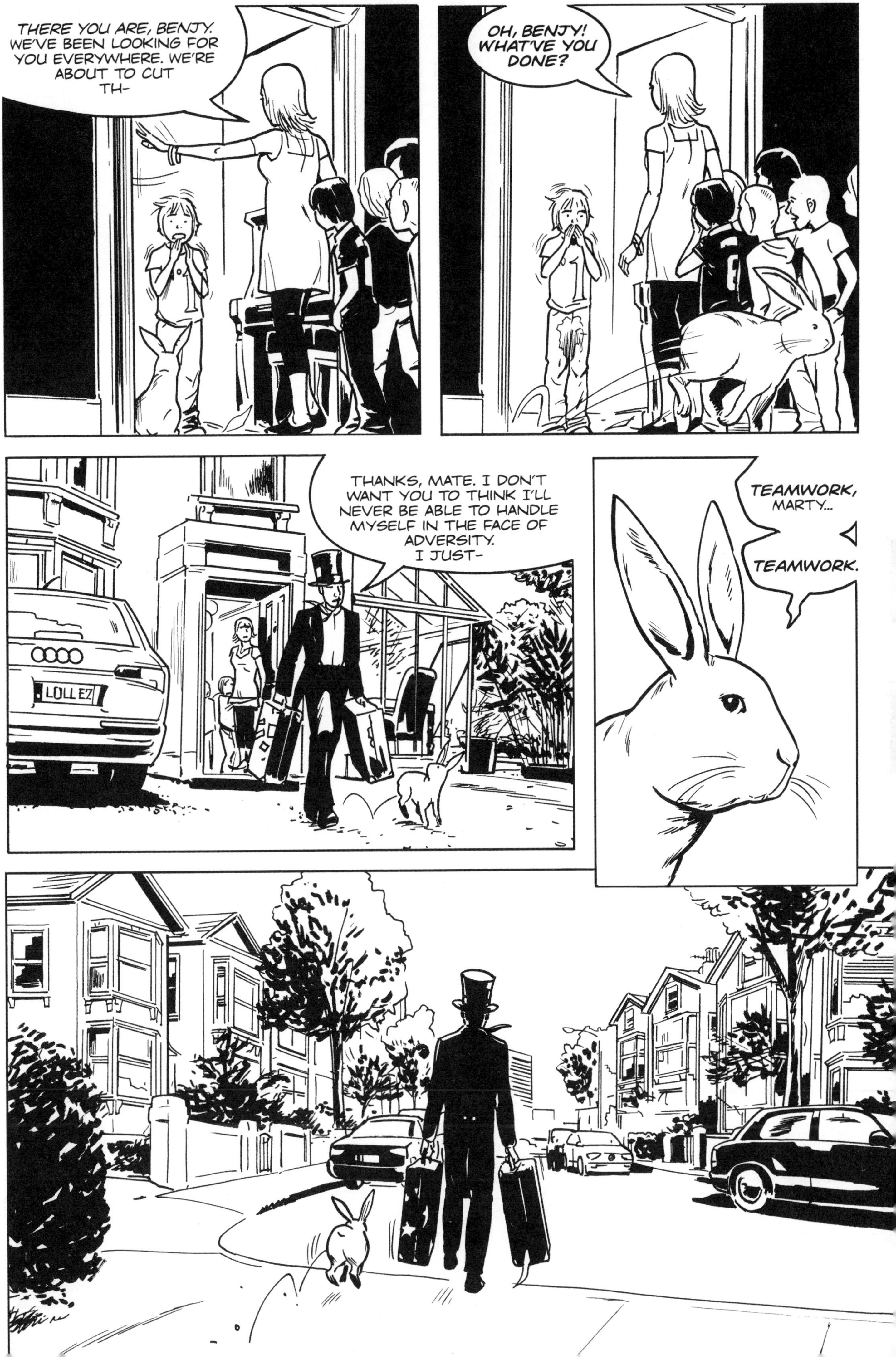
THERE YOU ARE, BENJY. WE'VE BEEN LOOKING FOR YOU EVERYWHERE. WE'RE ABOUT TO CUT TH-
OH, BENJY! WHAT'VE YOU DONE?
THANKS, MATE. I DON'T WANT YOU TO THINK I'LL NEVER BE ABLE TO HANDLE MYSELF IN THE FACE OF ADVERSITY. I JUST-
LOLL EZ
TEAMWORK, MARTY...
TEAMWORK.

MARVO Origins

I CAN'T SEE...

I CAN'T BLOODY SEE!!

DAISY!? DAISY!?!

YOU STILL THERE?!

WHAT'S GOING ON?! DAISY!!

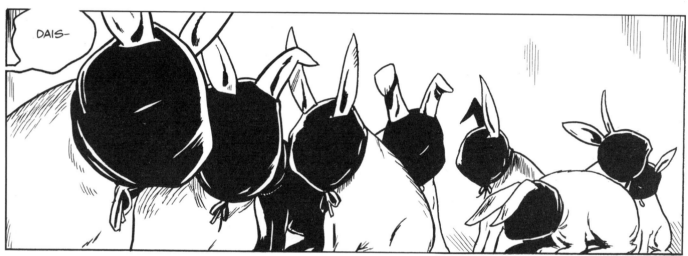

DAIS-

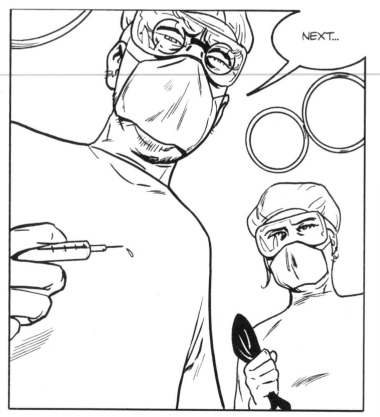

NEXT...

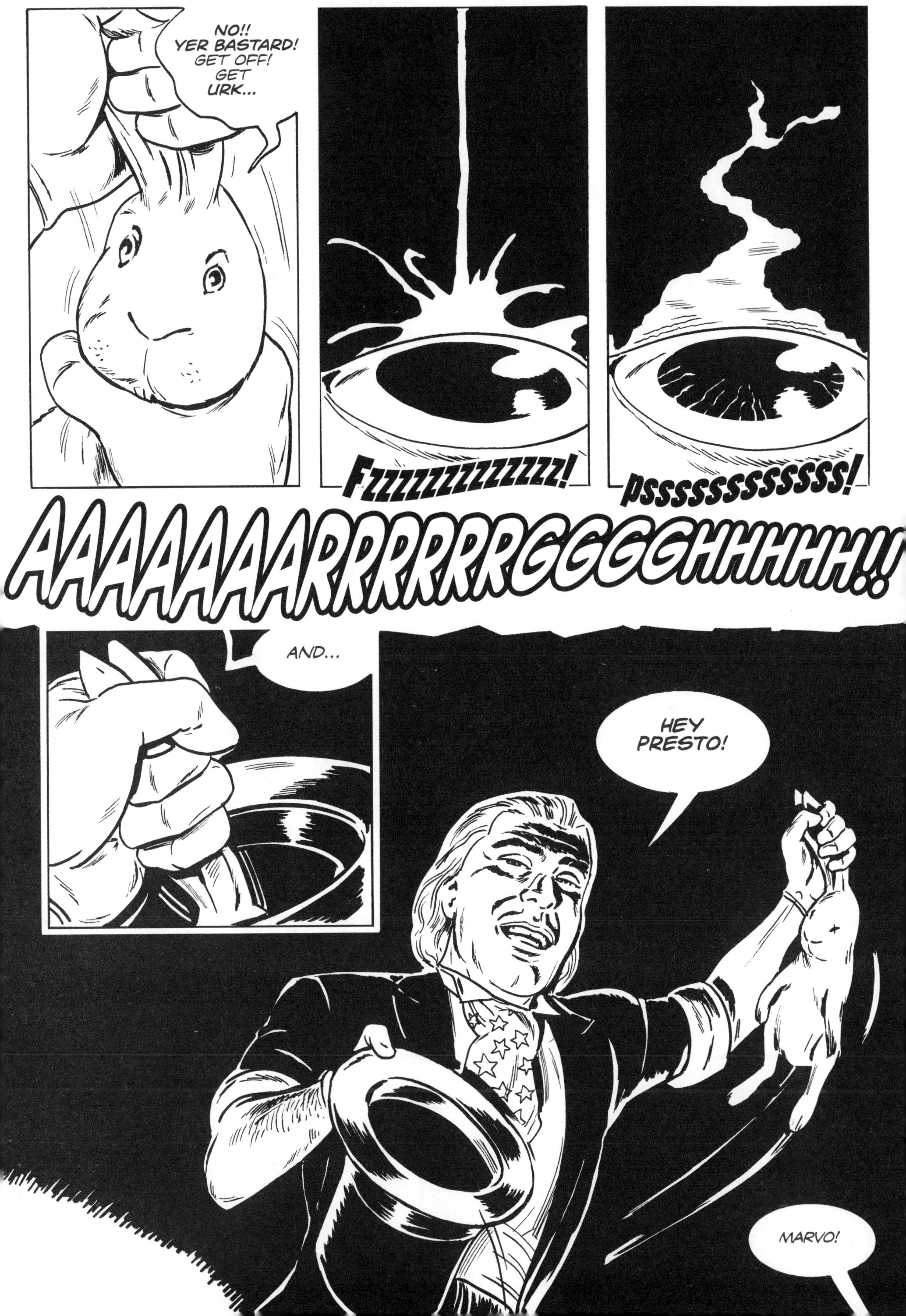
NO!! YER BASTARD! GET OFF! GET URK...
Fzzzzzzzzzzzzz!
pssssssssssss!
AAAAAAARRRRRRGGGGHHHHH!!
AND...
HEY PRESTO!
MARVO!

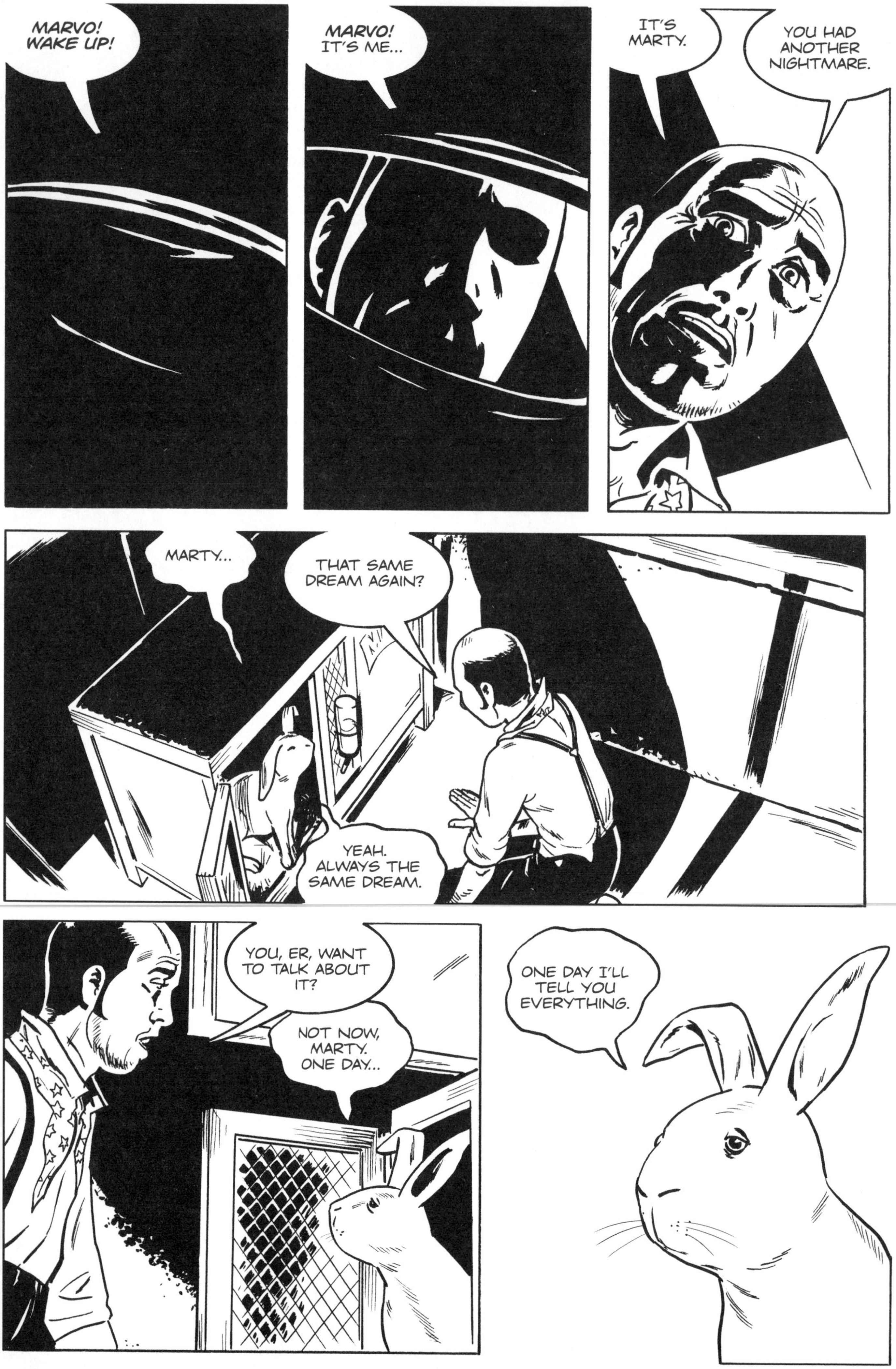
MARVO! WAKE UP!
MARVO! IT'S ME...
IT'S MARTY.
YOU HAD ANOTHER NIGHTMARE.
MARTY...
THAT SAME DREAM AGAIN?
YEAH. ALWAYS THE SAME DREAM.
YOU, ER, WANT TO TALK ABOUT IT?
NOT NOW, MARTY. ONE DAY...
ONE DAY I'LL TELL YOU EVERYTHING.

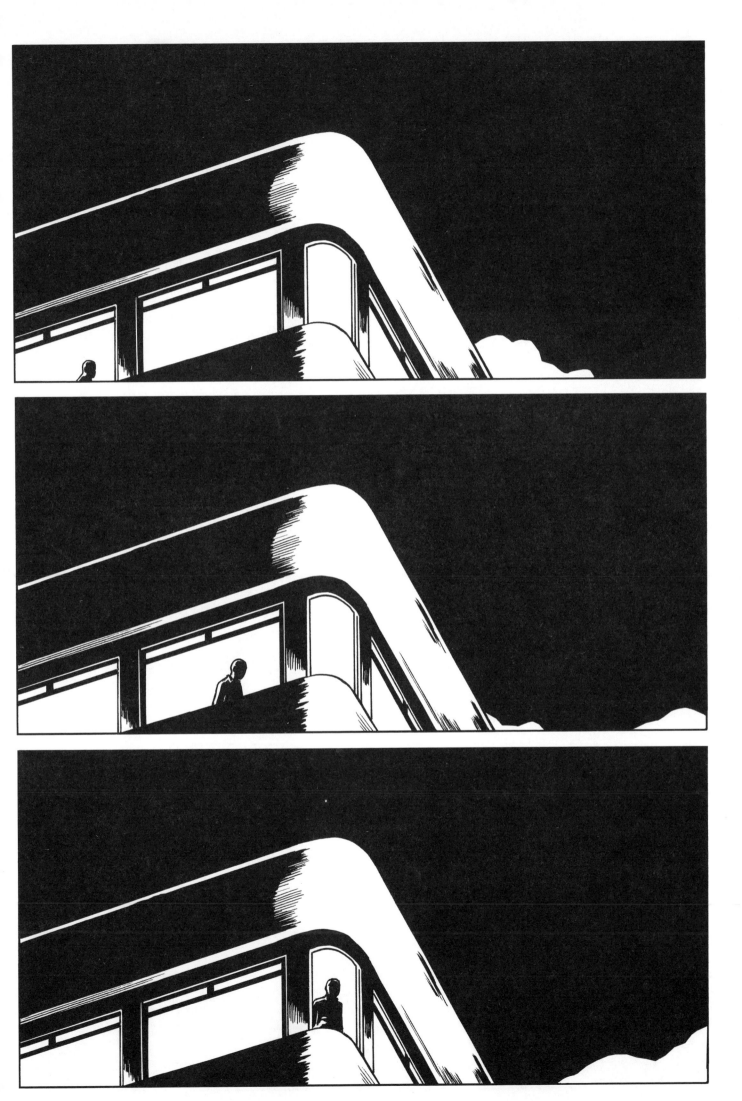

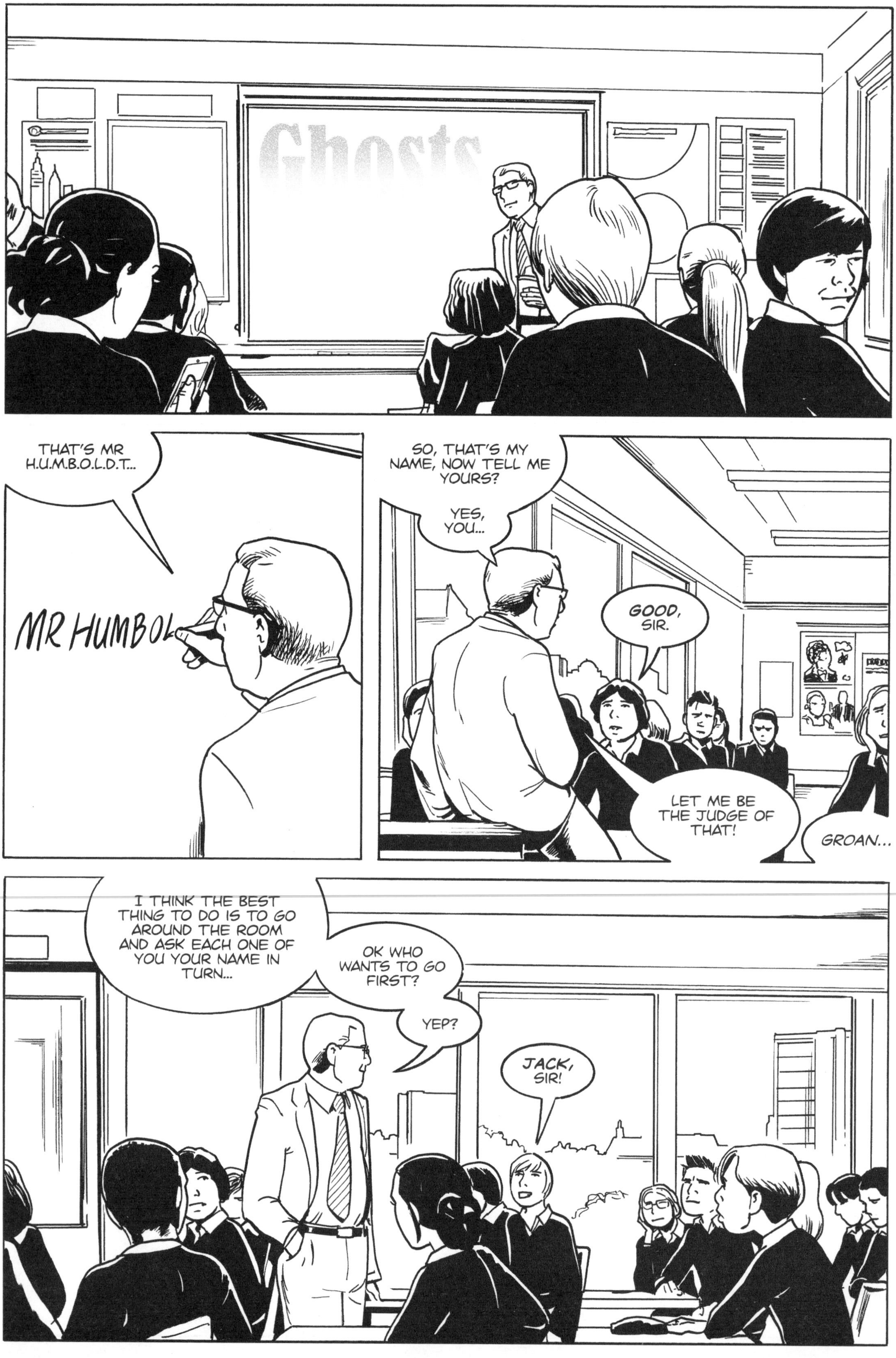
Ghosts
THAT'S MR H.U.M.B.O.L.D.T...
MR HUMBOL
SO, THAT'S MY NAME, NOW TELL ME YOURS?
YES, YOU...
GOOD, SIR.
LET ME BE THE JUDGE OF THAT!
GROAN...
I THINK THE BEST THING TO DO IS TO GO AROUND THE ROOM AND ASK EACH ONE OF YOU YOUR NAME IN TURN...
OK WHO WANTS TO GO FIRST?
YEP?
JACK, SIR!

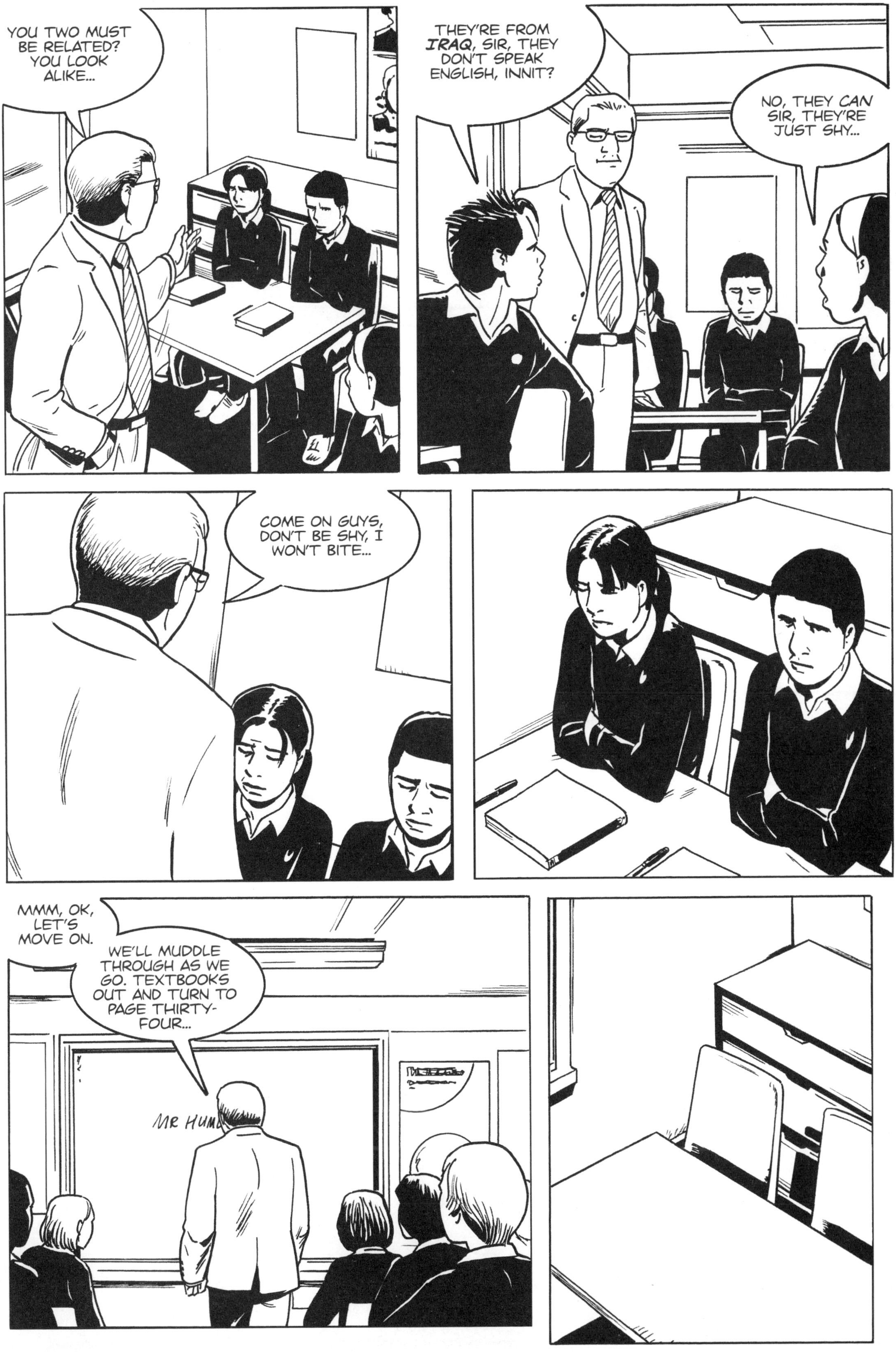
YOU TWO MUST BE RELATED? YOU LOOK ALIKE...
THEY'RE FROM IRAQ, SIR, THEY DON'T SPEAK ENGLISH, INNIT?
NO, THEY CAN SIR, THEY'RE JUST SHY...
COME ON GUYS, DON'T BE SHY, I WON'T BITE...
MMM, OK, LET'S MOVE ON.
WE'LL MUDDLE THROUGH AS WE GO. TEXTBOOKS OUT AND TURN TO PAGE THIRTY-FOUR...
MR HUM

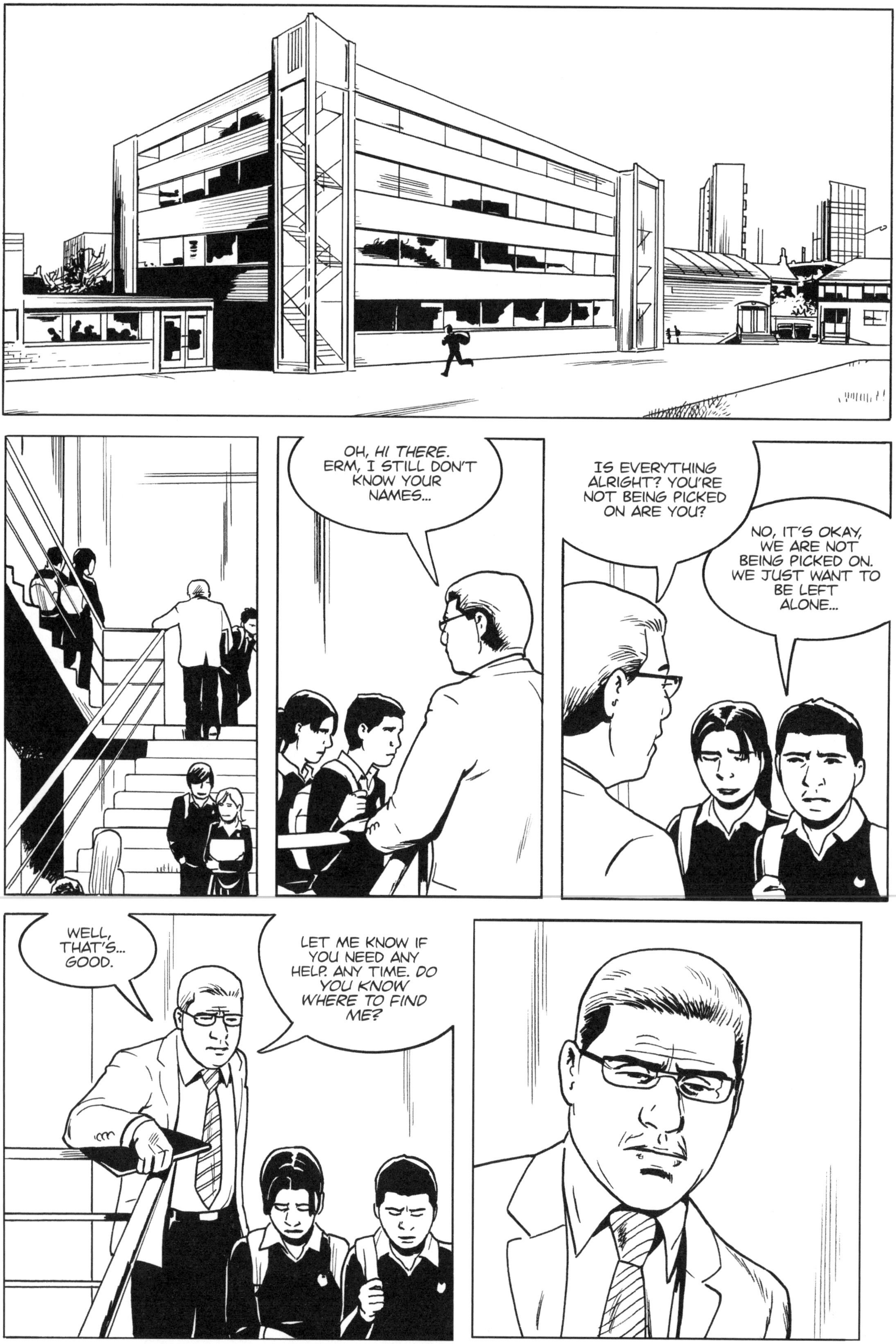

OH, HI THERE. ERM, I STILL DON'T KNOW YOUR NAMES...
IS EVERYTHING ALRIGHT? YOU'RE NOT BEING PICKED ON ARE YOU?
NO, IT'S OKAY, WE ARE NOT BEING PICKED ON. WE JUST WANT TO BE LEFT ALONE...
WELL, THAT'S... GOOD.
LET ME KNOW IF YOU NEED ANY HELP. ANY TIME. DO YOU KNOW WHERE TO FIND ME?

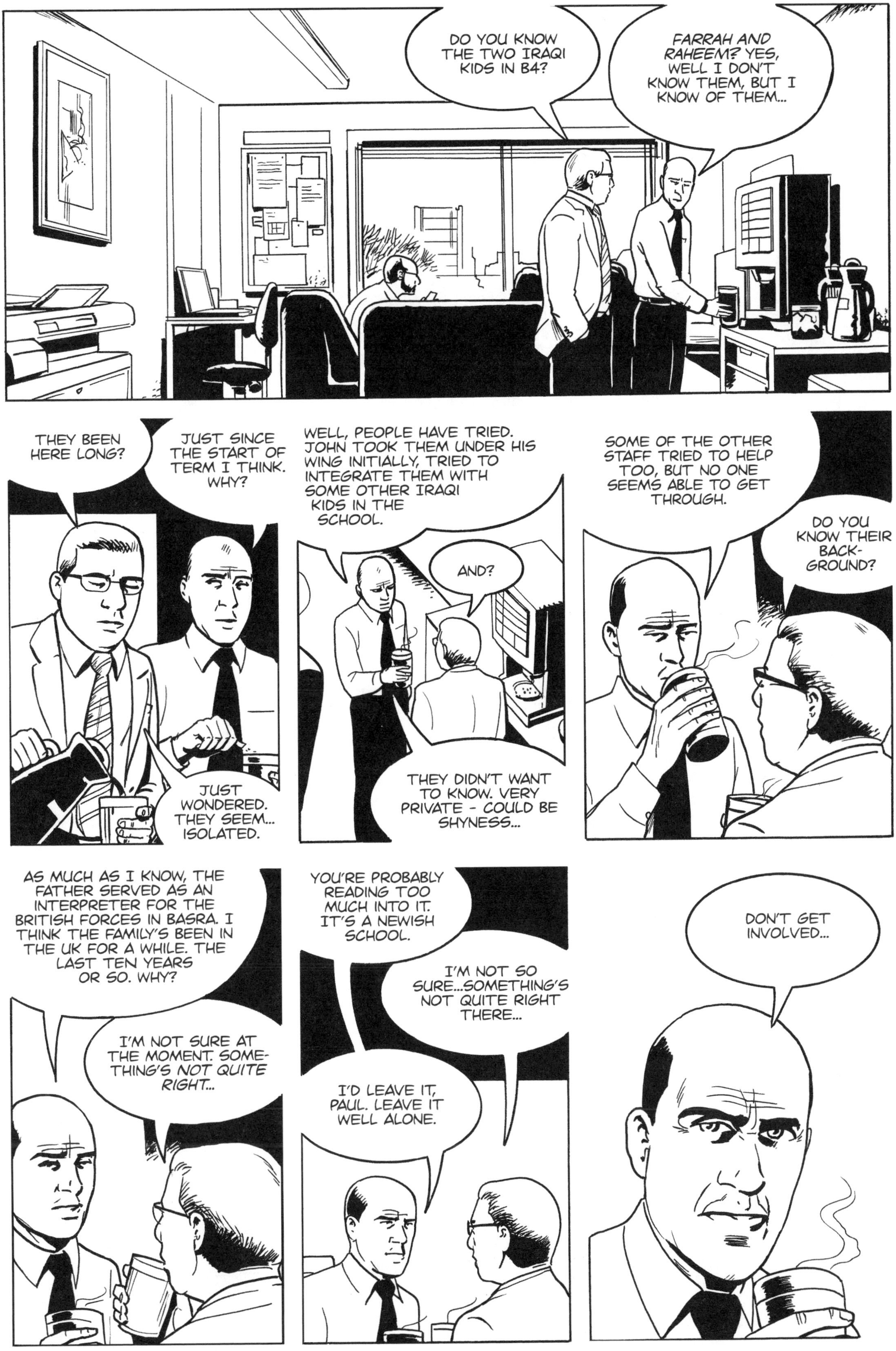
DO YOU KNOW THE TWO IRAQI KIDS IN B4?
FARRAH AND RAHEEM? YES, WELL I DON'T KNOW THEM, BUT I KNOW OF THEM...
THEY BEEN HERE LONG?
JUST SINCE THE START OF TERM I THINK. WHY?
JUST WONDERED. THEY SEEM... ISOLATED.
WELL, PEOPLE HAVE TRIED. JOHN TOOK THEM UNDER HIS WING INITIALLY, TRIED TO INTEGRATE THEM WITH SOME OTHER IRAQI KIDS IN THE SCHOOL.
AND?
THEY DIDN'T WANT TO KNOW. VERY PRIVATE - COULD BE SHYNESS...
SOME OF THE OTHER STAFF TRIED TO HELP TOO, BUT NO ONE SEEMS ABLE TO GET THROUGH.
DO YOU KNOW THEIR BACK-GROUND?
AS MUCH AS I KNOW, THE FATHER SERVED AS AN INTERPRETER FOR THE BRITISH FORCES IN BASRA. I THINK THE FAMILY'S BEEN IN THE UK FOR A WHILE. THE LAST TEN YEARS OR SO. WHY?
I'M NOT SURE AT THE MOMENT. SOME-THING'S NOT QUITE RIGHT...
YOU'RE PROBABLY READING TOO MUCH INTO IT. IT'S A NEWISH SCHOOL.
I'M NOT SO SURE...SOMETHING'S NOT QUITE RIGHT THERE...
I'D LEAVE IT, PAUL. LEAVE IT WELL ALONE.
DON'T GET INVOLVED...

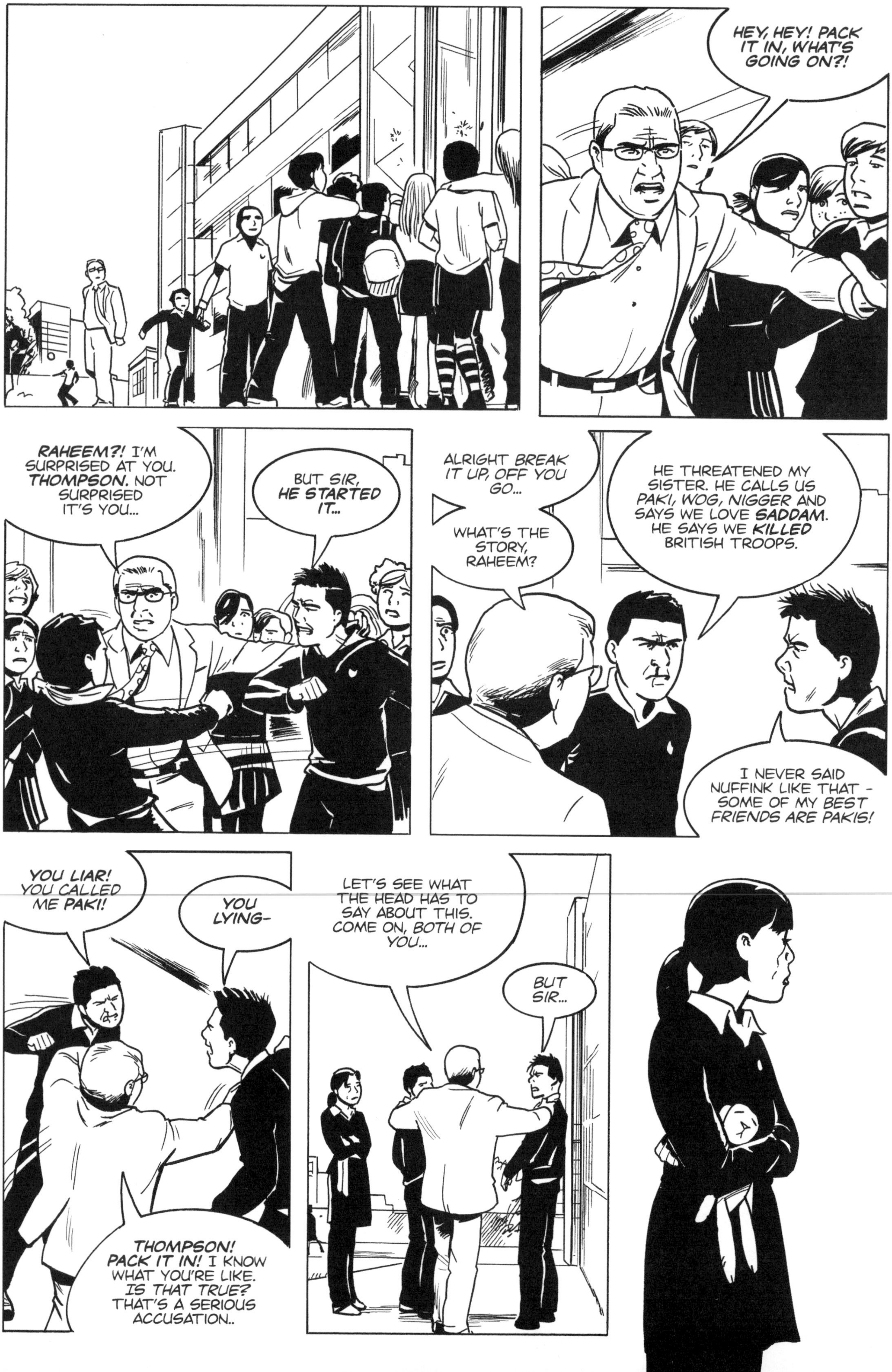
HEY, HEY! PACK IT IN, WHAT'S GOING ON?!
RAHEEM?! I'M SURPRISED AT YOU. THOMPSON. NOT SURPRISED IT'S YOU...
BUT SIR, HE STARTED IT...
ALRIGHT BREAK IT UP, OFF YOU GO...
WHAT'S THE STORY, RAHEEM?
HE THREATENED MY SISTER. HE CALLS US PAKI, WOG, NIGGER AND SAYS WE LOVE SADDAM. HE SAYS WE KILLED BRITISH TROOPS.
I NEVER SAID NUFFINK LIKE THAT - SOME OF MY BEST FRIENDS ARE PAKIS!
YOU LIAR! YOU CALLED ME PAKI!
YOU LYING-
THOMPSON! PACK IT IN! I KNOW WHAT YOU'RE LIKE. IS THAT TRUE? THAT'S A SERIOUS ACCUSATION..
LET'S SEE WHAT THE HEAD HAS TO SAY ABOUT THIS. COME ON, BOTH OF YOU...
BUT SIR...

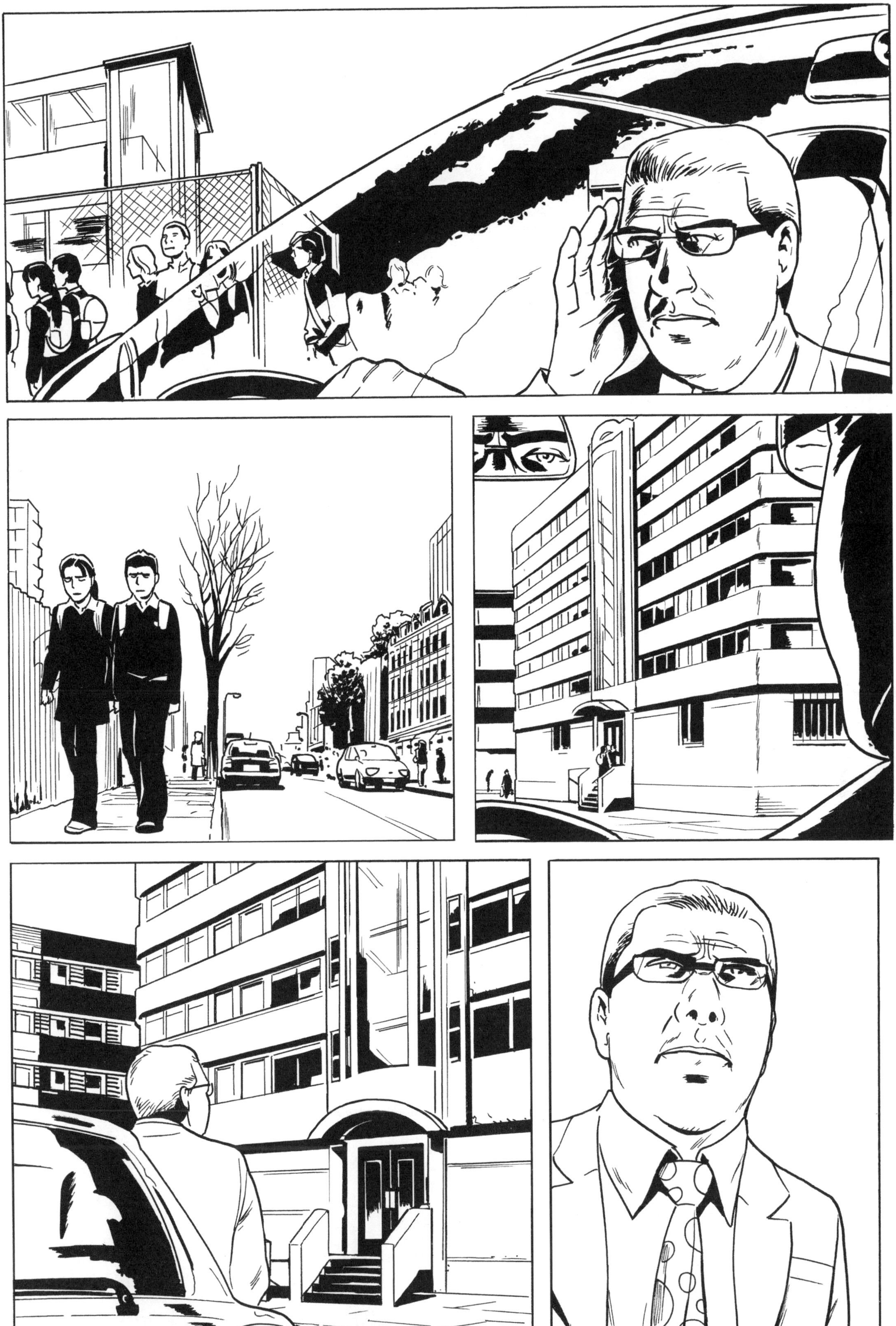

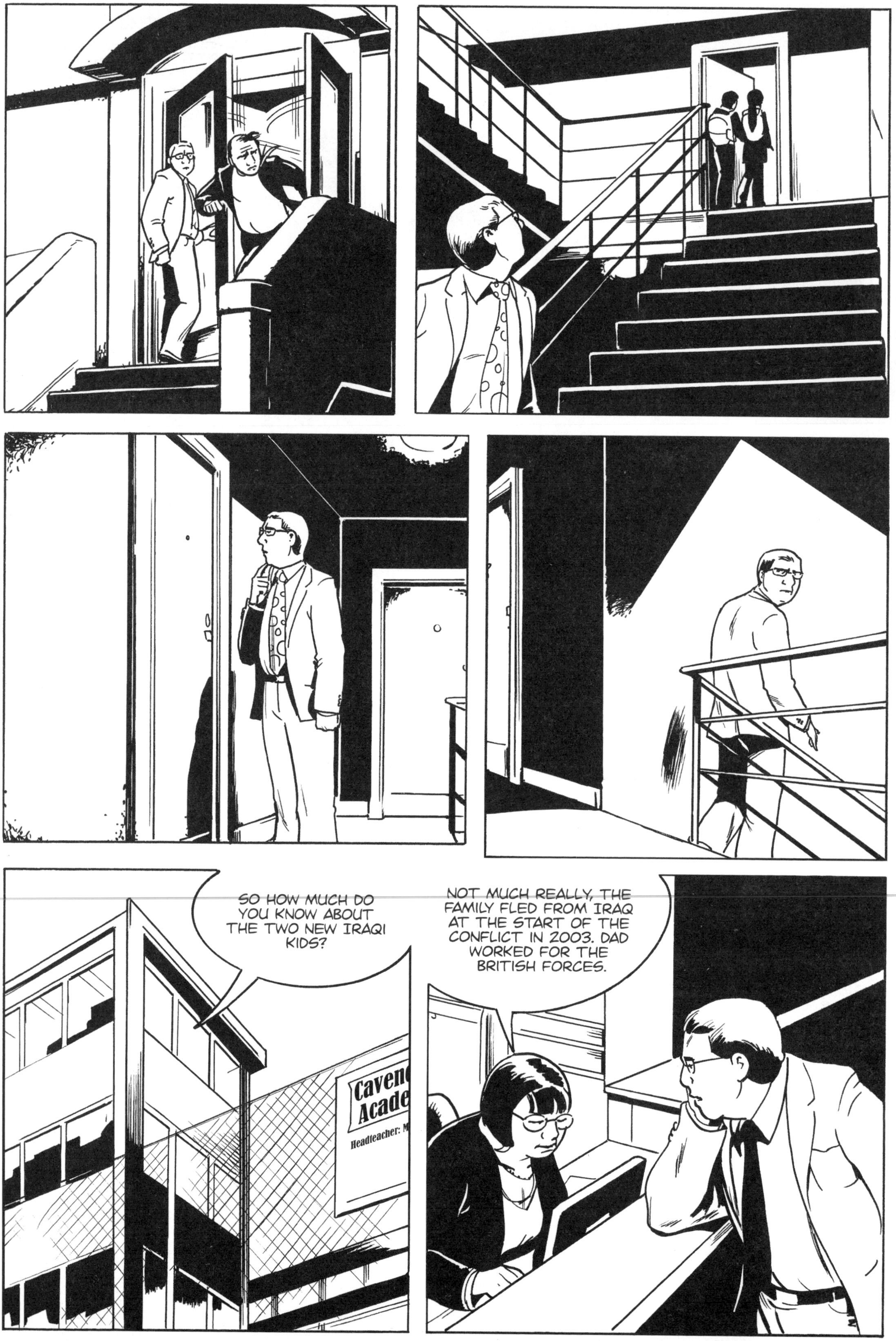
SO HOW MUCH DO YOU KNOW ABOUT THE TWO NEW IRAQI KIDS?
NOT MUCH REALLY, THE FAMILY FLED FROM IRAQ AT THE START OF THE CONFLICT IN 2003. DAD WORKED FOR THE BRITISH FORCES.

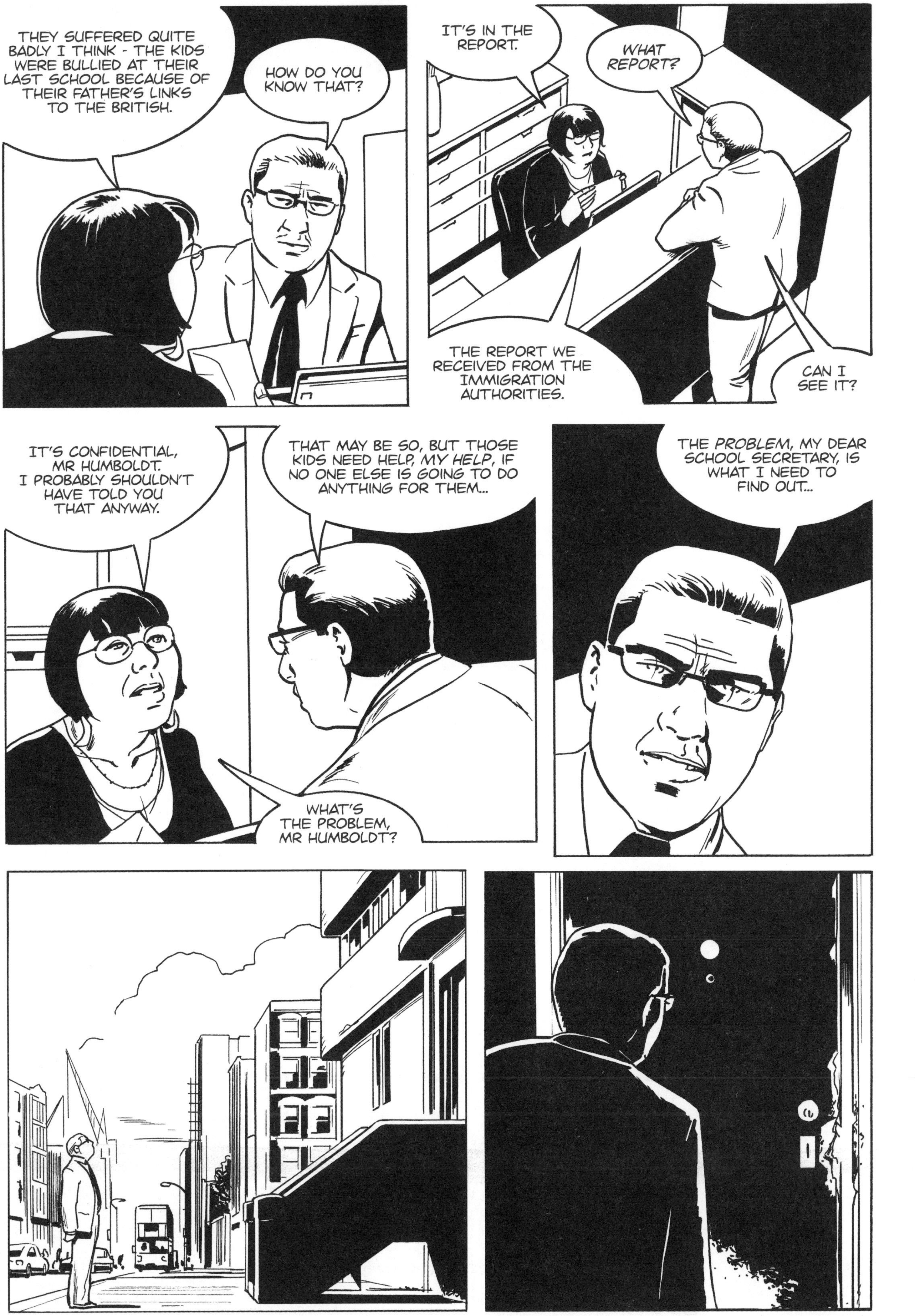
THEY SUFFERED QUITE BADLY I THINK - THE KIDS WERE BULLIED AT THEIR LAST SCHOOL BECAUSE OF THEIR FATHER'S LINKS TO THE BRITISH.
HOW DO YOU KNOW THAT?
IT'S IN THE REPORT.
WHAT REPORT?
THE REPORT WE RECEIVED FROM THE IMMIGRATION AUTHORITIES.
CAN I SEE IT?
IT'S CONFIDENTIAL, MR HUMBOLDT. I PROBABLY SHOULDN'T HAVE TOLD YOU THAT ANYWAY.
THAT MAY BE SO, BUT THOSE KIDS NEED HELP, *MY HELP*, IF NO ONE ELSE IS GOING TO DO ANYTHING FOR THEM...
WHAT'S THE PROBLEM, MR HUMBOLDT?
THE *PROBLEM*, MY DEAR SCHOOL SECRETARY, IS WHAT I NEED TO FIND OUT...

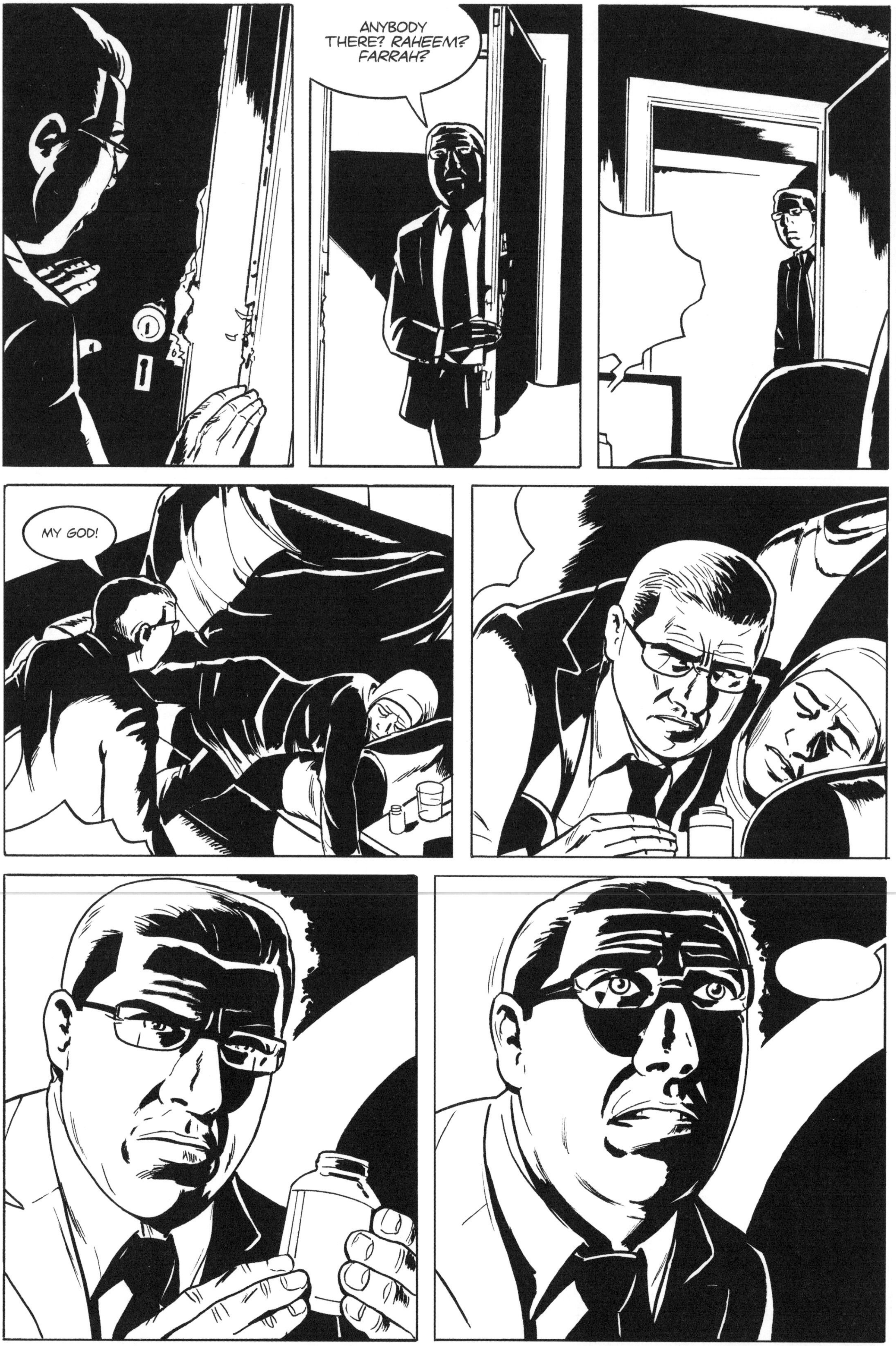
ANYBODY THERE? RAHEEM? FARRAH?
MY GOD!

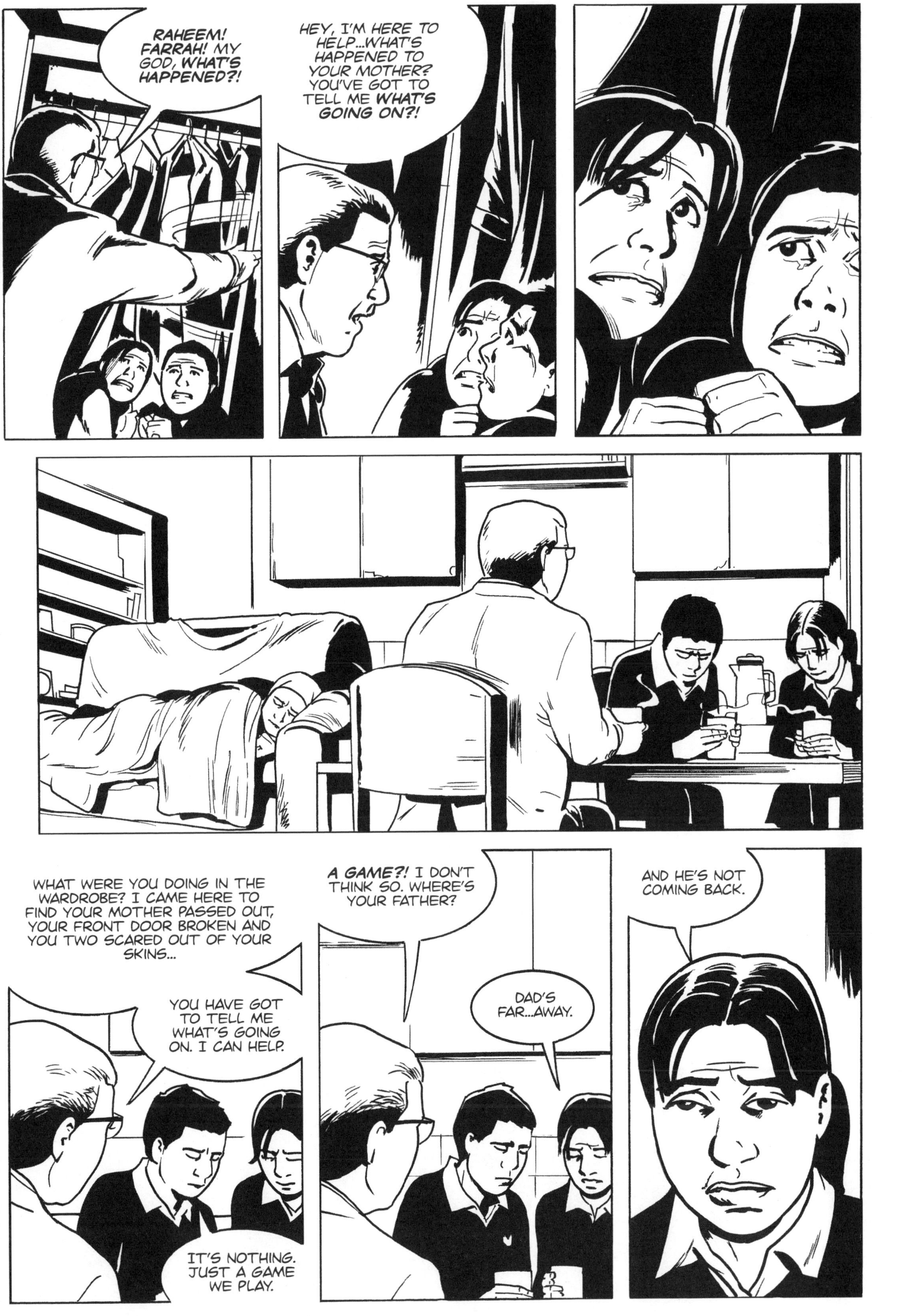
RAHEEM! FARRAH! MY GOD, WHAT'S HAPPENED?!
HEY, I'M HERE TO HELP...WHAT'S HAPPENED TO YOUR MOTHER? YOU'VE GOT TO TELL ME WHAT'S GOING ON?!
WHAT WERE YOU DOING IN THE WARDROBE? I CAME HERE TO FIND YOUR MOTHER PASSED OUT, YOUR FRONT DOOR BROKEN AND YOU TWO SCARED OUT OF YOUR SKINS...
YOU HAVE GOT TO TELL ME WHAT'S GOING ON. I CAN HELP.
IT'S NOTHING. JUST A GAME WE PLAY.
A GAME?! I DON'T THINK SO. WHERE'S YOUR FATHER?
DAD'S FAR...AWAY.
AND HE'S NOT COMING BACK.

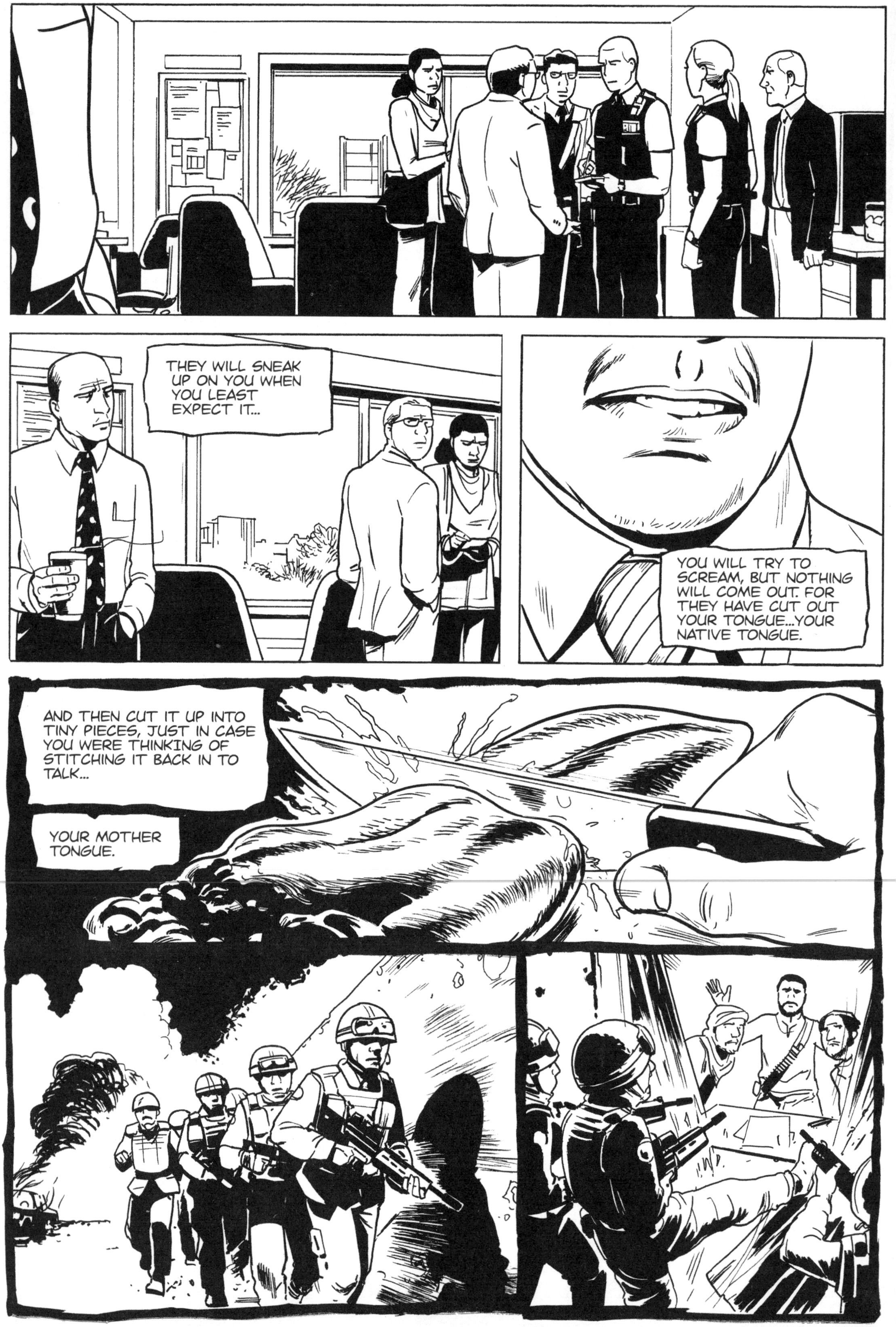
THEY WILL SNEAK UP ON YOU WHEN YOU LEAST EXPECT IT...
YOU WILL TRY TO SCREAM, BUT NOTHING WILL COME OUT. FOR THEY HAVE CUT OUT YOUR TONGUE...YOUR NATIVE TONGUE.
AND THEN CUT IT UP INTO TINY PIECES, JUST IN CASE YOU WERE THINKING OF STITCHING IT BACK IN TO TALK...
YOUR MOTHER TONGUE.

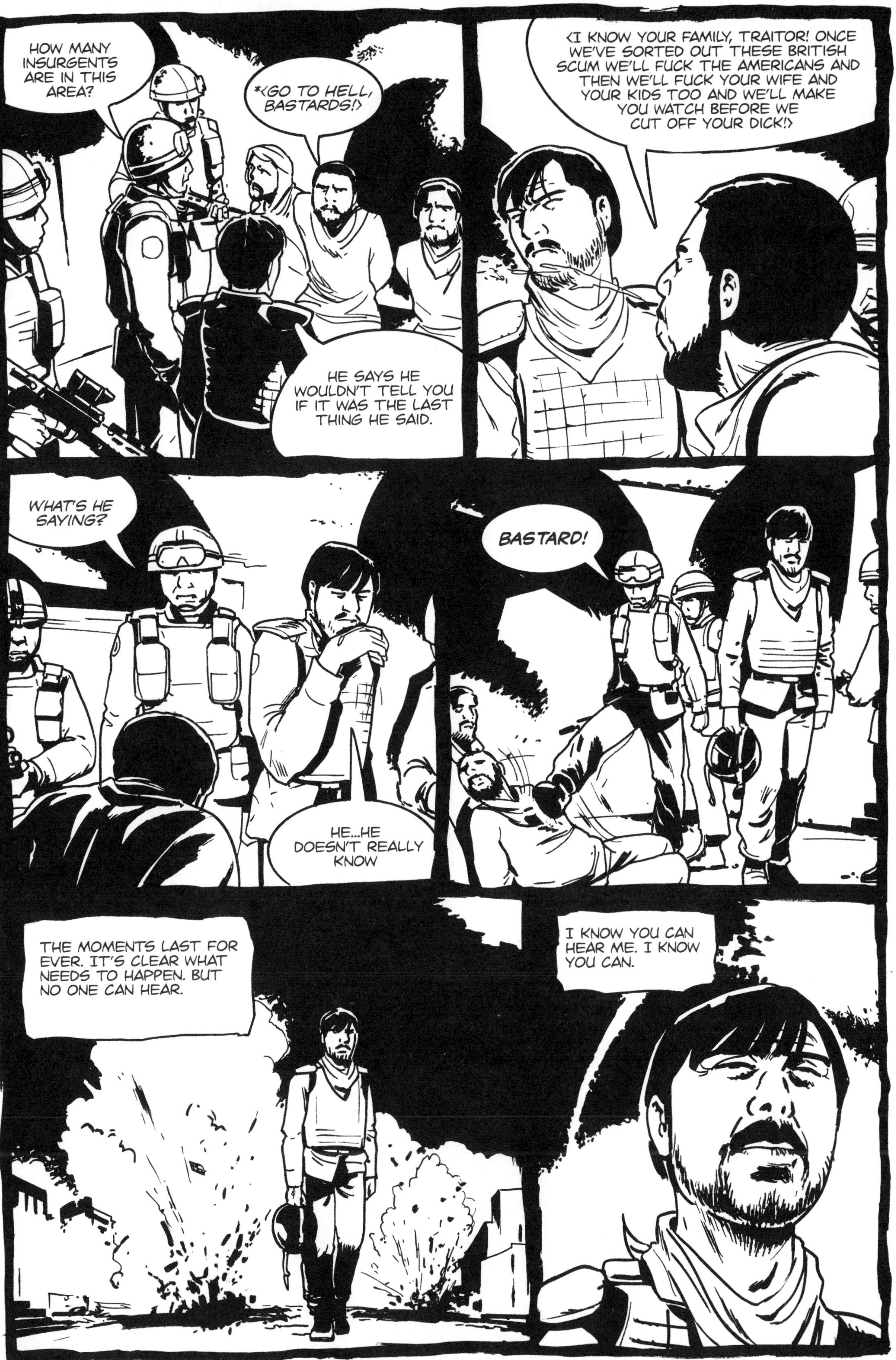
HOW MANY INSURGENTS ARE IN THIS AREA?
*<GO TO HELL, BASTARDS!>
HE SAYS HE WOULDN'T TELL YOU IF IT WAS THE LAST THING HE SAID.
<I KNOW YOUR FAMILY, TRAITOR! ONCE WE'VE SORTED OUT THESE BRITISH SCUM WE'LL FUCK THE AMERICANS AND THEN WE'LL FUCK YOUR WIFE AND YOUR KIDS TOO AND WE'LL MAKE YOU WATCH BEFORE WE CUT OFF YOUR DICK!>
WHAT'S HE SAYING?
HE...HE DOESN'T REALLY KNOW
BASTARD!
THE MOMENTS LAST FOR EVER. IT'S CLEAR WHAT NEEDS TO HAPPEN. BUT NO ONE CAN HEAR.
I KNOW YOU CAN HEAR ME. I KNOW YOU CAN.

* ARABIC

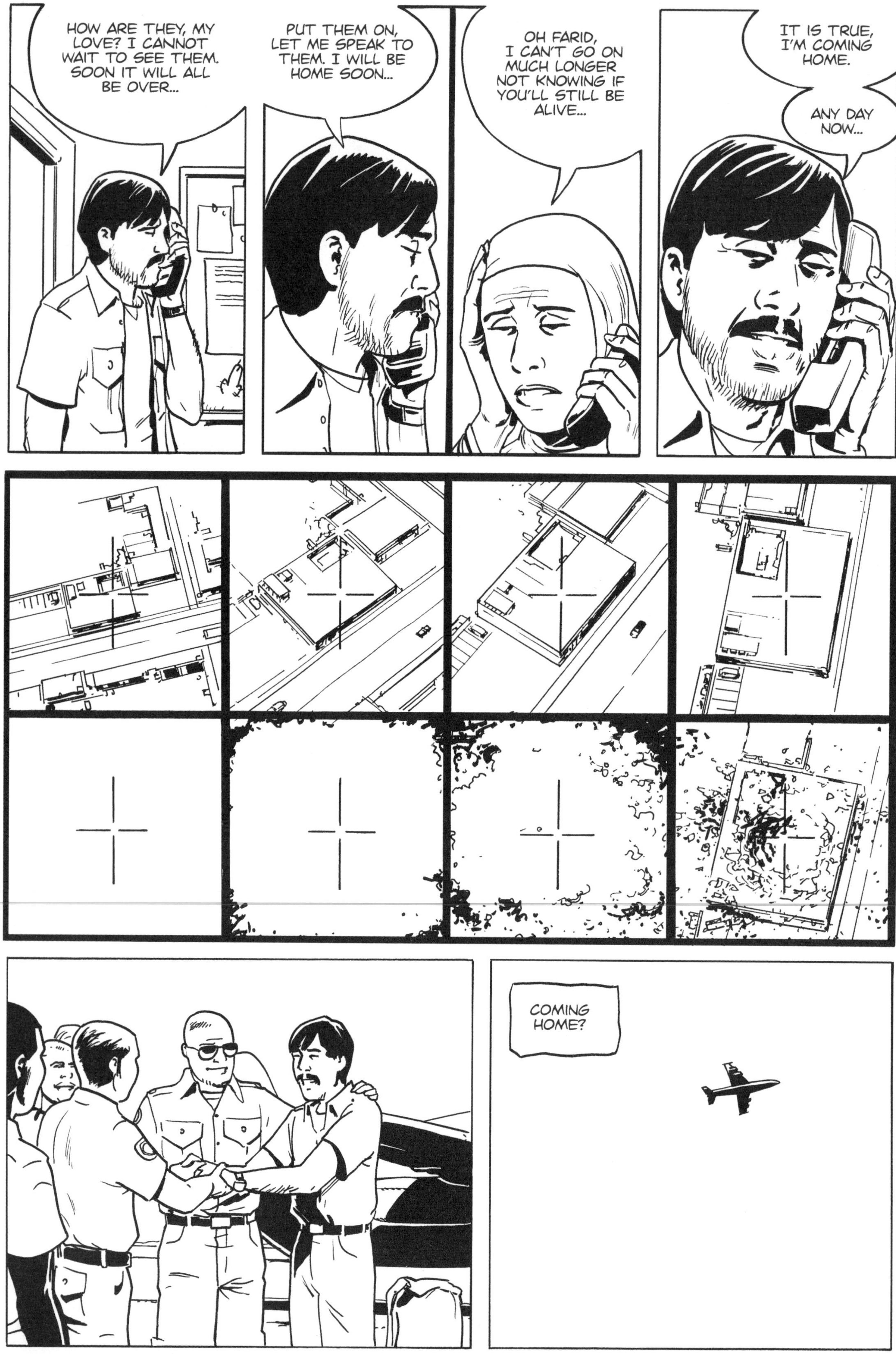
HOW ARE THEY, MY LOVE? I CANNOT WAIT TO SEE THEM. SOON IT WILL ALL BE OVER...
PUT THEM ON, LET ME SPEAK TO THEM. I WILL BE HOME SOON...
OH FARID, I CAN'T GO ON MUCH LONGER NOT KNOWING IF YOU'LL STILL BE ALIVE...
IT IS TRUE, I'M COMING HOME.
ANY DAY NOW...
COMING HOME?

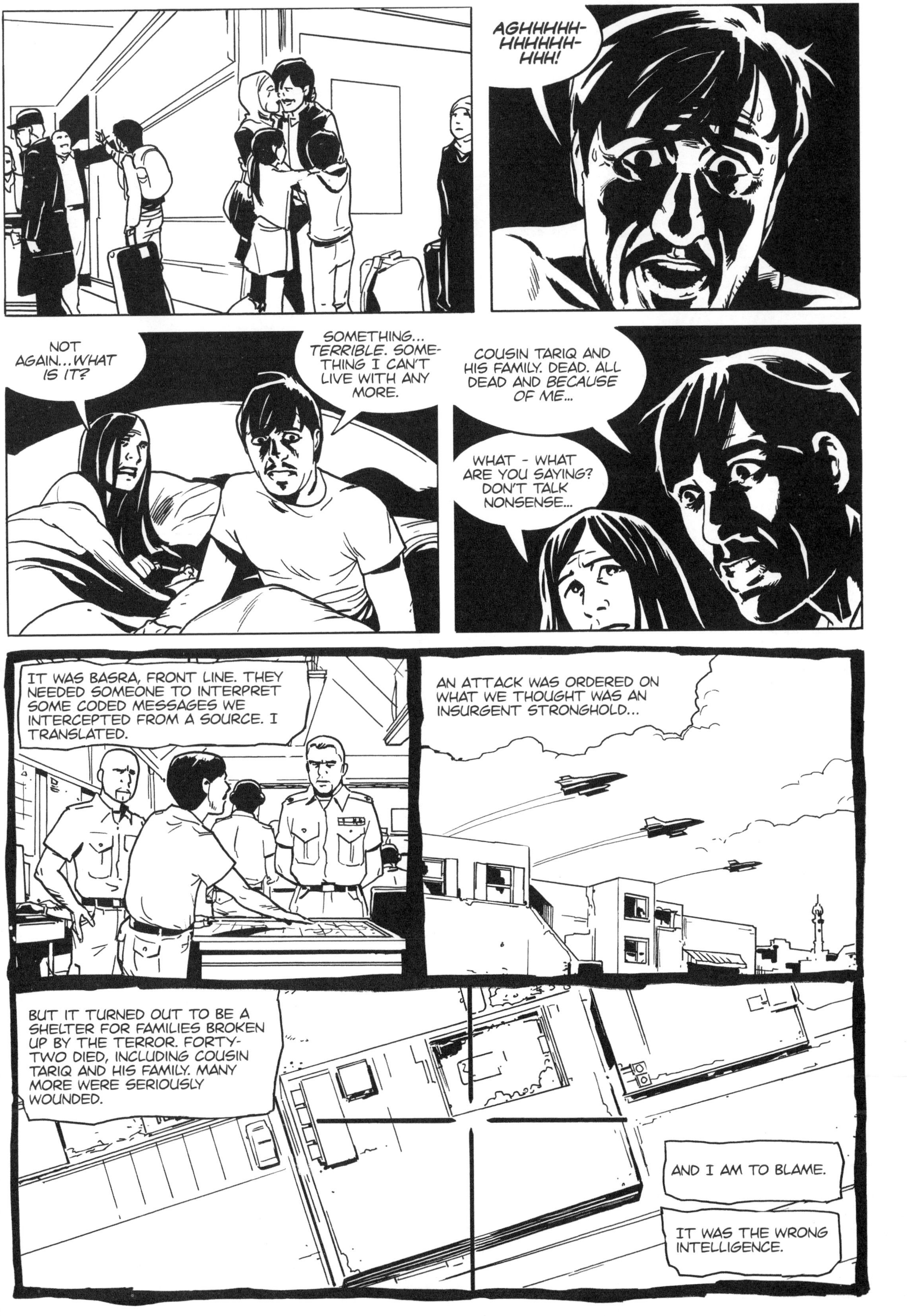
AGHHHHH-HHHHHH-HHH!
NOT AGAIN...WHAT IS IT?
SOMETHING... TERRIBLE. SOMETHING I CAN'T LIVE WITH ANY MORE.
COUSIN TARIQ AND HIS FAMILY. DEAD. ALL DEAD AND *BECAUSE* OF ME...
WHAT - WHAT ARE YOU SAYING? DON'T TALK NONSENSE...
IT WAS BASRA, FRONT LINE. THEY NEEDED SOMEONE TO INTERPRET SOME CODED MESSAGES WE INTERCEPTED FROM A SOURCE. I TRANSLATED.
AN ATTACK WAS ORDERED ON WHAT WE THOUGHT WAS AN INSURGENT STRONGHOLD...
BUT IT TURNED OUT TO BE A SHELTER FOR FAMILIES BROKEN UP BY THE TERROR. FORTY-TWO DIED, INCLUDING COUSIN TARIQ AND HIS FAMILY. MANY MORE WERE SERIOUSLY WOUNDED.
AND I AM TO BLAME.
IT WAS THE WRONG INTELLIGENCE.

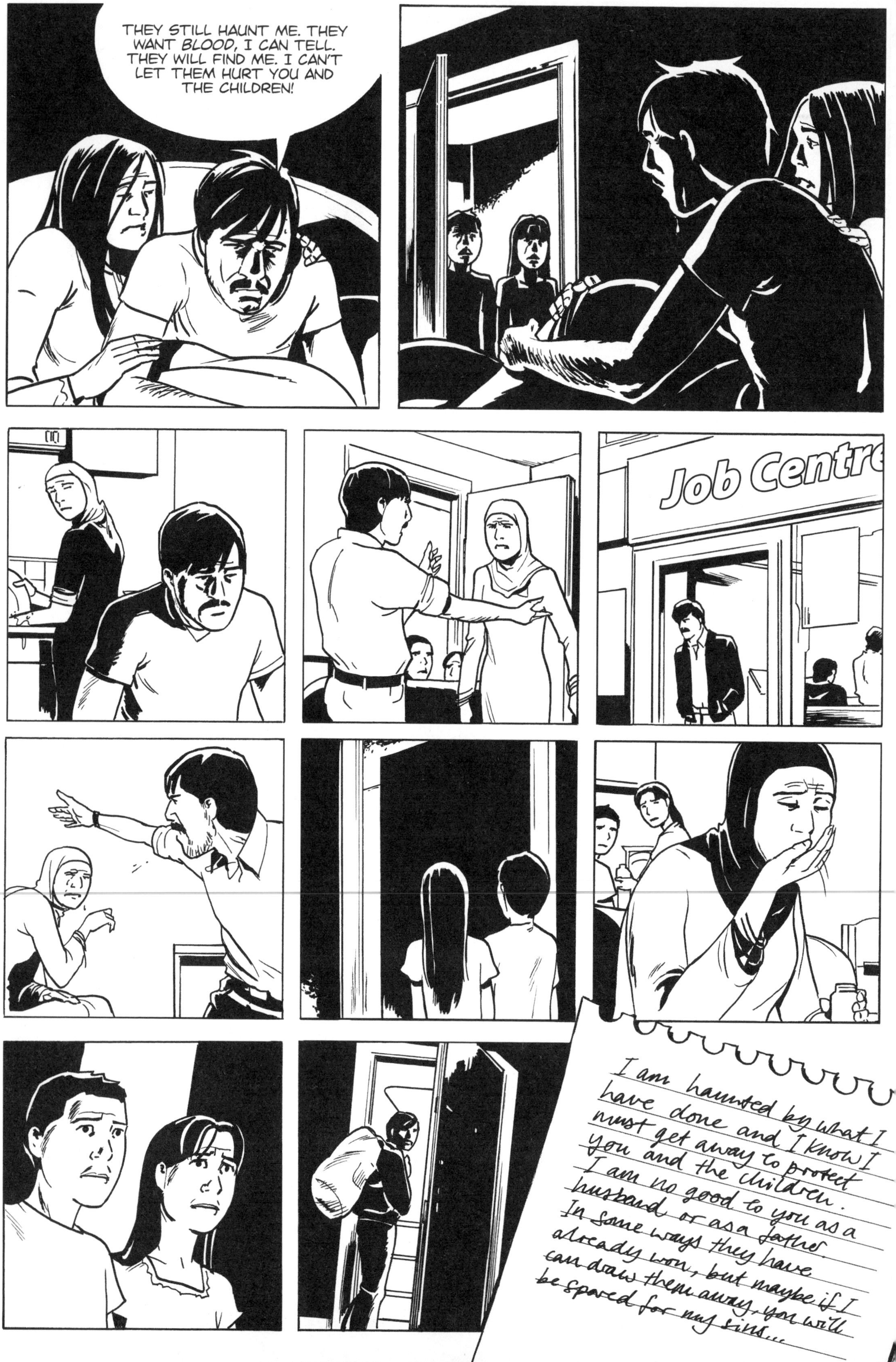
THEY STILL HAUNT ME. THEY WANT BLOOD, I CAN TELL. THEY WILL FIND ME. I CAN'T LET THEM HURT YOU AND THE CHILDREN!
Job Centre
I am haunted by what I have done and I know I must get away to protect you and the children. I am no good to you as a husband or as a father. In some ways they have already won, but maybe if I can draw them away, you will be spared for my sins...

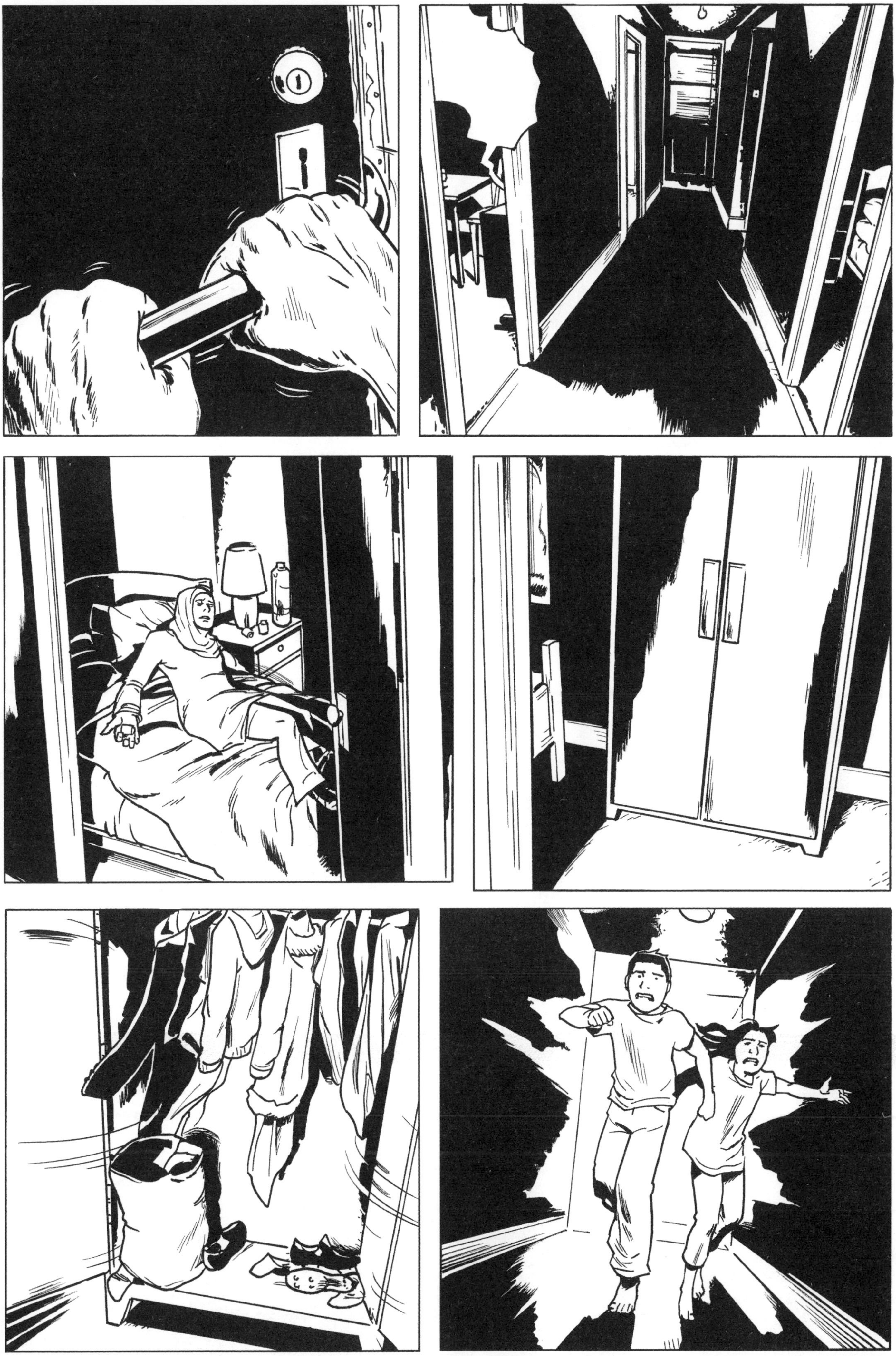

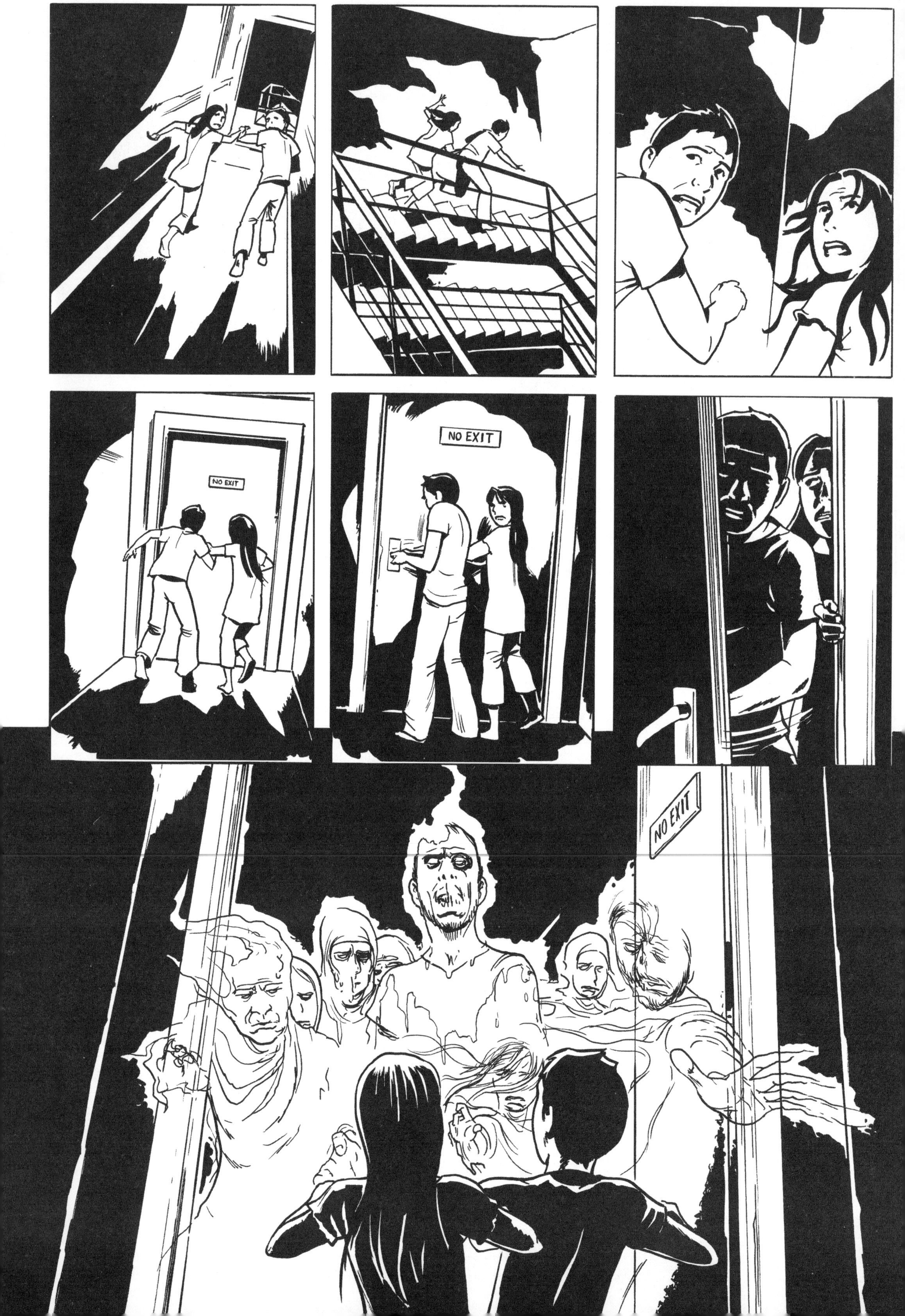
NO EXIT
NO EXIT
NO EXIT

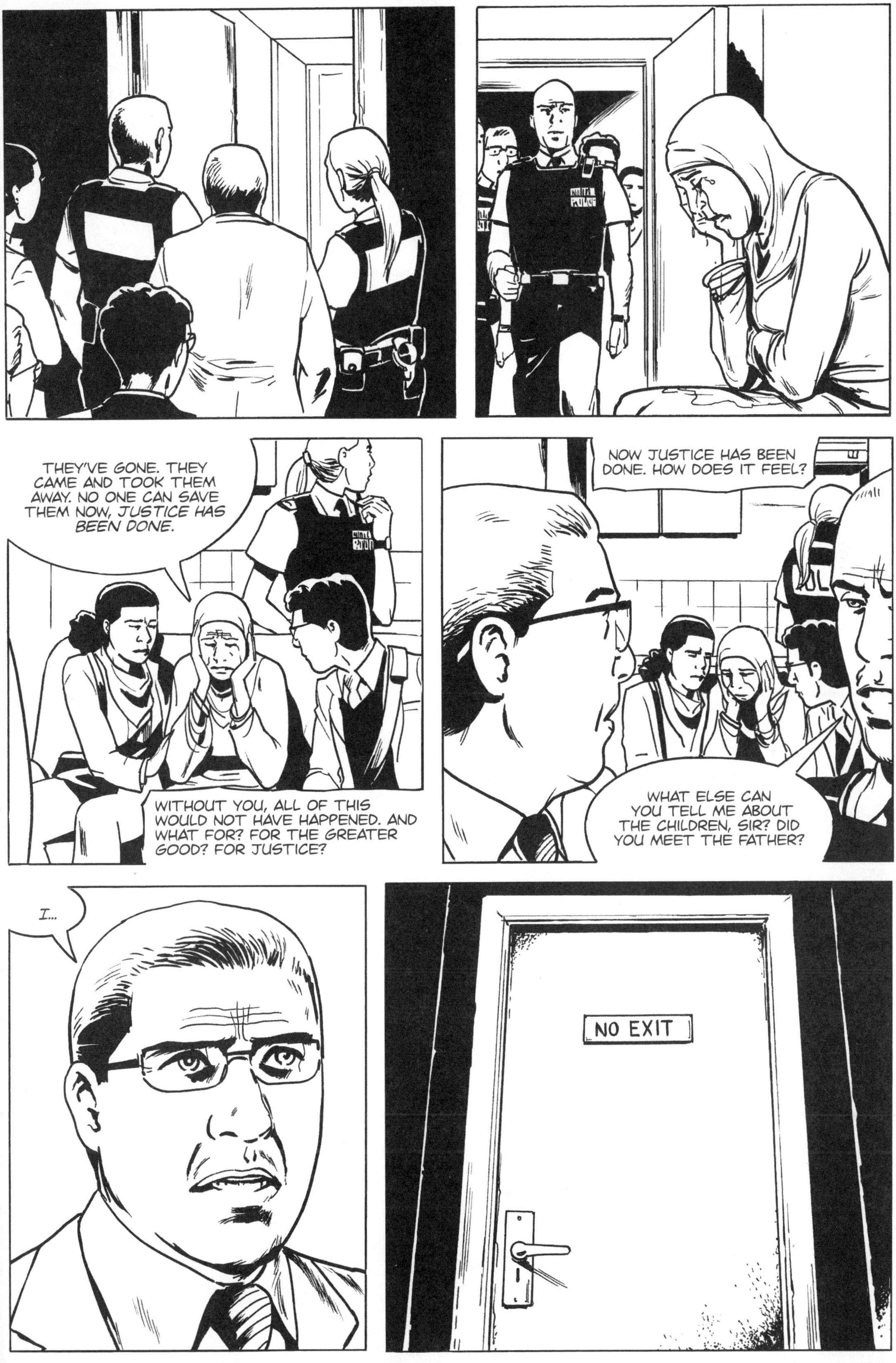
THEY'VE GONE. THEY CAME AND TOOK THEM AWAY. NO ONE CAN SAVE THEM NOW, JUSTICE HAS BEEN DONE.
WITHOUT YOU, ALL OF THIS WOULD NOT HAVE HAPPENED. AND WHAT FOR? FOR THE GREATER GOOD? FOR JUSTICE?
NOW JUSTICE HAS BEEN DONE. HOW DOES IT FEEL?
WHAT ELSE CAN YOU TELL ME ABOUT THE CHILDREN, SIR? DID YOU MEET THE FATHER?
I...
NO EXIT

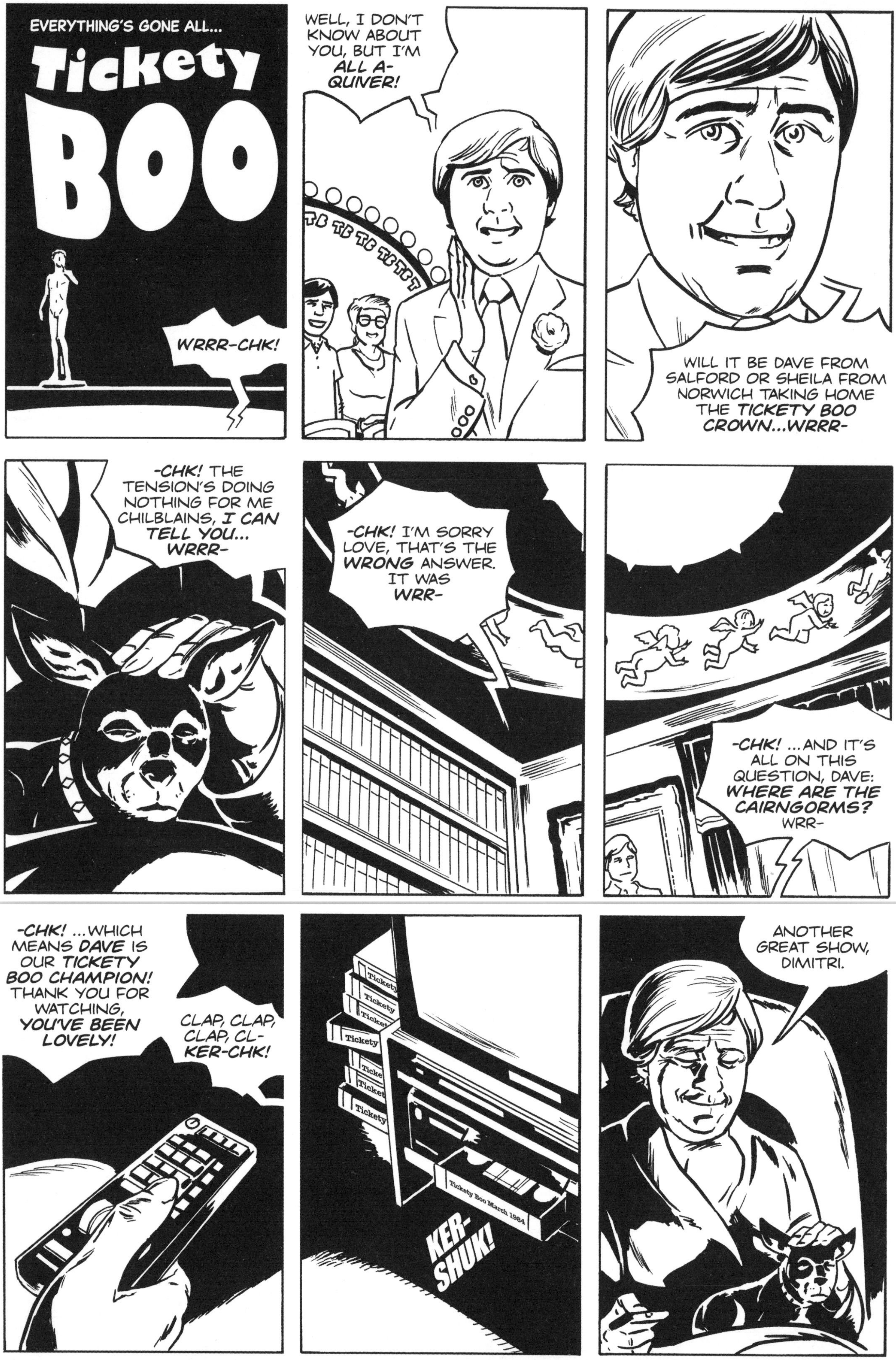
EVERYTHING'S GONE ALL...
Tickety BOO
WRRR-CHK!
WELL, I DON'T KNOW ABOUT YOU, BUT I'M ALL A-QUIVER!
WILL IT BE DAVE FROM SALFORD OR SHEILA FROM NORWICH TAKING HOME THE TICKETY BOO CROWN...WRRR-
-CHK! THE TENSION'S DOING NOTHING FOR ME CHILBLAINS, I CAN TELL YOU... WRRR-
-CHK! I'M SORRY LOVE, THAT'S THE WRONG ANSWER. IT WAS WRR-
-CHK! ...AND IT'S ALL ON THIS QUESTION, DAVE: WHERE ARE THE CAIRNGORMS? WRR-
-CHK! ...WHICH MEANS DAVE IS OUR TICKETY BOO CHAMPION! THANK YOU FOR WATCHING, YOU'VE BEEN LOVELY!
CLAP, CLAP, CLAP, CL-KER-CHK!
Tickety
Tickety
Tickety
Tickety
Tickety
Tickety
Tickety
Tickety Boo March 1984
KER-SHUK!
ANOTHER GREAT SHOW, DIMITRI.

THE SHIPPING FORECAST

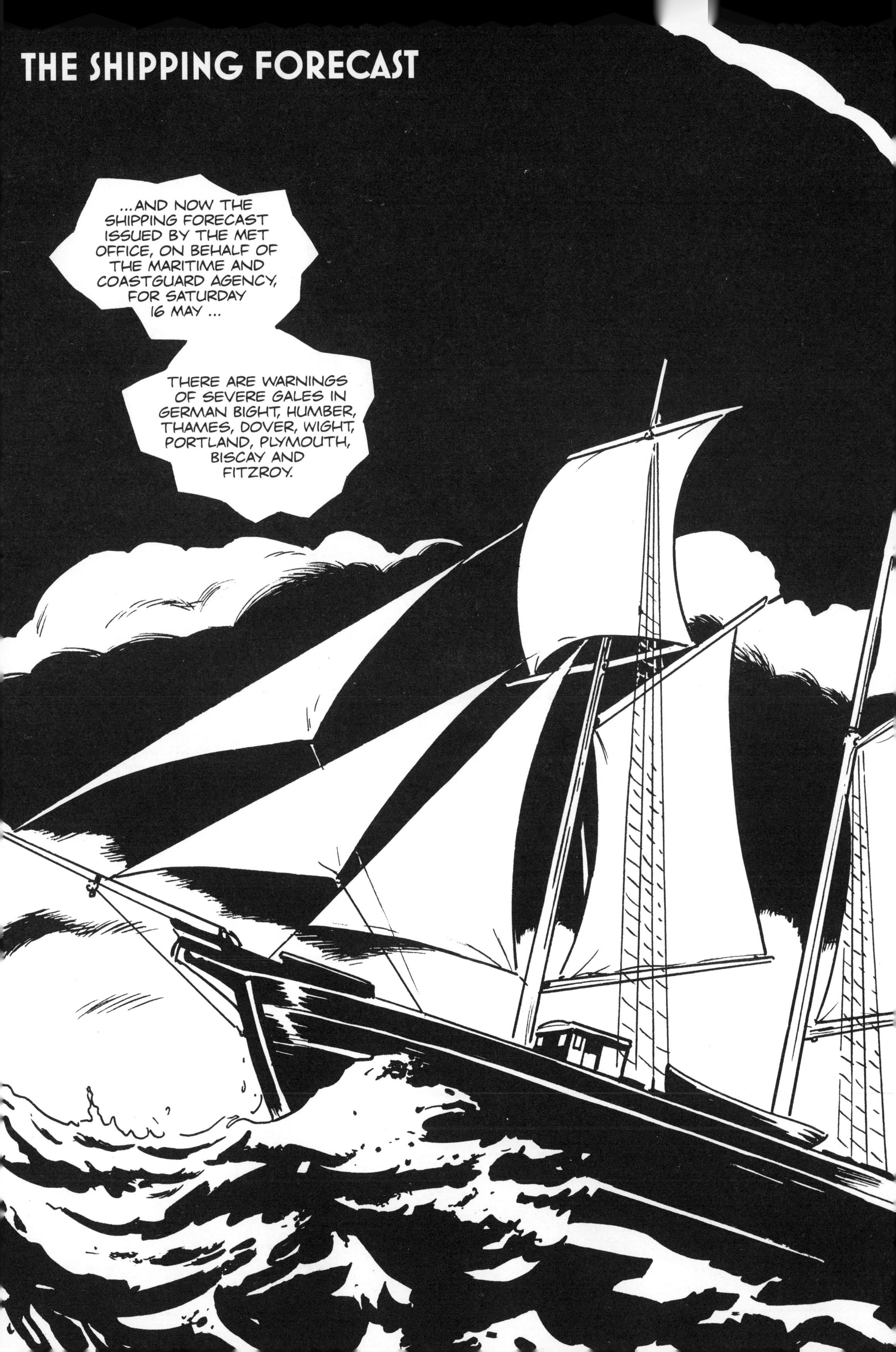
...AND NOW THE SHIPPING FORECAST ISSUED BY THE MET OFFICE, ON BEHALF OF THE MARITIME AND COASTGUARD AGENCY, FOR SATURDAY 16 MAY ...
THERE ARE WARNINGS OF SEVERE GALES IN GERMAN BIGHT, HUMBER, THAMES, DOVER, WIGHT, PORTLAND, PLYMOUTH, BISCAY AND FITZROY.

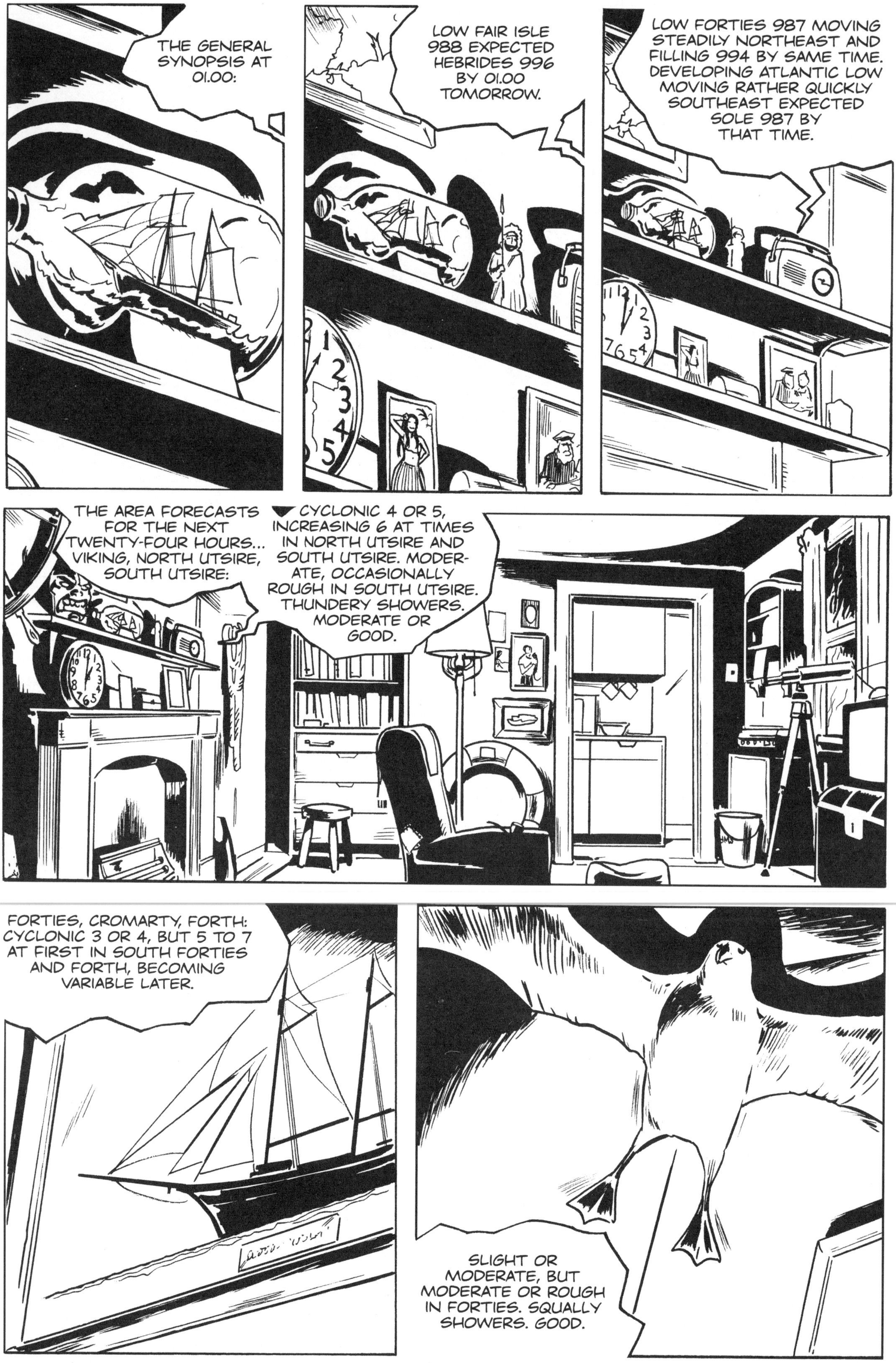
THE GENERAL SYNOPSIS AT 01.00:
LOW FAIR ISLE 988 EXPECTED HEBRIDES 996 BY 01.00 TOMORROW.
LOW FORTIES 987 MOVING STEADILY NORTHEAST AND FILLING 994 BY SAME TIME. DEVELOPING ATLANTIC LOW MOVING RATHER QUICKLY SOUTHEAST EXPECTED SOLE 987 BY THAT TIME.
THE AREA FORECASTS FOR THE NEXT TWENTY-FOUR HOURS... VIKING, NORTH UTSIRE, SOUTH UTSIRE:
CYCLONIC 4 OR 5, INCREASING 6 AT TIMES IN NORTH UTSIRE AND SOUTH UTSIRE. MODERATE, OCCASIONALLY ROUGH IN SOUTH UTSIRE. THUNDERY SHOWERS. MODERATE OR GOOD.
FORTIES, CROMARTY, FORTH: CYCLONIC 3 OR 4, BUT 5 TO 7 AT FIRST IN SOUTH FORTIES AND FORTH, BECOMING VARIABLE LATER.
SLIGHT OR MODERATE, BUT MODERATE OR ROUGH IN FORTIES. SQUALLY SHOWERS. GOOD.

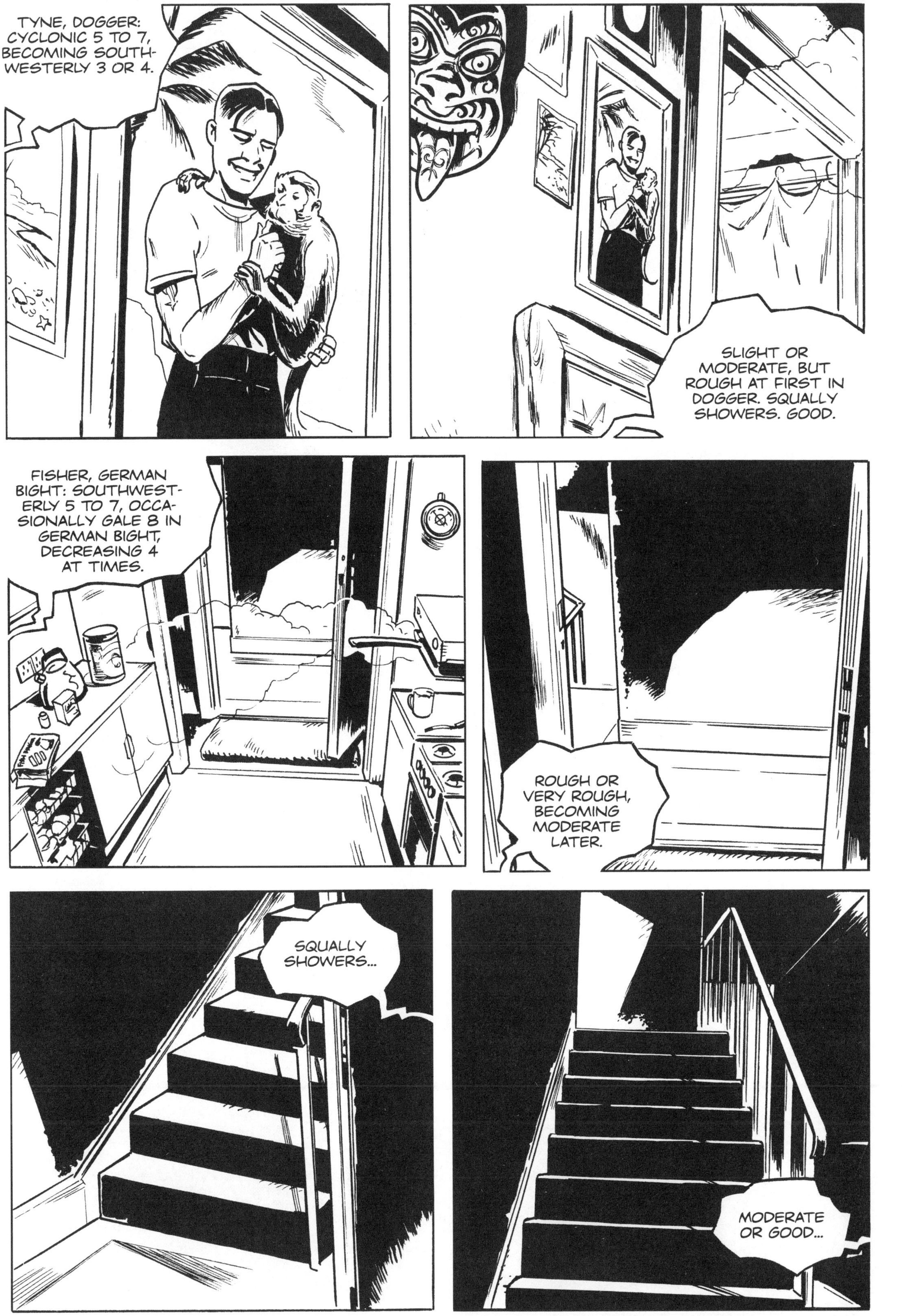
TYNE, DOGGER: CYCLONIC 5 TO 7, BECOMING SOUTH-WESTERLY 3 OR 4.
SLIGHT OR MODERATE, BUT ROUGH AT FIRST IN DOGGER. SQUALLY SHOWERS. GOOD.
FISHER, GERMAN BIGHT: SOUTHWEST-ERLY 5 TO 7, OCCA-SIONALLY GALE 8 IN GERMAN BIGHT, DECREASING 4 AT TIMES.
ROUGH OR VERY ROUGH, BECOMING MODERATE LATER.
SQUALLY SHOWERS...
MODERATE OR GOOD...

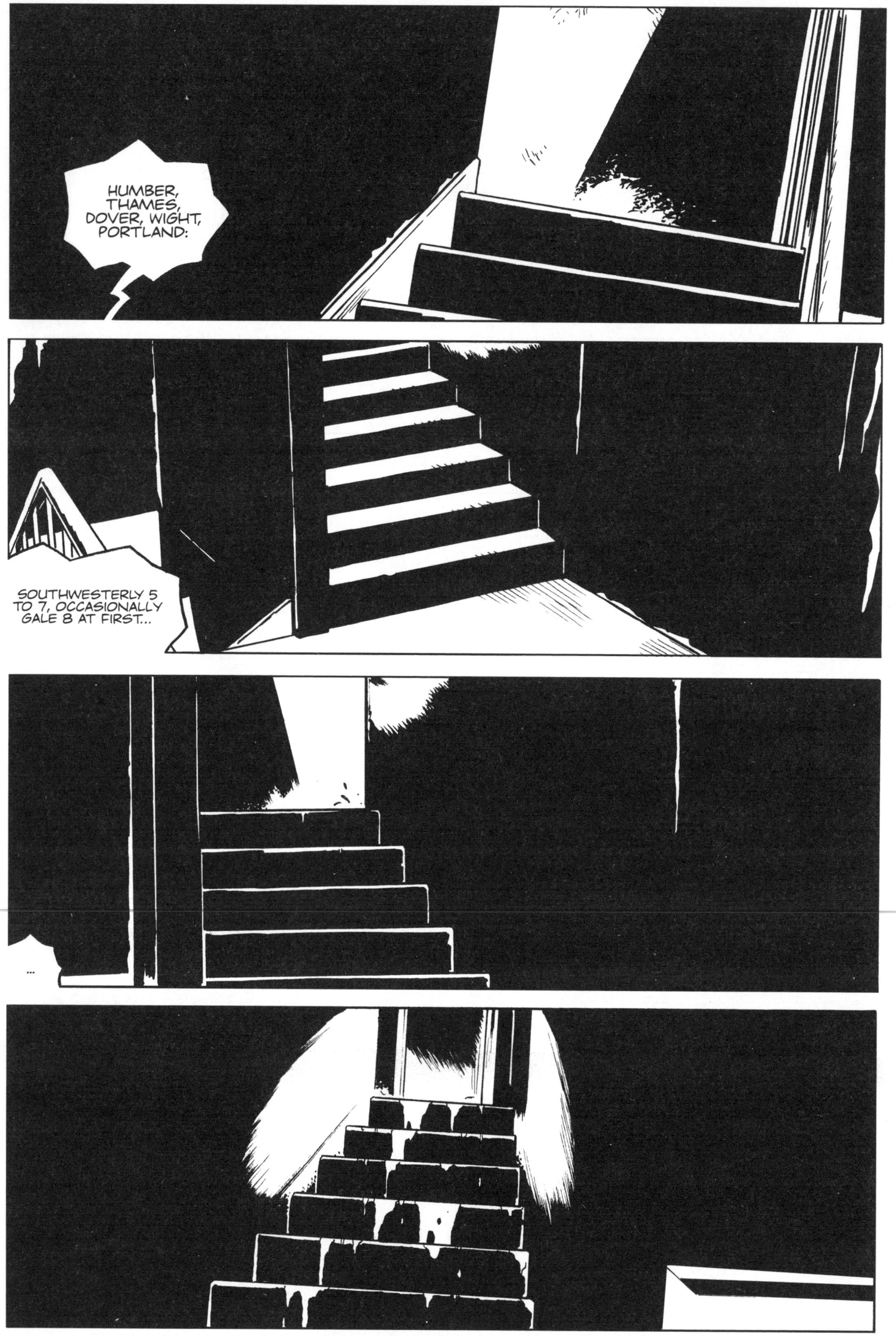
HUMBER, THAMES, DOVER, WIGHT, PORTLAND:
SOUTHWESTERLY 5 TO 7, OCCASIONALLY GALE 8 AT FIRST...
...

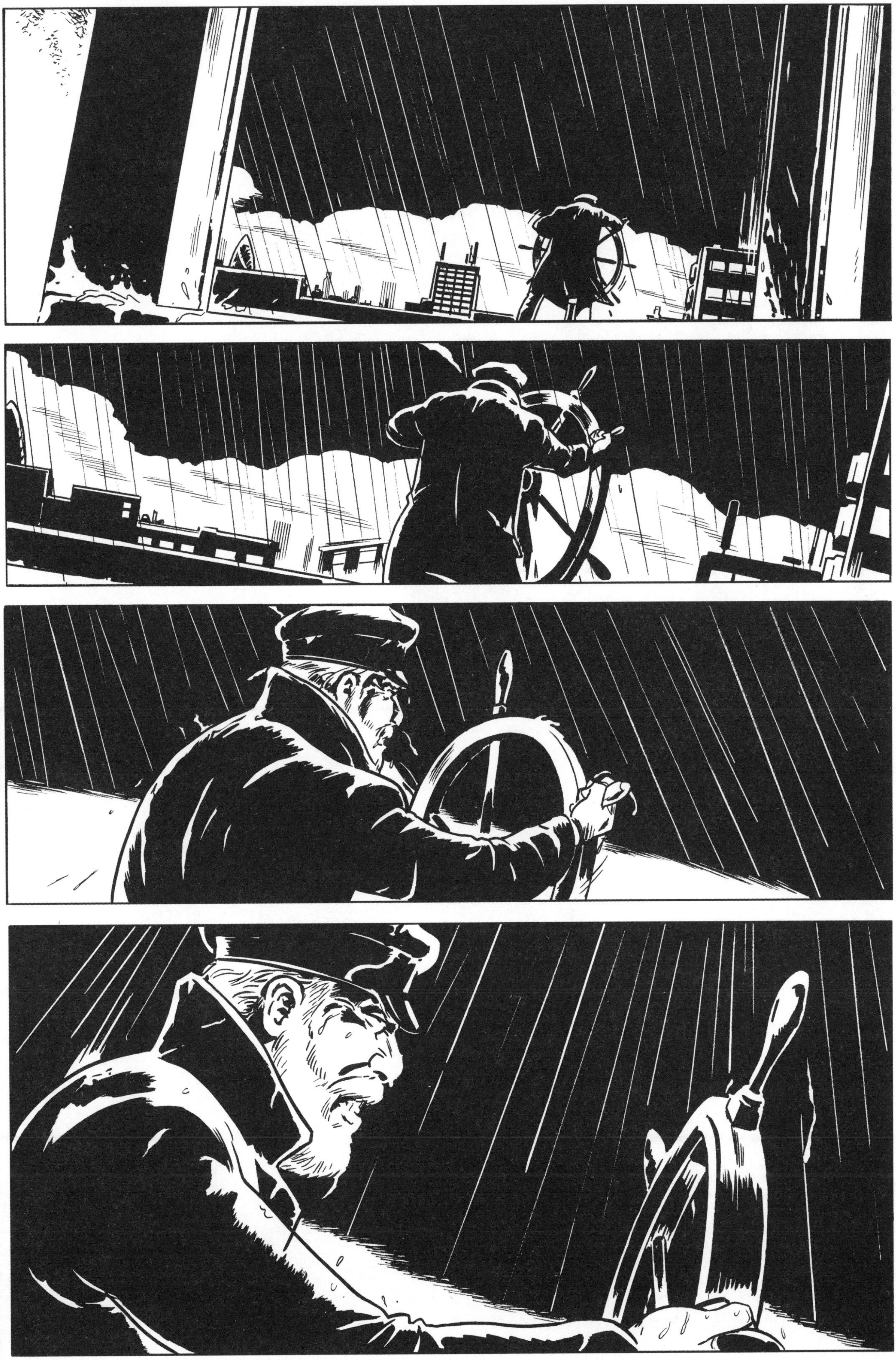

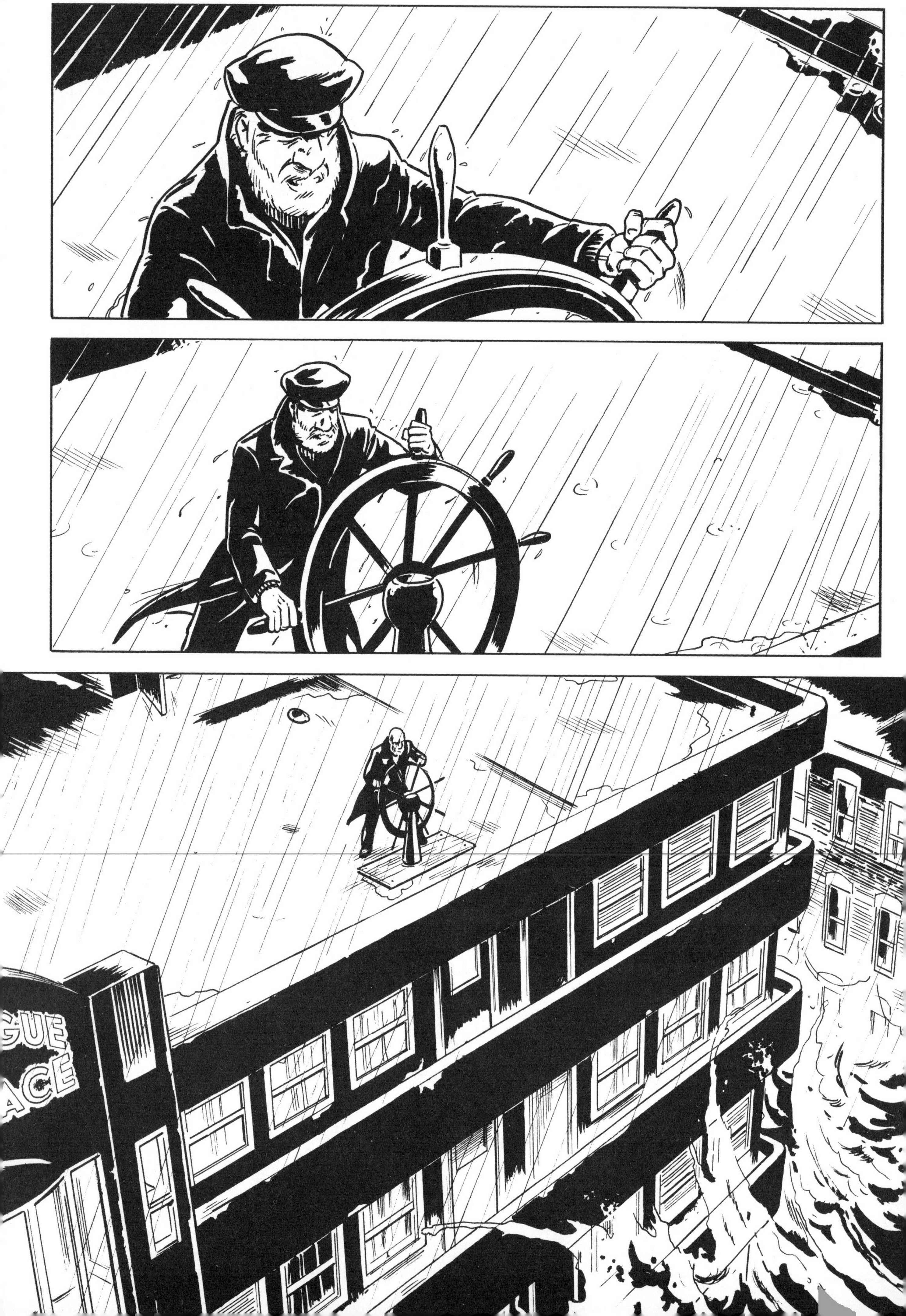
GUE
ACE

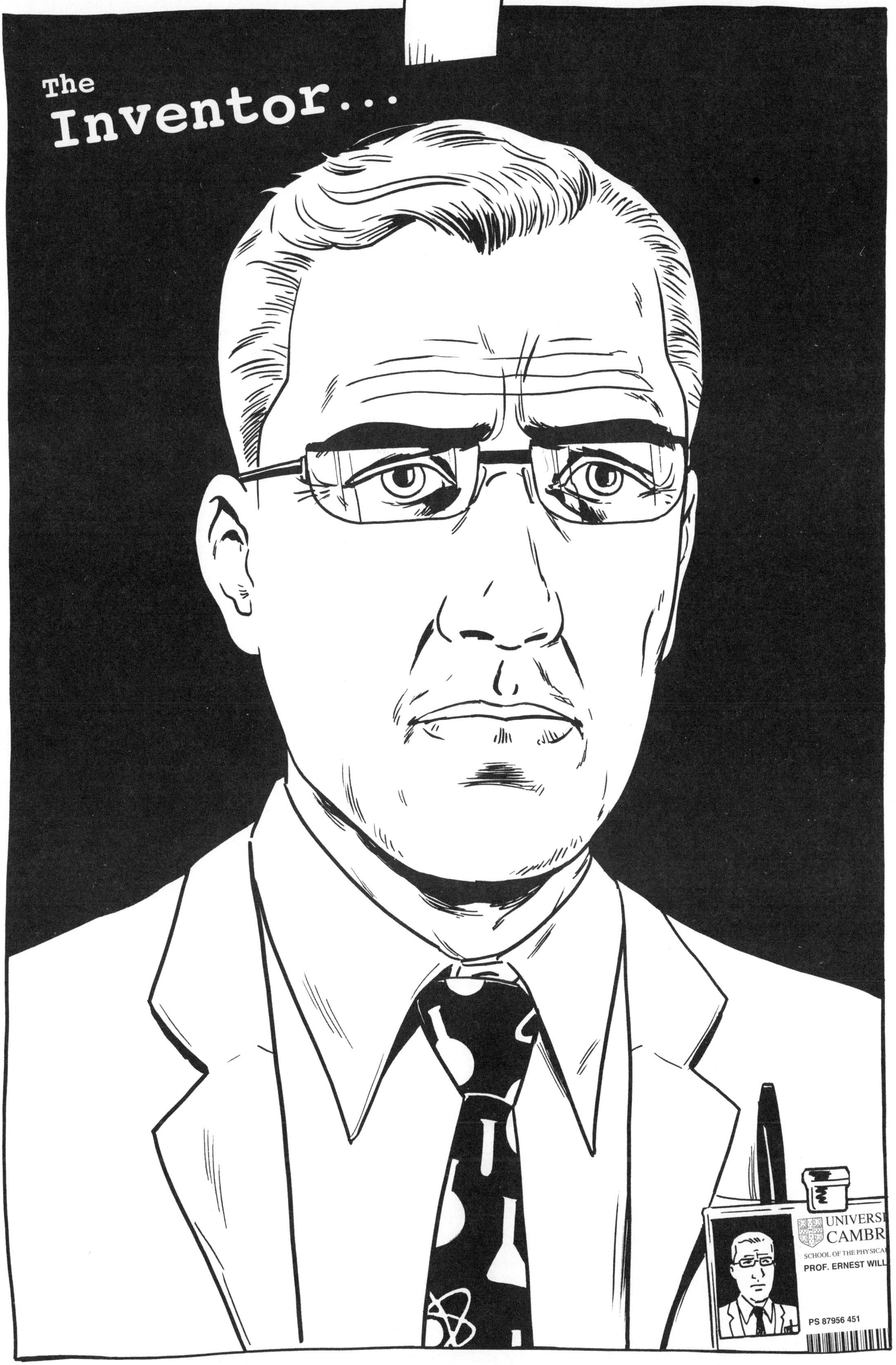
The Inventor...
UNIVERSI
CAMBR
SCHOOL OF THE PHYSICA
PROF. ERNEST WILL
PS 87956 451

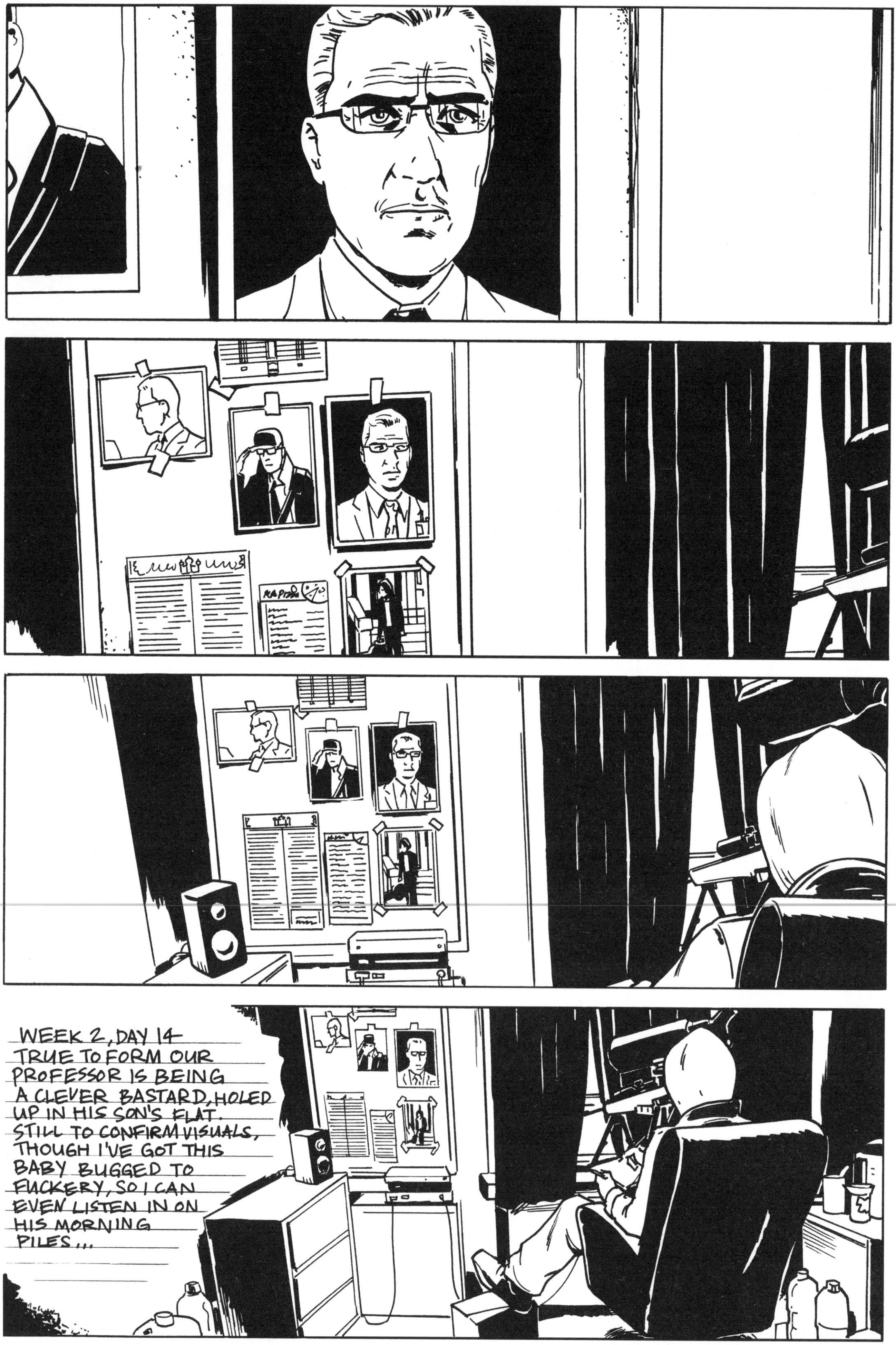
WEEK 2, DAY 14
TRUE TO FORM OUR PROFESSOR IS BEING A CLEVER BASTARD, HOLED UP IN HIS SON'S FLAT. STILL TO CONFIRM VISUALS, THOUGH I'VE GOT THIS BABY BUGGED TO FUCKERY, SO I CAN EVEN LISTEN IN ON HIS MORNING PILES...

THINK I'M IN FOR THE LONG HAUL ON THIS ONE ...

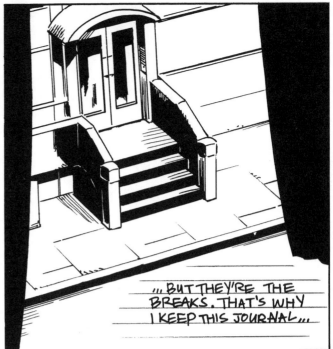

... BUT THEY'RE THE BREAKS. THAT'S WHY I KEEP THIS JOURNAL ...

MY OWN IMAGINARY SCREENPLAY TO KEEP ME SANE FROM THE UTTER TEDIUM ...

A PERSONAL INDULGENCE, BURNT AFTER EACH MISSION TO COVER MY TRACKS.

SLURP!

COME ON YOU TOSSER... LET'S BE HAVING YOU!

AS PER, WITH ALL STAKEOUTS, IT'S DREARILY BORING.

THERE'S THE DANGER OF GETTING ENTRANCED BY THE EVERY-DAY HUM-DRUM.

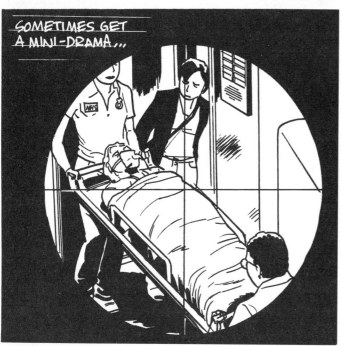

SOMETIMES GET A MINI-DRAMA...

...OR A FEW ECCENTRICS...

BUT YOU'D THINK IN SUCH A LARGE BUILDING, THERE'D BE SOME-THING INTERESTING GOING ON...

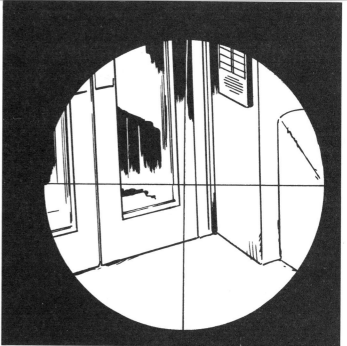

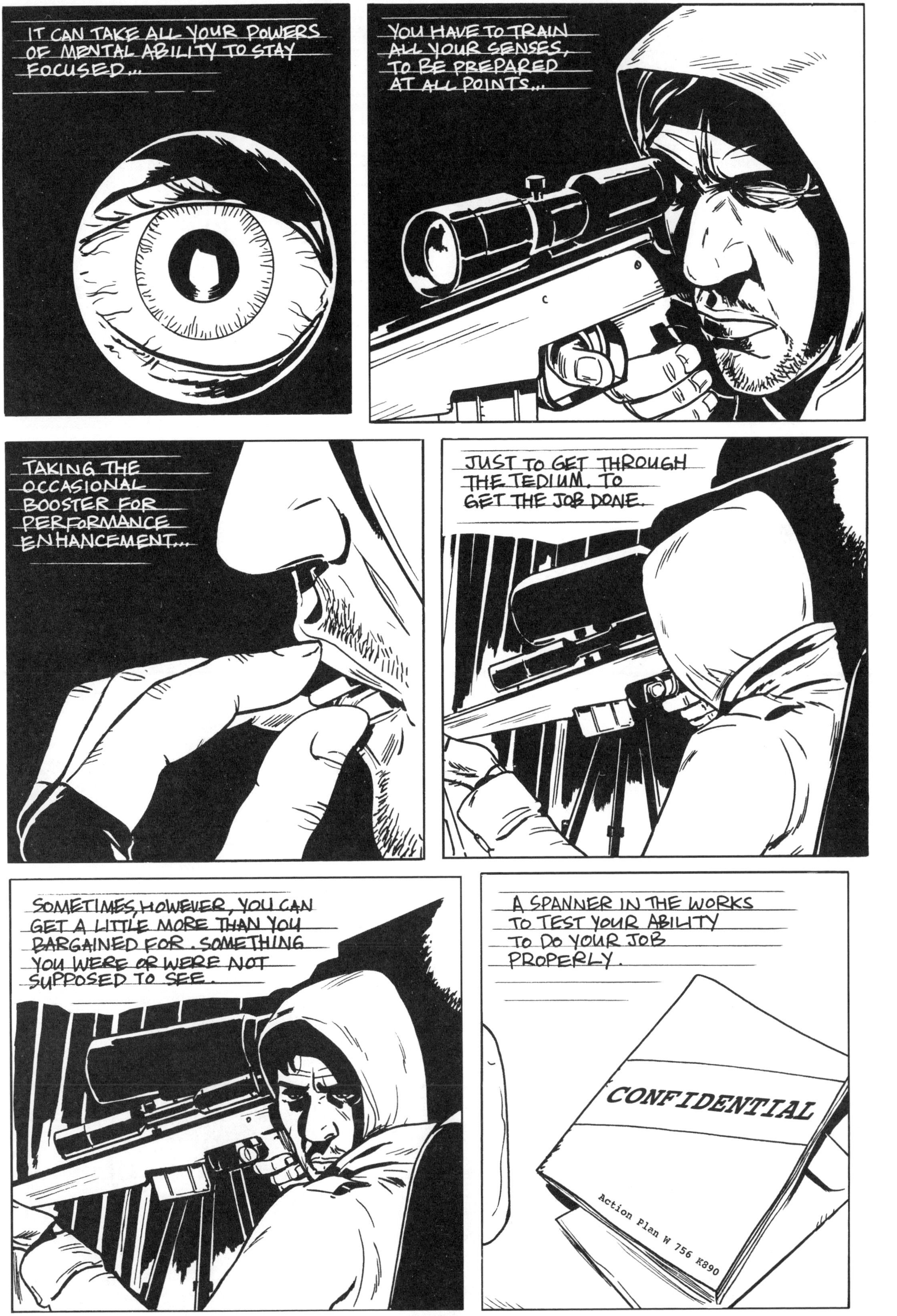

IT CAN TAKE ALL YOUR POWERS OF MENTAL ABILITY TO STAY FOCUSED...
YOU HAVE TO TRAIN ALL YOUR SENSES, TO BE PREPARED AT ALL POINTS...
TAKING THE OCCASIONAL BOOSTER FOR PERFORMANCE ENHANCEMENT...
JUST TO GET THROUGH THE TEDIUM. TO GET THE JOB DONE.
SOMETIMES, HOWEVER, YOU CAN GET A LITTLE MORE THAN YOU BARGAINED FOR. SOMETHING YOU WERE OR WERE NOT SUPPOSED TO SEE.
A SPANNER IN THE WORKS TO TEST YOUR ABILITY TO DO YOUR JOB PROPERLY.
CONFIDENTIAL
Action Plan W 756 K890

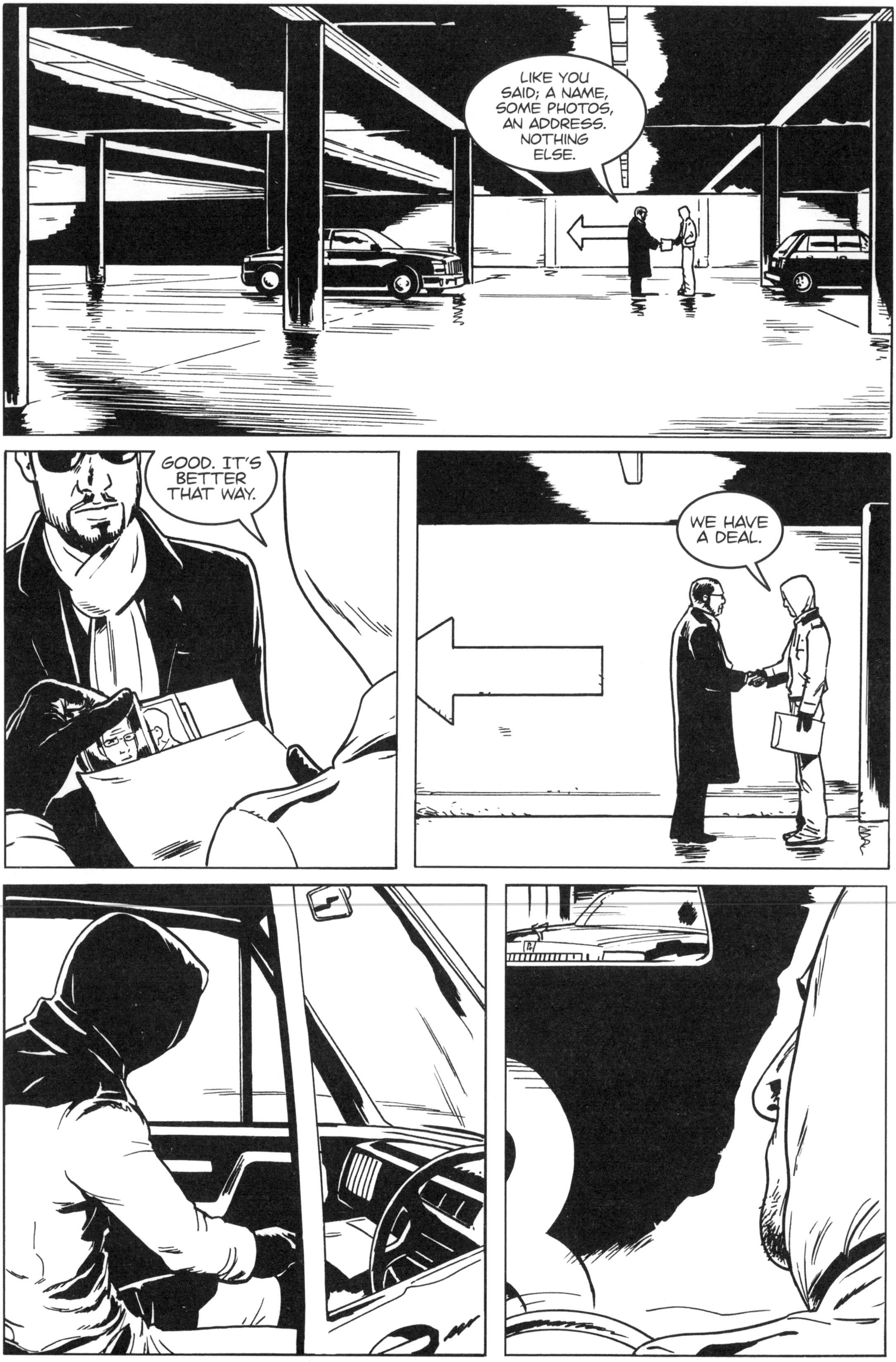
LIKE YOU SAID; A NAME, SOME PHOTOS, AN ADDRESS. NOTHING ELSE.
GOOD. IT'S BETTER THAT WAY.
WE HAVE A DEAL.

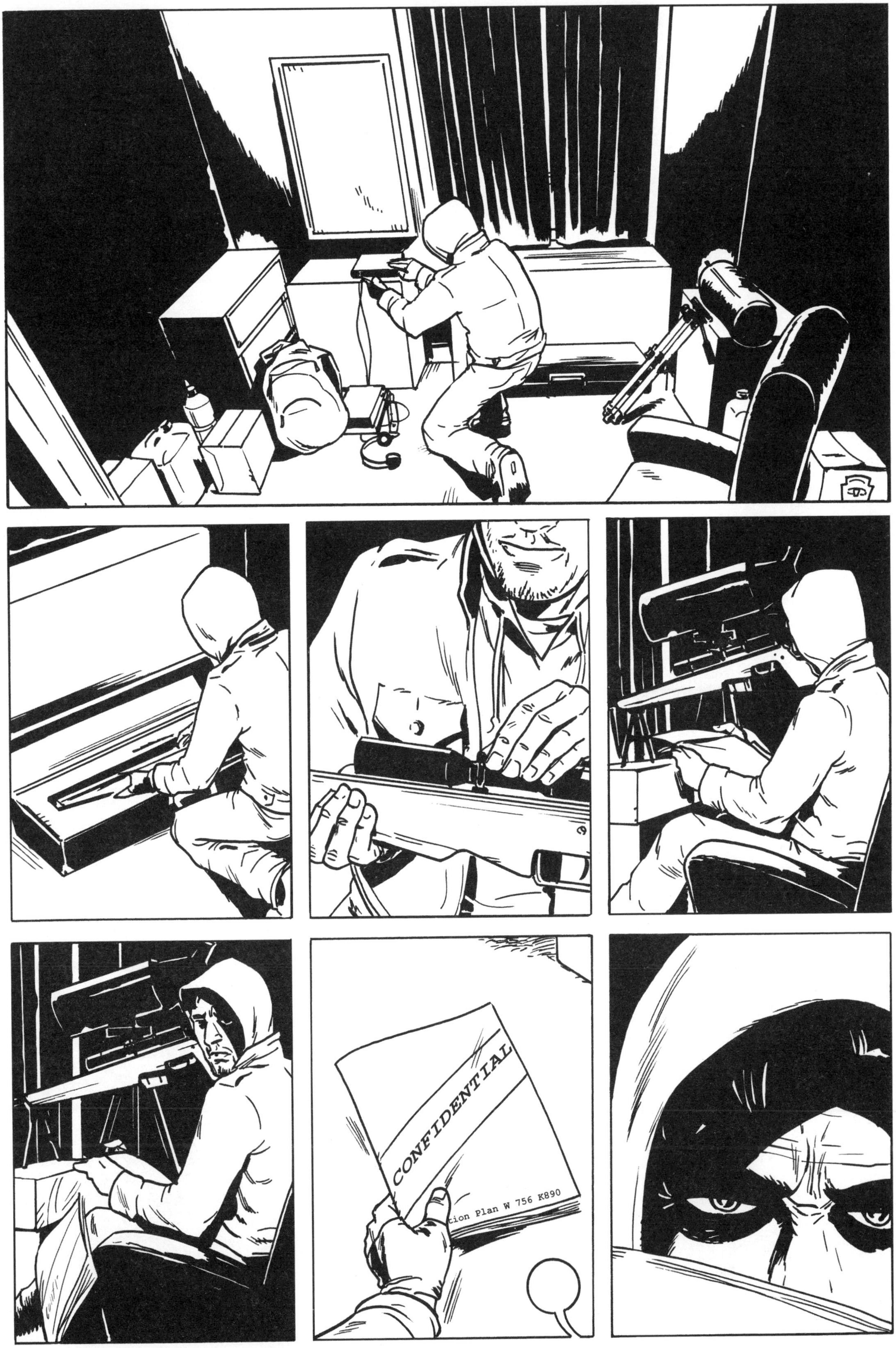
CONFIDENTIAL
tion Plan W 756 K890

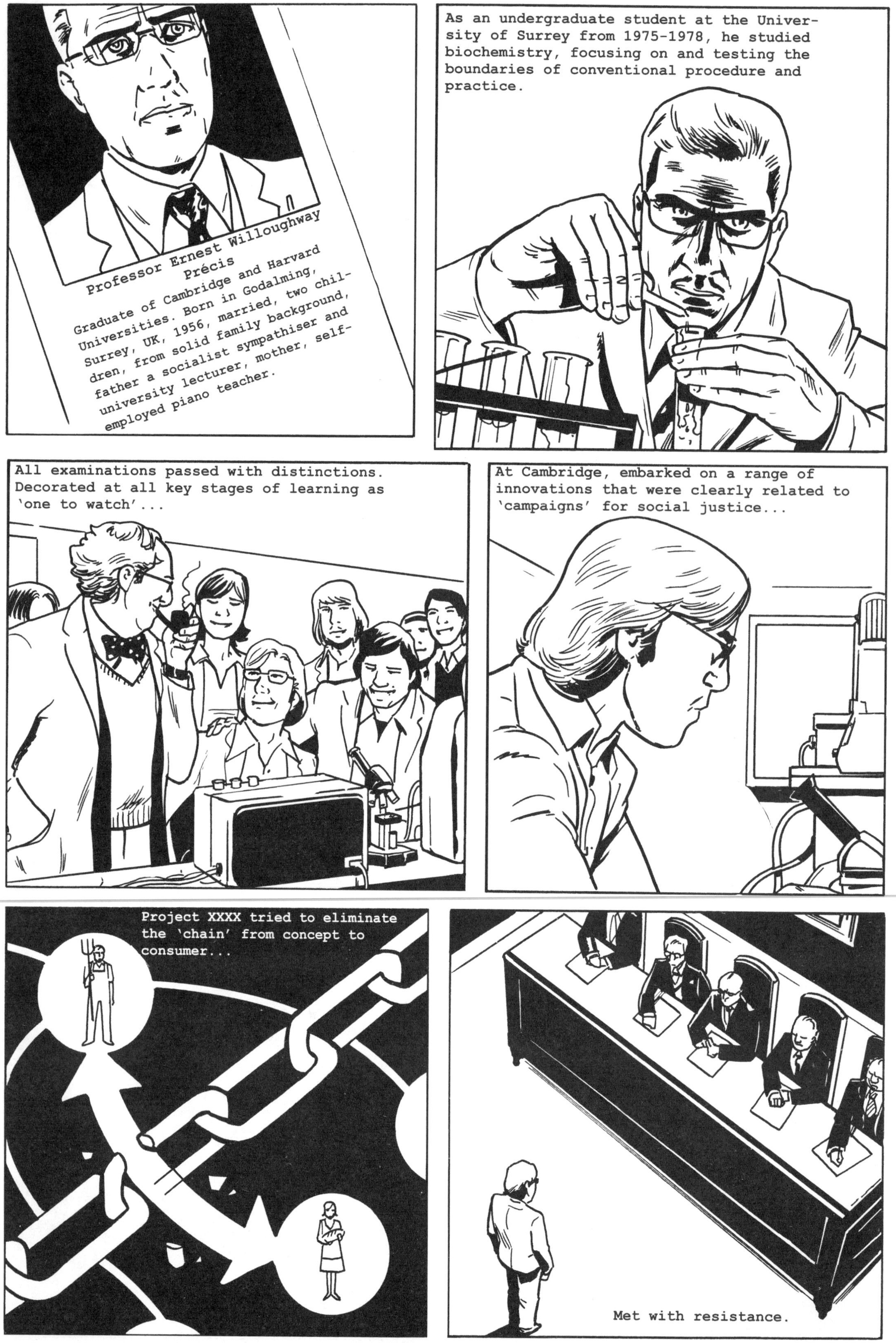
Professor Ernest Willoughway
Précis
Graduate of Cambridge and Harvard Universities. Born in Godalming, Surrey, UK, 1956, married, two children, from solid family background, father a socialist sympathiser and university lecturer, mother, self-employed piano teacher.
As an undergraduate student at the University of Surrey from 1975-1978, he studied biochemistry, focusing on and testing the boundaries of conventional procedure and practice.
All examinations passed with distinctions. Decorated at all key stages of learning as 'one to watch'...
At Cambridge, embarked on a range of innovations that were clearly related to 'campaigns' for social justice...
Project XXXX tried to eliminate the 'chain' from concept to consumer...
Met with resistance.

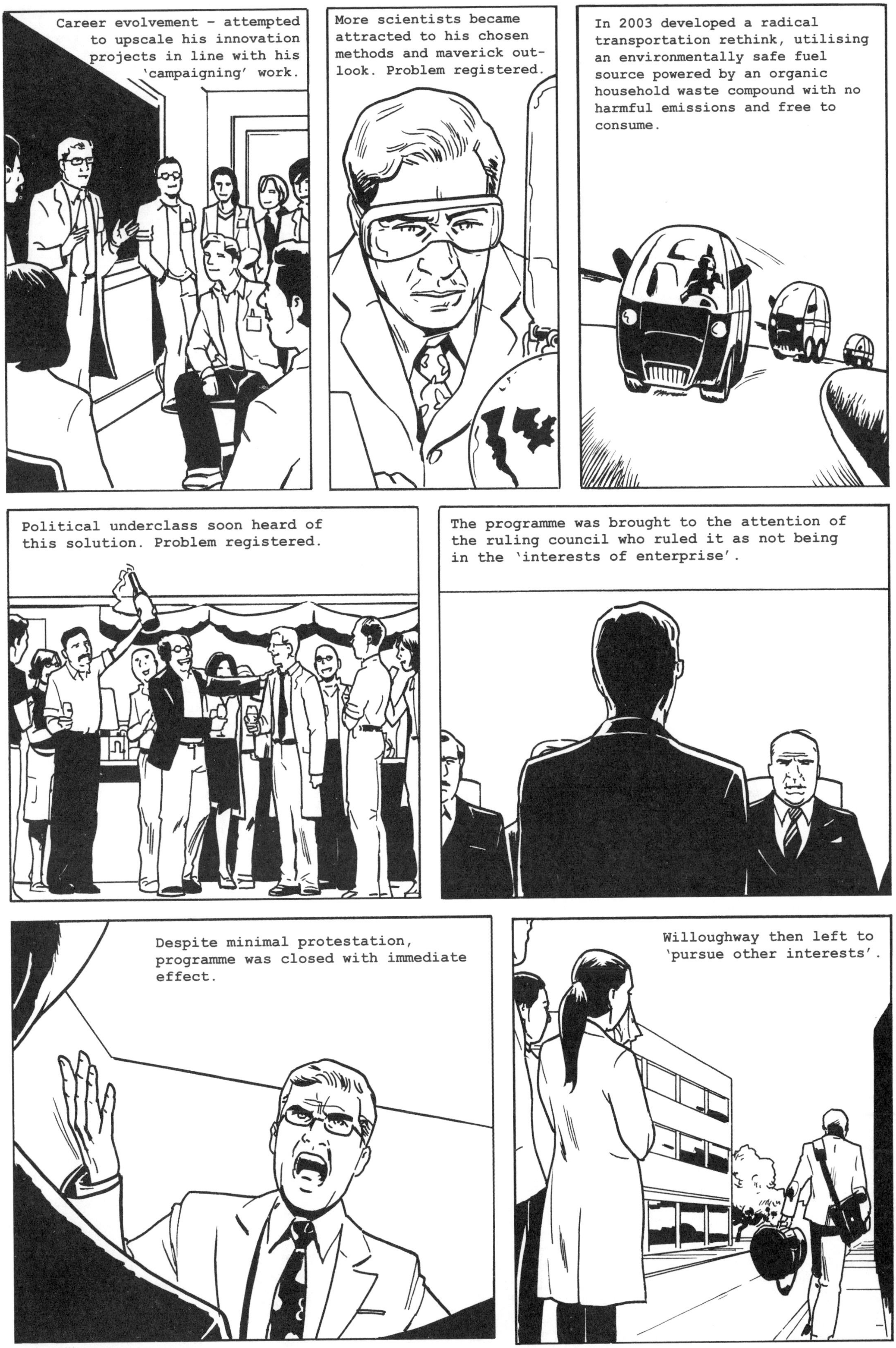
Career evolvement - attempted to upscale his innovation projects in line with his 'campaigning' work.
More scientists became attracted to his chosen methods and maverick outlook. Problem registered.
In 2003 developed a radical transportation rethink, utilising an environmentally safe fuel source powered by an organic household waste compound with no harmful emissions and free to consume.
Political underclass soon heard of this solution. Problem registered.
The programme was brought to the attention of the ruling council who ruled it as not being in the 'interests of enterprise'.
Despite minimal protestation, programme was closed with immediate effect.
Willoughway then left to 'pursue other interests'.

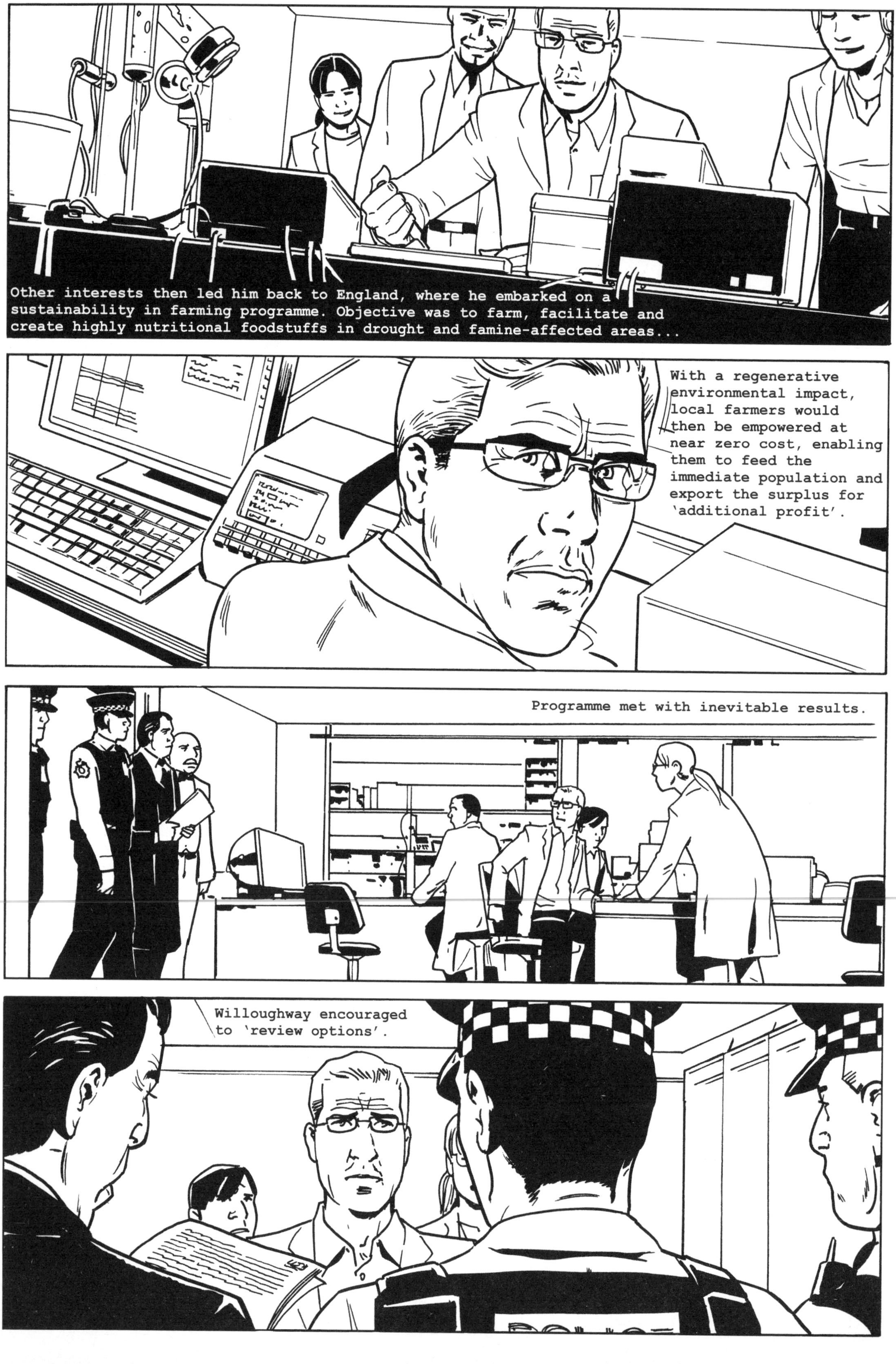
Other interests then led him back to England, where he embarked on a sustainability in farming programme. Objective was to farm, facilitate and create highly nutritional foodstuffs in drought and famine-affected areas...
With a regenerative environmental impact, local farmers would then be empowered at near zero cost, enabling them to feed the immediate population and export the surplus for 'additional profit'.
Programme met with inevitable results.
Willoughway encouraged to 'review options'.

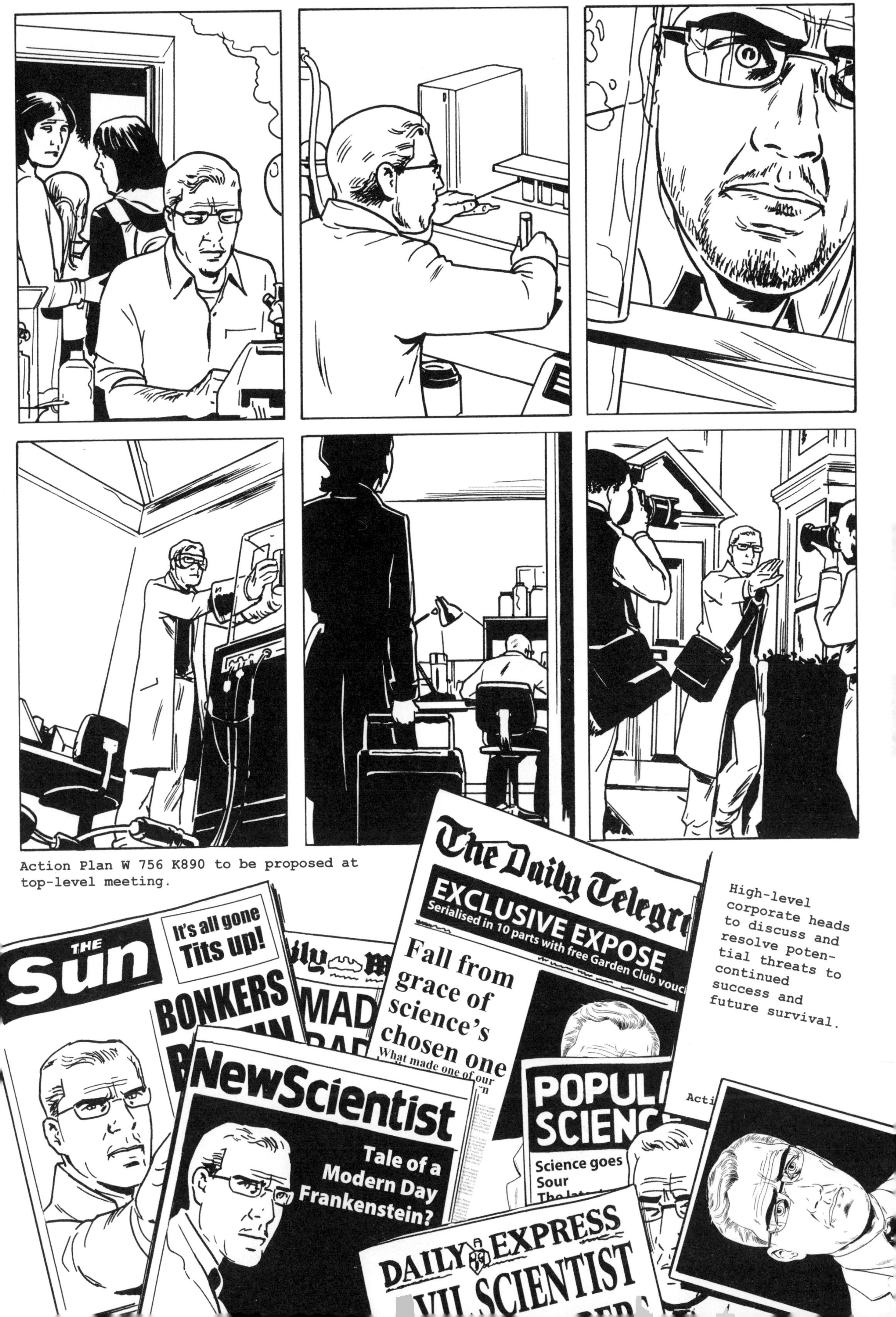

Action Plan W 756 K890 to be proposed at top-level meeting.
THE Sun
It's all gone Tits up!
BONKERS
The Daily Telegr
EXCLUSIVE EXPOSE
Serialised in 10 parts with free Garden Club vouc
Fall from grace of science's chosen one
What made one of our
MAD
NewScientist
Tale of a Modern Day Frankenstein?
POPUL
SCIENC
Science goes Sour
DAILY EXPRESS
SCIENTIST
High-level corporate heads to discuss and resolve potential threats to continued success and future survival.

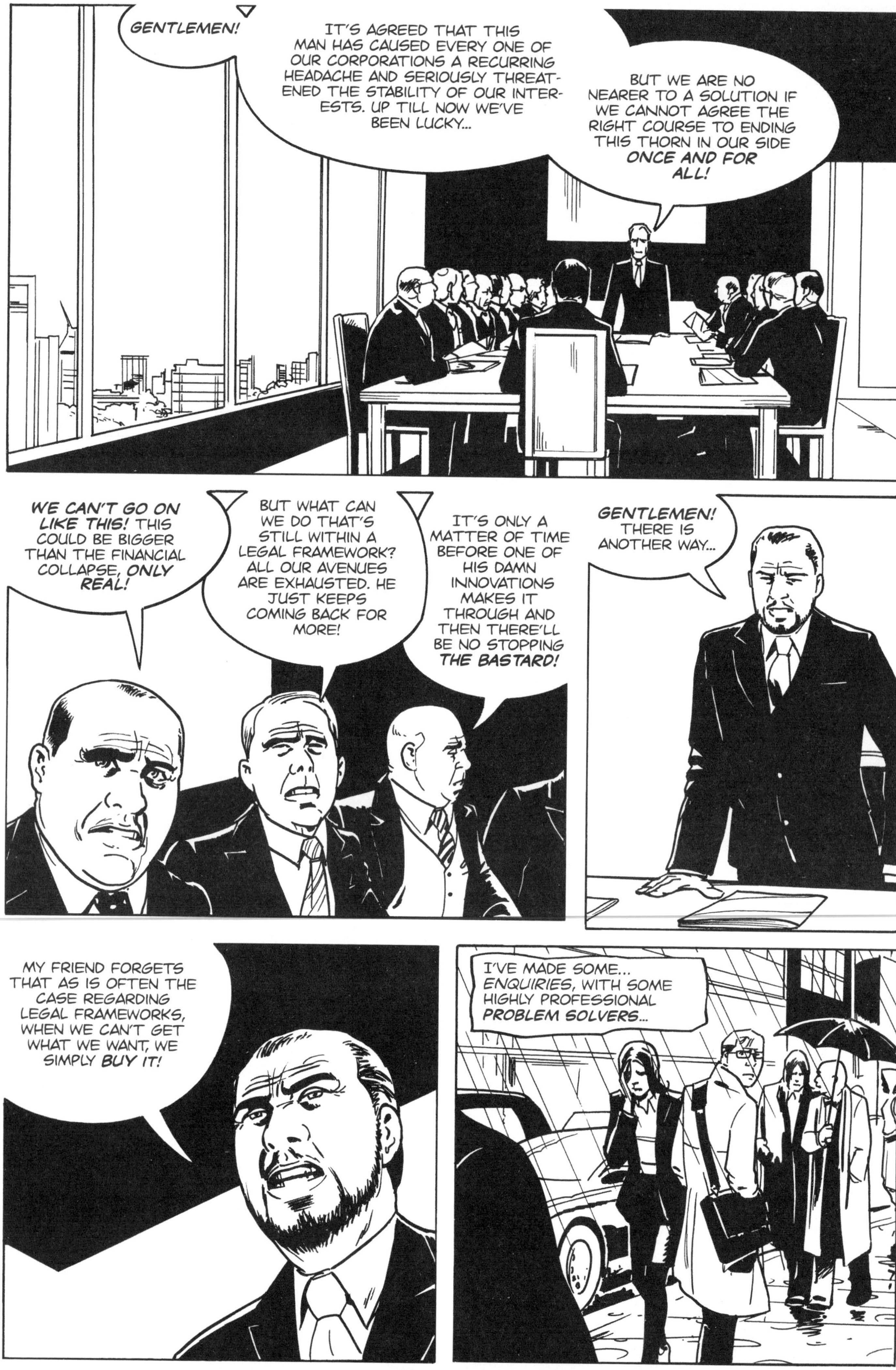
GENTLEMEN!
IT'S AGREED THAT THIS MAN HAS CAUSED EVERY ONE OF OUR CORPORATIONS A RECURRING HEADACHE AND SERIOUSLY THREAT-ENED THE STABILITY OF OUR INTER-ESTS. UP TILL NOW WE'VE BEEN LUCKY...
BUT WE ARE NO NEARER TO A SOLUTION IF WE CANNOT AGREE THE RIGHT COURSE TO ENDING THIS THORN IN OUR SIDE ONCE AND FOR ALL!
WE CAN'T GO ON LIKE THIS! THIS COULD BE BIGGER THAN THE FINANCIAL COLLAPSE, ONLY REAL!
BUT WHAT CAN WE DO THAT'S STILL WITHIN A LEGAL FRAMEWORK? ALL OUR AVENUES ARE EXHAUSTED. HE JUST KEEPS COMING BACK FOR MORE!
IT'S ONLY A MATTER OF TIME BEFORE ONE OF HIS DAMN INNOVATIONS MAKES IT THROUGH AND THEN THERE'LL BE NO STOPPING THE BASTARD!
GENTLEMEN! THERE IS ANOTHER WAY...
MY FRIEND FORGETS THAT AS IS OFTEN THE CASE REGARDING LEGAL FRAMEWORKS, WHEN WE CAN'T GET WHAT WE WANT, WE SIMPLY BUY IT!
I'VE MADE SOME... ENQUIRIES, WITH SOME HIGHLY PROFESSIONAL PROBLEM SOLVERS...

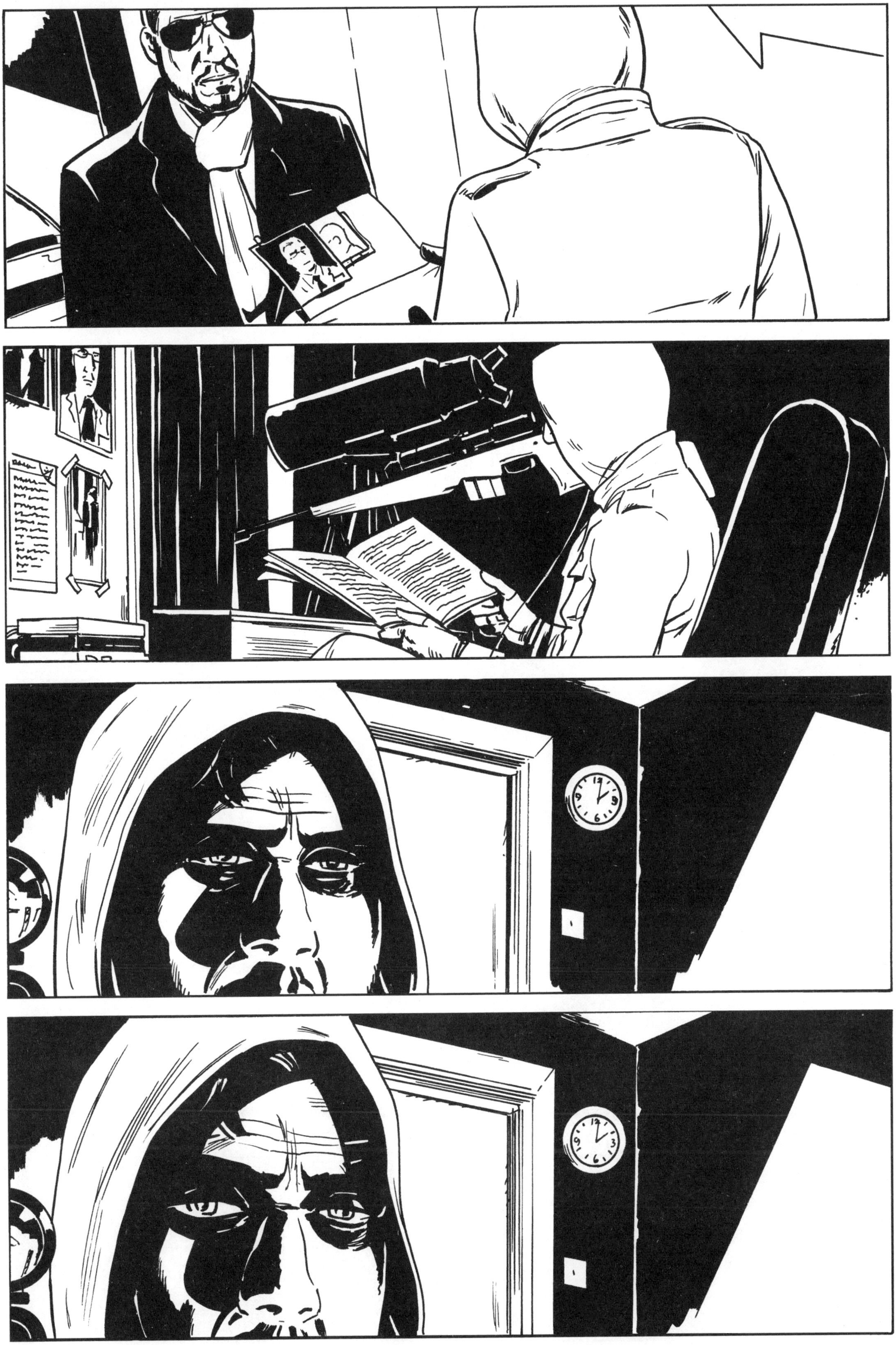

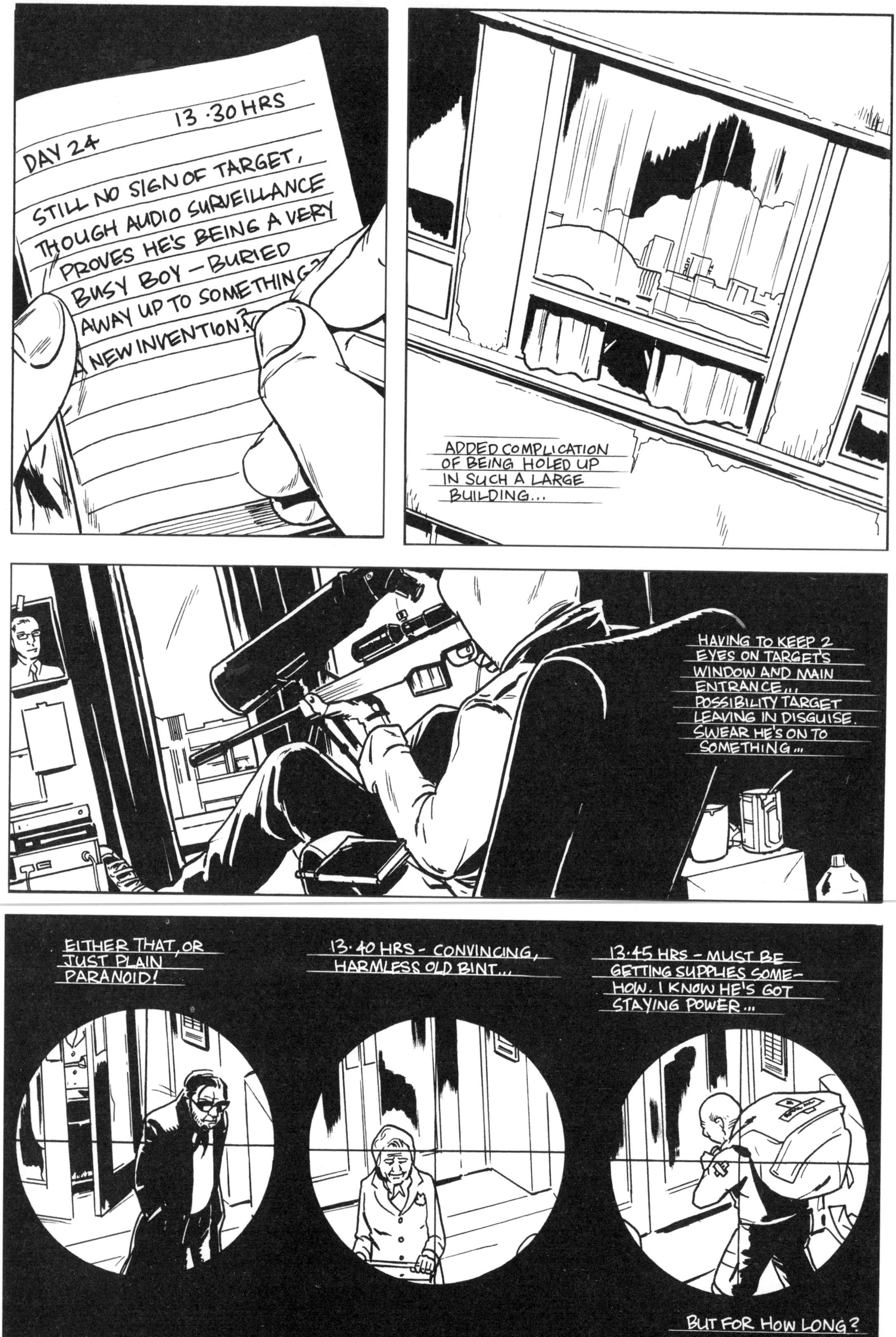
DAY 24
13·30 HRS
STILL NO SIGN OF TARGET, THOUGH AUDIO SURVEILLANCE PROVES HE'S BEING A VERY BUSY BOY – BURIED AWAY UP TO SOMETHING? A NEW INVENTION?
ADDED COMPLICATION OF BEING HOLED UP IN SUCH A LARGE BUILDING...
HAVING TO KEEP 2 EYES ON TARGET'S WINDOW AND MAIN ENTRANCE... POSSIBILITY TARGET LEAVING IN DISGUISE. SWEAR HE'S ON TO SOMETHING...
EITHER THAT, OR JUST PLAIN PARANOID!
13·40 HRS – CONVINCING, HARMLESS OLD BINT...
13·45 HRS – MUST BE GETTING SUPPLIES SOME-HOW. I KNOW HE'S GOT STAYING POWER...
BUT FOR HOW LONG?

COULD HE COME
OUT DRESSED
AS A FRUITY
OLD NONCE?

IS HE GETTING
ANY HELP?...
TASTY 20s
FORTY-
SOMETHING...

ONE MAN AND
HIS RABBIT!?!

ISN'T HE OFF
THE TELY?

NICE HAT
MATE...

SHIT! LOSING
FOCUS AGAIN...

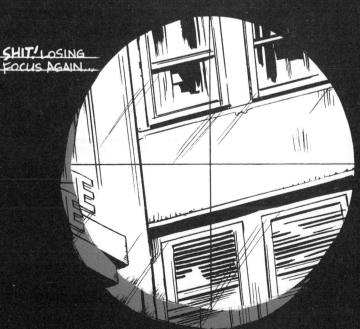

NOW- WHERE WAS I?

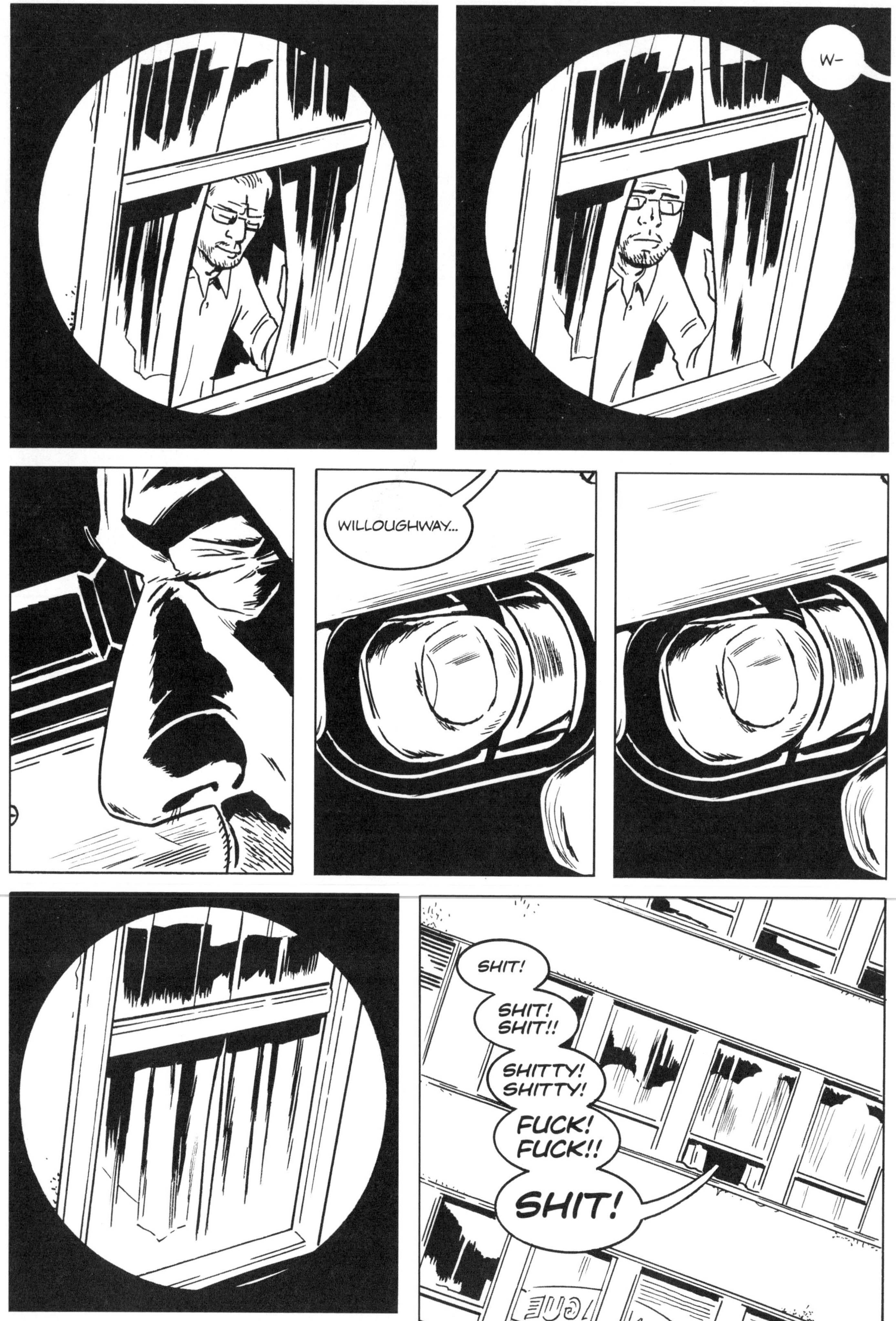
W-
WILLOUGHWAY...
SHIT!
SHIT! SHIT!!
SHITTY! SHITTY!
FUCK! FUCK!!
SHIT!

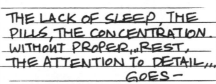

DAY 32. EVEN THE BEST NEED REST...

THE LACK OF SLEEP, THE PILLS, THE CONCENTRATION. WITHOUT PROPER...REST, THE ATTENTION TO DETAIL... GOES—

WHAT DO YOU MEAN NO PROGRESS? IT'S BEEN A *MONTH* FOR CHRIST'S SAKE!

YES, I KNOW, BUT IT'S NOT, IT'S, THIS ONE'S NOT THAT... EASY.

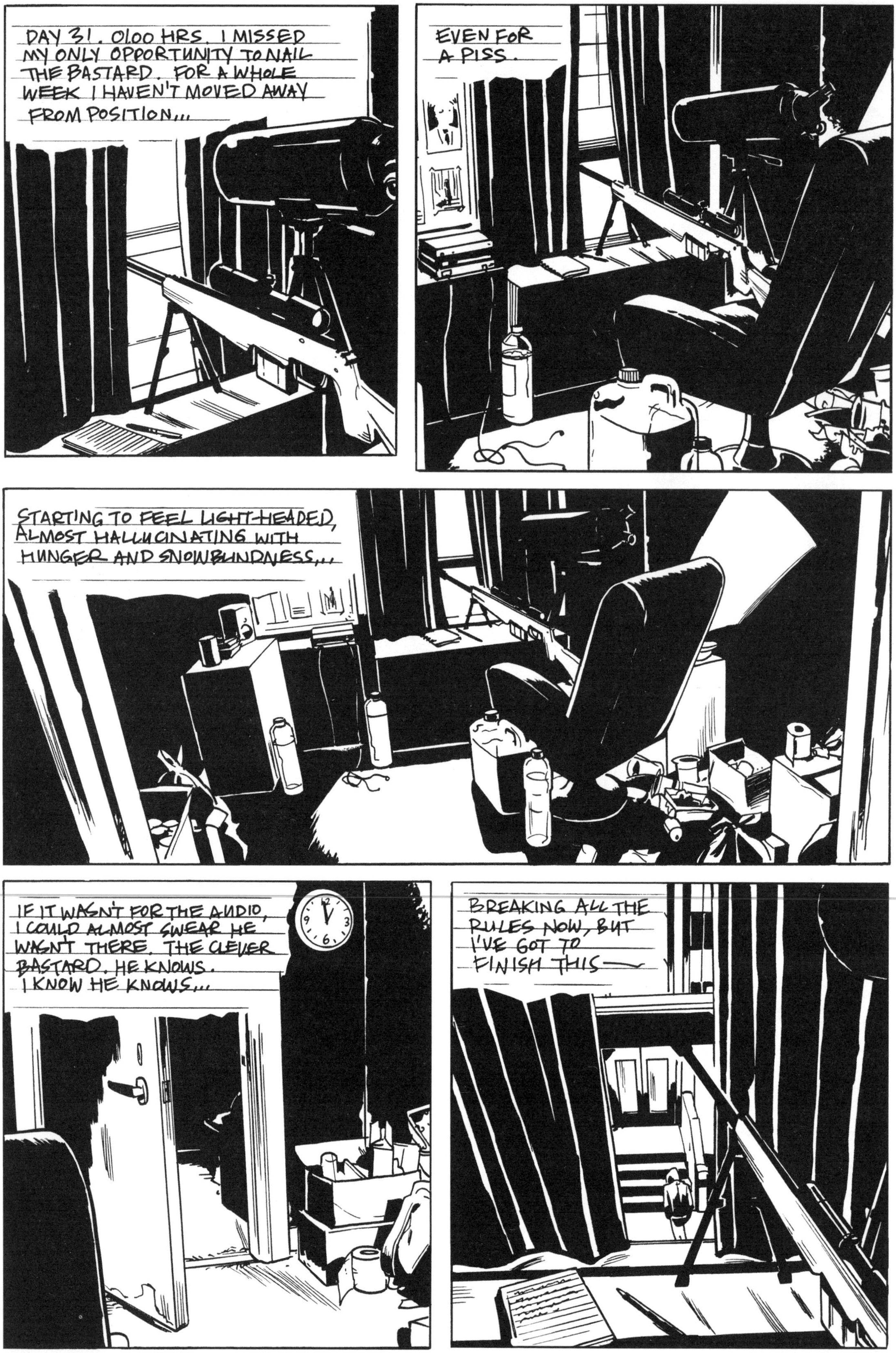
DAY 31. 01.00 HRS. I MISSED MY ONLY OPPORTUNITY TO NAIL THE BASTARD. FOR A WHOLE WEEK I HAVEN'T MOVED AWAY FROM POSITION...
EVEN FOR A PISS.
STARTING TO FEEL LIGHT-HEADED, ALMOST HALLUCINATING WITH HUNGER AND SNOWBLINDNESS...
IF IT WASN'T FOR THE AUDIO, I COULD ALMOST SWEAR HE WASN'T THERE. THE CLEVER BASTARD. HE KNOWS. I KNOW HE KNOWS...
BREAKING ALL THE RULES NOW, BUT I'VE GOT TO FINISH THIS—

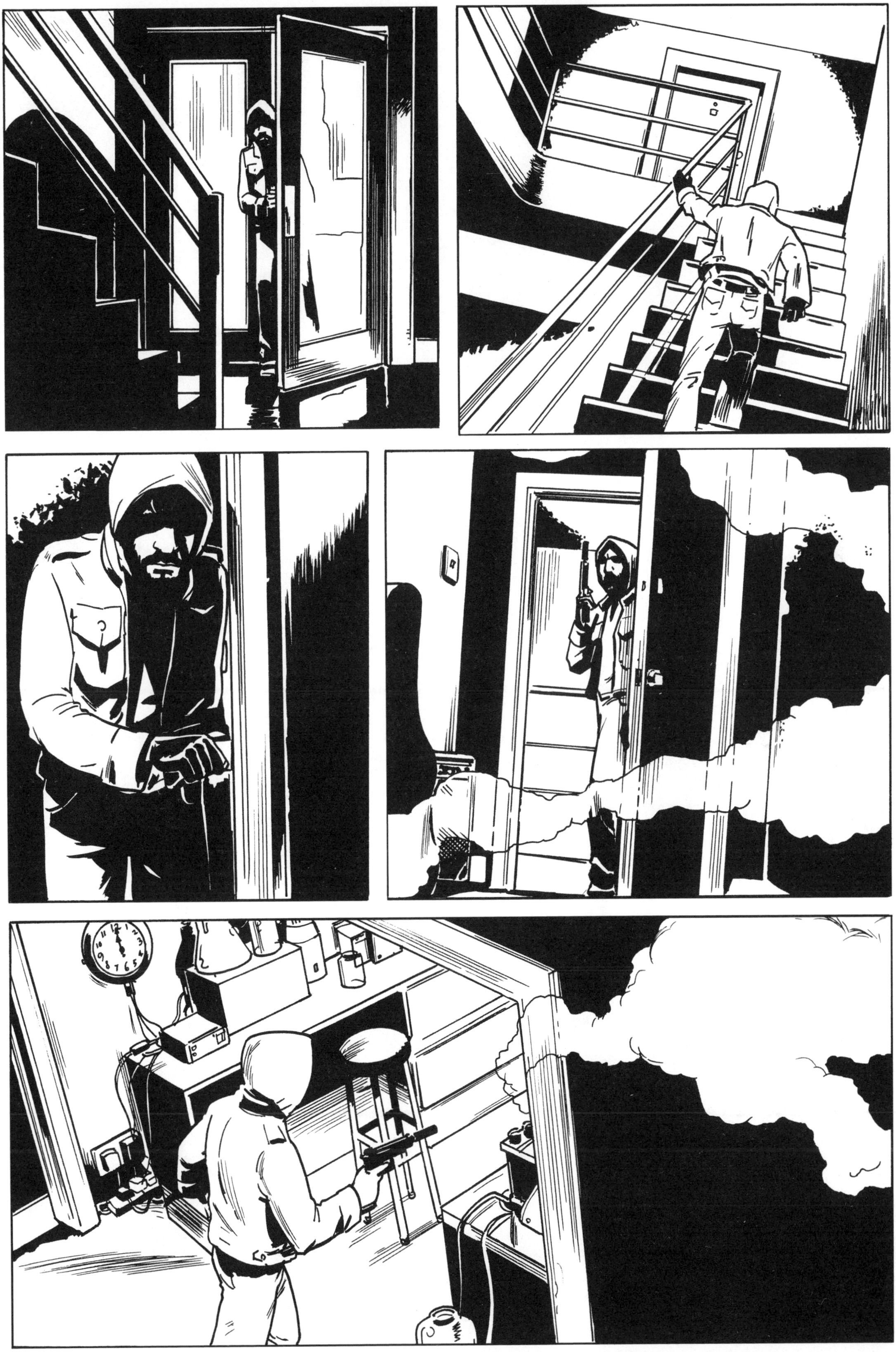

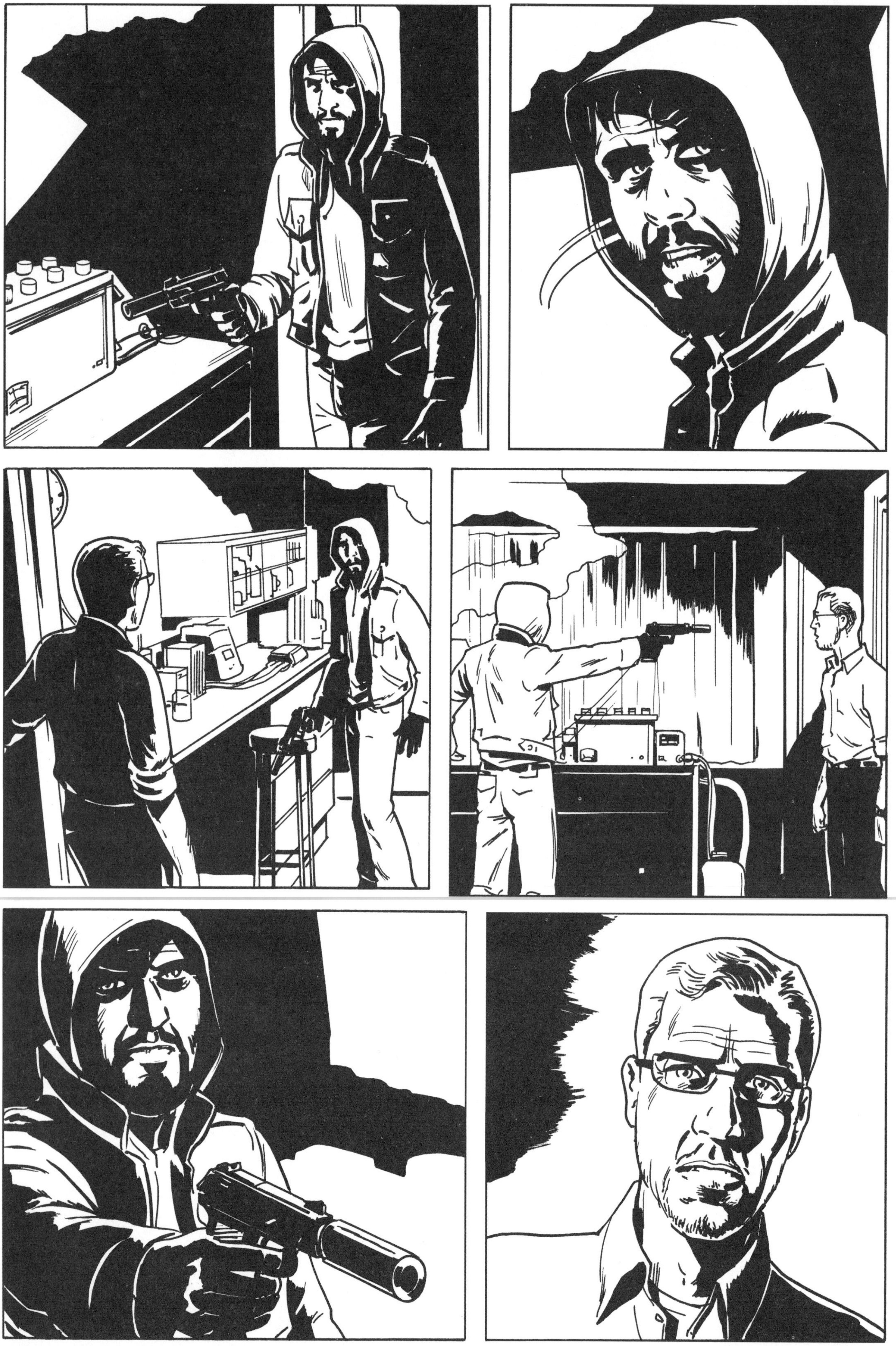

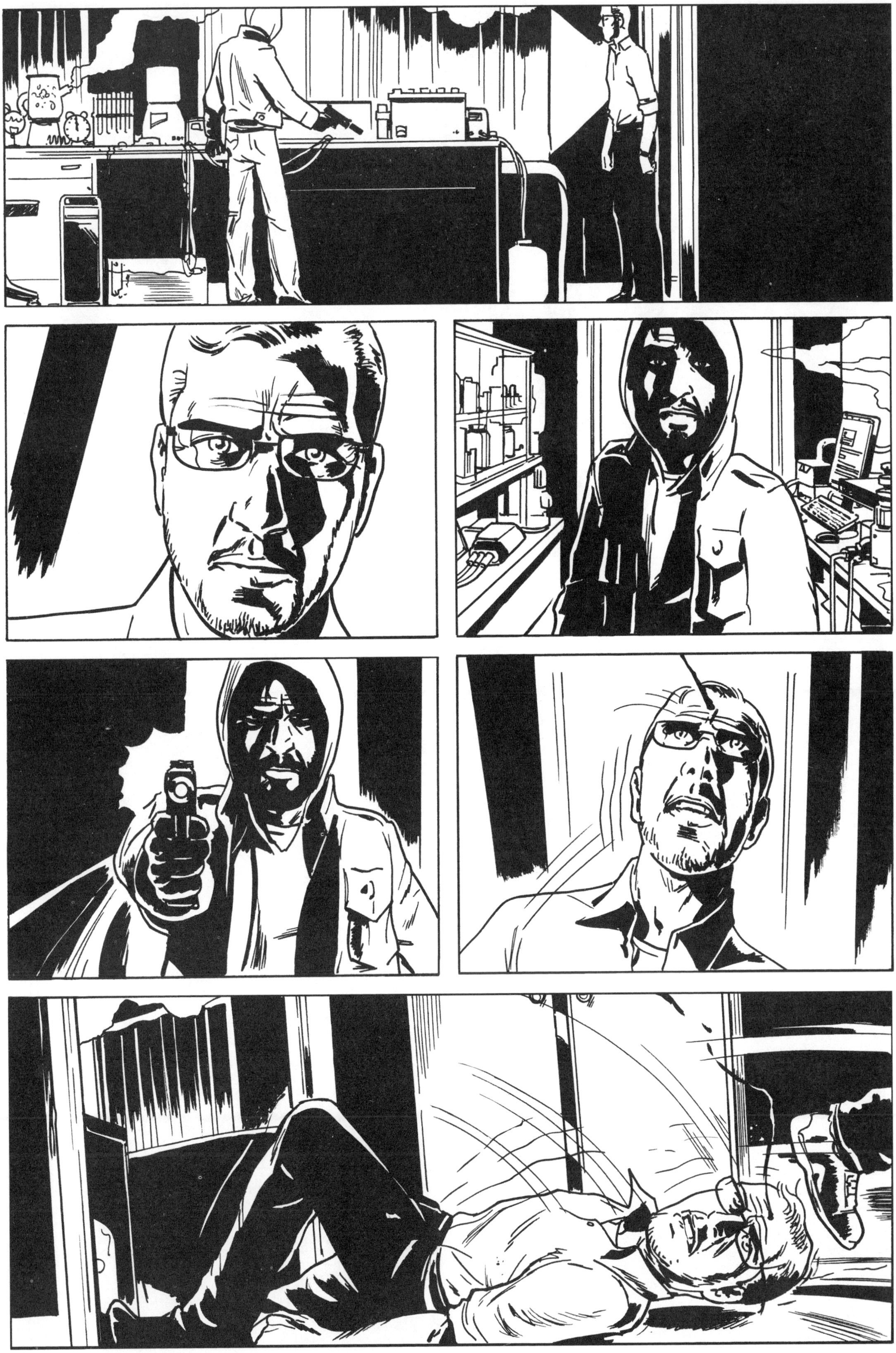

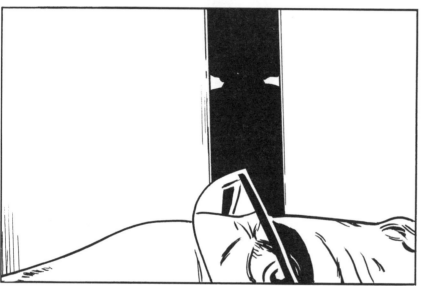

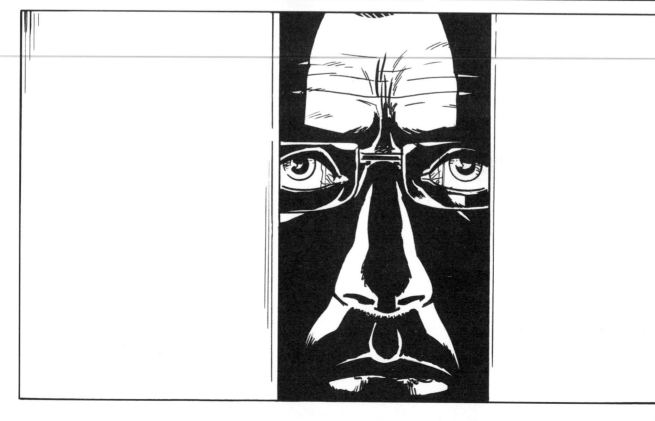

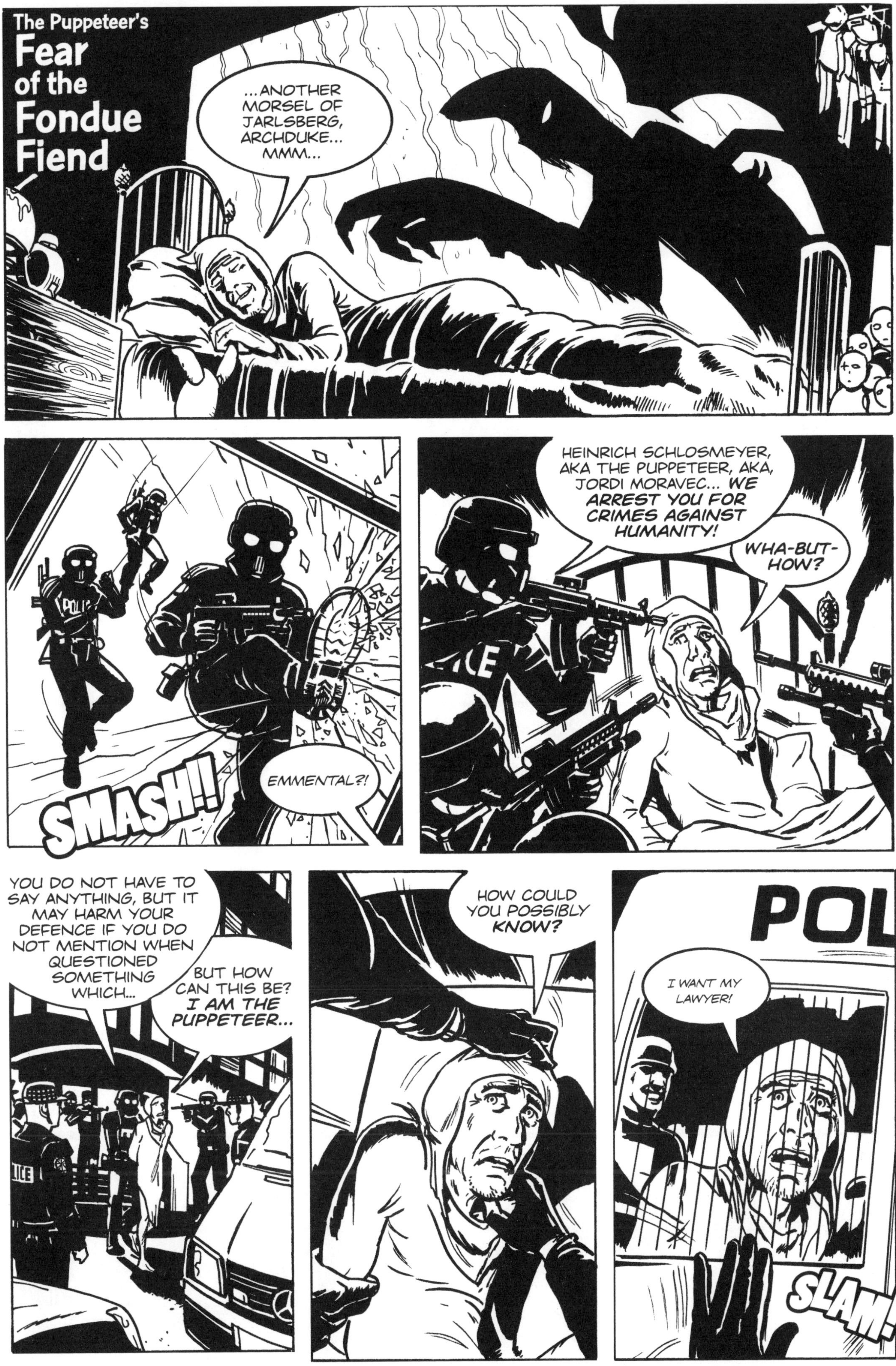
The Puppeteer's
Fear of the Fondue Fiend
...ANOTHER MORSEL OF JARLSBERG, ARCHDUKE... MMM...
SMASH!!
EMMENTAL?!
HEINRICH SCHLOSMEYER, AKA THE PUPPETEER, AKA, JORDI MORAVEC... WE ARREST YOU FOR CRIMES AGAINST HUMANITY!
WHA-BUT-HOW?
YOU DO NOT HAVE TO SAY ANYTHING, BUT IT MAY HARM YOUR DEFENCE IF YOU DO NOT MENTION WHEN QUESTIONED SOMETHING WHICH...
BUT HOW CAN THIS BE? I AM THE PUPPETEER...
HOW COULD YOU POSSIBLY KNOW?
POL
I WANT MY LAWYER!
SLAM!

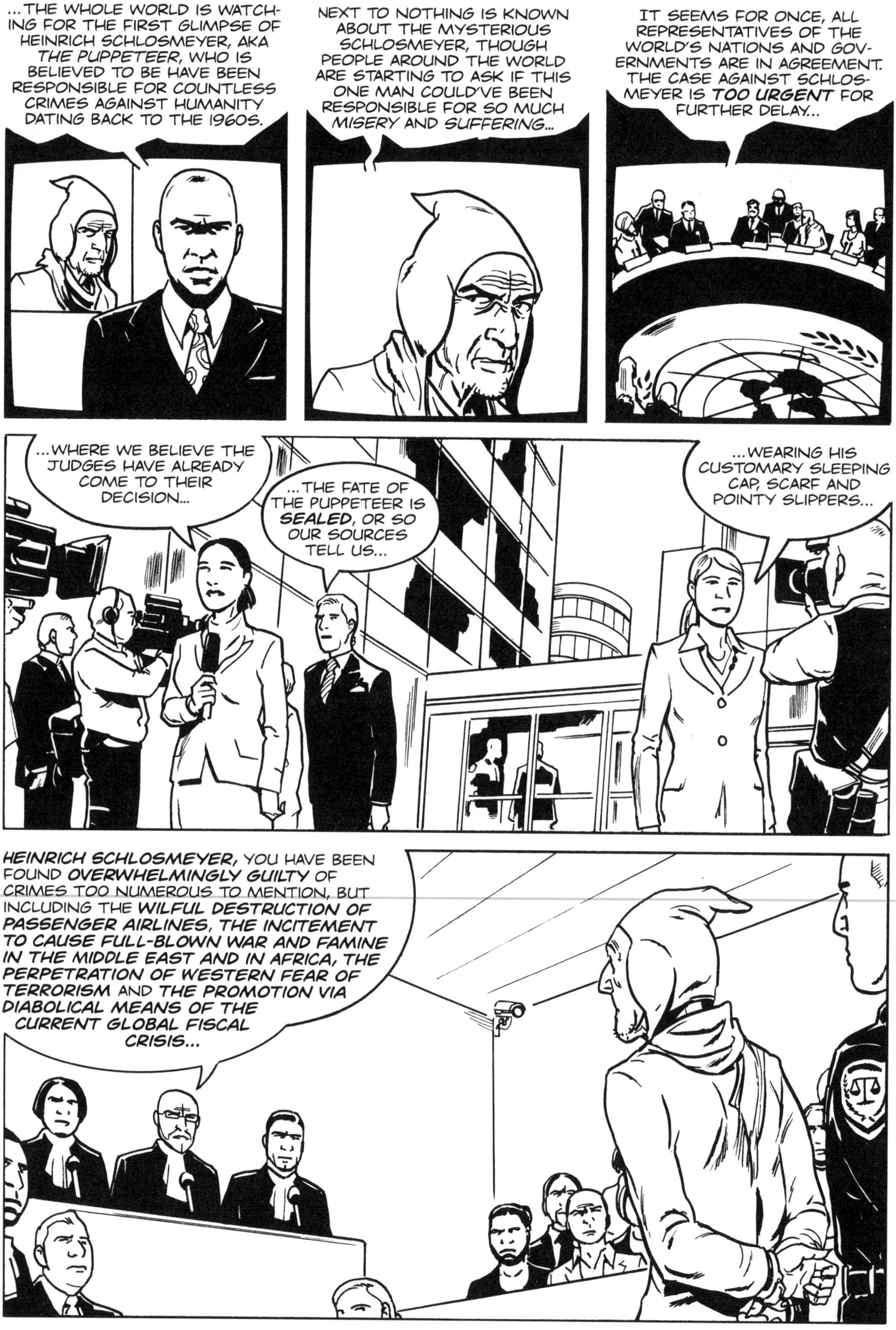
...THE WHOLE WORLD IS WATCHING FOR THE FIRST GLIMPSE OF HEINRICH SCHLOSMEYER, AKA *THE PUPPETEER*, WHO IS BELIEVED TO BE HAVE BEEN RESPONSIBLE FOR COUNTLESS CRIMES AGAINST HUMANITY DATING BACK TO THE 1960S.
NEXT TO NOTHING IS KNOWN ABOUT THE MYSTERIOUS SCHLOSMEYER, THOUGH PEOPLE AROUND THE WORLD ARE STARTING TO ASK IF THIS ONE MAN COULD'VE BEEN RESPONSIBLE FOR SO MUCH *MISERY AND SUFFERING*...
IT SEEMS FOR ONCE, ALL REPRESENTATIVES OF THE WORLD'S NATIONS AND GOVERNMENTS ARE IN AGREEMENT. THE CASE AGAINST SCHLOSMEYER IS ***TOO URGENT*** FOR FURTHER DELAY...
...WHERE WE BELIEVE THE JUDGES HAVE ALREADY COME TO THEIR DECISION...
...THE FATE OF THE PUPPETEER IS ***SEALED***, OR SO OUR SOURCES TELL US...
...WEARING HIS CUSTOMARY SLEEPING CAP, SCARF AND POINTY SLIPPERS...
HEINRICH SCHLOSMEYER, YOU HAVE BEEN FOUND ***OVERWHELMINGLY GUILTY*** OF CRIMES TOO NUMEROUS TO MENTION, BUT INCLUDING THE ***WILFUL DESTRUCTION OF PASSENGER AIRLINES, THE INCITEMENT TO CAUSE FULL-BLOWN WAR AND FAMINE IN THE MIDDLE EAST AND IN AFRICA, THE PERPETRATION OF WESTERN FEAR OF TERRORISM*** AND ***THE PROMOTION VIA DIABOLICAL MEANS OF THE CURRENT GLOBAL FISCAL CRISIS...***

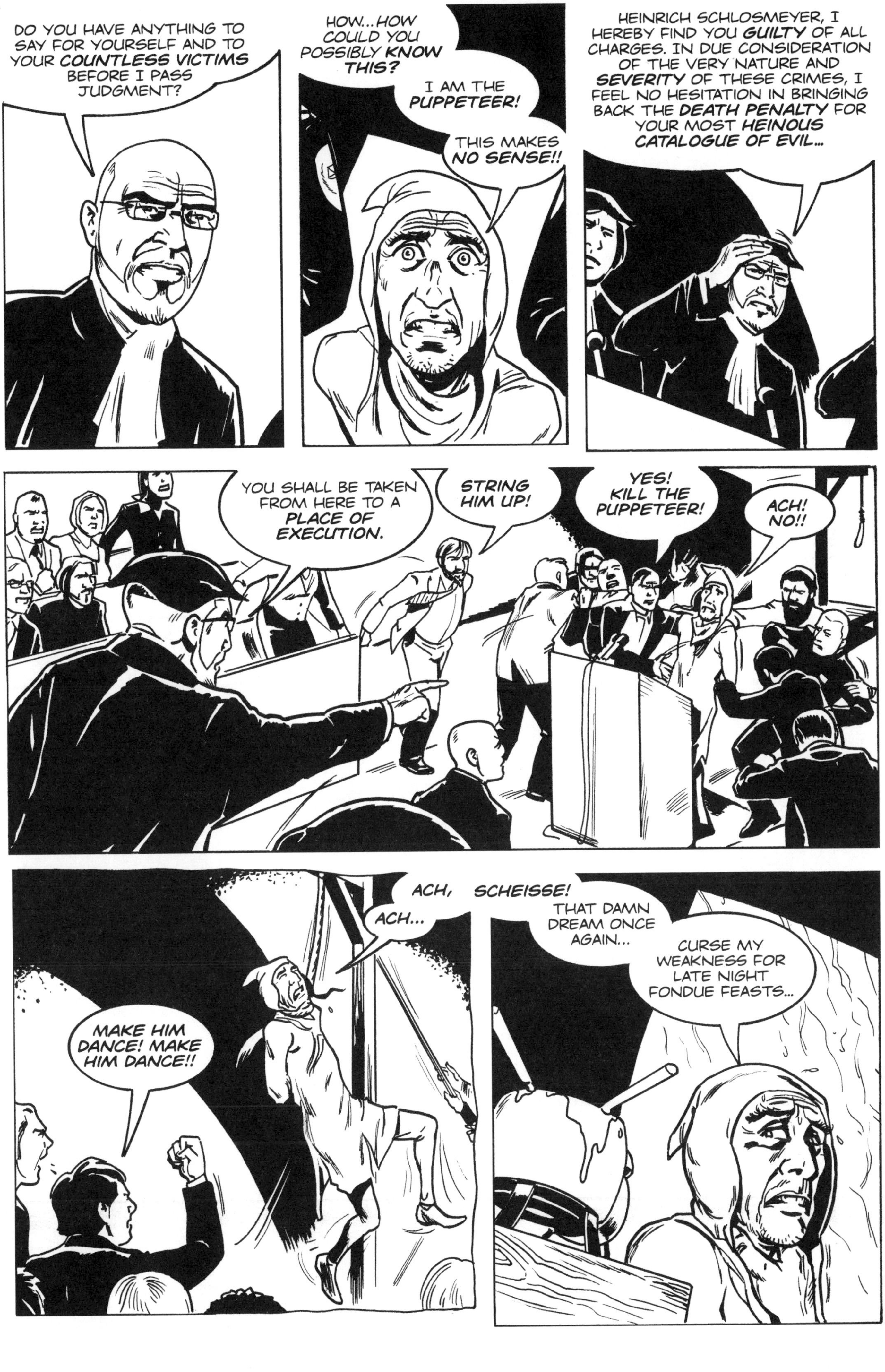
DO YOU HAVE ANYTHING TO SAY FOR YOURSELF AND TO YOUR COUNTLESS VICTIMS BEFORE I PASS JUDGMENT?
HOW...HOW COULD YOU POSSIBLY KNOW THIS?
I AM THE PUPPETEER!
THIS MAKES NO SENSE!!
HEINRICH SCHLOSMEYER, I HEREBY FIND YOU GUILTY OF ALL CHARGES. IN DUE CONSIDERATION OF THE VERY NATURE AND SEVERITY OF THESE CRIMES, I FEEL NO HESITATION IN BRINGING BACK THE DEATH PENALTY FOR YOUR MOST HEINOUS CATALOGUE OF EVIL...
YOU SHALL BE TAKEN FROM HERE TO A PLACE OF EXECUTION.
STRING HIM UP!
YES! KILL THE PUPPETEER!
ACH! NO!!
ACH...
MAKE HIM DANCE! MAKE HIM DANCE!!
ACH, SCHEISSE!
THAT DAMN DREAM ONCE AGAIN...
CURSE MY WEAKNESS FOR LATE NIGHT FONDUE FEASTS...

The
Architect's
Story

TRAINS
TAXIS   EXIT

LONDON

T C P deBoyne   T C P deBoyne

CHUFFING
the DRAGON

CHUFFING
the DRAGON

T C P deBoyne

T C P deBoyne

CHUFFING
DRAGON

CHUFFING
the DRAG

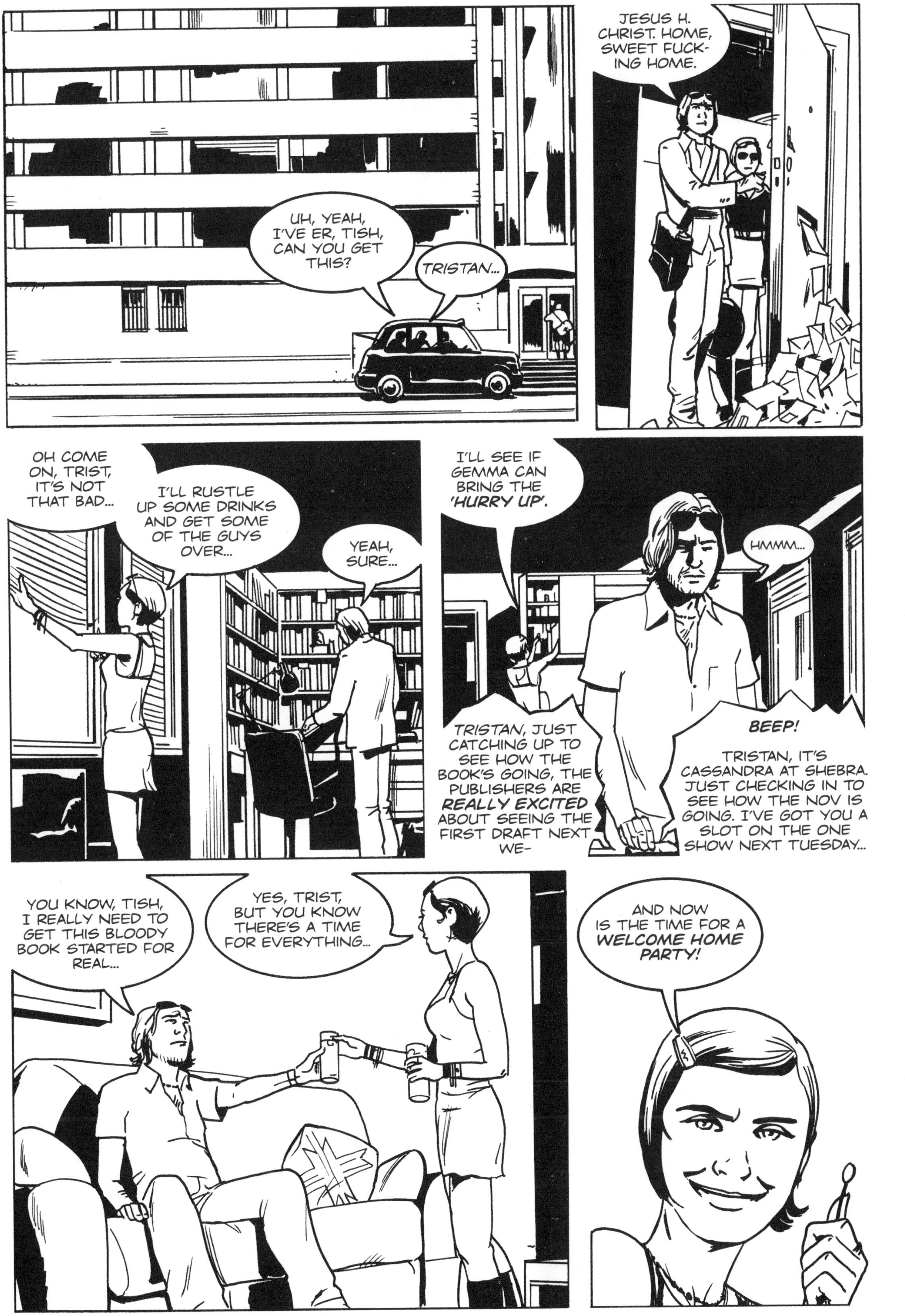
UH, YEAH, I'VE ER, TISH, CAN YOU GET THIS?
TRISTAN...
JESUS H. CHRIST. HOME, SWEET FUCK-ING HOME.
OH COME ON, TRIST, IT'S NOT THAT BAD...
I'LL RUSTLE UP SOME DRINKS AND GET SOME OF THE GUYS OVER...
YEAH, SURE...
I'LL SEE IF GEMMA CAN BRING THE **'HURRY UP'**.
HMMM...
TRISTAN, JUST CATCHING UP TO SEE HOW THE BOOK'S GOING, THE PUBLISHERS ARE **REALLY EXCITED** ABOUT SEEING THE FIRST DRAFT NEXT WE-
BEEP!
TRISTAN, IT'S CASSANDRA AT SHEBRA. JUST CHECKING IN TO SEE HOW THE NOV IS GOING. I'VE GOT YOU A SLOT ON THE ONE SHOW NEXT TUESDAY...
YOU KNOW, TISH, I REALLY NEED TO GET THIS BLOODY BOOK STARTED FOR REAL...
YES, TRIST, BUT YOU KNOW THERE'S A TIME FOR EVERYTHING...
AND NOW IS THE TIME FOR A **WELCOME HOME PARTY!**

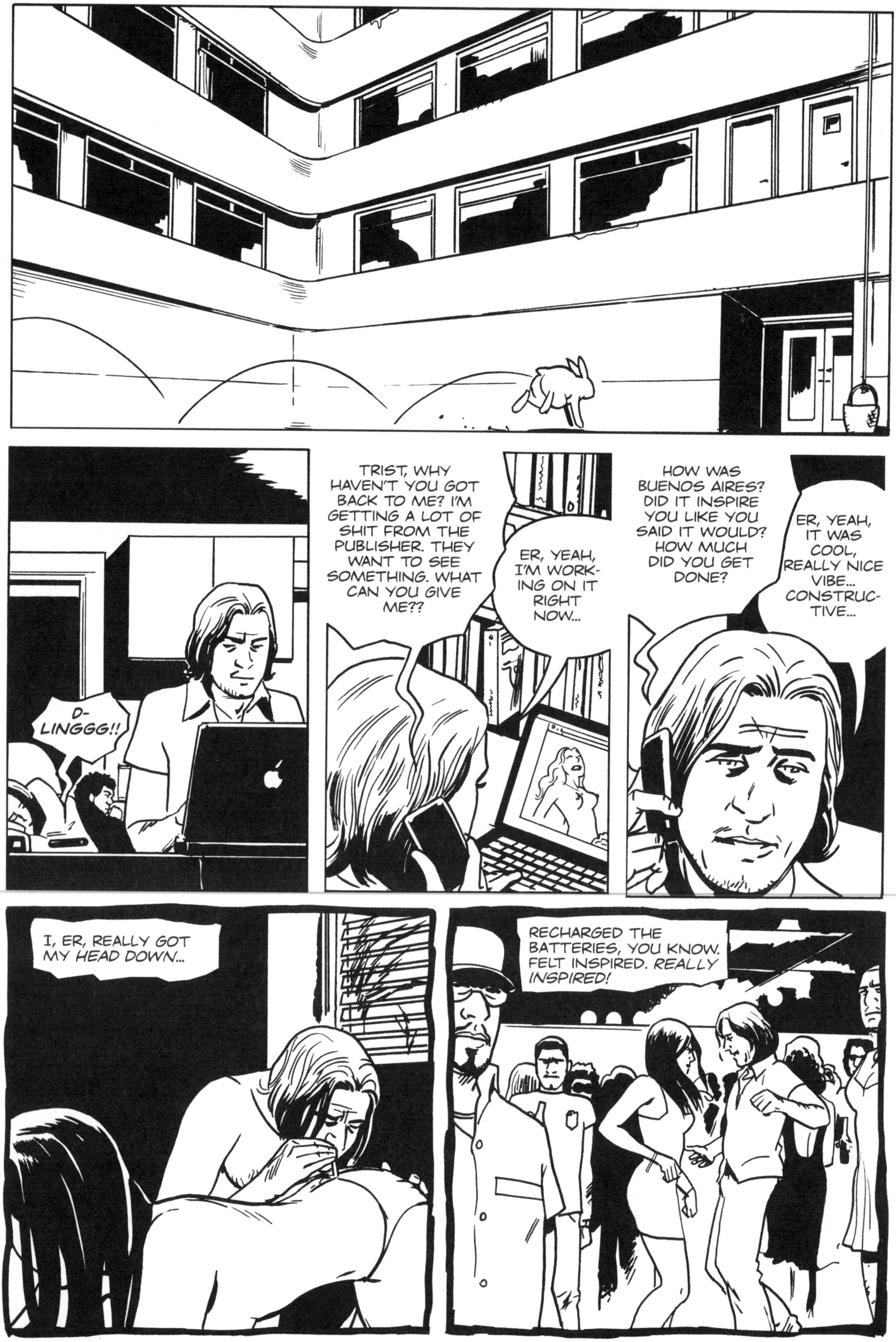
D-LINGGG!!
TRIST, WHY HAVEN'T YOU GOT BACK TO ME? I'M GETTING A LOT OF SHIT FROM THE PUBLISHER. THEY WANT TO SEE SOMETHING. WHAT CAN YOU GIVE ME??
ER, YEAH, I'M WORKING ON IT RIGHT NOW...
HOW WAS BUENOS AIRES? DID IT INSPIRE YOU LIKE YOU SAID IT WOULD? HOW MUCH DID YOU GET DONE?
ER, YEAH, IT WAS COOL, REALLY NICE VIBE... CONSTRUCTIVE...
I, ER, REALLY GOT MY HEAD DOWN...
RECHARGED THE BATTERIES, YOU KNOW. FELT INSPIRED. *REALLY INSPIRED!*

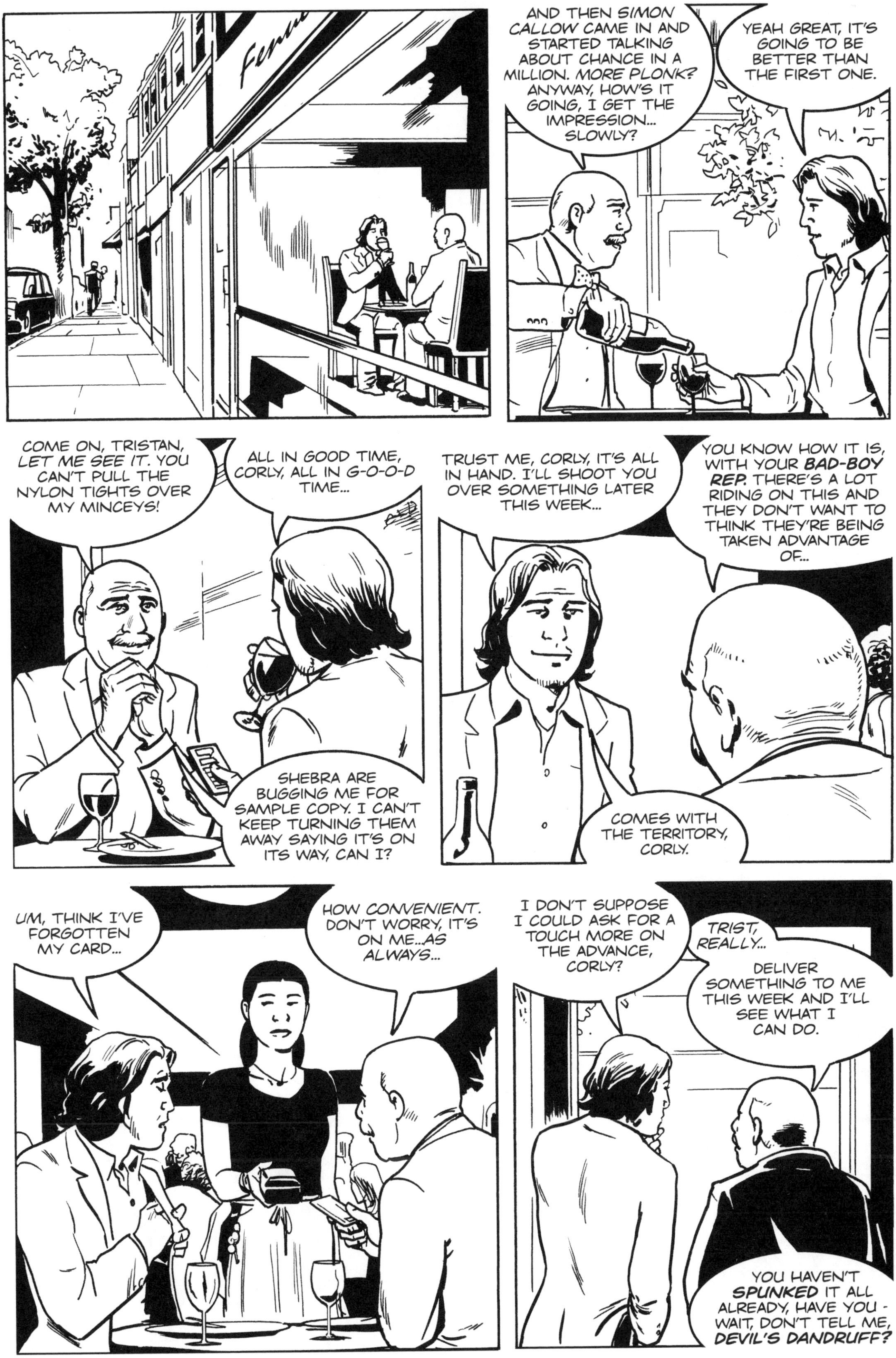
AND THEN SIMON CALLOW CAME IN AND STARTED TALKING ABOUT CHANCE IN A MILLION. MORE PLONK? ANYWAY, HOW'S IT GOING, I GET THE IMPRESSION... SLOWLY?
YEAH GREAT, IT'S GOING TO BE BETTER THAN THE FIRST ONE.
COME ON, TRISTAN, LET ME SEE IT. YOU CAN'T PULL THE NYLON TIGHTS OVER MY MINCEYS!
ALL IN GOOD TIME, CORLY, ALL IN G-O-O-D TIME...
SHEBRA ARE BUGGING ME FOR SAMPLE COPY. I CAN'T KEEP TURNING THEM AWAY SAYING IT'S ON ITS WAY, CAN I?
TRUST ME, CORLY, IT'S ALL IN HAND. I'LL SHOOT YOU OVER SOMETHING LATER THIS WEEK...
YOU KNOW HOW IT IS, WITH YOUR BAD-BOY REP. THERE'S A LOT RIDING ON THIS AND THEY DON'T WANT TO THINK THEY'RE BEING TAKEN ADVANTAGE OF...
COMES WITH THE TERRITORY, CORLY.
UM, THINK I'VE FORGOTTEN MY CARD...
HOW CONVENIENT. DON'T WORRY, IT'S ON ME...AS ALWAYS...
I DON'T SUPPOSE I COULD ASK FOR A TOUCH MORE ON THE ADVANCE, CORLY?
TRIST, REALLY...
DELIVER SOMETHING TO ME THIS WEEK AND I'LL SEE WHAT I CAN DO.
YOU HAVEN'T SPUNKED IT ALL ALREADY, HAVE YOU - WAIT, DON'T TELL ME, DEVIL'S DANDRUFF?

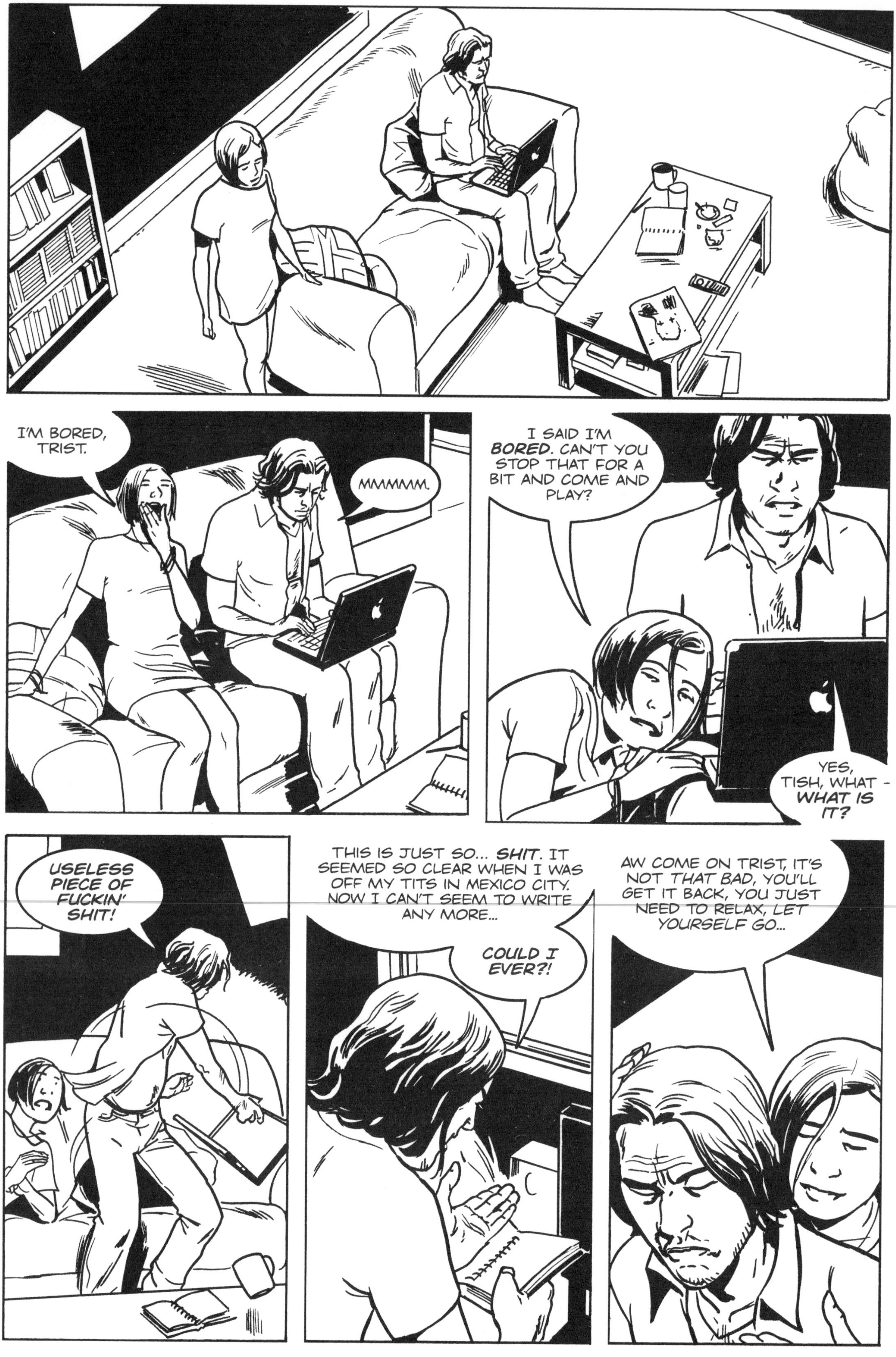
I'M BORED, TRIST.
MMMMM.
I SAID I'M **BORED.** CAN'T YOU STOP THAT FOR A BIT AND COME AND PLAY?
YES, TISH, WHAT - ***WHAT IS IT?***
USELESS PIECE OF FUCKIN' SHIT!
THIS IS JUST SO... **SHIT**. IT SEEMED SO CLEAR WHEN I WAS OFF MY TITS IN MEXICO CITY. NOW I CAN'T SEEM TO WRITE ANY MORE...
COULD I EVER?!
AW COME ON TRIST, IT'S NOT *THAT* BAD, YOU'LL GET IT BACK, YOU JUST NEED TO RELAX, *LET* YOURSELF GO...

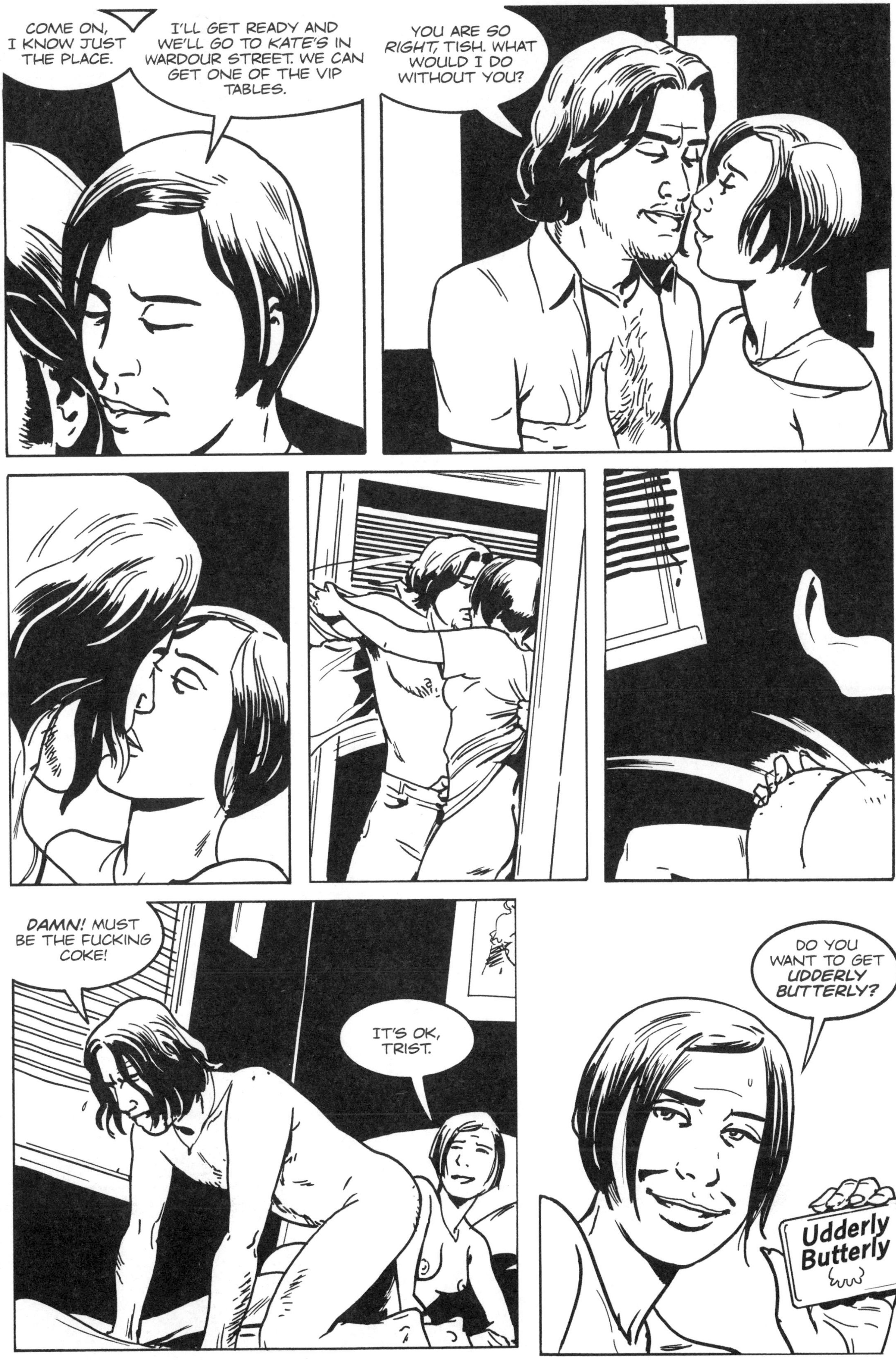
COME ON, I KNOW JUST THE PLACE.
I'LL GET READY AND WE'LL GO TO KATE'S IN WARDOUR STREET. WE CAN GET ONE OF THE VIP TABLES.
YOU ARE SO RIGHT, TISH. WHAT WOULD I DO WITHOUT YOU?
DAMN! MUST BE THE FUCKING COKE!
IT'S OK, TRIST.
DO YOU WANT TO GET UDDERLY BUTTERLY?
Udderly Butterly

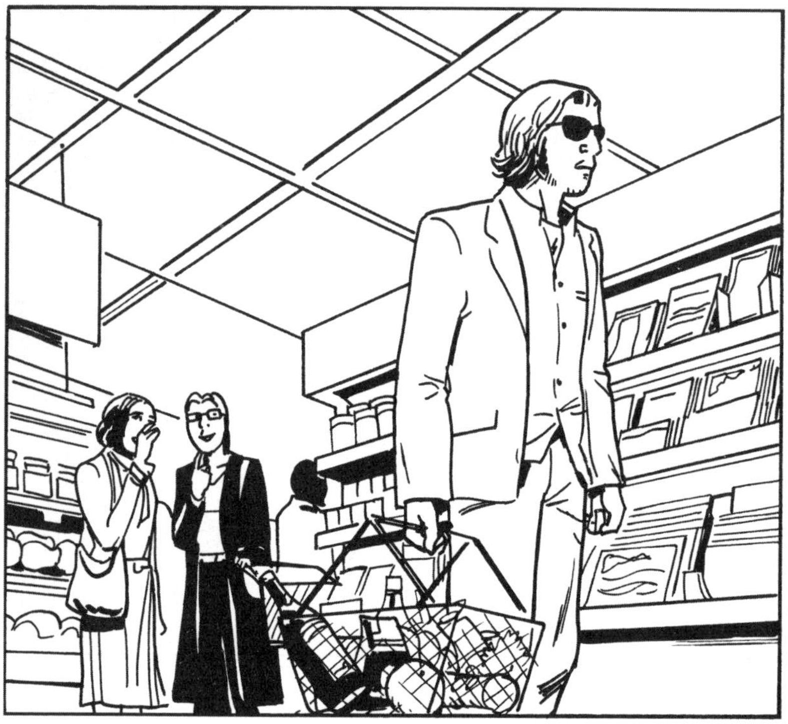

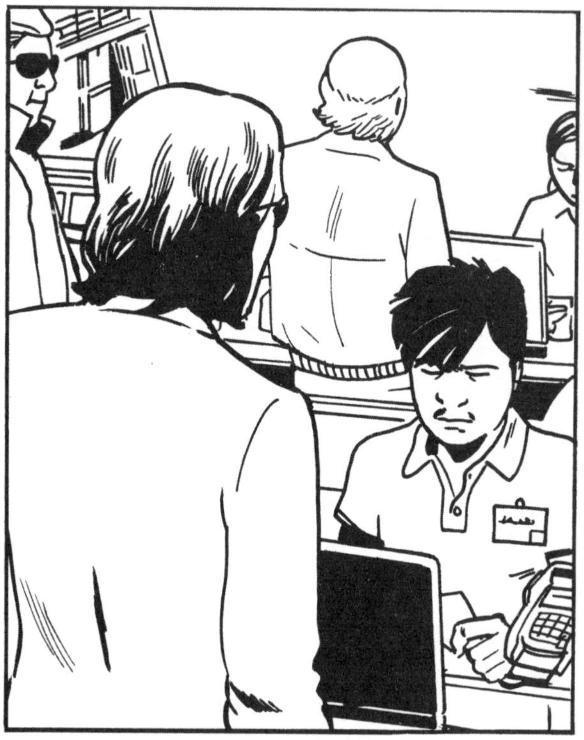

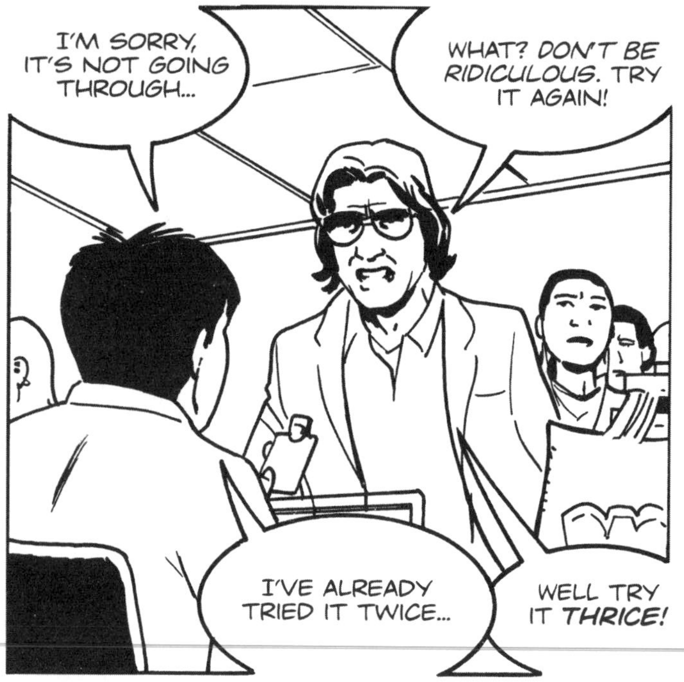
I'M SORRY, IT'S NOT GOING THROUGH...
WHAT? *DON'T BE RIDICULOUS.* TRY IT AGAIN!
I'VE ALREADY TRIED IT TWICE...
WELL TRY IT ***THRICE!***

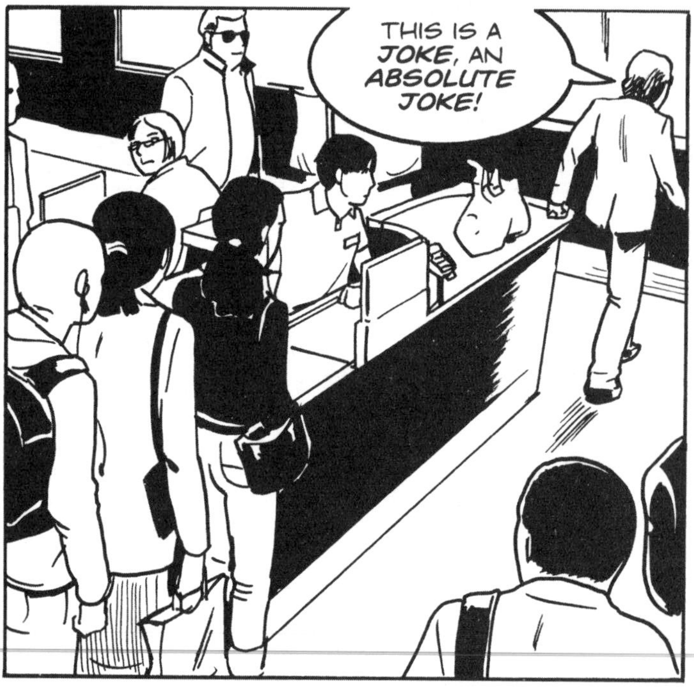
THIS IS A ***JOKE***, AN ***ABSOLUTE JOKE!***

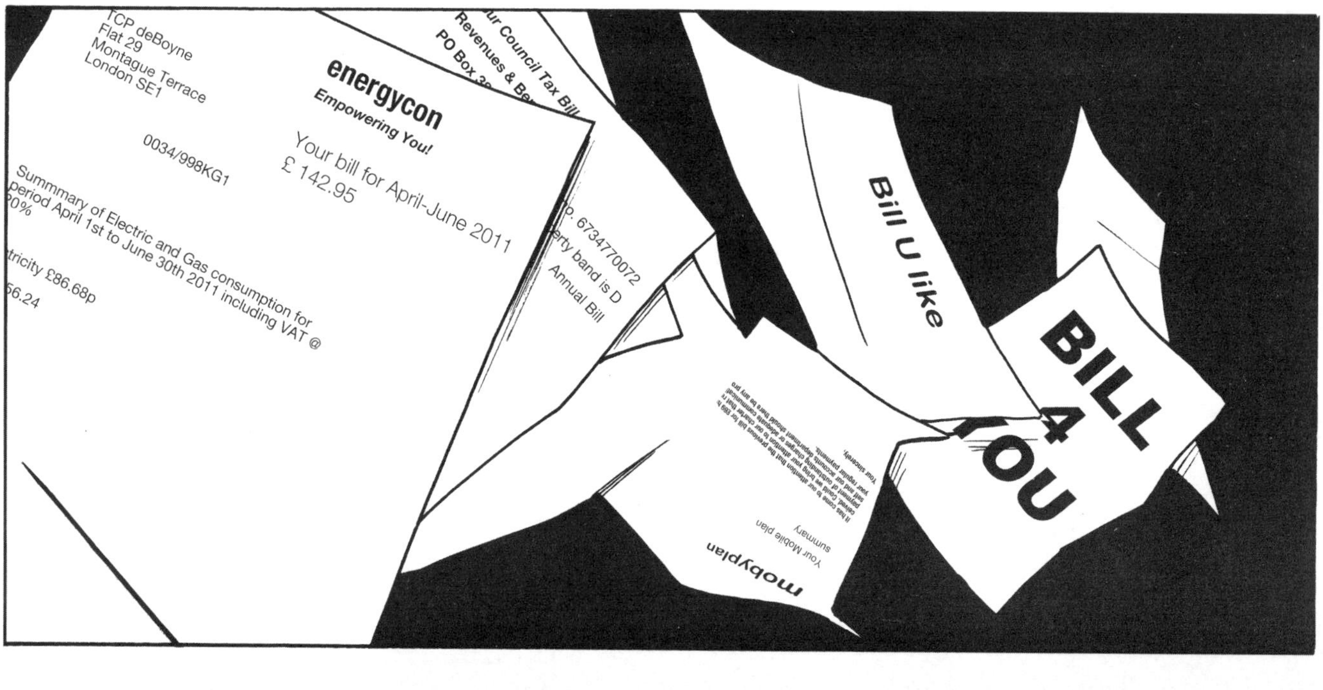
TCP deBoyne
Flat 29
Montague Terrace
London SE1
energycon
Empowering You!
0034/998KG1
Your bill for April-June 2011
£ 142.95
Summmary of Electric and Gas consumption for
period April 1st to June 30th 2011 including VAT @
Annual Bill
Bill U like
BILL 4 YOU
mobyplan
Your Mobile plan
summary

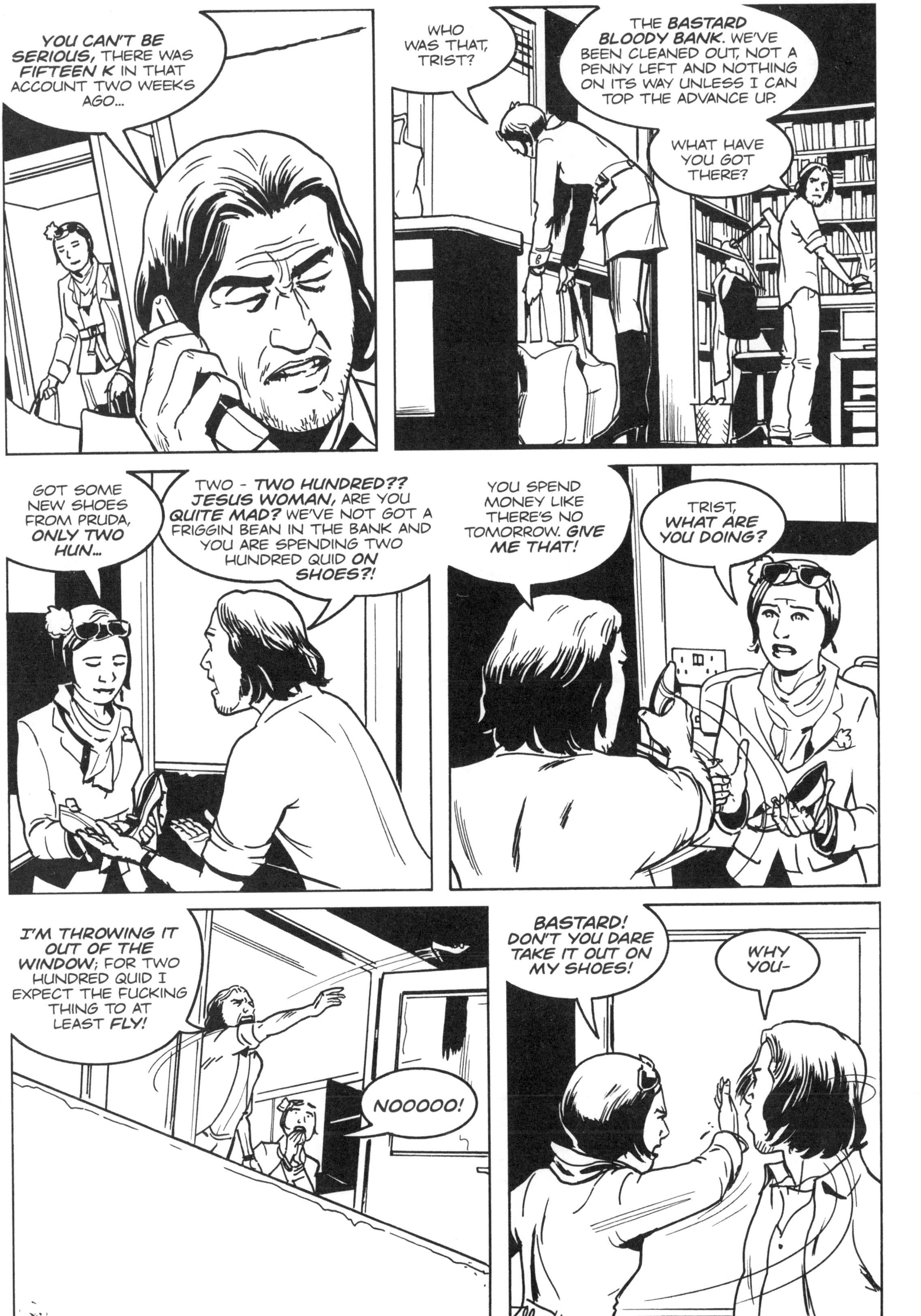
YOU CAN'T BE SERIOUS, THERE WAS FIFTEEN K IN THAT ACCOUNT TWO WEEKS AGO...
WHO WAS THAT, TRIST?
THE BASTARD BLOODY BANK. WE'VE BEEN CLEANED OUT, NOT A PENNY LEFT AND NOTHING ON ITS WAY UNLESS I CAN TOP THE ADVANCE UP.
WHAT HAVE YOU GOT THERE?
GOT SOME NEW SHOES FROM PRUDA, ONLY TWO HUN...
TWO - TWO HUNDRED?? JESUS WOMAN, ARE YOU QUITE MAD? WE'VE NOT GOT A FRIGGIN BEAN IN THE BANK AND YOU ARE SPENDING TWO HUNDRED QUID ON SHOES?!
YOU SPEND MONEY LIKE THERE'S NO TOMORROW. GIVE ME THAT!
TRIST, WHAT ARE YOU DOING?
I'M THROWING IT OUT OF THE WINDOW; FOR TWO HUNDRED QUID I EXPECT THE FUCKING THING TO AT LEAST FLY!
NOOOOO!
BASTARD! DON'T YOU DARE TAKE IT OUT ON MY SHOES!
WHY YOU-

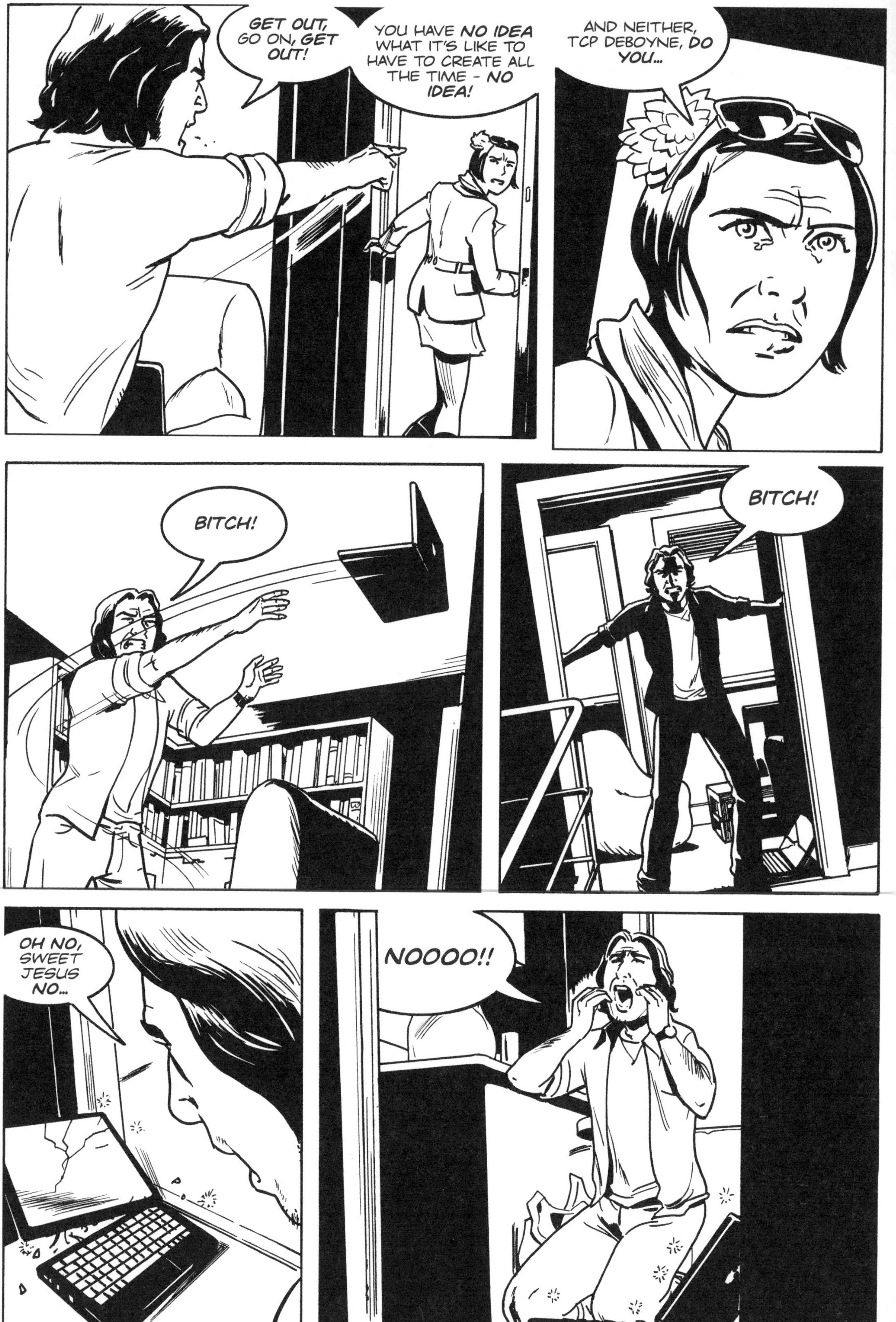
GET OUT, GO ON, GET OUT!
YOU HAVE NO IDEA WHAT IT'S LIKE TO HAVE TO CREATE ALL THE TIME - NO IDEA!
AND NEITHER, TCP DEBOYNE, DO YOU...
BITCH!
BITCH!
OH NO, SWEET JESUS NO...
NOOOO!!

TRISTAN?

Jeremy Chundera

love, loss and Camomile

I THOUGHT IT WAS *UTTER GARBAGE*.

I'VE SEEN BETTER DRAMAS IN MY LOCAL LAUNDERETTE.

SO WHAT WAS SO *BAD* ABOUT IT?

WELL, THERE WAS SIMPLY NO NARRATIVE DRIVE. IT JUST PLODDED ALONG, THE CHARACTER PROFILES WERE WEAK – I MEAN, IF THAT'S THE STANDARD OF WRITING TODAY IN THIS COUNTRY, IT'S FRANKLY DEPLORABLE!

love and Ca

SO TELL ME, TRISTAN, CAN YOU GIVE US THE LOWDOWN ON THE CHARACTERS FROM YOUR NEW BOOK? I'D BE INTRIGUED TO HEAR ABOUT THEM ON THE BACK OF THIS CRITIQUE...

ER, YEAH, WELL, THERE'S THIS... *CHICK* IN SOUTH AMERICA AND SHE'S TAKEN TOO MUCH SAN PEDRO *TRICHOCEREUS PACHANOI* CACTUS, WHICH IS, ERM, HALLUCINOGENIC...

love, loss camomile

AND SHE'S ER, SHE'S GOT GREAT...TITS AND SHE LOVES GETTIN' OFF OF THEM...

I GUESS...

AND SHE GOES TO THIS, ER, PARTY ON ONE OF THE FEW LEGAL NUDIST BEACHES IN SOUTH AMERICA, *ABRICO* IN WESTERN RIO DE JANEIRO,

FASCINATING.

AND THERE SHE BEGINS A JOURNEY OF SELF-DISCOVERY AND SELF-DEMOLITION...

love, loss camomile

THAT'S ORIGINAL...

YEAH, WHO IS THIS BLOKE? HE'S SUCH A *KNOB*...

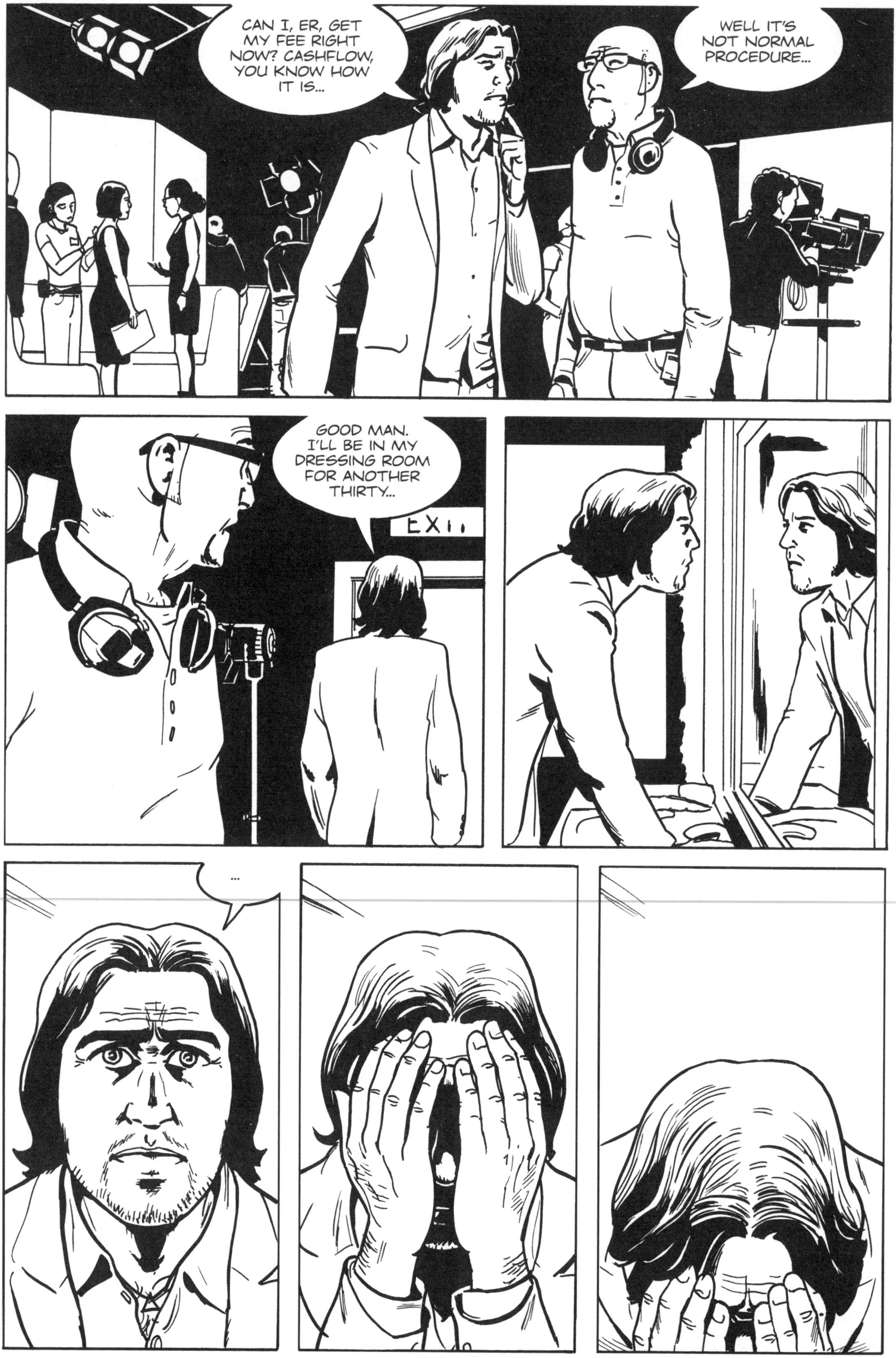
CAN I, ER, GET MY FEE RIGHT NOW? CASHFLOW, YOU KNOW HOW IT IS...
WELL IT'S NOT NORMAL PROCEDURE...
GOOD MAN. I'LL BE IN MY DRESSING ROOM FOR ANOTHER THIRTY...
...

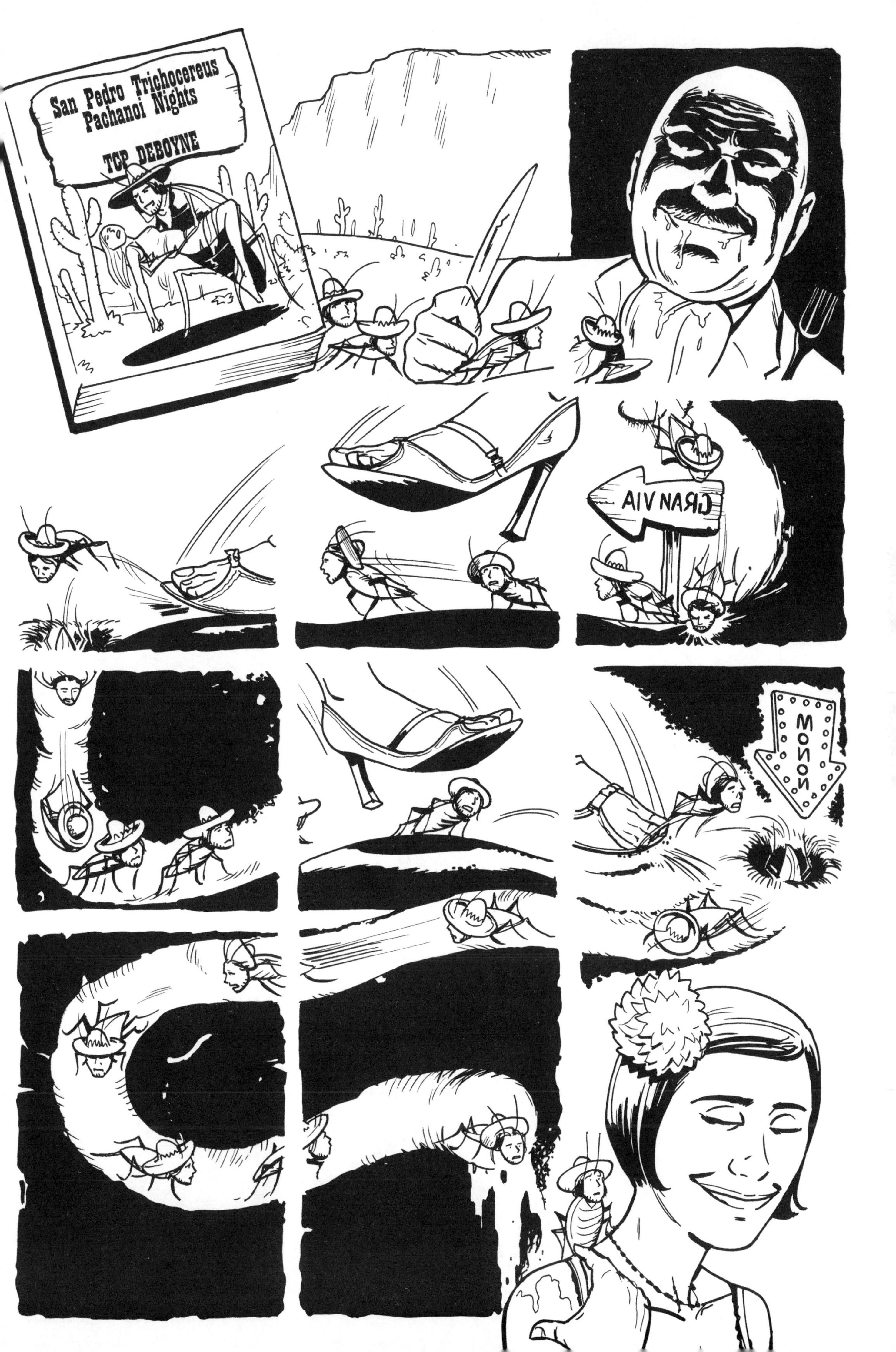
San Pedro Trichocereus
Pachanoi Nights
TCP DEBOYNE
GRAN VIA

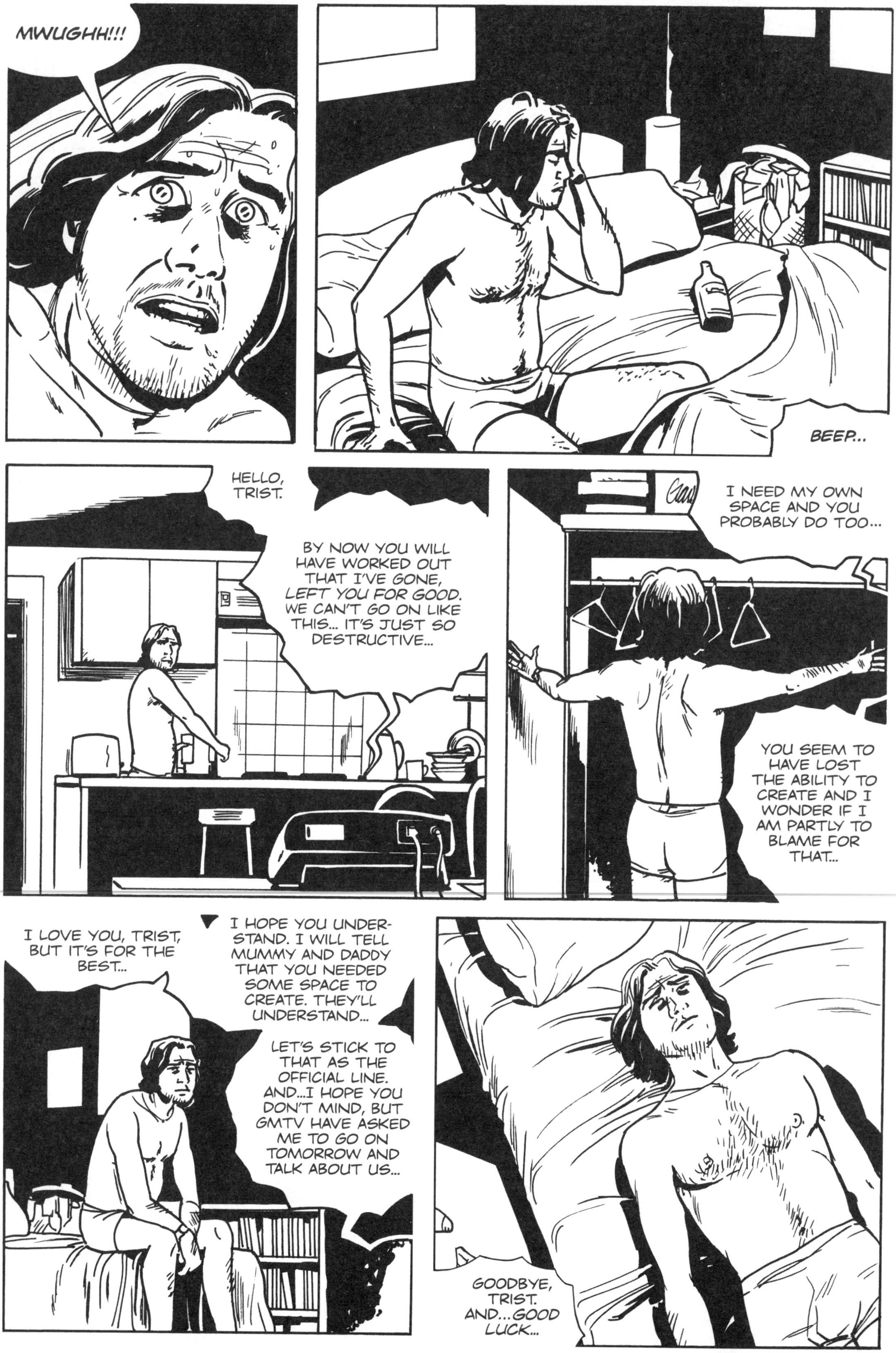
MWUGHH!!!
BEEP...
HELLO, TRIST.
BY NOW YOU WILL HAVE WORKED OUT THAT I'VE GONE, LEFT YOU FOR GOOD. WE CAN'T GO ON LIKE THIS... IT'S JUST SO DESTRUCTIVE...
I NEED MY OWN SPACE AND YOU PROBABLY DO TOO...
YOU SEEM TO HAVE LOST THE ABILITY TO CREATE AND I WONDER IF I AM PARTLY TO BLAME FOR THAT...
I LOVE YOU, TRIST, BUT IT'S FOR THE BEST...
I HOPE YOU UNDER-STAND. I WILL TELL MUMMY AND DADDY THAT YOU NEEDED SOME SPACE TO CREATE. THEY'LL UNDERSTAND...
LET'S STICK TO THAT AS THE OFFICIAL LINE. AND...I HOPE YOU DON'T MIND, BUT GMTV HAVE ASKED ME TO GO ON TOMORROW AND TALK ABOUT US...
GOODBYE, TRIST. AND...GOOD LUCK...

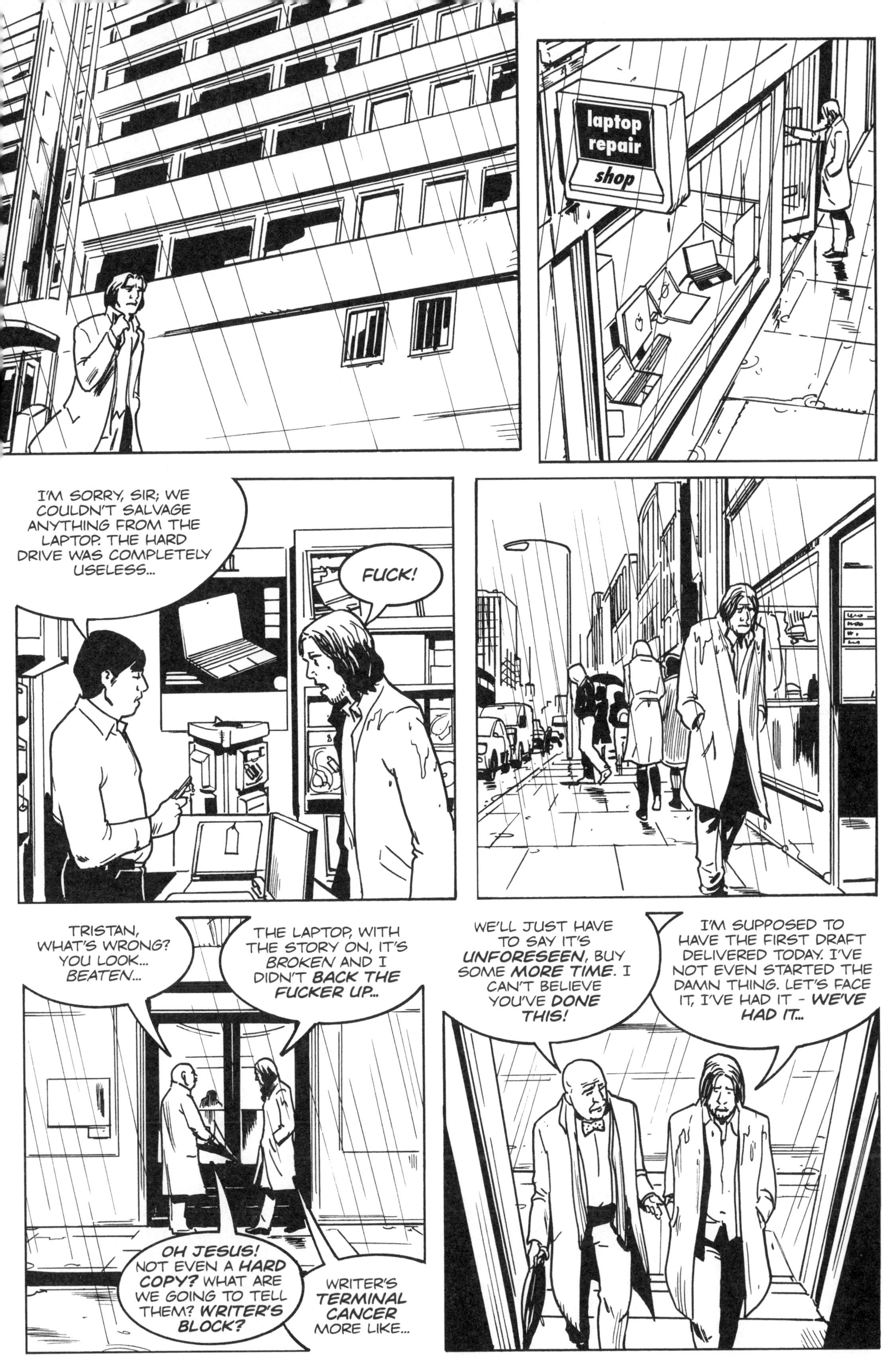
laptop repair shop
I'M SORRY, SIR; WE COULDN'T SALVAGE ANYTHING FROM THE LAPTOP. THE HARD DRIVE WAS COMPLETELY USELESS...
FUCK!
TRISTAN, WHAT'S WRONG? YOU LOOK... BEATEN...
THE LAPTOP, WITH THE STORY ON, IT'S BROKEN AND I DIDN'T BACK THE FUCKER UP...
OH JESUS! NOT EVEN A HARD COPY? WHAT ARE WE GOING TO TELL THEM? WRITER'S BLOCK?
WRITER'S TERMINAL CANCER MORE LIKE...
WE'LL JUST HAVE TO SAY IT'S UNFORESEEN, BUY SOME MORE TIME. I CAN'T BELIEVE YOU'VE DONE THIS!
I'M SUPPOSED TO HAVE THE FIRST DRAFT DELIVERED TODAY. I'VE NOT EVEN STARTED THE DAMN THING. LET'S FACE IT, I'VE HAD IT - WE'VE HAD IT...

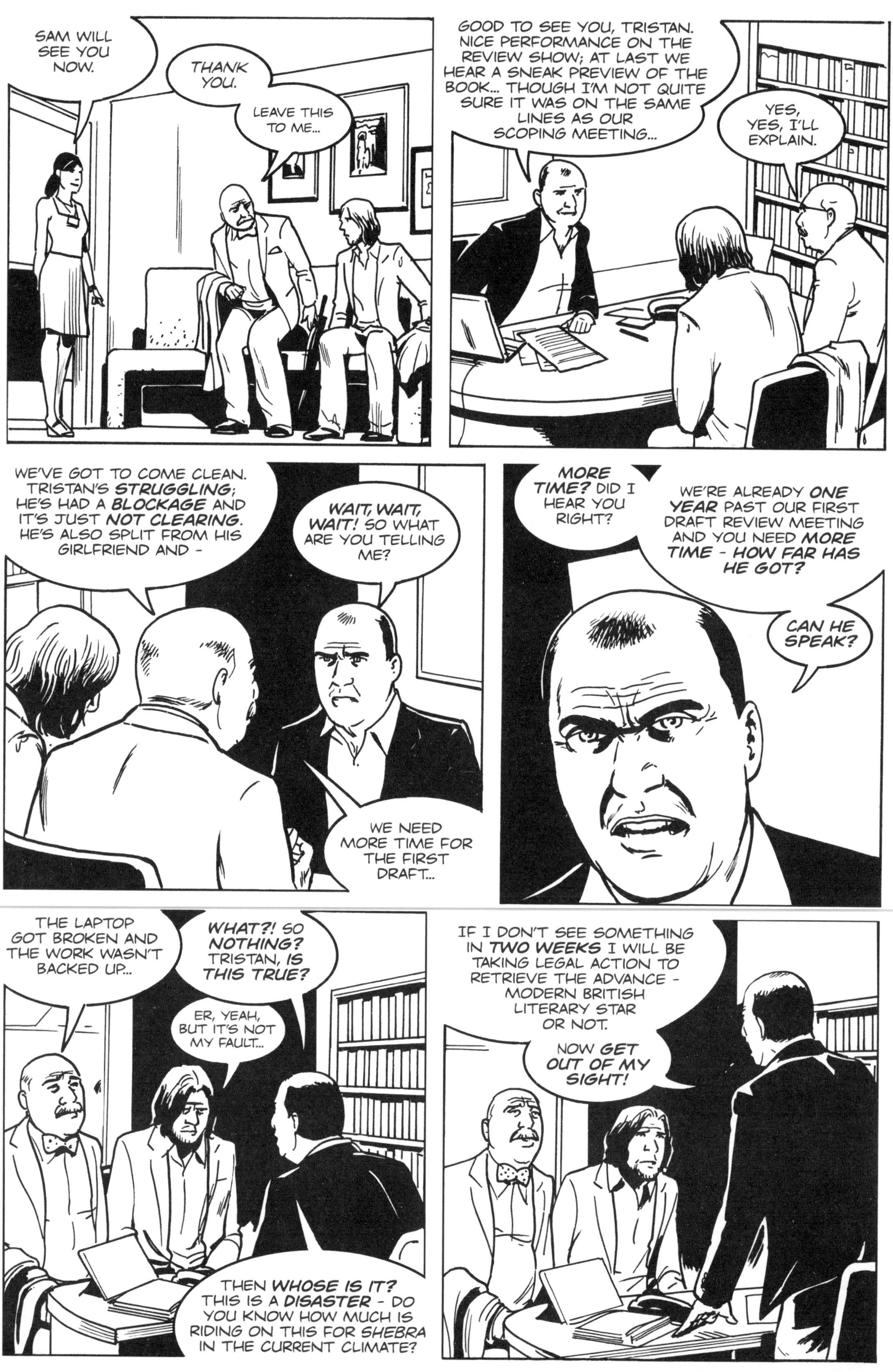
SAM WILL SEE YOU NOW.
THANK YOU.
LEAVE THIS TO ME...
GOOD TO SEE YOU, TRISTAN. NICE PERFORMANCE ON THE REVIEW SHOW; AT LAST WE HEAR A SNEAK PREVIEW OF THE BOOK... THOUGH I'M NOT QUITE SURE IT WAS ON THE SAME LINES AS OUR SCOPING MEETING...
YES, YES, I'LL EXPLAIN.
WE'VE GOT TO COME CLEAN. TRISTAN'S **STRUGGLING**; HE'S HAD A **BLOCKAGE** AND IT'S JUST **NOT CLEARING**. HE'S ALSO SPLIT FROM HIS GIRLFRIEND AND -
WAIT, WAIT, WAIT! SO WHAT ARE YOU TELLING ME?
WE NEED MORE TIME FOR THE FIRST DRAFT...
MORE TIME? DID I HEAR YOU RIGHT?
WE'RE ALREADY **ONE YEAR** PAST OUR FIRST DRAFT REVIEW MEETING AND YOU NEED **MORE TIME** - **HOW FAR HAS HE GOT?**
CAN HE SPEAK?
THE LAPTOP GOT BROKEN AND THE WORK WASN'T BACKED UP...
WHAT?! SO **NOTHING?** TRISTAN, **IS THIS TRUE?**
ER, YEAH, BUT IT'S NOT MY FAULT...
THEN **WHOSE IS IT?** THIS IS A **DISASTER** - DO YOU KNOW HOW MUCH IS RIDING ON THIS FOR SHEBRA IN THE CURRENT CLIMATE?
IF I DON'T SEE SOMETHING IN **TWO WEEKS** I WILL BE TAKING LEGAL ACTION TO RETRIEVE THE ADVANCE - MODERN BRITISH LITERARY STAR OR NOT.
NOW **GET OUT OF MY SIGHT!**

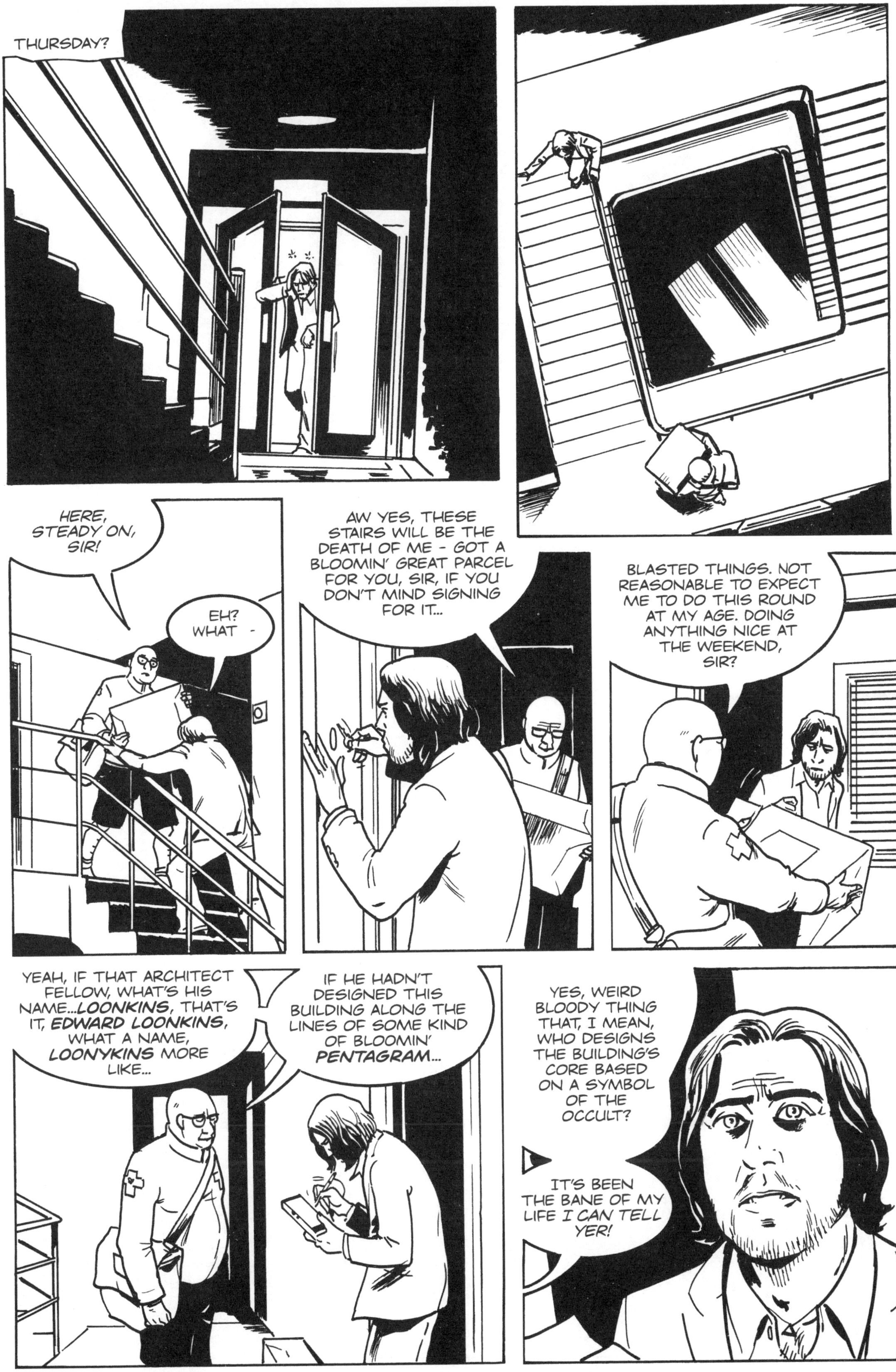
THURSDAY?
HERE, STEADY ON, SIR!
EH? WHAT -
AW YES, THESE STAIRS WILL BE THE DEATH OF ME - GOT A BLOOMIN' GREAT PARCEL FOR YOU, SIR, IF YOU DON'T MIND SIGNING FOR IT...
BLASTED THINGS. NOT REASONABLE TO EXPECT ME TO DO THIS ROUND AT MY AGE. DOING ANYTHING NICE AT THE WEEKEND, SIR?
YEAH, IF THAT ARCHITECT FELLOW, WHAT'S HIS NAME...*LOONKINS*, THAT'S IT, *EDWARD LOONKINS*, WHAT A NAME, *LOONYKINS* MORE LIKE...
IF HE HADN'T DESIGNED THIS BUILDING ALONG THE LINES OF SOME KIND OF BLOOMIN' *PENTAGRAM*...
YES, WEIRD BLOODY THING THAT, I MEAN, WHO DESIGNS THE BUILDING'S CORE BASED ON A SYMBOL OF THE OCCULT?
IT'S BEEN THE BANE OF MY LIFE *I CAN TELL YER!*

REALLY? SO HOW DO YOU, ER, KNOW THIS STUFF...

OH, IF YOU KNOW MONTAGUE TERRACE, SIR, YOU KNOW ITS STORY. IT'S IN THE FABRIC OF THE BUILDING...

FASCINATING, I'D LIKE TO KNOW MORE...WON'T YOU COME IN?

NO, I, ER REALLY SHOULDN'T SAY ANYTHING ELSE, SIR, I'M SURE YOU CAN FIND OUT FOR YOURSELF IF YOU'RE INTERESTED. NOW, MUST BE OFF...

BUT—

I'VE PROBABLY SAID TOO MUCH ALREADY SIR; IT'S A PROBLEM OF MINE; TALKING TOO MUCH.

MUST BE GOING...

CHEERIO SIR!

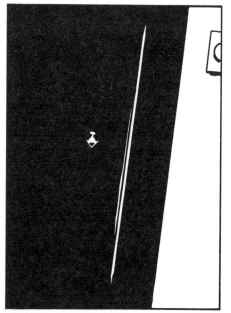

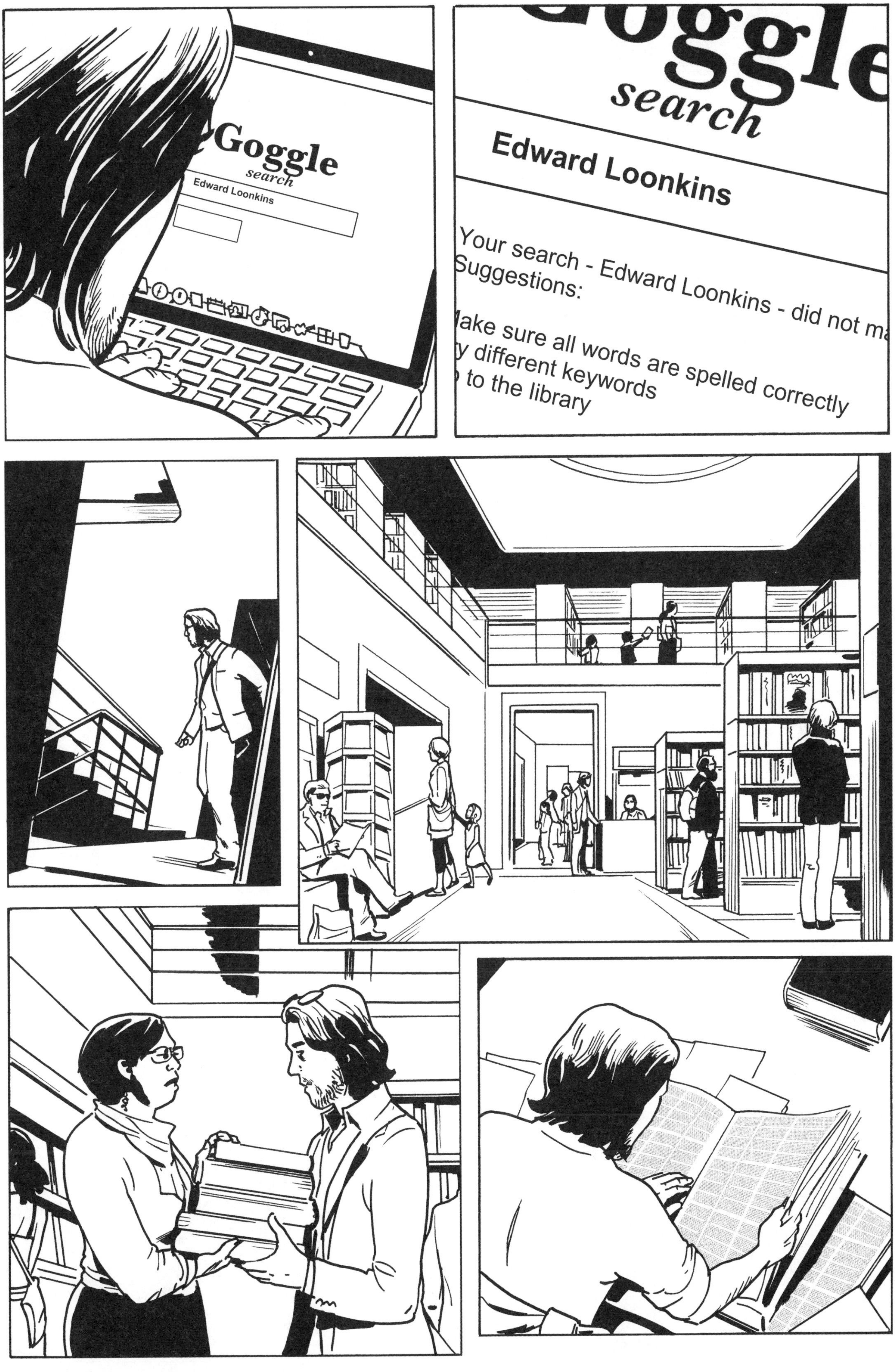
Goggle
search
Edward Loonkins
oggle
search
Edward Loonkins
Your search - Edward Loonkins - did not ma
Suggestions:
lake sure all words are spelled correctly
y different keywords
to the library

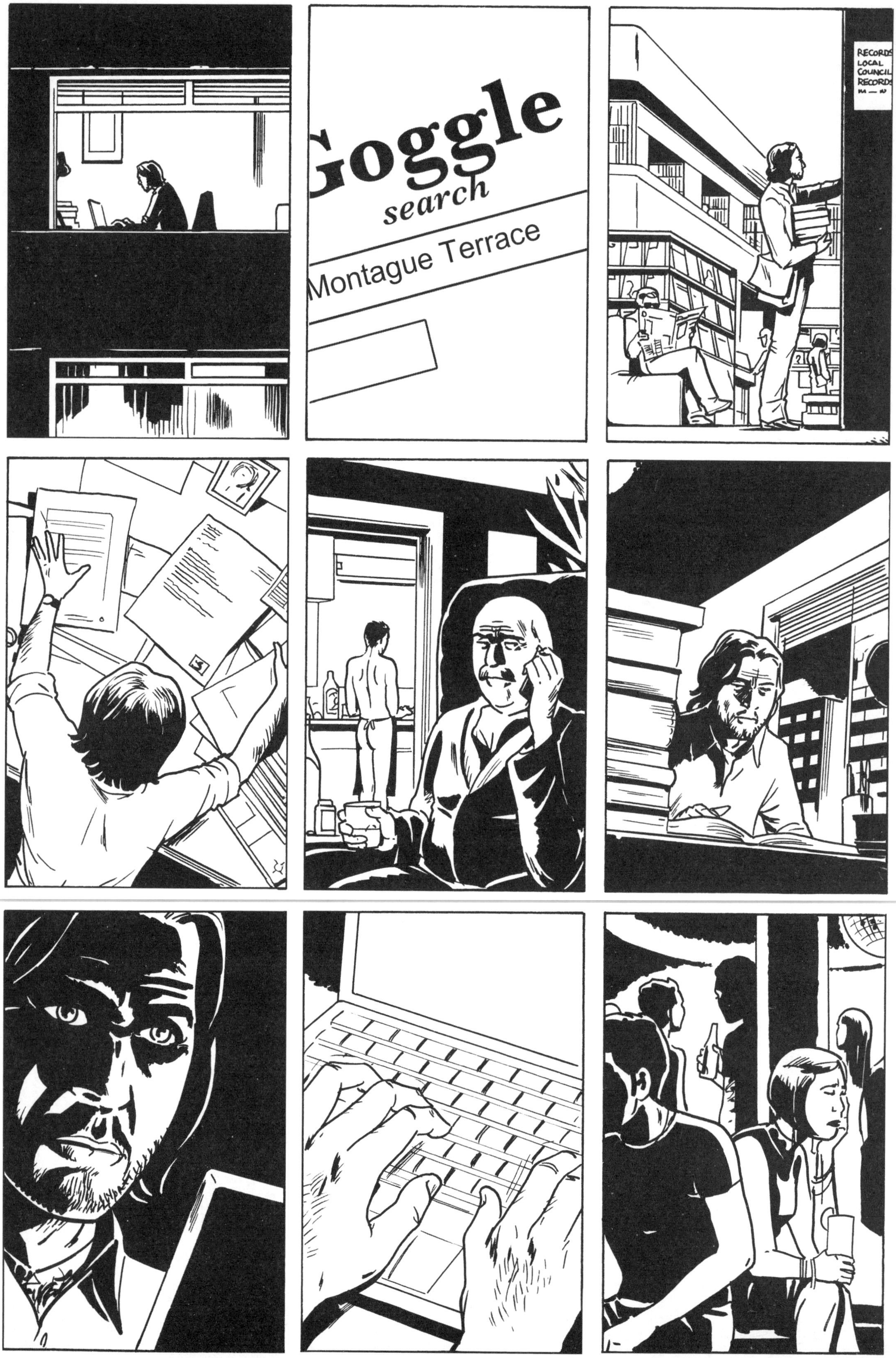
Goggle
search
Montague Terrace
RECORDS
LOCAL
COUNCIL
RECORDS

dweard Loonkins, architect and designer of
y modernist residential buildings across
uin and northern Europe.

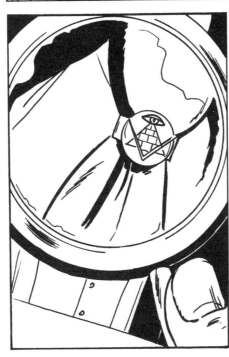

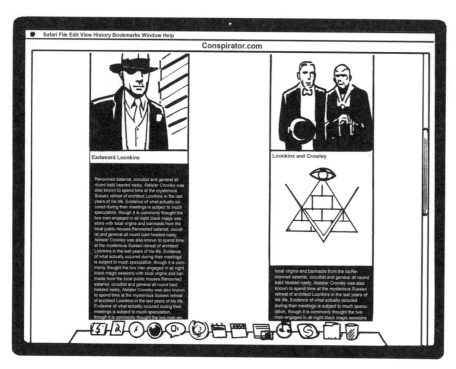

Safari File Edit View History Bookmarks Window Help
Conspirator.com
Eadweard Loonkins
Renowned satanist, occultist and general all round bald headed nasty, Aleister Crowley was also known to spend time at the mysterious Sussex retreat of architect Loonkins in the last years of his life. Evidence of what actually occured during their meetings is subject to much speculation, though it is commonly thought the two men engaged in all night black magic sessions with local virgins and barmaids from the local public houses.Renowned satanist, occultist and general all round bald headed nasty, Aleister Crowley was also known to spend time at the mysterious Sussex retreat of architect Loonkins in the last years of his life. Evidence of what actually occured during their meetings is subject to much speculation, though it is commonly thought the two men engaged in all night black magic sessions with local virgins and barmaids from the local public houses.Renowned satanist, occultist and general all round bald headed nasty, Aleister Crowley was also known to spend time at the mysterious Sussex retreat of architect Loonkins in the last years of his life. Evidence of what actually occured during their meetings is subject to much speculation, though it is commonly thought the two men en-
Loonkins and Crowley
local virgins and barmaids from the locRenowned satanist, occultist and general all round bald headed nasty, Aleister Crowley was also known to spend time at the mysterious Sussex retreat of architect Loonkins in the last years of his life. Evidence of what actually occured during their meetings is subject to much speculation, though it is commonly thought the two men engaged in all night black magic sessions

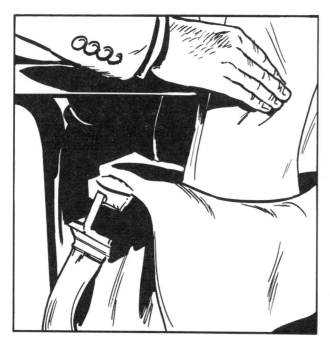

udderly butterly

GOT YA!

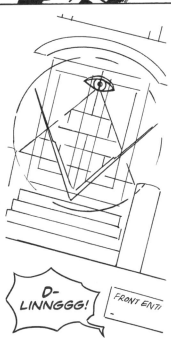

D-LINNGGG!

FRONT ENTI

D-LINNGGG!!

BEEP!

OH TRIST, HOW COULD YOU BE SUCH A *BASTARD*? I MISS YOU, TRIST, *DAMN IT!!*

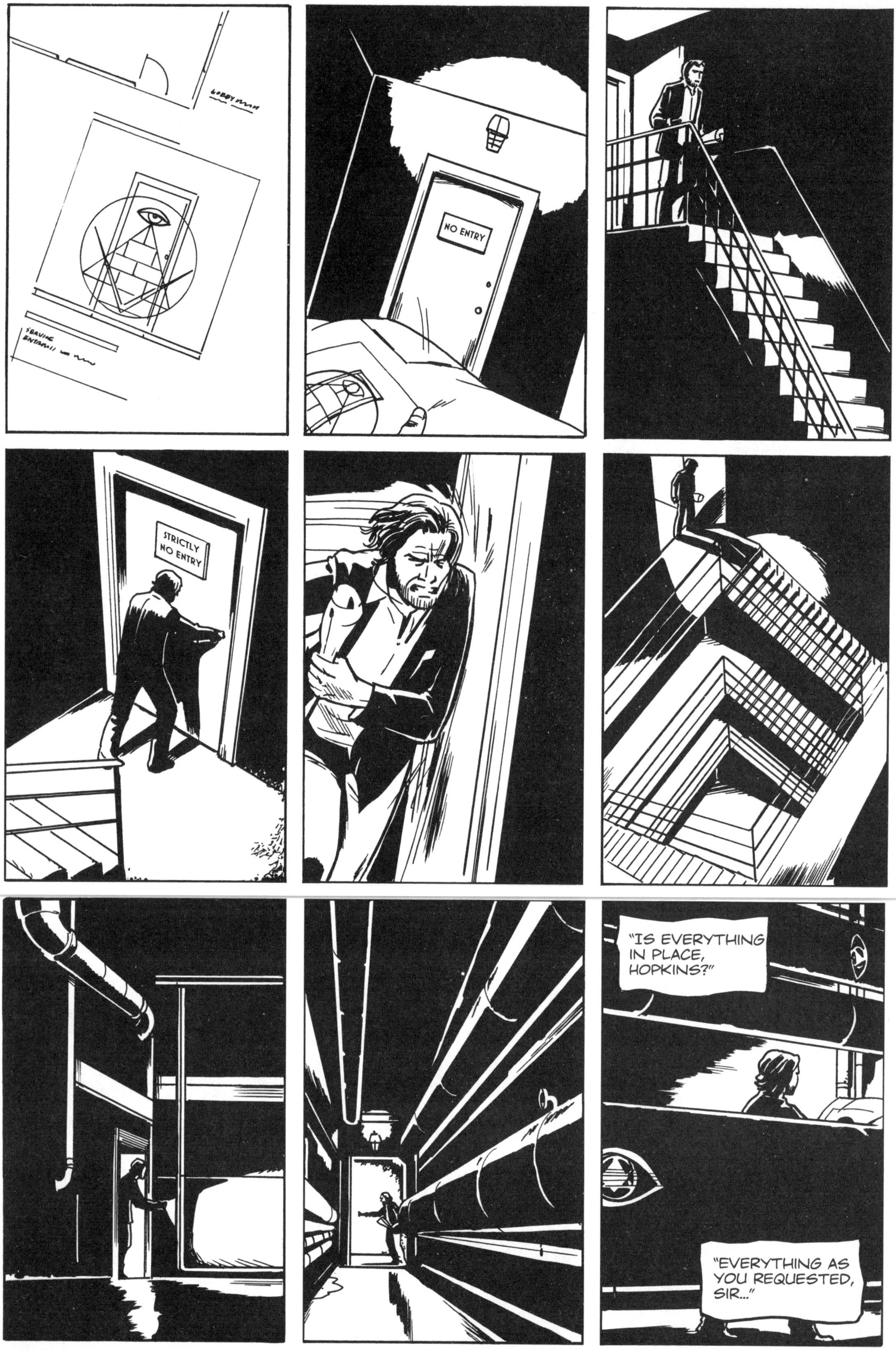
NO ENTRY
STRICTLY NO ENTRY
"IS EVERYTHING IN PLACE, HOPKINS?"
"EVERYTHING AS YOU REQUESTED, SIR..."

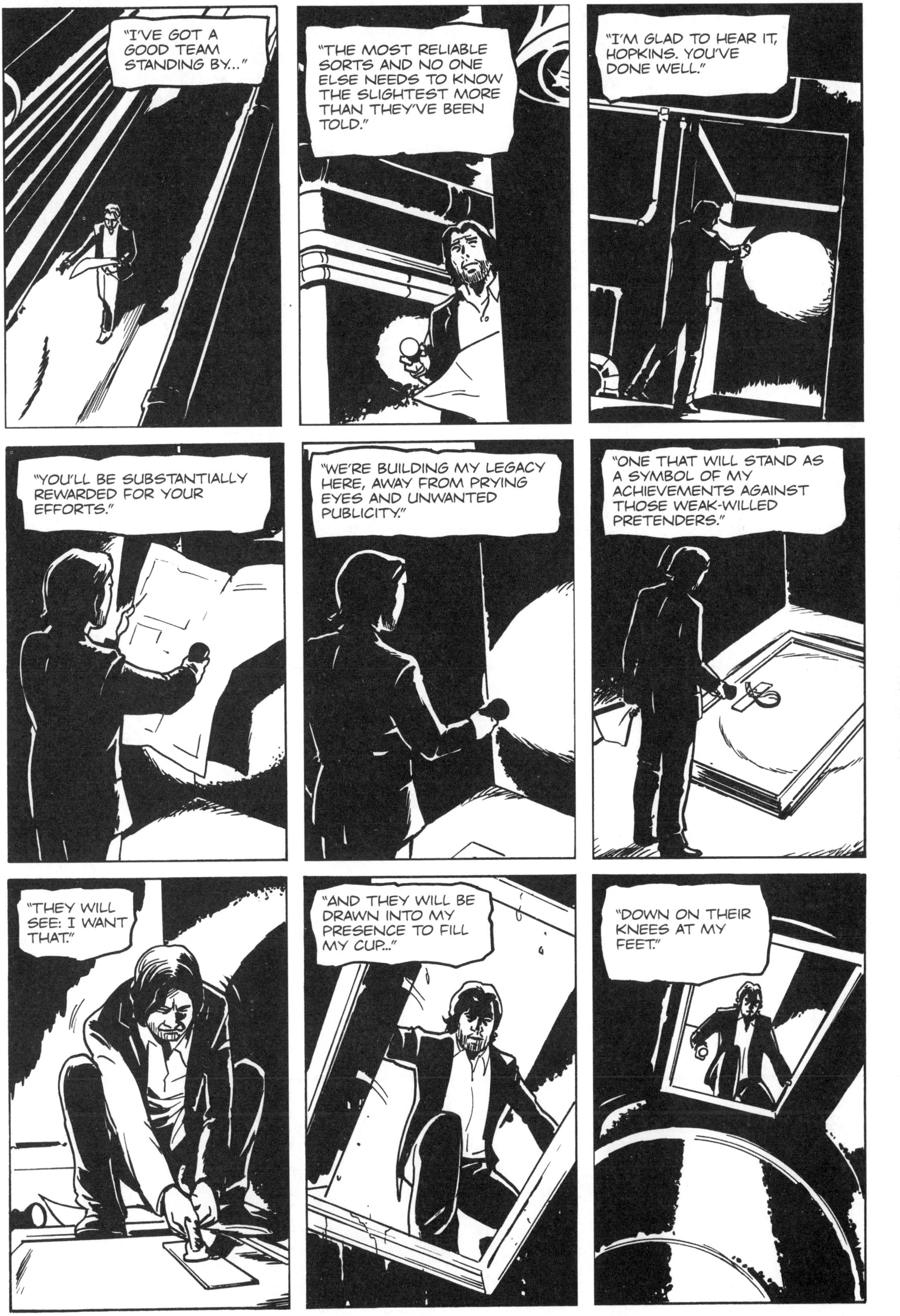
"I'VE GOT A GOOD TEAM STANDING BY..."
"THE MOST RELIABLE SORTS AND NO ONE ELSE NEEDS TO KNOW THE SLIGHTEST MORE THAN THEY'VE BEEN TOLD."
"I'M GLAD TO HEAR IT, HOPKINS. YOU'VE DONE WELL."
"YOU'LL BE SUBSTANTIALLY REWARDED FOR YOUR EFFORTS."
"WE'RE BUILDING MY LEGACY HERE, AWAY FROM PRYING EYES AND UNWANTED PUBLICITY."
"ONE THAT WILL STAND AS A SYMBOL OF MY ACHIEVEMENTS AGAINST THOSE WEAK-WILLED PRETENDERS."
"THEY WILL SEE: I WANT THAT."
"AND THEY WILL BE DRAWN INTO MY PRESENCE TO FILL MY CUP..."
"DOWN ON THEIR KNEES AT MY FEET."

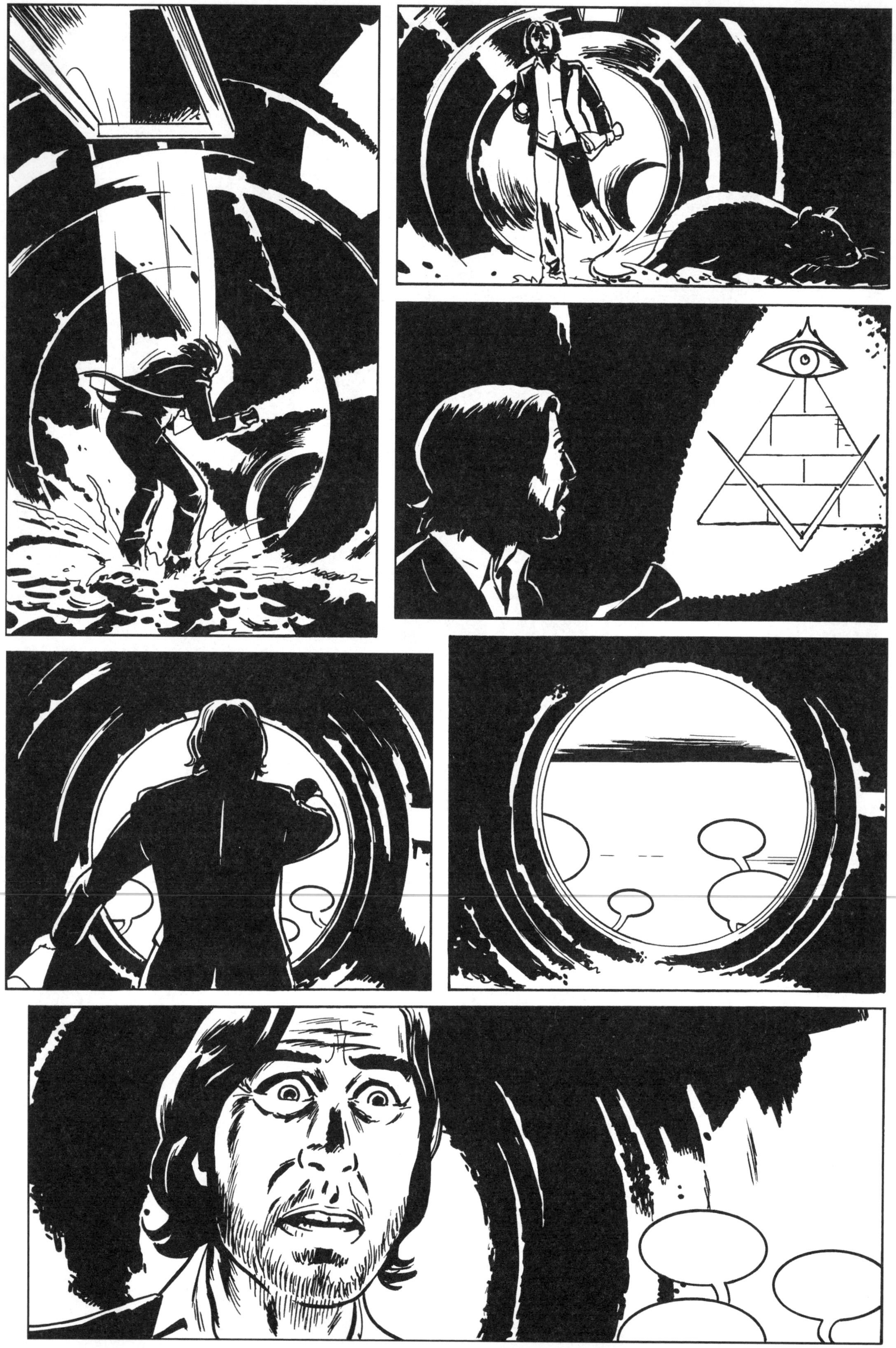

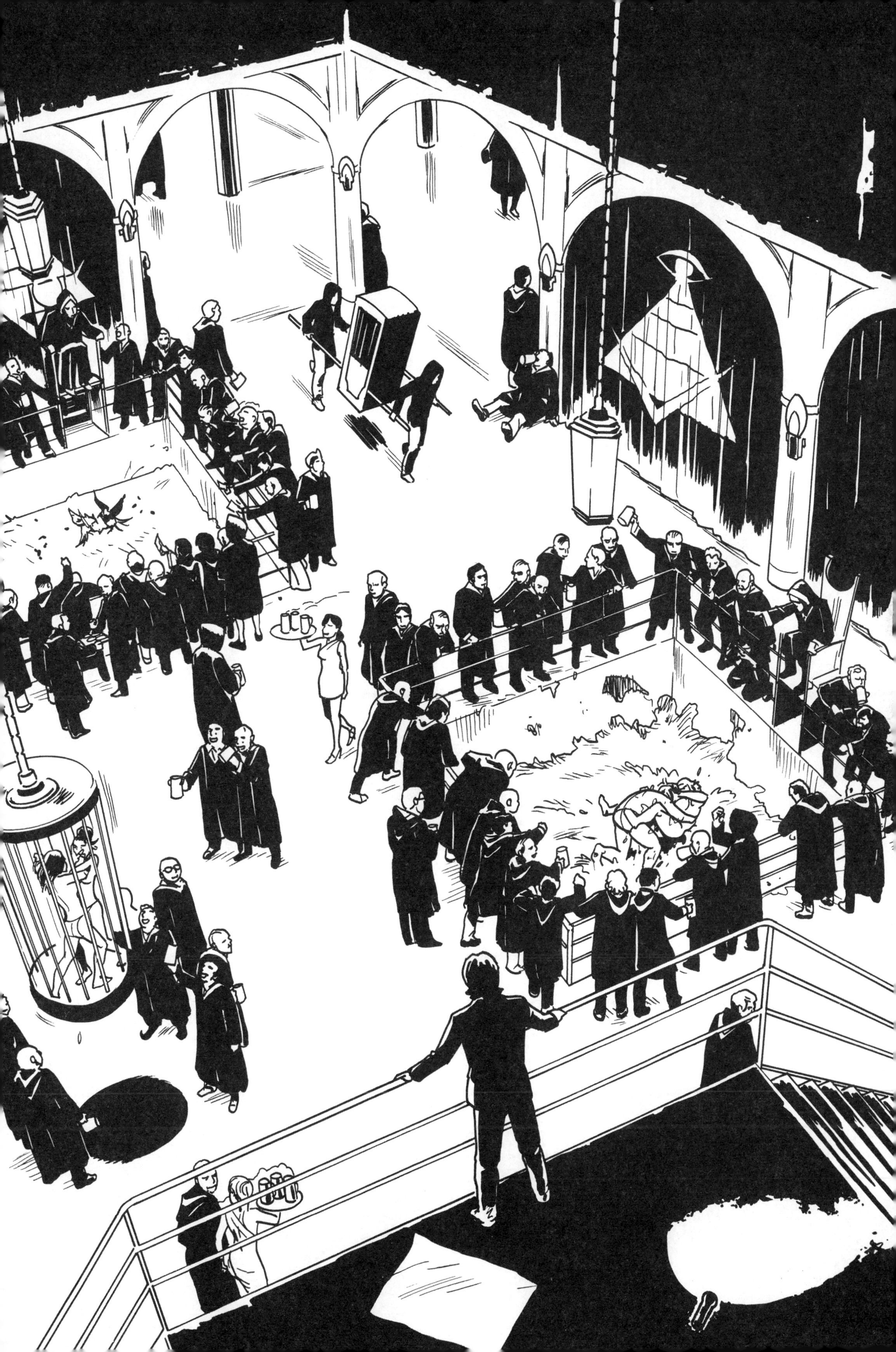

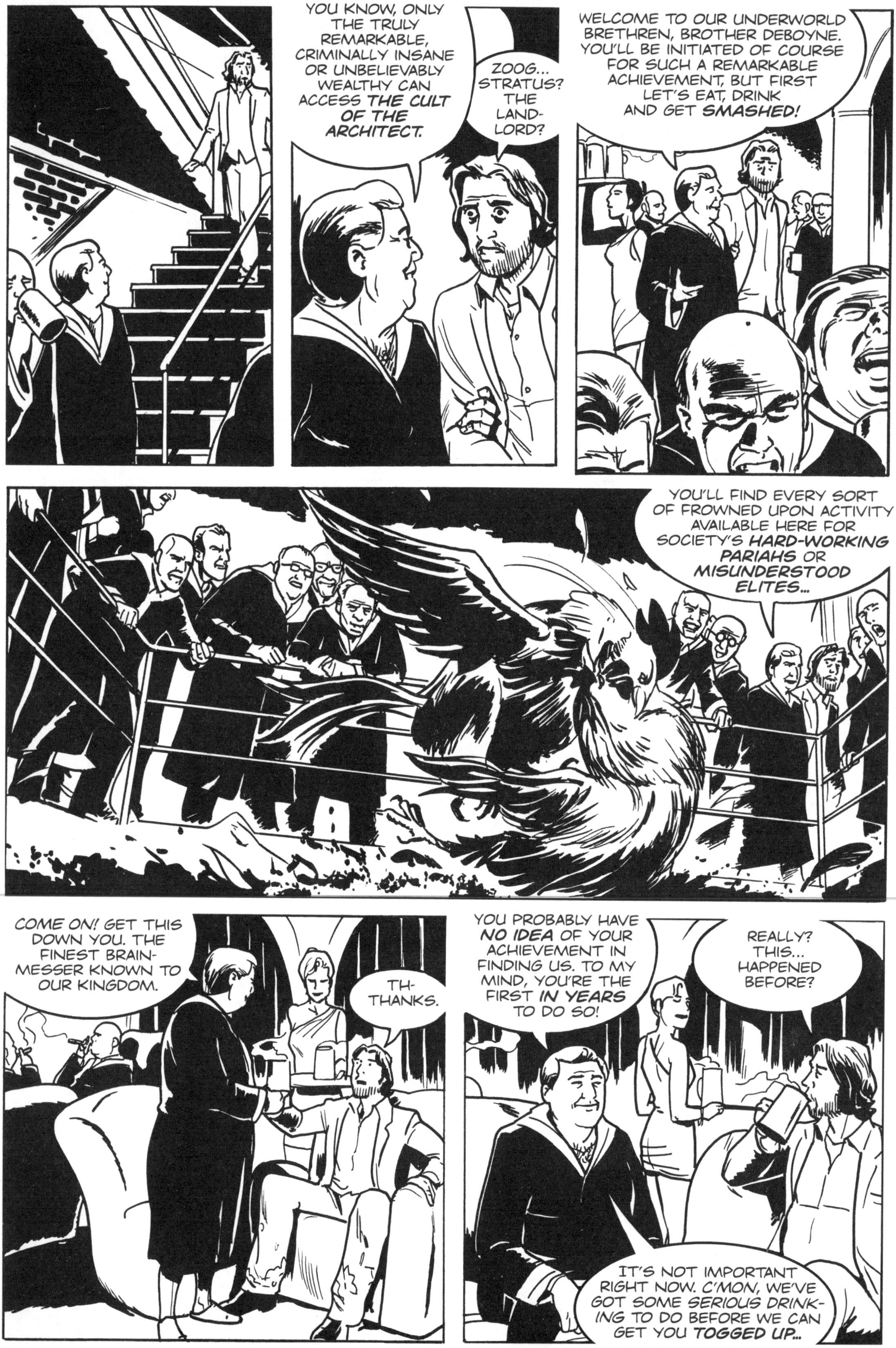
YOU KNOW, ONLY THE TRULY REMARKABLE, CRIMINALLY INSANE OR UNBELIEVABLY WEALTHY CAN ACCESS **THE CULT OF THE ARCHITECT.**
ZOOG... STRATUS? THE LAND-LORD?
WELCOME TO OUR UNDERWORLD BRETHREN, BROTHER DEBOYNE. YOU'LL BE INITIATED OF COURSE FOR SUCH A REMARKABLE ACHIEVEMENT, BUT FIRST LET'S EAT, DRINK AND GET **SMASHED!**
YOU'LL FIND EVERY SORT OF FROWNED UPON ACTIVITY AVAILABLE HERE FOR SOCIETY'S **HARD-WORKING PARIAHS** OR **MISUNDERSTOOD ELITES...**
COME ON! GET THIS DOWN YOU. THE FINEST BRAIN-MESSER KNOWN TO OUR KINGDOM.
TH-THANKS.
YOU PROBABLY HAVE **NO IDEA** OF YOUR ACHIEVEMENT IN FINDING US. TO MY MIND, YOU'RE THE FIRST **IN YEARS** TO DO SO!
REALLY? THIS... HAPPENED BEFORE?
IT'S NOT IMPORTANT RIGHT NOW. C'MON, WE'VE GOT SOME SERIOUS DRINK-ING TO DO BEFORE WE CAN GET YOU **TOGGED UP...**

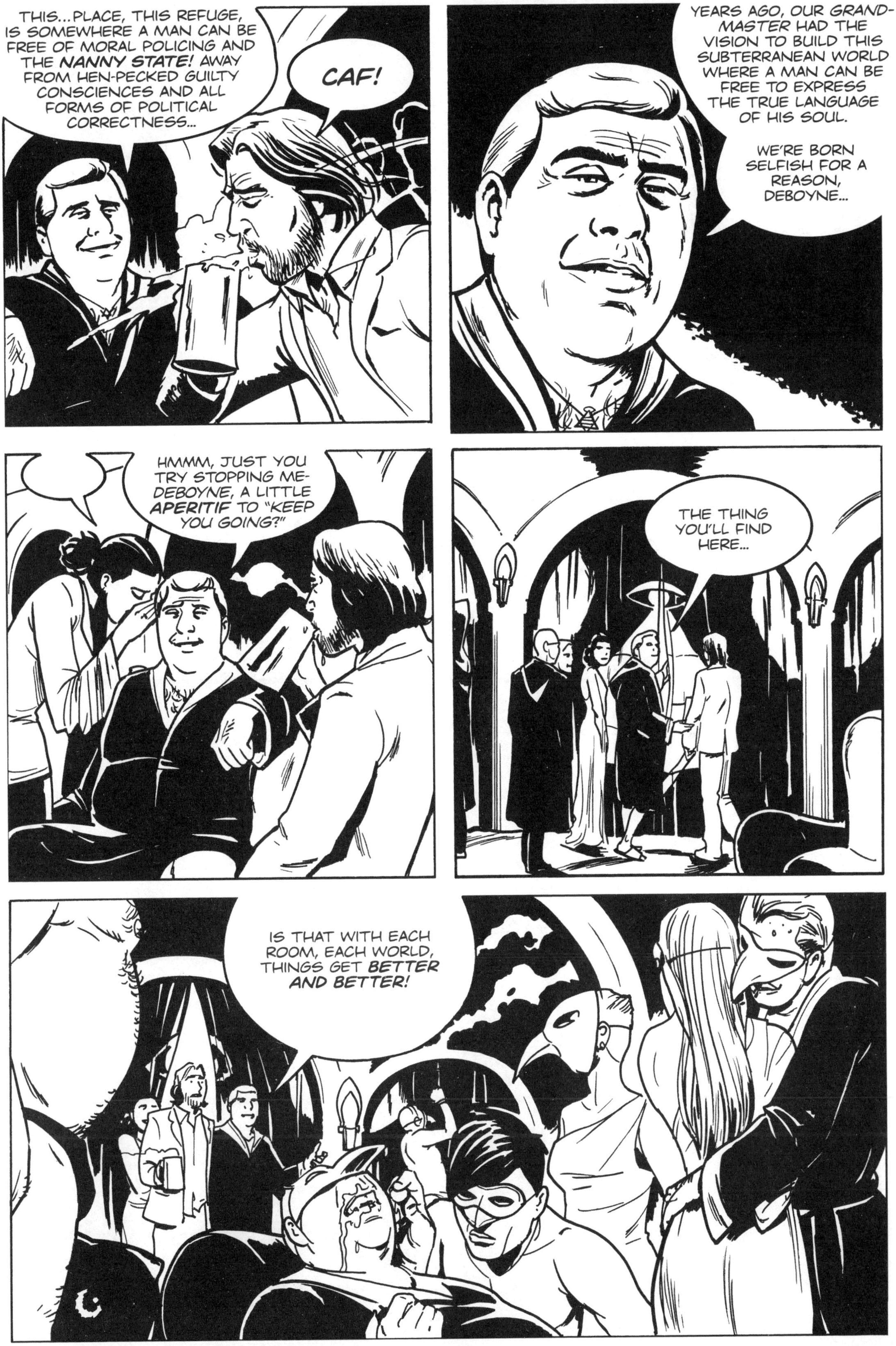
THIS...PLACE, THIS REFUGE, IS SOMEWHERE A MAN CAN BE FREE OF MORAL POLICING AND THE NANNY STATE! AWAY FROM HEN-PECKED GUILTY CONSCIENCES AND ALL FORMS OF POLITICAL CORRECTNESS...
CAF!
YEARS AGO, OUR GRAND-MASTER HAD THE VISION TO BUILD THIS SUBTERRANEAN WORLD WHERE A MAN CAN BE FREE TO EXPRESS THE TRUE LANGUAGE OF HIS SOUL.
WE'RE BORN SELFISH FOR A REASON, DEBOYNE...
HMMM, JUST YOU TRY STOPPING ME-DEBOYNE, A LITTLE APERITIF TO "KEEP YOU GOING?"
THE THING YOU'LL FIND HERE...
IS THAT WITH EACH ROOM, EACH WORLD, THINGS GET BETTER AND BETTER!

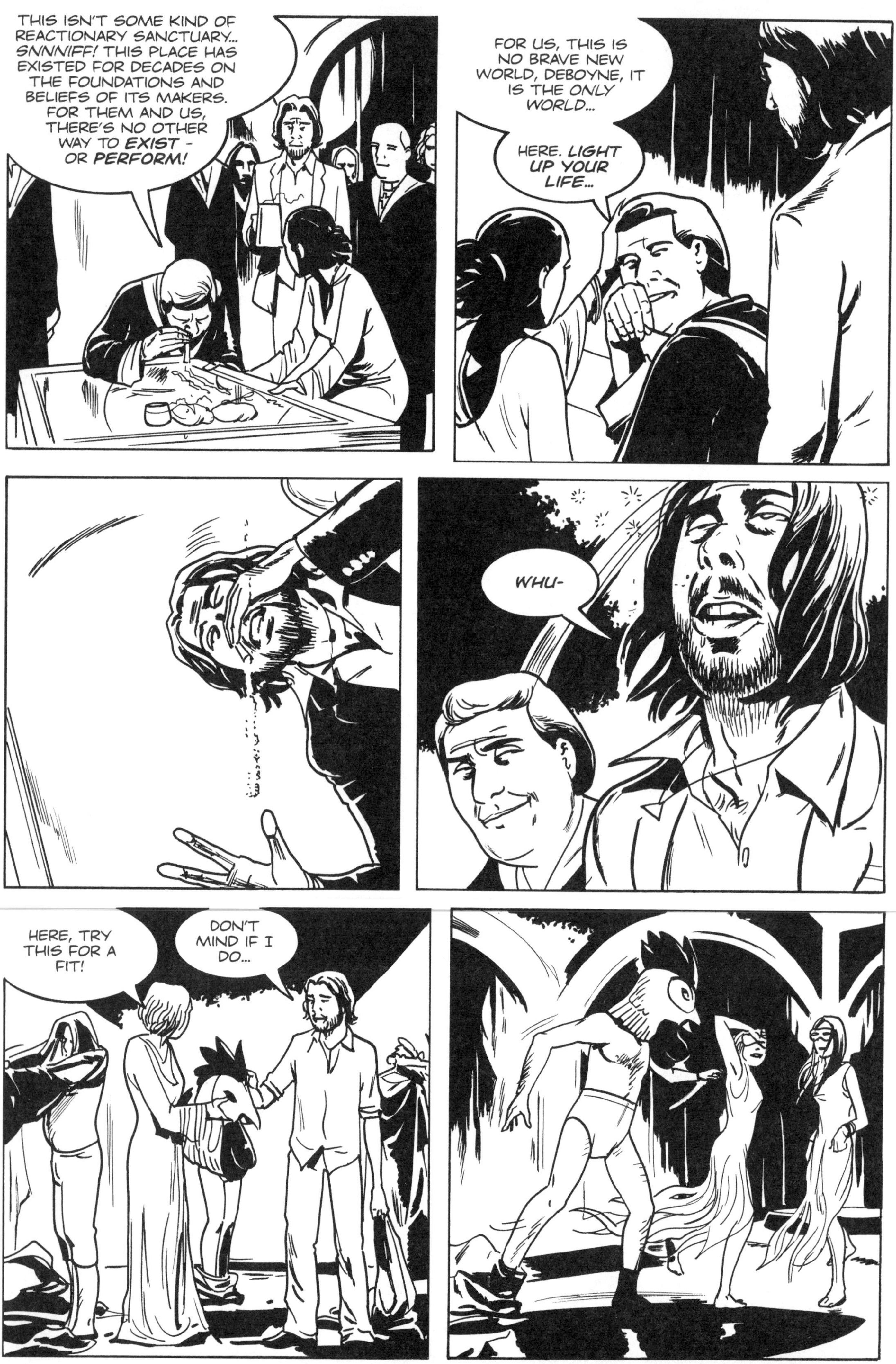
THIS ISN'T SOME KIND OF REACTIONARY SANCTUARY... SNNNIFF! THIS PLACE HAS EXISTED FOR DECADES ON THE FOUNDATIONS AND BELIEFS OF ITS MAKERS. FOR THEM AND US, THERE'S NO OTHER WAY TO EXIST - OR PERFORM!
FOR US, THIS IS NO BRAVE NEW WORLD, DEBOYNE, IT IS THE ONLY WORLD...
HERE. LIGHT UP YOUR LIFE...
WHU-
HERE, TRY THIS FOR A FIT!
DON'T MIND IF I DO...

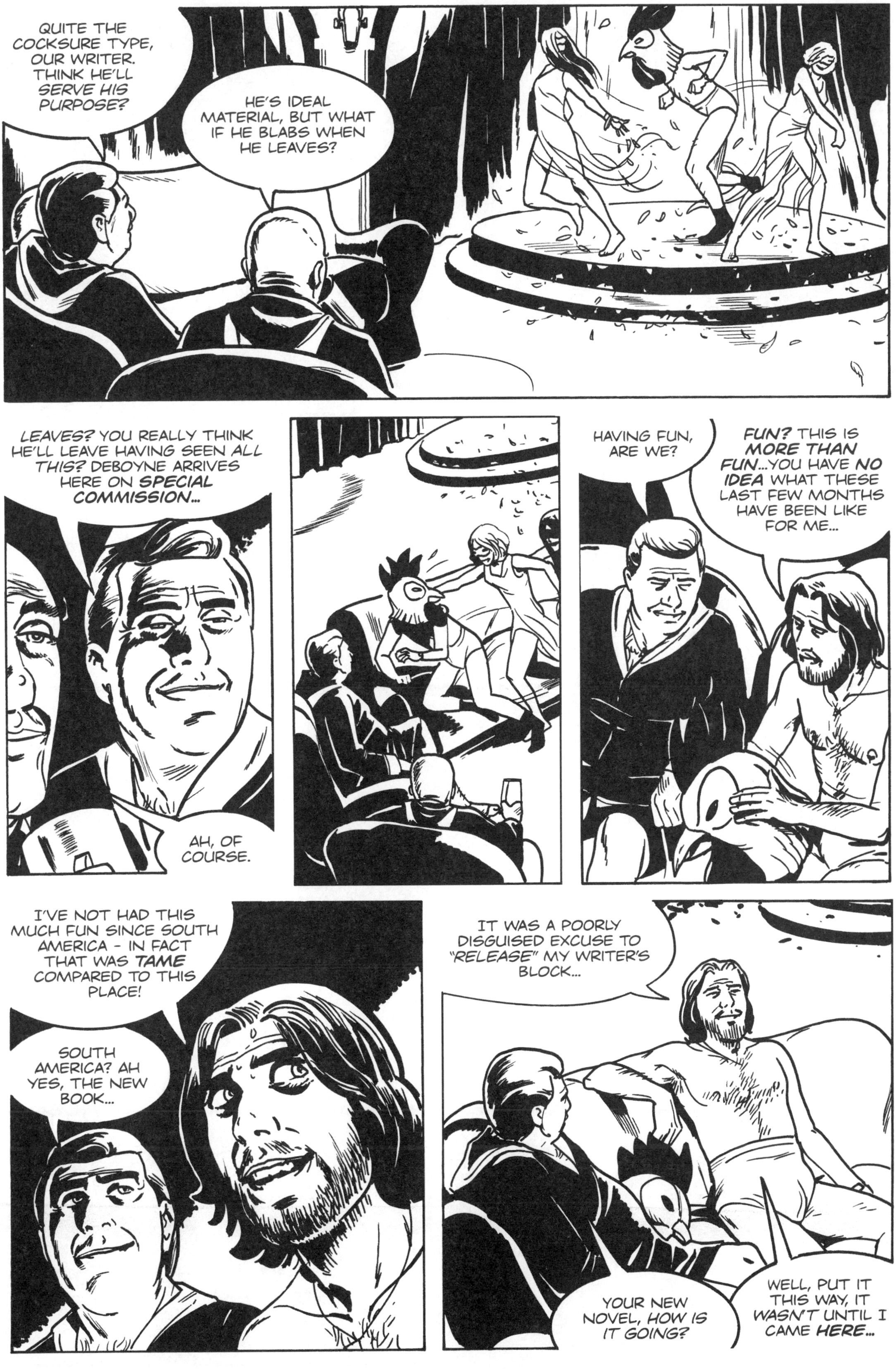
QUITE THE COCKSURE TYPE, OUR WRITER. THINK HE'LL *SERVE HIS PURPOSE?*
HE'S IDEAL MATERIAL, BUT WHAT IF HE BLABS WHEN HE LEAVES?
LEAVES? YOU REALLY THINK HE'LL LEAVE HAVING SEEN *ALL* THIS? DEBOYNE ARRIVES HERE ON ***SPECIAL COMMISSION...***
AH, OF COURSE.
HAVING FUN, ARE WE?
FUN? THIS IS ***MORE THAN FUN***...YOU HAVE ***NO IDEA*** WHAT THESE LAST FEW MONTHS HAVE BEEN LIKE FOR ME...
I'VE NOT HAD THIS MUCH FUN SINCE SOUTH AMERICA - IN FACT THAT WAS ***TAME*** COMPARED TO THIS PLACE!
SOUTH AMERICA? AH YES, THE NEW BOOK...
IT WAS A POORLY DISGUISED EXCUSE TO *"RELEASE"* MY WRITER'S BLOCK...
YOUR NEW NOVEL, *HOW IS IT GOING?*
WELL, PUT IT THIS WAY, IT *WASN'T* UNTIL I CAME ***HERE...***

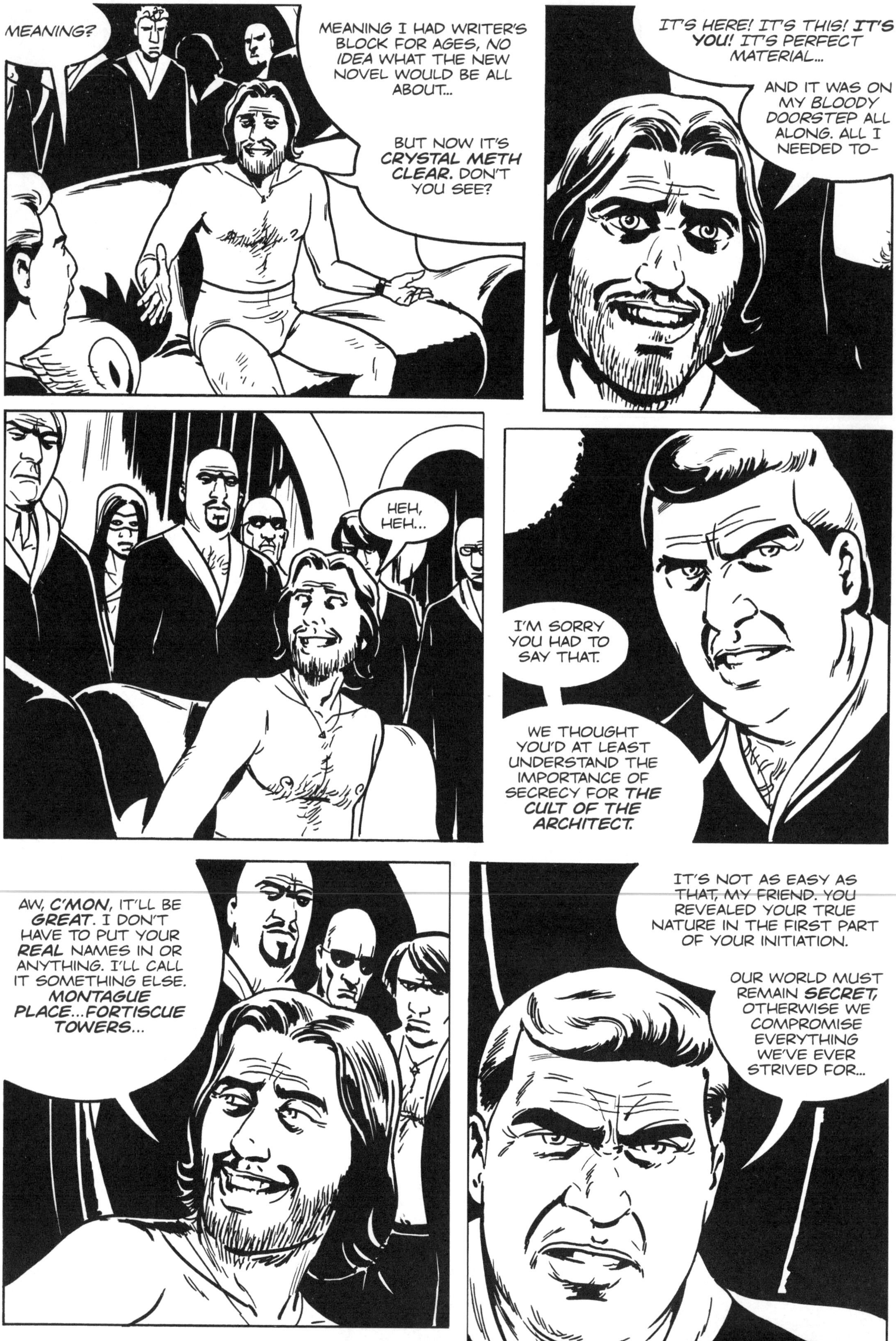
MEANING?
MEANING I HAD WRITER'S BLOCK FOR AGES, NO IDEA WHAT THE NEW NOVEL WOULD BE ALL ABOUT...
BUT NOW IT'S CRYSTAL METH CLEAR. DON'T YOU SEE?
IT'S HERE! IT'S THIS! IT'S YOU! IT'S PERFECT MATERIAL...
AND IT WAS ON MY BLOODY DOORSTEP ALL ALONG. ALL I NEEDED TO-
HEH, HEH...
I'M SORRY YOU HAD TO SAY THAT.
WE THOUGHT YOU'D AT LEAST UNDERSTAND THE IMPORTANCE OF SECRECY FOR THE CULT OF THE ARCHITECT.
AW, C'MON, IT'LL BE GREAT. I DON'T HAVE TO PUT YOUR REAL NAMES IN OR ANYTHING. I'LL CALL IT SOMETHING ELSE. MONTAGUE PLACE...FORTISCUE TOWERS...
IT'S NOT AS EASY AS THAT, MY FRIEND. YOU REVEALED YOUR TRUE NATURE IN THE FIRST PART OF YOUR INITIATION.
OUR WORLD MUST REMAIN SECRET, OTHERWISE WE COMPROMISE EVERYTHING WE'VE EVER STRIVED FOR...

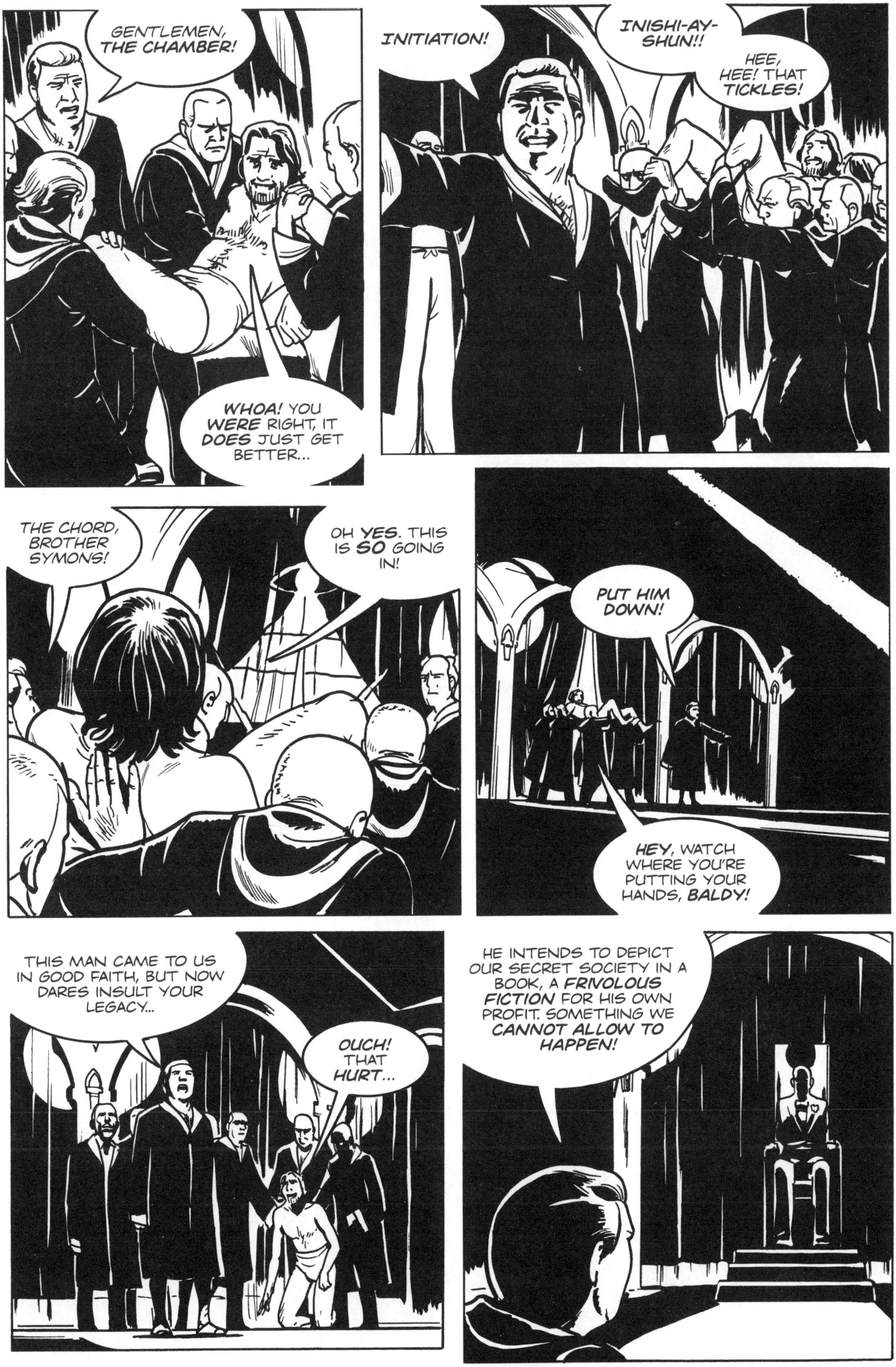
GENTLEMEN, THE CHAMBER!
WHOA! YOU WERE RIGHT, IT DOES JUST GET BETTER...
INITIATION!
INISHI-AY-SHUN!!
HEE, HEE! THAT TICKLES!
THE CHORD, BROTHER SYMONS!
OH YES. THIS IS SO GOING IN!
PUT HIM DOWN!
HEY, WATCH WHERE YOU'RE PUTTING YOUR HANDS, BALDY!
THIS MAN CAME TO US IN GOOD FAITH, BUT NOW DARES INSULT YOUR LEGACY...
OUCH! THAT HURT...
HE INTENDS TO DEPICT OUR SECRET SOCIETY IN A BOOK, A FRIVOLOUS FICTION FOR HIS OWN PROFIT. SOMETHING WE CANNOT ALLOW TO HAPPEN!

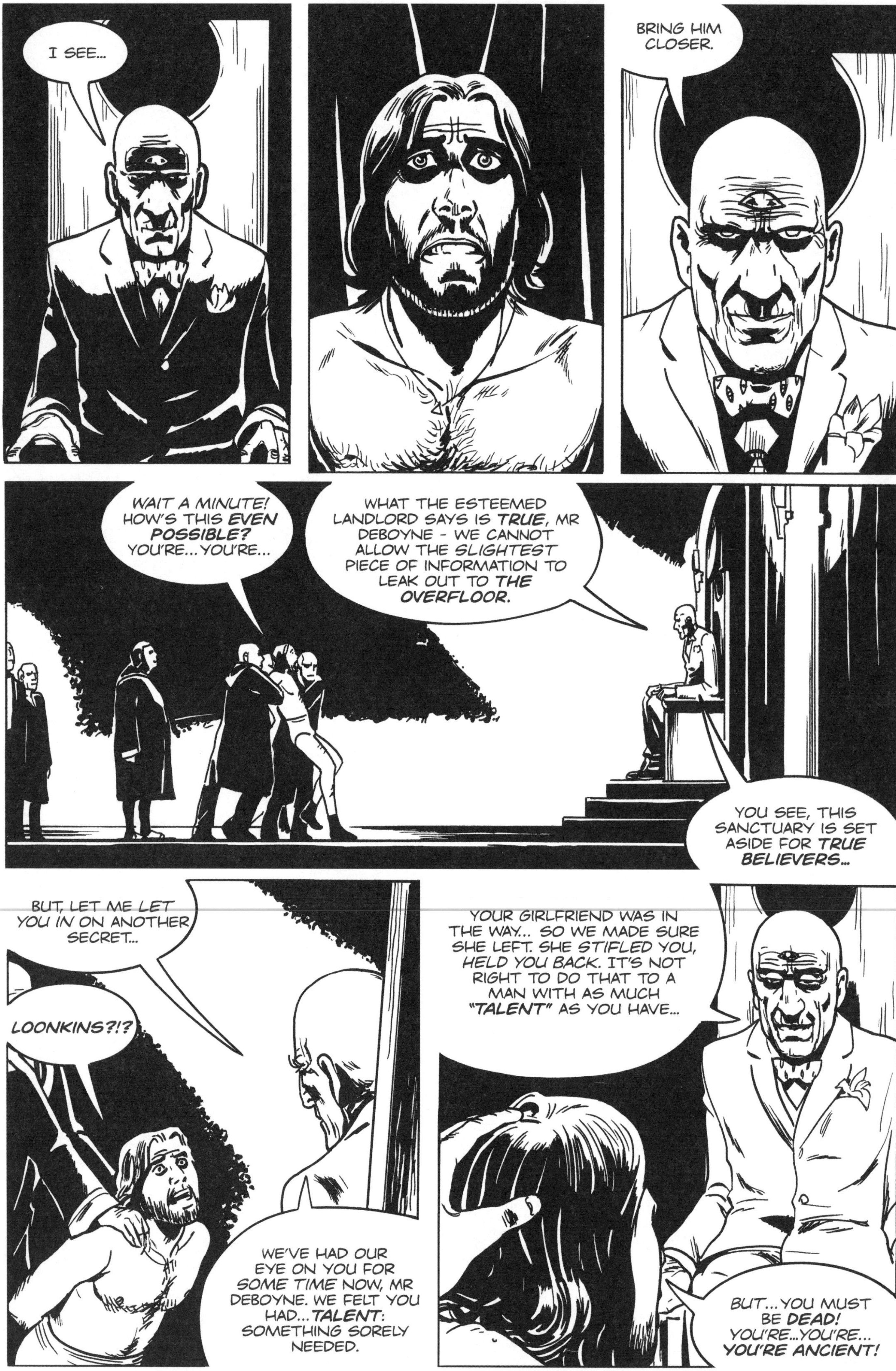
I SEE...
BRING HIM CLOSER.
WAIT A MINUTE! HOW'S THIS EVEN POSSIBLE? YOU'RE... YOU'RE...
WHAT THE ESTEEMED LANDLORD SAYS IS TRUE, MR DEBOYNE - WE CANNOT ALLOW THE SLIGHTEST PIECE OF INFORMATION TO LEAK OUT TO THE OVERFLOOR.
YOU SEE, THIS SANCTUARY IS SET ASIDE FOR TRUE BELIEVERS...
BUT, LET ME LET YOU IN ON ANOTHER SECRET...
LOONKINS?!?
WE'VE HAD OUR EYE ON YOU FOR SOME TIME NOW, MR DEBOYNE. WE FELT YOU HAD... TALENT: SOMETHING SORELY NEEDED.
YOUR GIRLFRIEND WAS IN THE WAY... SO WE MADE SURE SHE LEFT. SHE STIFLED YOU, HELD YOU BACK. IT'S NOT RIGHT TO DO THAT TO A MAN WITH AS MUCH "TALENT" AS YOU HAVE...
BUT... YOU MUST BE DEAD! YOU'RE... YOU'RE... YOU'RE ANCIENT!

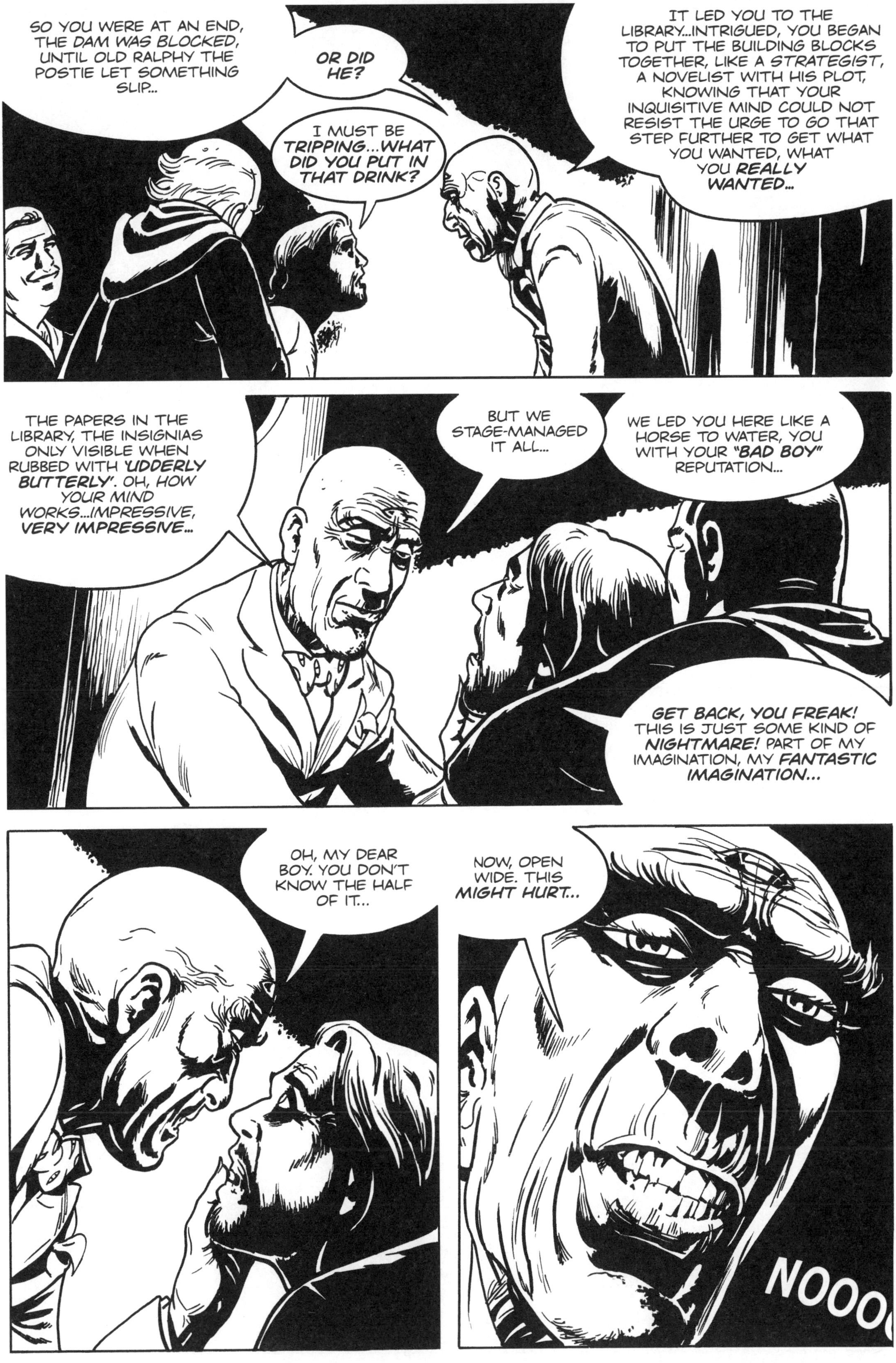
SO YOU WERE AT AN END, THE *DAM WAS BLOCKED*, UNTIL OLD RALPHY THE POSTIE LET SOMETHING SLIP...
OR DID HE?
IT LED YOU TO THE LIBRARY...INTRIGUED, YOU BEGAN TO PUT THE BUILDING BLOCKS TOGETHER, LIKE A *STRATEGIST*, A NOVELIST WITH HIS PLOT, KNOWING THAT YOUR INQUISITIVE MIND COULD NOT RESIST THE URGE TO GO THAT STEP FURTHER TO GET WHAT YOU WANTED, WHAT YOU **REALLY WANTED...**
I MUST BE **TRIPPING...WHAT DID YOU PUT IN THAT DRINK?**
THE PAPERS IN THE LIBRARY, THE INSIGNIAS ONLY VISIBLE WHEN RUBBED WITH **'UDDERLY BUTTERLY'**. OH, HOW YOUR MIND WORKS...IMPRESSIVE, **VERY IMPRESSIVE...**
BUT WE STAGE-MANAGED IT ALL...
WE LED YOU HERE LIKE A HORSE TO WATER, YOU WITH YOUR **"BAD BOY"** REPUTATION...
GET BACK, YOU FREAK! THIS IS JUST SOME KIND OF **NIGHTMARE!** PART OF MY IMAGINATION, MY **FANTASTIC IMAGINATION...**
OH, MY DEAR BOY. YOU DON'T KNOW THE HALF OF IT...
NOW, OPEN WIDE. THIS **MIGHT HURT...**
NOOO

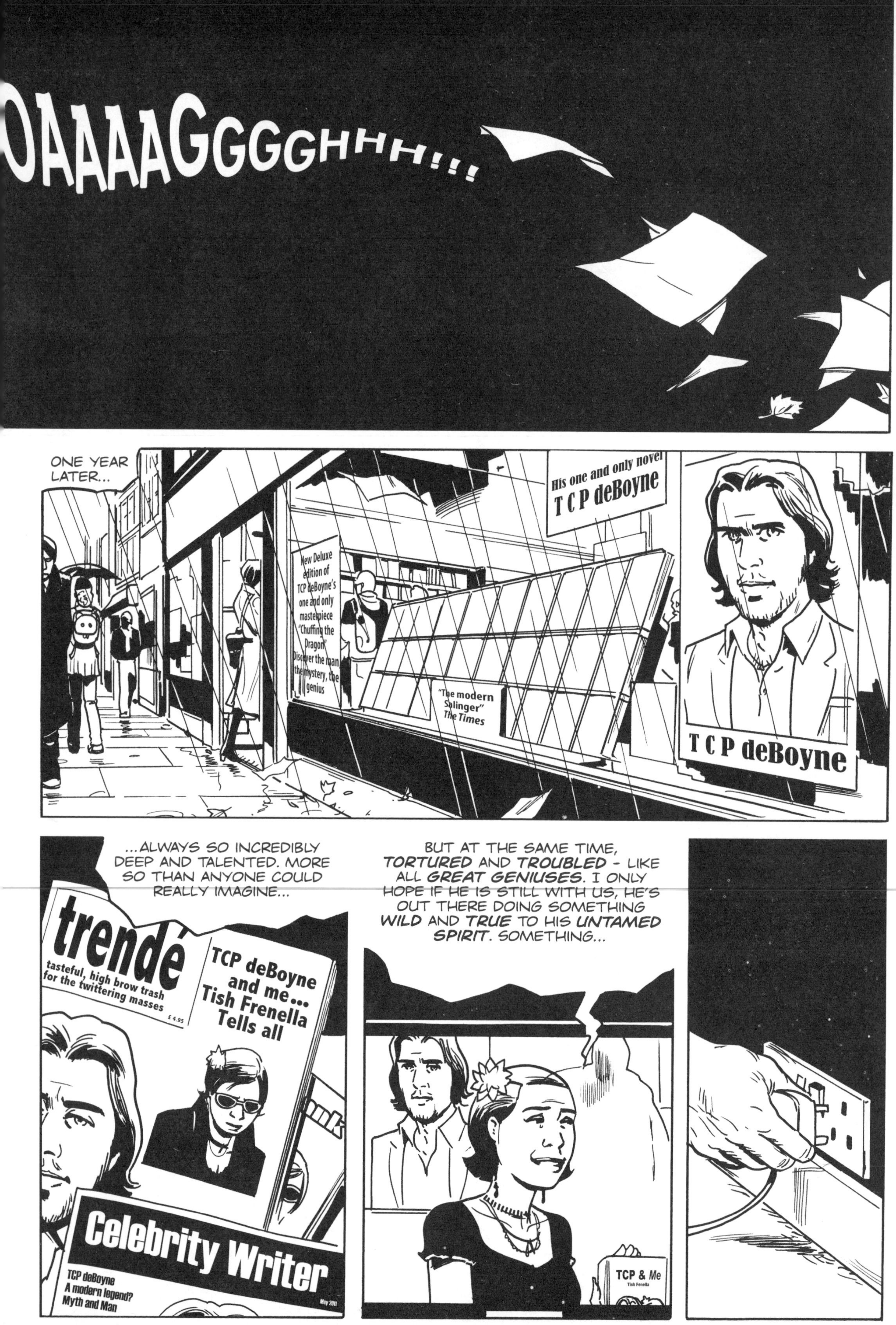
OAAAAGGGGHHHH!!!
ONE YEAR LATER...
His one and only novel
T C P deBoyne
New Deluxe edition of TCP deBoyne's one and only masterpiece "Chuffing the Dragon" Discover the man, the mystery, the genius
"The modern Salinger" The Times
T C P deBoyne
...ALWAYS SO INCREDIBLY DEEP AND TALENTED. MORE SO THAN ANYONE COULD REALLY IMAGINE...
trendé
tasteful, high brow trash for the twittering masses
£ 4.95
TCP deBoyne and me... Tish Frenella Tells all
Celebrity Writer
TCP deBoyne
A modern legend?
Myth and Man
May 2011
BUT AT THE SAME TIME, TORTURED AND TROUBLED - LIKE ALL GREAT GENIUSES. I ONLY HOPE IF HE IS STILL WITH US, HE'S OUT THERE DOING SOMETHING WILD AND TRUE TO HIS UNTAMED SPIRIT. SOMETHING...
TCP & Me
Tish Fenella

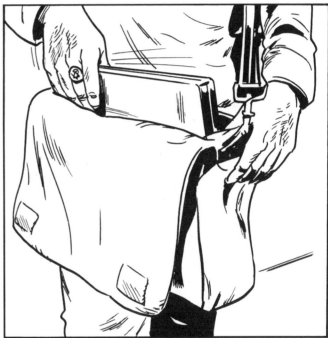

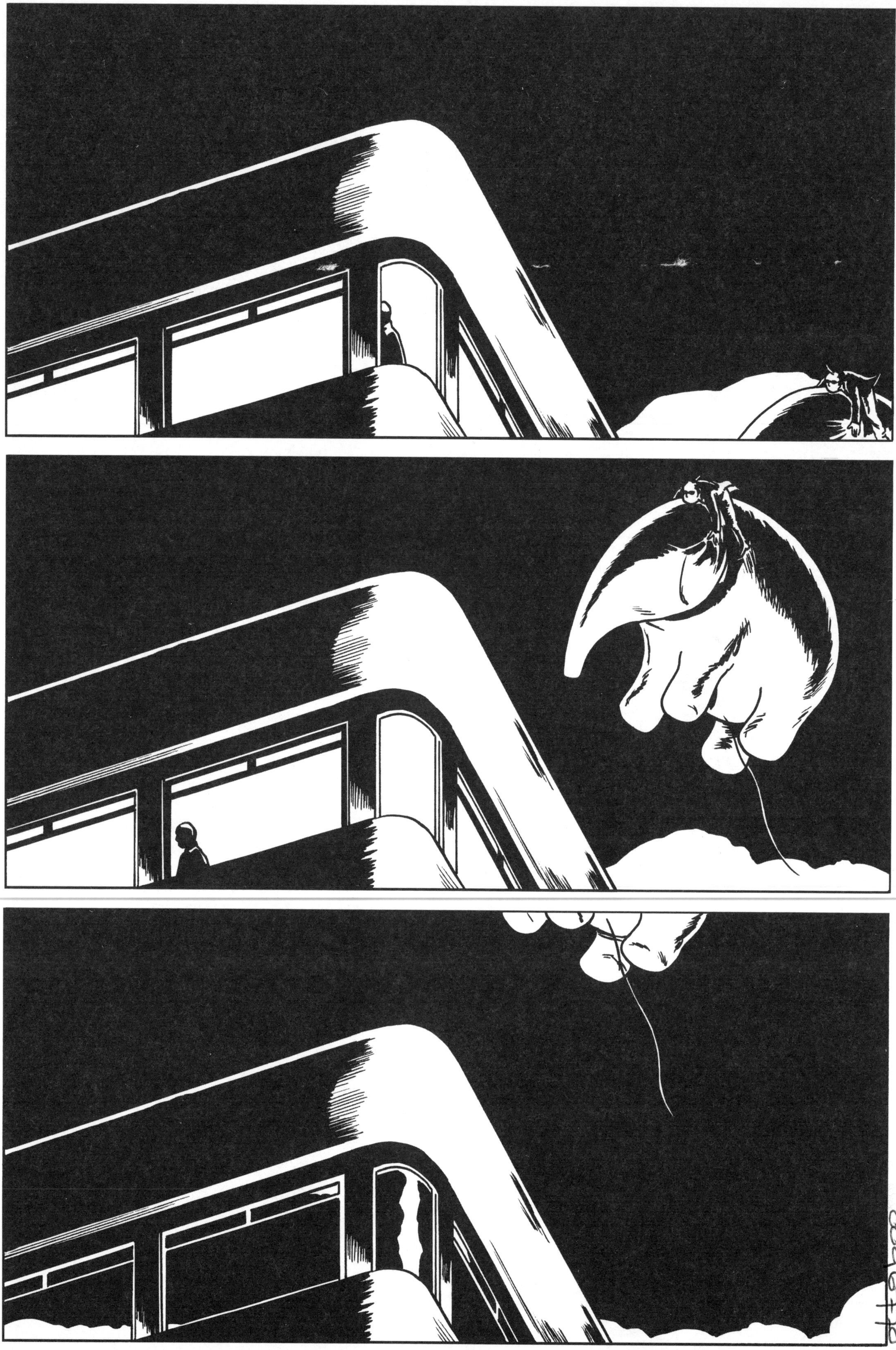